D1011316

A COOK'S TOUR
OF SAN FRANCISCO

The Best Restaurants and Their Recipes

＊＊＊＊＊＊＊A Cook's

ILLUSTRATIONS BY
Carolyn Cather

DORIS MUSCATINE

TOUR OF SAN FRANCISCO

The Best Restaurants and Their Recipes ✳✳✳

CHARLES SCRIBNER'S SONS

New York ✳✳✳

TITLE IS USED THROUGH THE COURTESY OF THOS. COOK AND SON,
"World's Oldest and Largest Travel Organization."

PICTURE CREDITS:

1. Broadway—PHOTOGRAPH BY PHIL PALMER, FROM *The Face of San Francisco*, PUBLISHED BY DOUBLEDAY & COMPANY.

2. Garden Court, Palace Hotel—PHOTOGRAPH BY STONE & STECCATI.

3. Ernie's—PHOTOGRAPH BY PHIL PALMER.

4. Fisherman's Wharf—PHOTOGRAPH BY PHIL PALMER.

5. Fisherman's Wharf—PHOTOGRAPH BY FRED LYON FROM RAPHO-GUILLUMETTE.

6. Pizza—PHOTOGRAPH BY FRED LYON FROM RAPHO-GUILLUMETTE.

7. Chinatown—PHOTOGRAPH BY PHIL PALMER FROM *Chinatown, San Francisco*, PUBLISHED BY HOWELL-NORTH BOOKS.

8. Johnny Kan's Restaurant—PHOTOGRAPH BY PHIL PALMER, FROM *Chinatown, San Francisco*, PUBLISHED BY HOWELL-NORTH BOOKS.

9. Sam's Anchor Cafe—PHOTOGRAPH BY HARRY V. PLATE.

To Charles ✳

SINE QUA NON

Acknowledgments ✳

MERELY to set down a list of the names of those who have aided and abetted the creation of this book seems too little compensation to them. It would be jollier and more fitting to invite them all to a great San Francisco banquet. But since a list it must be, let me acknowledge with appreciation and thanks the assistance, advice, and enthusiastic support of James D. Hart, Charlotte Jackson, Dr. Ludwig Immergluck, Florence Casaroli, Robert Lescher, Marlene Griffith, John Campbell Bruce, Earl Le Trace, Allan M. Roberts, Anita Lynn, Carl D. Brandt, Charles Leong, Elinor Parker, and those restaurant proprietors and chefs, most of whose names appear in the book, who were so generous in providing their stories and their recipes. How can I thank my children, Jeffrey and Alison, for their patience beyond the call of duty, or my husband, tireless dinner companion and literary critic, who has tried with me many of the restaurants and recipes here included, and, heroically, some that are not?

Contents ❋

CONTENTS

CONTENTS

A COOK'S TOUR
OF SAN FRANCISCO

The Best Restaurants and Their Recipes

I

Introduction

I N the wake of the catastrophe that leveled San Francisco by quake and fire in mid-April of 1906, two dozen gentlemen members of the Chit-Chat Club began plans for their next meeting. This group had been meeting monthly since 1874 to enjoy a good dinner and a paper by one of its members, and had never missed a session. In a bedroom beyond the burned-out area of the city, the May, 1906 meeting took place on schedule. A sidewalk kitchen, improvised for the event, yielded up a fine meal of oysters on the half shell, crab à la poulette, entrée, Roman punch, dessert, and coffee. The subject of the paper seems to be forgotten, but San Franciscans today still revere their food with the same passion.

For most of the city's history it has deserved a reputation for a cuisine of opulence and excellence. It has synthesized, in the best possible manner, an inheritance of foreign flavors with a local tradition for lusty eating first supported by gold-mine money and gold-miners' appetites. Supplied by an immediate and abundant source of sun-ripe fruits and vegetables, flanked by game forests, ranch lands, and an ocean full of sea food, circled by the best wineries in the country, and with its appetite urged on by an invigorating climate, San Francisco feasts.

OLD SAN FRANCISCO

To understand something of its gastronomic legacy, one needs to glance briefly at the city's history. The Spanish claimed the area in 1776, and well into the 1800's it remained a shanty settlement of not more than a few hundred people. They called it Yerba Buena—"good herb"—after a mint that scented its hillsides, and from which they brewed a good tea. Herbert Asbury, in his book on the Barbary Coast, reports that the settlement was of such minor importance as a trading post that "the Hudson's Bay Company abandoned it after vainly striving for five years to establish a profitable commerce." [1] At the end of the Mexican-American War in 1846, this Mexican province came under the American flag, and by 1847 it bore the name San Francisco.

Then gold was discovered. From that point on, the city developed at a terrific pace. Within a few years it was a metropolis, luxuriating in Babylonian excess and wickedness. In every sense it was the most lived in—and perhaps, most died in—city of the country. When the gold news spread, the rest of the country converged on the city like swarming bees. Hordes of seamen abandoned their ships—cargoes and passengers in the bargain— as soon as they hit the harbor, to take off for the gold fields. The bay was a clutter of stranded vessels. Many, beached along the waterfront, saw use as saloons and boarding houses, while one became the city's first jail, and another gave its hulk and its name to the Hotel Niantic. The big Comstock Lode strike in 1859 added further incentive for immigration. The completion of the transcontinental railroad in 1869 provided easier accessibility. By the '70's, the Nevada mines were operating at their peak—and most of their production went straight to San Francisco. The population in 1875 was 190,000; by the turn of the century, the

[1] Herbert Asbury, *The Barbary Coast*, Garden City, New York, Garden City Publishing Company, Inc., 1933, p. 4.

city had 350,000 residents, and a world-wide reputation as a leader of business and a center of culture.

Originally, accommodations could hardly keep up with this influx of beings. The early-day population was largely male and transient. The city had few private residences, in contrast to an epidemic rash of hotels, boarding houses, bars, and restaurants. San Francisco has never stopped being a city that "eats out." At first its food was abundant, but no one knew how to prepare it. According to one account, when the well-known southern cook Mammy Pleasant reached the city in the '50's, there was such great demand for her work that she put up her services at auction, and sold them for $500 monthly. This shortage of talent was corrected in short order. When wealthy easterners came by private railcars to inspect the scene of their investments, they brought their own chefs—fortunately for the city's culinary growth, Frenchmen—who deserted with the alacrity of the seamen, in this case to mine the fortunes of a hungry city. Further, when nouveau-riche Californians took up the broadening art of travel, they often returned with tastes awakened by the foods and customs of the Continent. By the 1870's, San Franciscans were dining on from a dozen to eighteen courses at a sitting, often spending a good six hours at table.

By the famous Nineties, the city was dubbed another Paris for the heights to which it had risen gastronomically, and for the depths to which it had sunk morally. The Barbary Coast was an area of depravity; Chinatown's tongs warred against each other, its population smoked opium and trafficked in slave girls, and its large contingent of responsible and upright Chinese suffered hideous treatment through guilt by association. Bohemians battened on its stimulations, and the wealthy indulged themselves in spiraling excesses of grandeur. Every San Franciscan was instantly ready to frolic and cavort, and in the wake of this gaiety pleasure domes prospered—beyond any reasonable count for a city of the size.

INTRODUCTION

Three elegant French restaurants led the parade. The Maison Riche, the Poodle Dog, and the Maison Dorée treated their customers to sauces and soufflés that did proud by their French ancestry. And for those who wanted more than vintage wine with their food, they provided private upstairs dining rooms fitted out with couches and locks on the doors. They did not ordinarily supply female companionship—though in later years some are reported to have kept a handy supply of appropriate telephone numbers—but only the setting, the facilities, and the inspiration. And, of course, a constant and discreet cloak of privacy, with the upstairs entrance always well separated from the family entrance downstairs.

Marchand's became known for its onion soup, The Pup for its fish cooked in wine by the owner himself, and Delmonico's for its elevator to the upstairs rooms. But the greatest of all the city's dining spots was the opulent Palace Hotel.

The Palace boasted—and not vainly—that it could prepare any dish requested by its guests, regardless of its origin. In 1876, the hotel received at breakfast the entire passenger list of a special transcontinental train. A New York theatrical troup, in a publicity stunt that handily outshines most current Madison Avenue shenanigans, decided to close its New York run, race across the continent, and open the same play in San Francisco in so recklessly short an interval that it required breaking all transportation records. The trip was attended by blasts of publicity and a bunch of daring passengers, who were to get besides the thrills of speed and notoriety, a week's room and board at the Palace. They made it, arriving a good several hours earlier than even their wild imaginings had presaged, and an hour and a half later sat down to a Palace breakfast. The staff provided them with Salmon Grille à la Maître d'Hôtel, Tom Cod Frit with Sauce Tartare, Cucumber Salad, Filet de Boeuf with Sauce Béarnaise, Côtelettes d'Agneau with Sauce Soubise, Escalope de Veau à la Genoise, Pomme de Terre Maître d'Hôtel, Rognons

Sauté au Champignons, Poulet Grillé au Cresson, Oeufs Brouillés au Point d'Asperges, Oeufs Frites au Temben, Pré Salé, Omelettes au Rhum, and Apricots, Raspberries, Strawberries, and Cherries.[2]

Christmas at the Palace was like a feast day in ancient Rome. Local families made it a tradition to appear annually for the banquet, the consuming of whose many courses took almost as many hours. The hotel's historians Lewis and Hall describe for us Pudding à la Sultan, the climax of the gastronomic orgy: "It was made of yellow corn flour, cooked in milk sweetened with brown sugar. Among its other ingredients were cinnamon, mint, sliced bananas, dates, and the yolks of eggs. It was served with a hot rum sauce, flavored with anise seeds, 'green tea essence,' mint, and sugar. . . . Pudding à la Sultan was regarded as a fitting climax to a Palace Christmas dinner. After so hearty a meal it was wise to finish with something light." [3]

There was a fine variety of lesser resorts that catered to the city's appetites. Across from Golden Gate Park, Dickey's Road House appealed to the wealthy Sunday breakfast crowd—and no wonder! "Never again, epicures assure us, will steaks be seen such as Dickey's. Before each celebrant was set a steak's small tender heart, a valentine of a steak, succulent, fragrant, dripping. Beside it a glistening broiled quail snuggled in its bed of golden toast and slivers of fried . . . but potato is too harsh and plebeian a word for such succulent, crisp and melting morsels! . . . Strong meat for breakfast was demanded by San Franciscans, many of whom remembered the fighting fifties when a man rejoiced in grizzly bear steak and broiled venison for breakfast!" [4] Besides an accompanying basket of fruit and nuts, and a pot of coffee, the meal was washed down with a good bottle of champagne.

[2] Oscar Lewis and Carroll D. Hall, *Bonanza Inn*, New York, London, Alfred A. Knopf, 1939, p. 49.

[3] *Bonanza Inn*, p. 77.

[4] Evelyn Wells, *Champagne Days of San Francisco*, New York, London, D. Appleton-Century Company, Inc., 1939, pp. 27, 28.

Another scene of sumptuous Sunday breakfasts was—and in a calmer way still is—the Cliff House. This institution, despite two gutting fires, has existed since the 1860's, jutting over the beach with a spectacular view of Seal Rocks.

After-theatre suppers had a particular vogue in the Nineties, and audiences arrived still applauding at Zinkand's on Market Street to cheer, in turn, its excellent German food. Some preferred theatre restaurants such as the Midway Plaisance, whose simple bill of fare makes it clear that its customers were kept far too busy ogling the undulations of its star, Little Egypt, to allow for lengthy gustatory diversions. Refreshments were served in the café, and, provided they bought a drink, hungry patrons could bolt down for a mere fifteen or twenty cents additional, oysters—Eastern or local, large or small, served raw on the half-shell, or steamed, fried, stewed, roasted, or baked in eleven different ways, including the oyster loaf—and a great variety of other short-order items including cold platters of pickled pigs' feet, roast of mutton with potato salad, a number of sandwiches, omelettes, and just plain hash.

As the Midway's menu would indicate, the oyster was a favorite San Francisco dish. Accompanied by a chilled Château Yquem, it heralded many a lordly banquet. Several restaurants specialized in its preparation, notably Goodfellow's Grotto, near the city hall, and a Sutter Street emporium that also served up a noteworthy boiled terrapin, Gobey's "Ladies and Gents Oyster Parlor." But the best place for such delectables was the bustling California Market, that jangled, in the words of Evelyn Wells, "like a great bazaar under a single roof, housing fish stands, vegetable and dairy stands, beer counters and restaurants. At Morgan's, one of the many restaurants specializing in fish dishes, one ate all the prawns, crab, and shrimp one could hold, oyster cocktails—a San Francisco invention—oysters on the half shell, a small steak, and a cup of coffee, all for twenty-five cents. Darbee and Immel's and the Pearl Oyster House served similar 'two-bit' meals in the California Market." [5]

An unusual restaurant of the day was The Castle, perched like an eagle's lair on the crown of Telegraph Hill, just where Coit Tower now stands. It was the first dining establishment on the hill, where today Julius' Castle (not even a poor relation) and the Shadows, a pleasant German-style place with good cooking, draw crowds because of the excitement of their setting. You may think that the automobile access is tortuous; the folk of the Nineties reached the lofty perch of The Castle by a special cable car. The restaurant had a short life, burning to the ground some years before the earthquake.

Artists and the literary-minded found the intellectual and physical atmosphere of San Francisco a boon and inspiration, and a large number of Bohemians decorated the scene. Their center was the Washington-Jackson-Montgomery territory, a locale blessed by a fringe of Italian and French eateries where the food was both well-prepared and inexpensive. Since restaurants and bars were often both the living rooms and the studios of the arts and letters crowd, nightly symposia packed such places as the Brooklyn Hotel and the Tour Eiffel—both noteworthy for good two-bit meals; or Luna's on Vallejo Street, a small Mexican house that fired its customers with spicy sausages, chile con carne, and hot-sauced enchiladas. There, of a foggy evening you might see Joaquin Miller or Frank Norris; and you would always find Ricardo, the sashed and mustachioed one-eyed waiter, who ran the show. Fifty-cent Italian dinners that offered infinite varieties of *pasta* and *risotto*, and several courses later, a warm and frothy *zabaglione*, drew the crowd to Steve Sanguinetti's, Luchetti's, and most popular of all, Papa Coppa's. Their French counterparts, The Fly Trap, the St. Germaine, and Jules' (the first place to install slot machines), gave their

[5] *Champagne Days of San Francisco*, p. 182.

customers eight courses and a bottle of wine for half a dollar. An even better bargain were the French family-style restaurants —still a familiar though somewhat changed San Francisco institution—where at long, common tables, you shared with your neighbors a tureen of hot soup, a salad, a fish dish, roasts, vegetables, bread, fruit, coffee, and sometimes cheese, dessert, and a bit of wine—all for twenty-five cents.

Coppa's deserves more than passing notice, for among all of the Bohemian gathering places, it was unique. The food was good; Giuseppe Coppa had learned his trade by cooking at several of the city's best restaurants, including the Poodle Dog. Diners with $1.75 in their pockets could order his great specialty, chicken in a coconut. This was a disjointed chicken stewed inside a sealed coconut where it inhaled a spicy sauce fortified with bits of bacon browned in olive oil, dice of peppers, onions, tomatoes, niblets of fresh corn, and slivers of coconut meat. The vessel, set in water, steamed for a long sixty minutes before being set whole before a quiveringly expectant *bon vivant*. San Franciscans can still feast on chicken in a coconut, but the ambrosial curried concoction dreamed up by Trader Vic has actually only its two basic ingredients in common with Coppa's chicken Portola.

Coppa's truest fame came, however, not from its hearty and abundant suppers, nor its cozy surroundings—both marks of distinction enough for an artistic clientele—but because Giuseppe gave instant credit to patrons who were down and out. This they so much appreciated that when he had the place badly repainted, just after the turn of the century, the work was redone gratis by just about all of the artists in the Bay Area. The result was a group fresco unique in San Francisco art. It took three months to complete. Oscar Lewis, in *Bay Window Bohemia*, chronicles its progress:

"Three men tried their hands at the project that first Sunday. Porter Garnett, working on the north wall, produced a ferocious-looking lobster, some five feet tall, standing rampant on an island labeled Bohemia. Robert Aitken, later a sculptor of note, whose San Francisco productions include the Dewey Monument in Union Square, drew two amiable-appearing nudes, while the third member, Perry Newberry, soon to become unofficial 'mayor' of Carmel, added his bit.

"Next Sunday the work continued. . . . Garnett drew, a foot or two below the ceiling, a frieze enclosed in a decorative border . . . On this border were lettered the names of those, past and present, whom the group considered eligible for inclusion in Bohemia's Hall of Fame. . . .

"Extending about the room just above that . . . was a line of stalking black cats, the handiwork of 'Marty' Martinez. . . . During the next several months the work went on until in the end every foot of wall space on three sides of the room was covered. The artists did not hesitate to include in their compositions caricatures both of themselves and their cronies. . . . Thus it became a favorite pastime of the Philistines . . . to try to identify the artists at the long central table with their likenesses on the walls."

There were even philosophical speculations in "English, Latin, Hebrew, and medieval French." Lewis reports that in order to get a large wall clock safely into the composition, a supine Father Time took shape, balancing the time piece on his legs, an hour glass on one hand, and a bottle of wine on the other! [6]

These intriguing interiors assured a full house for ever more, until disaster struck in the form of the great 1906 fire. Although Coppa remained active until he was almost eighty, none of his successive establishments—though painted to the rafters—ever caught the quality of the original. He finally retired in the late 1930's. Perhaps his greatest gesture was after the quake in 1906, when with some of his clients he searched out the remains of his

* Oscar Lewis, *Bay Window Bohemia*, Garden City, New York, Doubleday & Company, Inc., 1956, pp. 102–3.

restaurant, and as Albert Parry reports in *Garrets and Pretenders*, "there amid the ruins, he served dinner to his patrons, and what a dinner it was!" [7]

The Bohemian Club had its beginnings at such places as Coppa's. But what started as a confrérie of the day's most talented men of the arts—and which by its nature included many free spirits as well as many poor ones—encompasses today an elite that is certainly richer, perhaps no less talented, but comparatively docile. Once the club established itself in its own quarters, conservatism set in, and today it is one of the city's most staid congregations. Parry tells us, "Now the Bohemian Club agrees to allow modernistic paintings in its halls only after a stiff fight. . . . Now it requires the services of one hundred and fifty waiters and a number of high-priced chefs to cater to the hordes coming to the Bohemian Grove for the Midsummer Jinks. . . . Now the Club is a grand, dignified and costly affair. . . ." [8] Perhaps the truest link with the past is that these "Bohemian" gentlemen still enjoy their food—but today they partake of a cuisine that is as distinguished as any in the city.

In a town engulfed in a tidal wave of population, much of it en route to or from the gold fields or foreign ports, there grew up many lodging houses and hotels, and—the inevitable replacements for missing parlors—hundreds of bars. These ranged from the treacherous dives of the Barbary Coast to the more than twenty high-class saloons in the downtown area, and included such resorts as the Tivoli Gardens, which started as a humble beer hall, and ended up serving grand opera with its drinks. In North Beach today, the Bocce Ball—which is, alas, giving up its ball courts in the rear—is one of several spots that still satisfy both thirsts of imbibing opera-lovers.

With one bar to every hundred of its people, it is no wonder

[7] Albert Parry, *Garrets and Pretenders*, New York, N.Y., Dover Publications, Inc., revised edition, 1960, p. 236.
[8] *Garrets and Pretenders*, pp. 239–40.

that old San Francisco invented any number of drinks, and developed cocktail habits as epic as the Free Lunch. Along the cocktail route in the following years, gentlemen of the era drank, besides quantities of champagne, the Gold Rush Sazerac—reputedly the first cocktail ever made—a mixture of rye, bitters, absinthe and ice, and a faint suggestion of anisette. Johnny Farley, the proprietor of the Peerless Saloon, has a claim on history as one of the first bartenders to shake up a mixture with ice. Beginning in 1849, the El Dorado Gambling House, just off Portsmouth Square, had behind its counter the fortunate services of Professor Jerry Thomas, called America's greatest bartender. As the inventor of a drink that bears a near inversion of his name —the Tom and Jerry—he is at least America's most easily remembered one. In his time he authored a bartender's guide with the appropriate title "The Bon Vivant's Companion, or How to Mix Drinks." The drink that attained the greatest popularity of all—as early as the Seventies—was an invention of Duncan Nichol, overseer of the fabulous Bank Exchange Bar. He named his potent and exotic brew Pisco Punch, but never shared its formula, beyond the fact that it was based on a colorless Peruvian brandy. Those who had ever tasted as much as the naked brandy shared their elegiac responses with any one who would listen. "The first glass satisfied me that San Francisco was, and is, a nice place to visit . . . The second glass was sufficient, and I felt that I could face small-pox, all the fevers known to the faculty, and the Asiatic cholera, combined, if need be." [9] You can get Pisco Punch today at the Buena Vista, but there are no San Franciscans left who can compare it with the original.

Until the appearance in March, 1852, of Barry and Patten's Drinking House, there was no saloon of real elegance or more than a tinge of respectability. But here the paintings were fine rather than lewd, the furnishings elaborate and elegant, gam-

[9] Thomas Knox, The Underground World, Hartford, The J. B. Burr Publishing Company, 1877, p. 769.

bling was not tolerated, the upper floor was given over to a billiard parlor equipped with the finest tables available, and an abundant free lunch was set forth daily to accompany beverages of only the highest quality. It was the forerunner of a large number of similarly regal drinking houses. Nichol's Bank Exchange was one of the most sumptuous saloons of the Nineties' scene. The art that adorned its walls was valued at $100,000, and its customers trod pavements of marble. But the display of paintings that captured most attention was the collection of nudes that jammed Ernest Haquette's Palace of Art on Post Street. Today, in keeping with this feminist tradition, Larry Geraldi displays "Gloria" and her assorted undraped sisters in his Domino Club bar-restaurant. In the old days, the Palace of Art—quite daring, in spite of its splendid respectability—allowed entry to ladies. It served to all comers a noon-hour commercial lunch for a quarter (including drink), and a free lunch from 4 to 11 p.m. Under the crystal chandeliers, the later afternoon visitors heaped their plates from a table bowing under crab salad, clam juice, celery and radishes, pigs' heads, head cheese, clams from Bolinas Bay, beans, chili with meat, sausages, beef à la chile Colorado, fried clams, sardines, boiled ham, terrapin stew (a great San Francisco favorite), croquettes of veal and chicken, corned beef, stewed beef, and chipped beef, Saratoga chips, pork and beans, sliced tongue, smoked salmon, cracked crab, herring, cheese and crackers, pop corn, nuts, and fruit.

The Cardinal had a similar spread, as did the Grand Hotel's Hoffman Café, the Palace Bar, the Occidental, the Baldwin, and the Reception, where the adaptable terrapin or plump crab legs beckoned from a sauce of cream and sherry. The Yellowstone Bar, a Montgomery Street landmark, offered browsers no less than a dozen cheeses, shrimp in jellied crème de menthe, sweetbreads, caviar, venison, and a multitude of other delicacies. In these establishments, the hot dishes generally came from the kitchen twice daily—late afternoon and around midnight. Uniformed waiters assisted the guests, and it was the custom for gentlemen to keep their private bottles stashed away at the bar.

Several saloons owed their popularity to atmospheres of a less lavish nature and prices more in keeping with the sawdust on their floors. This is not to say that they stinted on the free lunch —or the nudes—but they were shy of crystal chandeliers and marble pavements. One such tavern, out on Meiggs' Wharf, enjoyed a seagoing clientele, and bore the odd name Cobweb Palace in recognition of garlands and veilings contributed over the years by resident spiders. They were not the only wild life represented: the place was a small-scale zoo and aviary, crammed with a jumble of caged parrots, monkeys, and anything else that some incoming sailor had to sell. According to Herbert Asbury, there was even a collection of carved walrus tusks and sperm whale teeth, now stored in the De Young Museum. Abe Warner, the salty proprietor, conducted the making of hot toddies—for which the bar was famous—from its 1856 opening until 1897, at which point the eighty-year-old bartender went into retirement. Three-Fingered Jack's also graced the waterfront; John Denny combined a bar and a grocery store that attracted a large number of political types to the corner of Pacific and Salmon Streets; Jimmy Gibbs' wholesale liquor store on Merchant Street sold its wares retail to the general public; and the Martin and Horton Saloon on Clay became a colorful catchall for the town's leading characters, of which there was an abundance. If, as you drive past the Hotel Stewart on Geary Street, you are startled by a man masquerading as some outrageous bygone dignitary, epaulettes squaring his shoulders, and plumes dancing on his hat, you will have some idea of how Joshua Norton, the town's greatest character of all, appeared a hundred years ago. Having lost first his fortune and consequently his sanity, he proclaimed himself Emperor of the United States and Protector of Mexico. In his honor the Hotel Stewart today has created the Emperor Norton Room (and doorman to match)—where every drink in the house "is one full ounce and costs six bits." Fondness for the Emperor Norton is an old San Francisco tradition. In his own day he so beguiled San Francisco that the entire city willingly entered his fantasy, addressed him as Emperor for the twenty years until his death, provided him with uniforms by proclamation of the council, welcomed him to all its bars and restaurants as an honored guest, and even, on those occasions when he issued fifty-cent bonds or checks, purchased or cashed them with the same dignity as if they had been issued by the United States Treasury.

The 1906 earthquake, followed by the devastations of uncontrolled fire, ravished the city completely, sweeping away with democratic impartiality the glittering palaces and the sin-infested shanties. There were many grave heads that shook in their conviction that the wicked and high-living city was only receiving its just deserts. And there were those wags who answered—and one who even put it into verse—that if that were the case, how come churches burned down and a famous distillery remained unscathed? The citizens staggered only briefly under this heavy blow, and then tried to take up, as fast as they could rebuild them, in the places where they left off.

The first restaurant of real consequence to open after the fire was the Louvre on the corner of Fillmore and Ellis—in the midst of the new business district. It was soon joined by other restaurants of note. Techau's Tavern, whose owner had operated Good Fellow's Grotto before it, was always bustling, and served excellent food. Tait's was a later offspring of Carl Zinkand, who had directed with such success the pre-fire establishment that bore his name. Felix's on Montgomery Street and the Poodle Dog-Bergez-Frank's on Bush gave the city some of its best French food. Girard's French Restaurant on Ellis Street employed a chef who had worked for twenty years with Victor Hirtzler at the St. Francis. Their greatest specialty was the salad dressing, eventually bottled and still on the market—although the restaurant no longer exists. There was Pierre's on Pine Street, and on Pacific, where Taj is today, was La Favorite, which started when a French family took boarders into their dining room.

Blanco's, one of the great names in the after-fire city, presented musical entertainment and fabulous cuisine in a florid gold, white and red-velvet setting. Blanco had owned the Poodle Dog when the fire razed it. When he started out on his new enterprise he brought along George Brauer, for many years the Poodle Dog chef. In a kitchen partly tucked under the musicians' balcony, Brauer prepared extraordinarily good dishes, the most famous of which was probably his Frog Legs Poulette. Ruth Teiser comments on the rococo trappings among which Blanco diners consorted. From her account one visualizes a palace, its walls embroidered with frescoes and intaglios, its ceilings dripping with fantastic Venetian glass chandeliers. Three sides of the hall carried a balcony of boxes, fashioned after those at the French Opera, resting on huge columns, and curtained in garnet drapings that could be pulled all across to provide privacy. The fourth side, on which the kitchen fronted, provided the space for the entertainers. The opening night performance included classical and Hawaiian music, and operatic excerpts trilled by a soprano, Mme. Oetzel, and a tenor, Signor Porcini. The menu, "a result of momentous conferences between Blanco and Brauer, emerged as a rich blend of Paris, San Francisco, Philadelphia, and Suisun gastronomical traditions." For two dollars first-nighters ate Toke Points with sauce mignonette, a creamed or clear soup, caviar canapes, almonds, anchovies, and olives, a fish course of paupiettes de bass, followed by filet de boeuf and sweetbreads, then an intermission of Pisco Punch—a sherbet reconstructed along the lines of the old Bank Exchange concoction. Next came Philadelphia squab, teal duck from Suisun with fried hominy, and poulet de grain aux cresson. The accompaniment was petits pois français, and last, before the sweets, came a green salad. For dessert there was a special ice cream, a cake, fruits, cheese, and black coffee.[10] In 1935 the Music Box restaurant took over the old premises but it never equalled Blanco's fame or success.

New Frank's on Clay was one of the most popular among the Italian places that opened after the fire. Campi's was another. It was run expertly by the Campagnolis, a former Italian opera singer and her musician husband. The Gianduja attracted a large clientele from its own neighborhood, the Latin quarter on Stockton Street. The Leon d'Oro was particularly famous for its snails, cooked tenderly in oil, onion, garlic, parsley, Marsala, meat stock, butter, and an unexpected fillip of anise. One pried these juicy morsels from their shells with toothpicks—just as they do in Chinatown today.

In the Upper Tenderloin—an area that had once supported numerous saloons, houses of prostitution, gambling halls, and the Cremorne (later the Midway Plaisance, and the scene of Little Egypt's gyrations)—there prospered an honest restaurant, the Bay City Grill, with excellent fare entirely cooked to order. Through its entrance on Turk Street, very near Market, the regulars crossed sawdust floors to counter or table seats downstairs or booths up above. The Bay City Grill, with its antique waiters and first-rate food, has unhappily faded from the midtown gastronomic scene, as have the two Solari's. Another former restaurant of some local renown was Herbert's Bachelor Grill on Powell, later called Herbert's when it relented in 1933 and allowed women on the premises. Its other claim to fame was a rudimentary catering service. At very little additional, one could order a hot dinner sent home. The staff would set it up, table service included, and clear it away at the end of the feast.

Out at the beach the Whitney brothers directed Playland and a number of establishments designed to curb appetites whetted by the vigorous sea air. Among the most popular havens was Topsy's Roost, where diners munched southern fried chicken. There was also corn pone and an orchestra for dancing. The Hot

[10] Ruth Teiser, *Bonanza Banquets*, No. 12, Book Club of California, 1950.

House, a counter dedicated with refreshing candor to a multitude of searing Mexican dishes, stimulated many a dull palate, and undoubtedly dulled quite a few more. The Pie Shop, which also featured light snacks, offered its customers a lush variety of more than a dozen pies among which wild blackberry was supreme.

A Bohemian establishment (with Portuguese overtones) that was dear to many San Francisco hearts, and one that still provokes memories, mouth-watering and otherwise, was Izzy Gomez' place on Pacific. The story was that three hundred pound Izzy—seldom seen without a black fedora on his somewhat pointed head—had opened his career as a Shanghaier in the Good Old Days. If he had turned to a more honest profession, he hadn't left too much of the old color behind him, and the pervading atmosphere of his place was always rip-roaring. Henry Evans recalls that "the place was noted for its dirt, profanity (which Izzy didn't like), excellent steaks, low-priced drinks and general color. Sunday morning, Teddy (who was bouncer as well as swamper) used to give the place a thorough cleaning. The broken teeth, glass, furniture and discarded garments would make a noticeable pile." [11] The place was in its heyday in the Thirties, when steady patrons stuffed themselves for a quarter on giant steakburgers between slabs of sour dough French bread, washed to their gullets by beakers of red wine for a dime. Today all that remains, beside the memories, is the old door, hanging—on a wall—in the off-beat café Vesuvio (a place with a good amount of color of its own, and known around town for its discreet sign in the front window announcing "Booths for Psychiatrists").

One Bohemian rendezvous that has survived to the present day—although many of the facts of its history have not—is the Iron Pot. Its location has shifted over the years, but it originated in the midst of the great Bohemian colony that prospered at the

[11] Henry Evans, *Bohemian San Francisco*, San Francisco, The Porpoise Bookshop, 1955, p. 3.

end of the century. For thirty years it has occupied its present quarters at 639 Montgomery Street, across from the Monky Block and next door to the defunct Artists Rendezvous above Prosperity Corner. The Monky Block—or Montgomery Building—was until its demise the oldest large building downtown, having kept its four-storied eye on San Francisco since it was put up by Henry Halleck in 1853. Its design was for its day revolutionary, its potential occupancy tremendous, and many thought it would achieve fame more as folly than as foresight. But because of its innovations, it became the swankiest professional address in town, and its offices lost their chic only in the mid-Eighties, when even more modern buildings marked the skyline. Then it housed the artists in its high-windowed rooms. Practically every noteworthy member of the art colony worked or slept there at some point in his career. The Bank Exchange was at the Washington Street corner of the Monky Block; Pappa Coppa's was at one time on the Merchant Street side. It housed two newspapers, stored the beginnings of the Sutro Library, and within its hospitable confines Sun Yat Sen planned the Chinese revolution against the Manchu Dynasty. Now commerce has fingered its way up the street and pushed before it the artisans of bygone days. Where the Monky Block stood, there is now—alas—a parking lot.

When the Monky Block's population was mostly Bohemian in makeup, musicians, writers, sculptors, and painters used to assemble at the Iron Pot, whose name derived from the venerable vessel always kept simmering with a good goulash on the back of the stove. If a painter couldn't pay cash for his meal, he could pay in kind, and the place became an informal gallery. When a painting sold at the Pot, it meant a gallon of *vino* and a celebration. Today the studios are gone—and most of the artists—but the Iron Pot strives to maintain something of the old atmosphere. There are checkered tablecloths and plenty of wine, and a jolly bunch of waiters. Taking paintings for meals is no longer the custom, but the walls remain galleries for contemporary artists. Bobbe Vargas, the present owner, says that the patrons still claim that they can't understand the paintings. But the Pot still offers solid, Italian-style food at moderate prices, although I don't think that the perpetual goulash is bubbling any more on the back of the stove.

There have always been men on the San Francisco scene who have earned reputations for their epicurean sensitivities. One of these was Raphael Weill, who founded the White House Department store in the 1850's, filled it with dazzling French merchandise, and his stomach with equally splendid French viands. As Herb Caen says, " 'Chicken à la Raphael Weill' is still to be found on menus from San Francisco to Paris." [12]

A gentleman who kept his contemporaries guessing at the magic of his culinary formulas was Major Joseph Tilden—one of the most noted epicures of his day. He shared his secrets with only a very few close friends. A rare volume, *Joe Tilden's Recipes for Epicures*, published in 1907 after his death, comes from the files of one of those intimates. The collection includes well-tested recipes for such dishes as Palestine soup, which makes use of the nowadays seldom employed Jerusalem artichoke; bisque of prawns or shrimp; venison soup; five excellent chowders, including Daniel Webster's; shrimps à la Bordelaise; crab à la Creole; salt codfish (bacalas) à la Viscaina; several simple but intriguing recipes for sole, haddock, salmon and flounder; and one for baking fish roe with anchovy paste, the yolks of hard-boiled eggs, parsley, butter, lemon juice and bread crumbs. Entrées range from sweetbreads with mushrooms, frogs à la poulette, and terrapin stewed in sherry and Madeira—all San Francisco favorites —to calves' head en tortue and calves' feet à la maréchale. Pheasants, quail, duck, and chickens receive a refreshing variety of interpretations, and besides recipes for beef, lamb, and pork, there

[12] *Herb Caen's Guide to San Francisco*, Garden City, New York, Doubleday & Company, Inc., 1957, p. 47.

are directions for a stewed cold mutton, Mexican tripe, and barbecued whole pig, which the author noted was a very old dish. There are accounts of sauces, vegetables, salads, and even cheese straws to go with the latter. Desserts and cakes are not neglected. They run an international gamut that embraces zabaglione, pastry Genoise, omelette soufflé, Lady Baltimore cake, and Amherst pudding. The book concludes with the rules for obtaining a good champagne cup—or rather five good champagne cups—and other prescriptions for wine punches, cups, and toddies. Here is how Major Tilden constructed a timbale of macaroni for twelve:

> Boil one-half pound of macaroni in water for five minutes. Cut in inch length pieces and simmer for twenty minutes in one quart of milk, being careful that it does not boil. Season with salt, pepper, mace and cayenne. Add one cup of cream, stir until very smooth, add the beaten yolks of eight eggs and one can of mushrooms sliced. Stir well and then add the macaroni with one pound of sweetbreads, cut in small pieces and two dozen Eastern oysters. Let this cool, then cover with pastry and bake in the oven until brown.

And to make lamb chops à la Nesselrode, he gave these directions:

> Trim carefully one dozen young lamb chops. Fry in butter three tablespoonfuls of marrow, some chopped mushrooms and eschalots. Then add a glass of sherry and stir it well before adding also a cup of rice, four cups of stock, several sweet Chili peppers chopped and some salt. Cook for half an hour or until pasty. Pour it out in a pan to the thickness of half an inch and let cool. Then with a biscuit cutter, cut into rounds about the size of a chop. On each one of these rounds place a chop and cover the top with Bechamel sauce. When cold dip in egg and bread crumbs and fry a light brown.
>
> A good recipe for the Bechamel sauce is the following: One

ounce of butter browned with one ounce of flour. To this add half a glass of sherry, some finely chopped truffles, one cup and a half of stock, salt and pepper, and cook for ten minutes. Add the juice of a lime, take from the fire and stir in the well-beaten yolks of two eggs.

A volume that saw print a few years earlier was *The Landmarks Club Cook Book, a California Collection of the Choicest Recipes From Everywhere, Including a Chapter of the Most Famous Old Californian and Mexican Dishes*. Its scope is a great deal broader, but thereby less discriminating than Major Tilden's. But it does incorporate such oddities as a salad of rose leaves ("pound in a mortar and pestle the leaves of three large red," etc.), which the contributor comments was given to her "by a member of the Sultan's household"; a Norwegian fruit soup for children's lunch; German tamales; fig sandwiches; and a nasturtium sauce to accompany boiled mutton.

Another early cook book was that of Victor Hirtzler, a native of Strasbourg who came to San Francisco in 1904, his preeminence in the art of cooking already well established. Many of the crowned heads of Europe knew his feats, and he had left his culinary imprint at Sherry's and the Waldorf-Astoria before settling in as chef de cuisine at the Hotel St. Francis in San Francisco. The Hotel, first built in 1849, then rebuilt within two years after the fire, assured its guests of perfect appointments, not the least noteworthy of which was its table. *The Evening Post* initiated a daily printing of M. Hirtzler's recipes. In 1910 the book stalls offered a volume covering his complete repertoire, bits of cooking advice, and advertisements for the widow Finke's champagnes and sparkling Burgundies, and for Mrs. McCarthy's Ellis Street Employment Office. The first section of his book deals with model menus; the second part contains "Extraordinary and Secret Compositions in Culinary Art (Hitherto Unpublished) for Which the Hotel St. Francis is Famed Written Especially for Housewives and Private Cooks The Whole Covering MORE THAN TWO THOUSAND DISHES." Among the recipes typical of the times is this one for marrow bones on toast:

> The best marrow is found in the round, the second best in the hind legs. Have it sawed off in two or three-inch lengths. Wrap in cloth and plunge in boiling broth, well seasoned, cooking for about twenty minutes. The broth may be used for soup just the same. Drain off, and serve the bones containing the marrow on a folded napkin, serving slices of fresh bread toasted, or take out the marrow and serve on the toast, without the bones, as you prefer. A favorite dish with many epicures.

Mr. Hirtzler offered his guests souffléed potatoes, a dish that has disappeared from all but a few of the most enterprising Bay Area menus:

> Have two kettles of fat, one having fresh kidney suet, clean and white. Slice your peeled potatoes into pieces of equal size through the entire length of the potato. Put into cold water for half an hour. Drain, and shake in a cloth to remove water. Plunge these slices, which should be about an eighth of an inch thick, into a kettle of lard of less temperature than smoking hot. Fry until they begin to become soft, but not discolored. Skim out with a wire spoon and plunge into the second kettle, having fat of smoking temperature, waiting long enough for potatoes to cool slightly. They should puff up immediately.

Between the courses of a large meal it was customary to serve digestives, light ices laced with alcohol. A favorite was Lalla Rookh:

> Fill a sherbet glass with water ice, and scoop out a big spoonful from the center, filling this with crème de menthe cordial.

Mr. Hirtzler suggested that brandy was a good alternative to crème de menthe, and further, that a delicious Thanksgiving treat was obtained by mixing semi-frozen rich vanilla ice cream in equal proportions with brandy. The Roman punch that Jack's serves today is much the same thing except that they use rum. On the more serious side, Mr. Hirtzler told housewives and private cooks how to boil terrapin. After boiling it alive for two minutes, and removing the skin with a towel, they were to immerse it whole into a kettle of water along with an onion, a carrot, a bay leaf, and one clove, to boil until the feet were tender. This took anywhere from fifteen minutes to several hours, depending on whether they were preparing papa or junior. The tender meat, including the liver, was removed from the shell, and put in jars together with its broth—first reduced to a cupful—and a whiskey glass of sherry. It was then ready for use in any one of a number of vigorous combinations. One of the favorite terrapin dishes was served from a chafing dish, in which it was immersed in a sauce of heavy cream thickened further with egg yolks, and enlivened with nutmeg, salt and pepper, a generous glob of butter, and half a glass of very dry sherry—terrapin à la Maryland. For those who preferred a browner dish, Mr. Hirtzler suggested terrapin Baltimore:

> One cup of terrapin with the liver. Put into a saucepan with salt, pepper, nutmeg, celery salt, a glass of dry sherry and boil for five minutes. Now mash the liver in a salad bowl, adding two raw yolks, one ounce of sweet butter, straining through fine sieve. Now add a cup of brown sauce to the simmering terrapin, then add the liver prepared as above, pouring in gradually. Barely heat this enough to thicken. Before serving add half a glass of dry sherry.

THE SAN FRANCISCO MENU TODAY

SAN FRANCISCO at present parades a legion of restaurants. Some embody past glories, others the tastes and contributions of a cosmopolitan population, and all a real love for good food. The city has, like any good cook, abstracted some of the best accents from widely differing cuisines, but the resulting menu has a strictly San Francisco flavor.

There are several foods you should certainly try. Seafood, for instance, is generally prepared in San Francisco with the imagination and care that make a dinner choice no easy matter. One of the most marvelous foods is the Dungeness crab, that turns up cooked or cold in a splendid assortment. There is also the giant king crab, flown in from Alaska, but it's not for me —not in the season when the crab pots bring in the local crustacean. So many restaurants serve cracked crab as part of the hors d'oeuvres—or as a separate course—that eight rosy legs, two pincer claws, white body wedges, and quartered lemons couchant on a field of cracked ice might well be considered the San Francisco coat of arms.

A dish in which crab generally stars, but sometimes is understudied by shrimp, is the city's most popular salad—crab Louis. A simple meal in itself, needing only the complement of a chilled white wine and a basket of crusty sour dough French bread, this dish consists of a mountain of delicate chilled crab meat resting on lettuce and covered with a piquant Louis dressing. In her superb *West Coast Cook Book*, Helen Evans Brown reports that a 1914 menu from Solari's listed this old favorite.[13]

When you're at Fisherman's Wharf, try the local fish stew, *cioppino*, according to some accounts a dish originally improvised by early Italian fishermen. One of the best versions is made largely with crab, but there are endless numbers of sea creatures which adapt themselves to a garlicky swim among its steaming tomatoes, onions, peppers, flecks of oregano, parsley and bay leaves.

Tiny Bay shrimp (fished these days from Bodega or Morro

[13] Helen Evans Brown, *West Coast Cook Book*, Boston, Little, Brown and Company, 1952, p. 134.

Bay) have an excellent flavor. They are under an inch in length, and it takes an army of them just to make a shrimp cocktail. They are often what you get when you order the latter, so if you have in mind something you can bite in two, you had better specify prawns. The Japanese restaurants serve a particularly fine dish of fried prawns called Tempura. Abalone, a giant among the mollusks, is native to California waters. Local chefs generally prepare it in steak-size slabs, browned quickly lest they become tough, but delicate when cooked with care. The Chinese sauté thin strips with a mélange of quick-cooking ingredients. Everybody makes it into chowder. Since the fresh meat cannot be shipped outside the state—the danger of the abalone's extinction having long been imminent—visitors should try some while they may.

Fresh salmon, to my mind one of the greatest of delicacies, has a local season like the native crab. Most city chefs prepare it enchantingly well, poached in delicate court bouillon, broiled so that its skin crackles, glazed with butter, onions, and carrots, or more formally posing under an aspic cover, en Bellevue. But then, you will be faced with such pleasant alternatives as turbot stuffed with crabmeat, creamy coquilles Saint-Jacques, golden-fried sand dabs (the most delicate member of the flounder family), sherried clams Elizabeth, broiled sea bass, crisp brown small fry (whitebait)—a specialty of the Nuggett Grill on Sutter Street—or filet of sole Marguery—everybody's masterpiece. True lobsters are sometimes imported from Atlantic waters, but San Franciscans generally dabble in their drawn butter with chunks of *langoustes*—or spiny lobsters. These creatures are almost all body, and unlike their Eastern counterparts have no meaty claws.

We have seen that oysters have nourished San Franciscans from early days; they have also produced a few legends. Hangtown Fry, so says one story, got its name by being requested as the last meal of a miner condemned to swing from a gallows

in Hangtown, California (now more discreetly named Placer-
ville). By the time the distant fresh oysters reached the scene,
the prisoner—with help from his friends—had left it. There
was nothing to do but cook up the dish anyhow, and like all
such merchandise in all such stories, it was phenomenally good
and has never since lost its popularity. The subject of this great
episode in culinary criminology is only an omelette, but one
that encloses a panful of delicately browned oysters topped off
with a garnish of bacon. Another oyster dish with more than
ordinary notoriety is the oyster loaf, reputedly so delectable it
could pacify the most wrathful of spouses, soothe the most in-
jured of feelings, reduce instantly the highest of dudgeons. What
better charm could a straying husband employ? I have read that
in the last century penitent San Franciscans called it a "squarer,"
and took it home to their wives in a paper bag to keep it hot.
It was much more effective than later generations' boxes of
candy or bunches of posies. Although I have also read that the
oyster loaf originated in San Francisco, the concoction was
known in eighteenth century England, and very early in New
Orleans—where it was called "La Médiatrice." The basic recipe
always starts with a loaf of bread, its top sliced off for a lid, its
innards scooped out. It is painted generously with butter, and
toasted ruddy and crisp in the oven. Then it is filled with sautéed
oysters, which are sometimes coated with cracker or bread
crumbs, and dunked in egg or cream. The hollow now crammed
full, the top fitted into place, the loaf languishes in the oven
until time for its glorious demise. Morrison Wood prints his
own version—the most interesting variation I've ever tried—in
his fine volume, *Fisherman's Wharf Cook Book*. He uses a
French bread swelled out with sherry-flavored oysters browned
crusty in cornmeal, then topped with slivers of dill pickles.[14]
Although until recently there was an Oyster Loaf Restaurant in

[14] Morrison Wood, *The Fisherman's Wharf Cook Book*, San Carlos, California, Nourse Publishing Company, 1955, p. 105.

28

San Francisco, today it is hard to find the dish on a city menu. Maye's Oyster House still serves it, either on the premises or to take out.

Californians are great salad lovers, feeding on an almost infinite variety of lettuce and greens that they punctuate with all manner of non-leafy tossables. In the mid-1700's the Franciscans planted the silver-leafed olive which today provides an excellent oil for salad dressings. I have Italian friends who prefer the California product. Many restaurants serve the salad as a first course —often with assorted hors d'oeuvres. Hearts of palm, Belgian endive, limestone lettuce, watercress, and hearts of Romaine brighten San Francisco salads. Green Goddess, always a favorite, originated at the Palace Hotel when the chef invented it to honor George Arliss, the star of William Archer's dramatic vehicle of the same name. Celery Victor, named after its creator, came out of Victor Hirtzler's imagination and the Hotel St. Francis kitchens. You can get these tender hearts poached in a broth then bathed in dressing, not only at their place of origin, but at good restaurants all over town.

San Francisco lives in the center of a vast garden, so a word should be said about the abundance of other fresh produce and fruit. Among them are artichokes, and some markets (though few restaurants) offer the tiny member of the family, which is even more delicious than the full grown one. Avocados are plentiful; San Franciscans generally prefer them chilled in company with seafood—the perfect foil for crab, lobster, prawns, or tiny bay shrimp. Sorrel, a rare but deserving green, turns into one of my favorite soups, and Jack's, one of my favorite restaurants, knows the proper incantations to mumble over the pot. Like all the best San Francisco places, they also have a magic eye when it comes to picking fruit for their tables, and you can be sure of voluptuous figs, melons, and berries. Californians also eat pomegranates, persimmons, papayas, and kumquats, though more often at home than in restaurants. If you yearn for tropical fruit, Trader Vic's supply is always of exceptional quality. Pineapple, in his hands, is a different—and better—fruit.

San Francisco is excellent for meat and poultry eating too. You can find chicken prepared in sauces of red wine or sour cream, broiled over charcoal or turned on the spit, curried, fried, or sautéed—and even baked in clay or hidden inside a coconut. Meats turn up as fondue Bourguignonne, spicy kebab, steak and kidney pie, saltimbocca, rack of lamb, and Burgundy beef. Variety meats are transformed into delicacies, and you will find kidneys, tripe, brains, and sweetbreads enough to delight a gourmet's heart. Several restaurants offer game, and will cook your catch if you happen to have been lucky in field or stream. I don't know what they would do if you turned up with a terrapin.

Eggs, in the form of Joe's Special, are an old San Francisco favorite. The story goes that this dish was invented late one night at New Joe's when all that was left in the kitchen was a bit of hamburger, some spinach, and a dozen eggs. A batch of hungry patrons came in, the chef put all his resources together, added a few condiments—and *ecco!*—the famous Joe's Special was born. (To make up a batch that will feed four, brown a pound of hamburger in olive oil and butter over a good flame. Add a handful of chopped scallions or minced onions, stirring as they cook, a sprinkle of marjoram, basil or oregano, and salt and pepper. Add a cup of chopped spinach, and continue to cook and stir. Scramble four beaten eggs into the meat mixture, and continue to mix as they set, but don't let them overcook.)

Nearby Petaluma supplies the city with eggs and poultry and the fine "Rouge et Noir" Camembert. Another good California cheese is the mild semi-soft Jack, and closely related, creamier Teleme, both from Monterey. Fortunately for Italian cookery, the local ricotta is first-rate.

Salami, pasta, and chocolate factories supply the city's inhabitants and its chefs with quality manufactures. But the local product which has earned the city its most loyal and devoted following—bordering at times on religious mania—is its sour dough French bread. Sour dough has come down from mining days, but it has improved all the way. A friend of mine reported that when he returned to the area last summer after several years in New York, he gained—in the short period of four weeks —fifteen pounds, all of them, he swears happily, on sour dough French bread. Until recently, this San Francisco staff of life sustained only Bay Area residents or visitors. Now TWA flights whisk a precious 300 loaves at a time from Larraburu Bakery to the Hotel Plaza in New York. My friend can reside at peace in either community.

On the caloric side, San Franciscans like to add to their girth with paklava, French pastries, petits coeurs à la crème, cherries jubilee, crêpes suzette, and cheesecake. But two other specialties appear with the greatest frequency: fried cream and banana fritters. Fried cream, a firm custard square rolled in fine crumbs or nutmeats, then fried in butter, goes down easily whether doused with a tangy cherry sauce, or set in flames under a ladle of warm brandy. Helen Evans Brown has an early recipe from a San Diego cookbook; it was called "Bonfire Entré." Fried cream was cut in "sticklike pieces and stacked up on individual plates like miniature and roofless log cabins. A couple of lumps of sugar, brandy-soaked, went into the center of each pile of 'logs,' and matches graced the side of each plate. The lights were lowered, and everyone lit up. Whoopee!" [15] Things have changed a bit in California; now the waiters set the fires. Banana fritters are equally distingué. The bananas, dipped in a flavorful batter, sizzle gently in butter or fry in deep fat until they are amber, and arrive puffy and hot in a long silver boat with a cargo of whipped cream. (If you want to try them, split one banana for each two portions, first the long way and then in half. Put to soak in a mixture of rum or brandy, two or three tablespoons of confectioner's sugar, and the juice of half a lemon, and a little

[15] *West Coast Cook Book*, p. 66.

grated peel. Make a batter by adding to two well beaten egg yolks, one cup of sifted flour, ½ teaspoon salt, ¾ cup of milk, and a tablespoon each of the liquid from the bananas and melted butter. When mixed smooth, add the egg whites beaten stiff. Drain the bananas, dip until well coated in the batter, and fry. This amount of batter will do nicely for eight portions.)

Cappuccino—in San Francisco a drink of hot chocolate, milk, and brandy, and no relation, except in name, to the Italian coffee with milk—puts a glowing finish to many a meal. Some restaurants serve it, and many bars, particularly La Tosca in North Beach. I can't think of a happier stand against a chilling fog—unless, possibly, it be that other San Francisco protector, Irish coffee.

SOME ETHNIC VARIATIONS

BECAUSE San Francisco is made up of many smaller communities, you won't really get a feel of the city until you experience directly the excitement that its different groups contribute. Leonard Austin, in *Around the World in San Francisco* (Fearon, 1959), lists sixty-six racial and ethnic groups resident in the city. You will begin to know San Francisco when you poke into her streets and ways, and sit at table with a crew of former Basque shepherds, or with the varied descendants of Italians, Armenians, Slavs, Japanese, Germans, Indians, Frenchmen, Chinese, and fifty-seven others.

Many of these citizens, to preserve customs from their mother cultures, patronize special markets that stock the supplies needed for their own styles of cooking. The streets of Chinatown are edged with a continuous market. Chinese groceries have traditionally exhibited their produce in open stalls fringing the sidewalks. Recently the San Francisco Police Department, embarked on a health kick, began enforcing a generally ignored ordinance that may result in the closing down of open air displays—not only in Chinatown, but also in the Italian neighborhoods. You will have to hunt inside for the water chestnuts, snails, bunches of long, thin string beans, Chinese broccoli and cabbage, and fresh ginger roots. But the Peking ducks will still swing in the windows, and the fish will continue to swim unaware in their glass houses.

In the Italian neighborhood there are red and green peppers, purple *melanzane*, pale green zucchini and dark green broccoli, artichokes with scalloped skirts, bitter dandelions and *cardoni*, and aromatic bunches of sweet fresh basil. In the fall, great barrels of chestnuts squat beside the doors. Italians can buy spring suckling lamb, or *capretto* for an Easter feast of kid roasted with oil, rosemary, and garlic. There are dried salt cod-fish, and mobiles of salami. Blood sausages, *mortadella*, and *coppa* fill the cases, and all the zesty cheeses are there, from gorgonzola to craggy mountains of very old Parmesan—to be grated fresh at home.

The Greeks keep up the tradition of their coffee houses, in some of which they down an anise-flavored fire-water called Ouzo. They support a restaurant on Columbus called La Grecque, and another half-dozen in the Tenderloin district, among them the Minerva Café and the Greek-American Coffee House. The Danish, whose Bay Area concentration is one of the largest in the country, have had a favorable influence on a number of baked goods. They have a luxury restaurant dedicated to their style of cooking. Camille's, an old San Francisco establishment with a French background, has recently been metamorphosed as Copenhagen, with Viking spears, a chef and a menu from Copenhagen.

Spanish-speaking peoples in San Francisco—Mexicans, Latin and Central Americans, Spaniards, and New Mexican Hispanos —still congregate in North Beach, upper Broadway, and around the base of Telegraph Hill. Restaurants and nightspots with a

33

Latin beat add to the pulse of the neighborhood, among them the Mexican Xochimilco on Powell Street, El Patio Andaluz with its flamenco artists, and La Bodega, a modest but charming place that has hours as casual as its proprietors, Helen and Harry Clarke. While the food holds out at La Bodega, you can have salad, some variation of a *paella,* French bread, and with your dark roast coffee served Spanish-style in a glass, either a semi-dry Jack cheese that resembles Spanish Manchego, or a delicious rum petit four. Occasionally customers drain their Spanish wine from a *porron,* a glass jug with a narrow protruding spout. Non-professional guitarists frequent La Bodega; they often join in a *jaleo,* and night-owls hear their music drift across the street. Segovia, Sabicas, and Montoya have all visited here. There is another hangout in the neighborhood for aficionados, mostly non-Spanish variety, up around the corner on Broadway. It is the elegant bar owned by author-bullfighter Barnaby Conrad, filled with a collection of just about everything from the bull ring, and called the Matador.

Russians came to San Francisco early, even before the Gold Rush. Some Russian sailors died on a warship that touched the port in 1848, and were buried on the slopes of what is consequently now called Russian Hill. The graves are still there. That ship sailed on, but others returned, and by 1869 San Francisco housed a Russian colony large enough to have its own church. Today there are bakeries and restaurants that specialize in Russian foods, among them the Ukraine Bakery, which once served food, but now limits itself to the production of sturdy ryes and dark black pumpernickels, salt sticks, onion rolls, egg twists, and the like. Among the restaurants are the Luchina on Clement, the Renaissance on Geary Blvd., (which also provides live Russian music), the Miniature Bakery-Delicatessen on Clement (which makes especially good piroshki), and the Park Presidio Bakery and Delicatessen on Clement. At the modest, inexpensive and excellent Boris and Mary's (301 Balboa) there is no live Russian music, but the juke box has a choice of one hundred Russian records. Boris and Mary Savitsky, who came to this country in 1951 by way of China and the Philippines, converted what was once a regular American coffee shop into a haven for devotees of good home-cooked Russian meals. The menu changes daily, and includes such dishes as stchee (cabbage and potato soup), borscht (cabbage, beets, and potatoes), beef à la Stroganoff (beef simmered in sour cream), koreika (roast pork with sauerkraut), kitochki (ground chicken patties), shashlik (barbecued lamb Caucasian-style), pilav (lamb stew with rice, also Caucasian), cutlet à la Kiev (boned and breaded chicken breast, stuffed with spicy butter), cheese cake and rum cake.

Edinburgh Castle, a huge Scottish pub at 950 Geary, lures many patrons who speak their English with a burr. They drink their ale or stout to the whine of the pipes, and watch dart games in progress in the back of the hall.

A contingent of Swiss reside in the city, and their gathering spot until recently was the William Tell Hotel (William Tell Haus) at 630 Clay Street. There to the strains of an accordion-led band dressed in lederhosen and jaunty hats, the crowd jigged or whirled in a polka or a waltz. They now dance on Friday, Saturday and Sunday in Fugazi Hall, and the old building, still hospitable, accommodates Turk Murphy, his superb jazz band, and a whole new set of dancers.

A few Jewish delicatessens, mainly along McAllister and Golden Gate in the Fillmore, cater to tastes formed in such borscht-and-sour-cream centers as New York and Chicago—and to a Western legion of inspired followers. Lisa's Kosher Style Restaurant on Eddy Street isn't fancy, but the food is good. David Apfelbaum, a survivor of two concentration camps, presides over David's Restaurant-Delicatessen. The place fills after show time with many of the stars from the legitimate theatres across Geary Street. The perfume of pickled herring, sweet and sour stuffed cabbage, chopped chicken livers, onion rolls, hot pastrami, corned beef, and pickled dills is enough to make a strong man quaver. People, on entering, can't resist going into a series of deep-breathing exercises. Occasionally when I have been waiting for a table, a merciful hand has extended from behind the counter, bearing a plate of triangles lavishingly spread with chicken livers —to nibble on until a place was free. Before David took over this location, yearners after lox and bagels frequented a shop at the same address known as the "Bon Vivant." I always admired its listing of one of my favorite foods, in what was a true San Francisco amalgamation, "blintzes avec sour cream."

But I have not yet begun to mention some even greater foreign influences on the San Francisco cuisine. The Japanese, Chinese, French, Italian, Indian, Armenian, and German restaurants are so important that each will have to have its own section in the restaurant chapter that follows.

SOME MISCELLANEOUS INSTITUTIONS

SAN FRANCISCO's best sidewalk cafe—and its nearest thing to the Via Veneto—is Enrico's. This big, swanky emporium occupies a choice spot on Broadway, half indoors, half out. Most of its patrons are elegant coffee loungers or bar flies, but you can eat your way through a substantial al fresco dinner at one of its travertine tables. Like its Roman counterparts, it provides a perch just out of the passing parade, but close enough for good ogling.

Outdoors enthusiasts in the middle of town can soak up sun in the Hotel Canterbury's Garden Patio, which serves from an à la carte menu all day long, and is also heated—just in case. On Sutter Street, not far from Union Square, this pleasant umbrella-shaded oasis seems miles from any business district. The Starlite Roof of the Sir Francis Drake leaves the hubbub far behind by going twenty-one stories straight up. It provides a good smorgasbord lunch with an excellent city view, cocktail service and dancing into the wee hours. The Mark Hopkins Hotel's Top of the Mark serves only drinks, and San Franciscans are delighted when they have out-of-towners to lure to this glass-walled observatory. There is also nightly dancing. Across the street, the new twenty-nine story Fairmont Tower with its Crown Room now shares the Mark's monopoly on the skyline; you can see for fifty spectacular miles from either place. The Fairmont has at least two other noteworthy rooms. The Pavilion Room, a glass-enclosed Persian wonder, overlooks a roof garden terraced like those of private Nob Hill residences of the turn of the century. Subtropical trees and shrubs and a Monterey pine surround a pool and animated fountain. The 2,000 feet of enclosed space easily accommodates a gilded chandelier of wrought iron that stretches twenty-four feet across and supports forty-five pendant lanterns. San Franciscans go here for dancing, which begins during the cocktail hour. The hotel's Tonga Room is a sort of California Street South Seas. Not only is there a pool, but the orchestra (no doubt heavily plied with Dramamine) floats in it aboard a raft; not an hour goes by but that a tropical storm thunders through the beams.

The St. Francis Hotel on Powell opposite Union Square proceeds in quieter fashion. There, just a few steps up from the lobby, stretches a pleasantly serene spot called The Terrace Room. It serves excellent cocktails, lunch, dinner, and late suppers, in a stately modern setting. The waitresses move softly about, their Japanese kimono-clad figures looking like so many lovely dolls.

Two other San Francisco landmarks are Goldberg-Bowen, a fancy grocery that has dispensed gourmet foods and wines locally since 1850 (and now includes a main floor restaurant), and

INTRODUCTION

Blum's, a confectionery that has satisfied the city's sweet tooth since 1890 (and now also serves, in several locations, salads, sandwiches, and other light foods).

San Francisco still has a prodigious number of drinking places and can provide for any taste or mood. The newest fad is for fanciful revivals of the saloon of bygone days. The most lavish of these is the Roaring Twenties. Revelers in its decorated chambers can try out their vocal cords around honky-tonk pianos, boost their egos by hitting the targets in the downstairs shooting gallery, or be titillated by watching a bevy of fringe-swishing waitresses take turns sliding down brass fire-poles and pumping red velvet swings.

Lucius Beebe, the city's Epicure General, bellicosely points out that there is little similarity between the Twenties' speakeasy and its modern stage-set. "I find it difficult," he writes in his *San Francisco Chronicle* column, "to reconcile the contemporary recreation of the Roaring Twenties with its properties ravished from Venetian palazzos, Moorish mosques, Nob Hill mansions of the Eighties and red velvet swings that are Harry K. Thaw-Stanford White, with the factual reality as I knew it, man and beast, for a decade and a half all the way from Honest Parker Shannon's in Avery Street, Boston, to Izzy Gomez's, nearer the scene of these later dazzlements. Izzy had scant use for quartered marble table tops and Parker Shannon kept a ball bat behind the bar into whose business end a quantity of melted lead had been poured."

At Bustles and Beaus, a downtown saloon that includes among its customers tired lady shoppers, the costumes come from another decade altogether, but the mood is precisely the same. Here the young ladies sometimes come down those 18-karat poles head first. Gold Street, another "turn-of-the-century" dispensary, sells sandwiches for a nickel. Drinks come somewhat higher. The Crazy Horse and the Red Garter serve beer with banjo music.

The Library, a book-lined bistro on Clement and 11th, is a cross between second-hand bookstore, Lonely Hearts Club, and telephone exchange. The books are actually for sale, but they remain for the most part decorative; the customers are usually far too busy calling each other up, via Central, on one of the thirty telephones installed around the place. It is a gimmick that guarantees that no one will sit alone for long without an offer, over the wire, of a drink from the other end of the bar. The downtown bar with a phone on every table is Extension 21 on Geary. Its owner, Harry Hanneman, says he got the idea from a Berlin uncle who operated the Razi Bar in that city.

A typical San Francisco institution is the cellar theatre-bar. Once a quarter bought your way into a barely decorated basement where you sat on a camp chair, sipped an inexpensive drink, and enjoyed the performance of talented but unknown local entertainers. So refreshing and original were many of them —most notably Mort Sahl and the Kingston Trio—that they brought fame to themselves, and to the hungry i and the Purple Onion. Nowadays things are different: the seats are more comfortable, the drinks are higher, and the hungry i has a restaurant on the premises. When Mort Sahl plays there it's $3.50 a throw, plus drinks—if you can get in.

Perhaps the most fashionable nightery—really a supper club —is Station J, an elegantly decorated old power house at Commercial and Montgomery streets. Things start bouncing here at the cocktail hour, when a small ensemble provides music for dancing. Later in the evening there is a thirteen-piece orchestra. The big, high-ceilinged power plant interior has been cut down to intimate size, yet retains enough of the original scale to achieve an almost Palace-of-Versailles grandeur. If you think it is done with mirrors, you are right: one wall reflects endlessly in a darkly veined glass a myriad of flickering lights from several hanging crystal chandeliers of substantial proportions. The bar and a scattering of tables are adjacent to the small dance floor, but diners ascend to a balcony that looks over the entire scene. They have a choice of lobster (broiled or thermidor), steak (filet with béarnaise or New York cut sirloin), and chicken (Cordon Bleu). All dinners include relishes, soup, salad, potato, vegetable, dessert and beverage, and they are expensive. Whether you come here for late supper, a predinner drink, or a snifter of brandy after, come here you should, for the spirit is contagious, and the design something to see.

One of the newest entertainments takes place at Gigi, a theatre-restaurant-bar on Broadway. Pasha's Sultan Band or the Haji Baba Combo play music of the Middle East, but this is only a background for the authentic belly dancers.

Jazz enthusiasts find the whole range from Dixieland to Progressive. Fans of the modern style congregate at the Jazz Workshop on Broadway, and devotees of the blues crowd into Sugar Hill. New Fack's, which is really more of a supper club, has generally excellent music. Old timer Turk Murphy holds forth in his own place, called Earthquake McGoon's, which has recently taken over the old William Tell Hotel. They have maintained a restrained 1890 saloon quality in the decor, and have even gone to the trouble of matching the old paint. They serve a limited dinner menu: steaks, chops, hamburgers, and steak sandwiches, special fish chowder, and a Louis Armstrong recipe for red beans and rice. Along with the main course they bring salad, garlic French bread, French fried potatoes, and coffee. The strains of Dixieland also prevail at an Embarcadero spot, On the Levee. Right across the street at Pier 23 Burt Bales plays a low-down piano; the pick-up band that joins him can change not only from night to night, but even through the course of an evening. Before he was nearly removed from the scene by a passing motorist, Burt used to cook up a good Southern fried chicken. It's a rare occasion when the bartender at Pier 23 doesn't execute a nostalgic old ditty in what is one of the most unlikely voices in the Western hemisphere. The customers love it.

The Old Spaghetti Factory Cafe and Excelsior Coffee House on Green Street actually does serve noodles and coffee (and a number of other things besides). But the main interests here are its classical and flamenco concerts, its popular musical review, and its decor—an accumulation of marvelous junk and humorous portraits that you can look through for hours.

San Franciscans flourish among their eateries, palaces, honky-tonks, and cafés. They drink steam beer (it originated in the city, and one brewer still remains). They toss dice for their check or the drinks. They thrive on the culinary variety their city provides them, delight in the prospect of *tripe à la mode de Caen* for lunch, kouzou kzartma for supper. They are equally at home eating pheasant amid Ernie's Edwardian splendors, or biting into sardines and onions on French bread at the counter in Mike's Billiard Parlor. For resident and visitor alike, San Francisco cooking has something of the effect reported by Alice B. Toklas, when she and Gertrude Stein (once an Oakland girl) revisited the city in 1935:

> In San Francisco we indulged in gastronomic orgies—sand dabs *meunière*, rainbow trout in aspic, grilled soft-shell crabs, *paupiettes* of roast fillets of pork, eggs Rossini and *tarte Chambord*. The *tarte Chambord* had been a specialty of one of the three great French bakers before the San Francisco fire. To my surprise, in Paris no one had ever heard of it.
>
> At Fisherman's Wharf we waited for two enormous crabs to be cooked in a cauldron on the side-walk, and they were still quite warm when we ate them at lunch in Napa County.[16]

[16] *The Alice B. Toklas Cook Book*, New York, Harper and Row, 1954.

II

Restaurants

I

N 1855, Frank Soulé, John Gihon, and James Nisbet reported
in *The Annals of San Francisco* that within two or three years
of the gold strike the number of establishments in the city devoted to eating was enormous and furthermore of a vast variety:

> There were the American *dining-rooms*, the English *lunch
> houses*, the French *cabarets*, the Spanish *fondas*, the German
> *wirthschafts*, the Italian *osterie*, the Chinese *chow-chows*, and
> so on to the end of a very long chapter.[17]

There is still the same variety and plenty in the land, but when
it comes to settling on a way of classifying the multitude of eat-
ing-houses, such clear-cut categories as *osterie* and *chow-chows*
do not always present themselves. The arrangement that follows
is as sensible as I can make it, and I try to note those restaurants
that fit into more than one category.

Before deciding on which establishments to include, I tried
or retried each one personally and anonymously, paid for all of
my meals myself, and, in spite of what is a growing custom, took
no compensation in any form for mentioning any place in this
book. I must confess to two exceptions: Vic Bergeron once

---

[17] Frank Soulé, John Gihon, and James Nisbet, *The Annals of San Francisco*,
New York, 1855, p. 640.

45

treated me to a lunch, but, as anyone who knows him will testify, besides being a charming and stubborn gentleman, he couldn't care less whether or not he was mentioned in someone's book. I also accepted one after-dinner drink at the urging of a proprietor who recognized me; but in the final analysis I decided against including his place, so I guess that's fair enough. After a good many meals and the addition of several pounds, I settled on those restaurants that I judged to be the best or most interesting in San Francisco. Of course, there will always be differences of taste and opinion—and I regret any errors of omission. But barring some few inevitable changes in management and fortune, I think the reader will find that each place included is at least good in one way or another. I would be grateful for the reader's comments, for I intend to keep my list as reliable as possible. As a general rule I have included no place that hasn't had time to prove itself.

Each restaurant is classified according to expense in one of three categories:

inexpensive (less than $3.00)
moderate (most dinners between $3 and $5)
expensive (over $5)

Drinks, tips, and tax are additional. Since restaurant hours and closing days vary considerably, and reservations are becoming increasingly necessary, the reader will be wise always to phone ahead. A directory of the restaurants described will be found at the end of this volume.

The recipes have all been tested; [18] they constitute a small but authentic San Francisco cook book, including most of the regional specialties. Occasionally they call for ingredients that may be unavailable in some areas. The following food suppliers will

---

[18] Some of the instructions that follow are reductions of recipes originally intended for very large numbers, and consequently in these few cases they may not be the exact equivalent of the restaurant dish.

fill mail orders: for Chinese food products, Chong Kee Jan, 957 Grant Avenue, San Francisco, California; for all Japanese food products, Uoki Fish Market, 1684 Post Street, San Francisco, California; for shallots, mussels, pâté de foie gras, truffles, babas au rhum, and other fancy products, Les Echalottes, 706 Lafayette Street, Paramus, New Jersey (catalogue available). The following substitutions can be made, although the results will not be as faithful as when the original ingredients are used:

For fresh herbs, use dried herbs, but cut the amount to one half.

For shallots, use green onions.

For fresh green ginger, use canned ginger (not crystallized) or soak dried ginger root in cold water before using.

For stock use canned bouillon, bouillon cubes, or stock bases such as the chicken and beef stocks put out by the Spice Island Company.

For meat extract (glace de viande), use bottled extracts such as Wilson's B-V extract of beef.

Where wine, brandy, rum, or the like are called for, the better the product, the finer the result.

There are two precautions; Japanese and Chinese soy sauce are not the same thing, and cannot be used interchangeably. Packaged herbs that are finely pulverized lose their oils, and consequently most of their flavor; those that are packaged in cardboard will contribute little more to the dish you are cooking than a musty flavor.

A Note on Ordering California Wine

SAN FRANCISCANS are great wine drinkers, living as they do within a few miles of the best winegrowing area of the country, and so almost all the listed restaurants have a good offering of imported and local wines. California wines are usually a better bargain, though none is comparable to the greatest vintages of France and Germany. When ordering California wines, be sure to order by the varietal name rather than by the generic. The best California wines, that is, are always made from the best European wine grapes and named after the principal grape used in their making. Names like *Burgundy, Claret, Sauterne, Chablis, Rhine Wine*, and *Vin Rosé* on a bottle of California wine are absolutely no guarantee of what is in the bottle. But names like *Pinot Noir, Cabernet Sauvignon, Pinot Chardonnay*, and the like, are protected by law, and guarantee that the wine in the bottle contains at least fifty-one percent of that grape. Since the climate is steadier than in Europe, the quality of California wine varies less from year to year, and there is less significance in the date of a wine except as denoting its age. Often the date is omitted altogether. Reputable vintners can be trusted not to market their wine before it is ready to drink. Here is a list of the best California dinner wines and some of the best wineries that produce them. The equivalent European genre is indicated in parenthesis.

RED WINES:

Cabernet Sauvignon (Red Bordeaux; Claret):
Beaulieu, Inglenook, Charles Krug, Louis Martini, Martin Ray
Pinot Noir (Red Burgundy):
Beaulieu, Inglenook, Louis Martini, Martin Ray
Gamay (Beaujolais):
Inglenook, Charles Krug, Digardi
Barbera (Chianti):
Louis Martini, Sebastiani

WHITE WINES:

Pinot Chardonnay (White Burgundy; Chablis):
Wente Bros., Inglenook, Beaulieu, Martin Ray

Pinot Blanc (Chablis; White Burgundy):
Wente Bros., Almadén
Dry Semillon (Sauternes; Graves—but dryer):
Wente Bros., Concannon
Sauvignon Blanc (Sauternes; Graves—but dryer):
Wente Bros., Concannon, Beaulieu
Johannisberg Riesling (Rhine; Moselle):
Louis Martini, Beaulieu, Almadén
Traminer (Alsatian):
Inglenook, Charles Krug, Louis Martini, Almadén
Sylvaner (Alsatian; Rhine):
Louis Martini, Almadén
Grey Riesling (from the French Chauché gris grape):
Wente Bros., Charles Krug, Almadén
Chenin Blanc (Vouvray):
Charles Krug, Louis Martini, Almadén

PINK WINES:

Grenache Rosé (Tavel):
Beaulieu, Almadén
Gamay Rosé (Rosé):
Inglenook, Charles Krug, Louis Martini

1. FRENCH

As early as the 1850's, San Francisco spoke with a French accent; its presently large Gallic population makes it a leading center of that culture in this country. It supports a French newspaper, hospital, and department store—the City of Paris—and a number of first-rate resorts devoted to the pleasure of eating *à la française*. Since it was in the first place the French chefs in the entourages of traveling Eastern nabobs who started off San

51

Francisco's long-standing affair with good cooking, it is only right that some of her finest restaurants should be dedicated to French cuisine.

✳ *Jack's*

615 SACRAMENTO STREET

expensive

A GOOD MANY SAN FRANCISCANS CONSIDER JACK'S THE FINEST restaurant in the city. When he is in town, financier Louis Lurie has come in for lunch every day for the last forty-four years. At the same corner table, he has hosted over the decades a legion of friends, and just about every visiting celebrity to the city. He was even once served a subpoena there, to testify before the Federal Housing Expediter on a matter of local hotel classifications—done in by his predictable habit of lunching at Jack's.

A Hollywood producer once starred Jack's in the dining scenes of one of his movies because it looked more like a restaurant than any place he knew. One of San Francisco's most exclusive stores has reproduced a replica of Jack's matchbook cover for local ladies' sweaters. A United States Senator requested its menu to decorate his Washington, D.C. dining room. After a devastating fire in 1958, the messages of condolence almost flooded the place. One day recently, several businessmen, enjoying themselves too much to tear themselves away, lingered over their lunch, then over their brandies, suddenly to discover that it was dinner time. They ordered up their second meal and finally departed at half past nine that evening.

How does all this come about? Primarily, through this venerable restaurant's tradition of impeccable cooking. Its kitchen employs only one modern gadget—a spinach chopper. Otherwise, all the blending, straining, puréeing, and other operations are performed in the old classic manner—with plenty of hand labor. Even the bartender juices his oranges, grapefruits, and lemons on a fine old-fashioned squeezer. Classic delicacies cram the single-page menu, which, owing to mercifully bright lighting, you can read without the slightest squint.

Reluctance to depart from honest decor is to my mind another of Jack's virtues. When you dine here, the backdrop is nothing more obtrusive than light walls bordered by a frieze in the gustatory tradition: over-flowing cornucopias, game, garlands of flowers, and spillings of grapes. The linens are white, the chairs have cane seats and looped backs, and there are hatracks along the walls. Diners who wish to celebrate some festive occasion can feast in splendid privacy in the red-curtained salons on the floor above. Guests are served by a corps of exceptional waiters —most of them as venerable as their surroundings.

Jack's has been functioning since 1864. Jacques Monique, the owner from 1884, sold the premises at the end of the century to Edward Blanquie. He resisted putting his name on the marquee, so Jack's Rotisserie it remained for the next several years. Then, during alterations to shift the kitchen from its position in front of the dining room to a location in the rear, the owners simplified the name to its present form.

Michel Redinger, who started working at Jack's in 1889, and who died only recently, bought an interest from Blanquie after the earthquake and fire, and together they operated in a temporary location on Golden Gate Avenue until the Sacramento Street premises could be rebuilt. The 1907 downtown scene was still a tangle of ruins when the doors reopened at the present site. For the last forty years the Redinger family alone has been running the business. Michel's brother Paul, whose tenure dates back to 1903, his brother Emile, and Paul's son Jack, have been managing things for the dozen years since the senior owner retired.

RESTAURANTS

It was Paul Redinger who, rummaging through the ruins of the 1906 catastrophe, dug up a few old sugar bowls, and a menu dated April 17, 1906. Customers that fateful day fortified themselves unawares, a few hours before disaster struck, with tripe à la mode de Caen, green turtle steak, pickled calf's head, or ragout of spring duck; they doled out seventy-five cents for their dinners, and got half a bottle of wine in the bargain. If they followed that with cognac or kirsch, the additions came to twelve and a half cents.

Although turtle steaks no longer enhance California menus, Jack's still serves up a splendid calf's head vinaigrette every Thursday, and tripe and duck are commonplace on their menu. Monday specialties are lamb stew à la française or braised beef with vegetables; on Tuesdays Jack's bakes lamb; Wednesday is beef day—boiled, or corned with cabbage; and on Thursday the chef collects accolades for roast leg of lamb with lentils, and braised ox-joints with vegetables; Friday's specialty is a combination of seafood baked au gratin en coquille St.-Jacques; and Saturday's triumph is the sorrel soup. Every day there is filet of sole à la Marguery, a dish I could eat happily for the rest of my days if Jack's did the cooking. There are always imported escargots, steaming pungently Bordelaise-style; frogs' legs sautéed à sec or poulette—a favorite since the '90's; sweetbreads lavished with mushrooms, or broiled and served up plump on toast; and boiled salmon bathed in hollandaise. At Jack's your appetite will be whetted with Olympia oysters, Romanoff caviar, imported pâté de foie gras; teased further by a taste of mock turtle soup redolent with sherry, or a shimmery cold jellied consommé; appeased by sand dabs or rex sole, meunière; satisfied by a buttery rump steak or mutton chop, a rack of spring lamb, or a chicken sautéed in white wine with artichokes and mushrooms; and finally silenced altogether by a rum omelette, the best crêpes suzette in the city, a seductive wedge of cheesecake, a slice of fresh pineapple glistening with kirsch, or camembert or Danish blue with crackers.

Roasted brown guinea hen in orange sauce, squab broiled crackling or snuggling in a casserole among a coterie of vegetables, steamed clams Bordelaise, or lamb kidneys broiled with bacon—what a happy confusion of choices! There is a generous complement of seasonable vegetables, and a half dozen sauces to spoon over them. Jack's will provide you with that once famous digestive, Roman punch, these days preferred at the end, rather than in the middle, of the repast; or with imported Bar-le-Duc jelly to spread on your French pancakes. If you prefer a slightly less exotic selection, there is a daily dinner which includes soup, salad, entrée, roast, vegetables, and dessert, all for a remarkably moderate sum.

Like any artist, the chef at Jack's creates without rigid formulas. The procedures he goes by are not written down, except in his memory, and his measurements are known only to his instincts. However, the restaurant has kindly provided me with reliable approximations of two of his masterpieces.

FILET OF SOLE MARGUERY

2 lbs. filet of sole (folded double)
1 cup sliced mushrooms
12 crab legs
½ cup shrimps
2 shallots, finely chopped

½ cup dry white wine
½ cup fish stock (or water)
salt and pepper
½ cup cream
2 tbsp. hollandaise sauce

In a well-buttered baking dish place filets of sole, sliced mushrooms, crab legs, shrimps, shallots, white wine, stock, and salt and pepper to taste. Bake in a moderate oven. When fish is cooked (about 15 minutes) remove all ingredients to an ovenproof platter or baking dish. To the liquid remaining in the dish, add ½ cup of cream, reduce to a thick sauce, then add 2 tbsp. hollandaise sauce. Mix well, but do not boil again. Pour the sauce over the fish and glaze under the broiler or in a hot oven. Serves four.

➤ CHICKEN MASCOTTE

1 2¾-lb. chicken, disjointed
butter
a few mushrooms, cut in
  wedges
2 hearts of artichokes, cut in
  wedges

1 clove of shallots, chopped
salt and pepper
⅓ cup sherry
1 cup brown stock

Melt enough butter in a skillet to sauté the chicken, then cook
the pieces until golden brown. When well colored, remove them.
Sauté the mushrooms, artichokes, and shallots in the same pan,
cooking until yellow, but not brown. Add chicken, salt, pepper,
sherry, and stock, and simmer until tender—about 20 or 30 minutes. Serve in a preheated casserole. Will serve two persons.

✳ *Fleur De Lys*

777 SUTTER STREET

expensive

ALTHOUGH YOU WOULDN'T SUPPOSE THAT A FRENCH RESTAURANT
in San Francisco would cause much stir in Paris, Fleur de Lys
has managed to do just that. It started with a column that Louis-
Piechaud wrote for *Le Figaro*, but before it was through it
involved Larousse, Littré, verse by Ronsard, members of the
French Society of Letters, and correspondents from Paris,
Cannes, and Bordeaux. They were one and all concerned with
how to pronounce the name of a fine restaurant carrying on the
tradition of Gallic cookery in far-off California. The experts
never could agree on whether to call the heraldic lily Fleur de
"Lease" or Fleur de "Lee," but the proprietors themselves pronounce the "s"—and that's definitive enough for me.

If you have a penchant for Gallic sophistication, Fleur de Lys will please you. Not only is the cooking *haute cuisine*, but the appointments and service are both exceptional. The tables twinkle like a window display, regally set with service plates and goblets of heavy silver, dinnerware of porcelain, stemware from Bavaria. At the bar you sip from Swedish or Czechoslovakian crystal.

The *cuisiniers* who preside over every elegant inch of this transplanted French acreage are a beautiful blonde and a handsomely bearded gentleman, Chérie and Robert Charles. The second world war interrupted Robert's medical studies at Grenoble, and after a five year stint in the French Army he gave up a career dedicated to surgery. Blessed be for us! He and Chérie set up as restaurateurs in the little village of Gourdon, near Cannes. Before long, the *Club des Sans Club* took notice of their talents, the *Guides des Touristes Gastronomes* recommended them to its readers, and the *Guide Michelin* placed two revered stars next to their *Le Nid d'Aigle*.

In 1955, the Charleses came to the United States for their first visit. A little over a year later they were back, and in business in San Anselmo, California. The first Fleur de Lys, operating on a spare budget, seated 28 patrons on beer kegs. But they dined off lavish silver utensils—wedding presents of the proprietors. The food was sumptuous. The couple couldn't afford advertising, but no matter, for the delights of dining chez Charles spread rapidly by word of mouth. Soon San Franciscans were traveling to the Marin village in droves to indulge their love of good food.

Finally Fleur de Lys moved to San Francisco. (The Charleses promised to return to their village, and have recently opened a second Fleur de Lys in San Anselmo.) To match the splendors of their new city restaurant, they sent to the Hotel Raphaël in Paris for a bartender *par excellence*, Maurice Amzallag. He has emerged recently from behind the bar to a post as Assistant Manager.

The first Charleses' menu carried a few words of their own composition that are still the best introduction to the foods that follow:

La cuisine est un art.
Celui qui la prépare ou la sert le fait avec amour.
Vous qui la dégustez, sachez la savourer avec amour aussi.
(Cooking is an art.
One who prepares it or serves it does so with love.
You who taste it should taste it, too, with love.)

The menu is à la carte, and there is an exceptional wine list. Robert is a member of the *Confrérie des Chevaliers du Tastevin*. You are in good hands.

A good start is a house specialty, Salade Niçoise, an invention from southern France that contains Boston lettuce, fresh tomatoes and cucumbers, broiled green peppers, string beans, tuna fish, anchovies, hard boiled eggs, black olives, "garlic chapon," an assortment of herbs, and a tangy French dressing. Or you might try an unusual appetizer, the Bébés Abalone "Diane," abalones no larger than an inch across, soaking up a dressing of olive oil and fresh lemon juice, a sprinkling of chopped chives, roughly grated black pepper, and appropriate spices. Perhaps, if you plan an elaborate follow-up, a simple green salad should start you off. The Charleses' own wine vinegar with an abundance of fresh basil and other herbs makes a splendid vinaigrette dressing.

Four hors d'oeuvres chauds tax your powers of decision. Should it be Crevettes Pondichéry—shrimps in curried pancakes—or mushrooms stuffed with snails? Or would oysters be even better —miniature Kislings in a mignonette sauce—or Eastern oysters baked in their shells, bubbling in a bath of fish bouillon, egg yolks, heavy cream, melted butter, and champagne? If there weren't so many delights to follow, I would be inclined to have shrimp, snails, and oysters all!

Half a dozen soups include cold vichyssoise and steaming green turtle. Fish and shellfish range from scallops en coquilles, and sole dieppoise—filets poached in a wine and cream sauce —to frogs' legs infused with garlic and fennel, and Langouste Cardinal—the lobster done up in a sauce of truffles. You can order next a breast of capon cooked in vin rosé and mushrooms, or rolled around whole truffles and goose liver, breaded, sautéed in sweet butter, flamed in cognac, and baked in the oven. Robert invented this last dish for a hostess who was entertaining the Prince Pierre de Polignac (Prince Rainier's parent), whose name it bears. If you prefer an entrée from the grill, try the skewered filets gilded with béarnaise sauce. Or, with a like-minded companion order a Filet de Boeuf Périgourdin for two—the heart of the filet encasing truffles and goose liver. Tournedos "Klaus" (one of my favorites) is the heart of the filet enclosed in a short pastry crust served with béarnaise sauce. There are excellent sweetbreads simmered in port wine with truffles, veal kidney chops rich with hunter's sauce, and the classic beef stewed in red Burgundy. Quail roasted garlicky and sauced with Madeira, flaming pheasant for two, or partridge in a game sauce enliven the menu when they are available. And I recommend the haricots verts as an accompaniment. They are cooked with all the care expended on more elaborate dishes, and it tells.

If you can face anything more than a café filtre and a fresh fruit in season, there are sugary glazed chestnuts, apple tarts tangy with apricot sauce, crêpes or baked Alaska, and miniature cream puffs—Délices des Rois—bursting with vanilla ice cream, afloat in a chocolate sauce over which the chef has turned a bottle of Grand Marnier, and dabbed a glob of whipped cream.

The Charleses, themselves authors of the charming volume *Of Tales and Recipes* (favorite dishes and accompanying anecdotes), have been most generous in supplying me with recipes.

The first, not on the regular Fleur de Lys menu, is

➤ PROVENÇALE FISH SOUP

6 different salt water fish	2 orange peels
½ qt. various shellfish	1 qt. water
4 oz. olive oil	slices of bread, enough to line
4 chopped onions	four small tureens
thyme, laurel, fennel, salt, pepper	1 cup Aïoli (recipe below)

SOUP: Cut fish in large chunks, sautée them and the shellfish in a casserole with the oil and onions, add the spices and orange peels, cover with the water, and cook uncovered for fifteen minutes. Strain the bouillon, set the fish aside.

BREAD: Toast the bread and use it to line four individual tureens. Moisten each slice with some of the bouillon.

AÏOLI: Peel, chop, then pulverize 8 garlic cloves with a mortar and pestle; add one cup of mayonnaise, stir together.

Pour the hot, strained bouillon slowly over the Aïoli, stirring continuously with a wooden spoon, then heat over a low fire, still stirring without interruption, until the sauce thickens slightly. Divide the fish among the soup bowls, and pour the sauce over the bread and fish. For four.

➤ FROGS' LEGS "GISELE"

(The Charleses made this dish at Gourdon, using *fenouil* from the slopes of the Alpes-Maritimes. You can imagine their delight when they found fennel abounding on the sides of California's Mount Tamalpais.)

6 dozen frogs' legs, as small as possible (best from Texas or Southern states)	½ cup finely chopped fennel and parsley
4 oz. butter	juice of 3 lemons
salt, ground black pepper	

Season the frogs' legs heavily, then sautée in a frying pan in very hot butter. Cook approximately ten minutes, one side first, then the other, until golden brown. Arrange on a hot platter, and keep warm. Add the chopped fennel, parsley, and lemon juice to the sauce in the pan. Cook two minutes over a high flame, pour over the frogs' legs. Serve immediately, garnished with parsley branch and quartered lemons. Serves six. This dish is best eaten with the fingers.

COEUR DE FILET PÉRIGOURDINE

1 choice filet of Eastern steer
2 lbs. goose liver (foie gras d'Alsace)

1 lb. truffles (truffes du Périgord)
4 oz. butter

for the sauce:

1 pt. beef glaze
salt, pepper, thyme, one laurel leaf
2 oz. finely chopped fresh mushrooms

4 oz. chopped truffles
1 oz. cognac
3 oz. tawny port wine

Trim and denerve the filet of beef until entirely lean. Pierce a hole all the way through the middle, then stuff it alternately with one slice of goose liver and one whole truffle. Season and roast with butter in a very hot oven to a rare state.

SAUCE: Remove all fat from the gravy, add the beef glaze, spices, and mushrooms, cook for ten minutes. Add the truffles, cognac, and port, heat through but do not boil.

Slice the roast into thick slabs and serve covered with the sauce.

Ritz Old Poodle Dog ✳

65 POST STREET

expensive

THE RITZ OLD POODLE DOG CLAIMS TO BE THE OLDEST SAN FRANcisco French restaurant. History certainly shows it to have been the naughtiest. In more sophisticated times, clients of the Poodle Dog dined in a family restaurant on the ground floor, banqueted in special rooms on the second, or feasted and cavorted in private rooms on the next three levels. Once through the special side entrance, one ascended by elevator to the salons on Floor Three, or the suites on the fourth and fifth floors—with elegantly appointed parlors, bedrooms, and baths.

In the '90's (when it was only a rip-roaring three stories) private parties took over the top two floors. San Francisco was the second city in the world to boast a complete phone network, and one of the precious few early instruments was at hand at the Poodle Dog—especially convenient if some lonely male guest felt the need for pretty company. Carriages with shades drawn deposited and fetched veiled ladies at the private entry. Although the staff—and the coachmen—were notable for their miserable memories, one scandal did not escape notice of the entire city, an all-night dinner hosted by a distinguished banker, an equally distinguished judge, and a most respected Senator. The high point of their evening was a dance by Little Egypt, who shimmied and swayed in her veilings—and then, it is reported, out of them.

For seventy-three years, the Poodle Dog survived scandal and raid, but Prohibition almost proved its undoing. It was unthinkable that such an establishment could serve its famous French cuisine without wine to accompany it. And so it closed until 1933, but since then has been operating continuously—with spirits, but without private upstairs salons.

The first of the Poodle Dogs was a real Gold Rush enterprise, set up in 1849 by a French family from New Orleans. That café on Clay and Dupont (now Grant Avenue) bore the name *Poulet d'Or* or *Poule d'Or*, which the miners without delay transformed to Poodle Dog. In 1868 the business moved to Bush and Grant and the three-story mode of operation. Soon its diners were consuming quantities of frogs' legs and terrapin, and willingly paying out one dollar for their dinner. In its heyday at the end of the century, patrons dined on twenty-three courses, with almost as many wines and liqueurs. A single meal often lasted several hours. At that moment in history a great chef, Calixte Lalanne, arrived from Bordeaux, joined forces with proprietors Allarme and Blanco, and together they prospered until the 1906 disaster completely destroyed the establishment. Two years later a merger of three old San Francisco restaurants created Bergez-Franks-Old Poodle Dog on Bush Street, a five-storied dome of pleasure. It was this resort that fell victim to Prohibition. When Calixte Lalanne returned to business in 1933, his patrons dined at the Ritz French Restaurant, a name that remained until his death in the '40's. Then his son, the present proprietor Louis, restored Poodle to the name.

The elegant Versailles Room—the main dining room—dates from a 1958 $135,000 job of redecorating. Panels of black walnut alternate with ruby damask. Great mirrors reflect chandeliers dripping crystal pendants, or hundred year old bronze candelabra. The antique glasses in the wall case, the pictures, and the bunches of grapes on the bar and at the top of the stairs, come from the pre-fire restaurant. The most unusual decoration is the old hat stand. It is really a French bread rack.

Variety meats are among the best specialties of the house. Chef Henri Tarnac, who has presided over the copper-clad kitchen these last twenty years, sends forth a fine tripe à la mode de Caen (prepared with calf's feet and wine, sealed tight, and oven-steamed for forty-eight hours), calf's head vinaigrette (boiled bite-size slices, with a piquant dressing, piping hot), sweetbreads sautéed with wine and mushrooms, and braised oxtails—a Tuesday lunch special. His scallops sautéed with fresh mushrooms and chopped shallots, then baked with cheese, cream, and sherry, and served in the shell, are delicious. Except with snails and Caesar salad, the Poodle Dog avoids the use of garlic. They believe that it dulls the taste of all subsequent food (how we disagree!), so they use only shallots in their cooking.

Here are three recipes from the Poodle Dog.

63

➤ ## CRAB LEGS "POODLE DOG"

1 tbsp. butter	1 shallot (or 2 green onions),
¼ lb. fresh mushrooms,	chopped
sliced	1 lb. crab legs
¼ lb. boiled ham, in julienne	¾ cup white wine or dry
strips	sherry

Slice mushrooms and brown slightly in 1 tbsp. butter. Add ham strips, chopped shallots or onions, and simmer for 30 seconds. Then add crab legs and sauté to blend ingredients. Add wine and simmer for a few minutes until thoroughly hot, so crab absorbs some of the liquid. Serve on toast. Serves four.

Lobster or scallops can be substituted for crab. If scallops are used, sauce should be thickened at the last minute with 1 tbsp. cornstarch.

➤ ## REX SOLE

4 lbs. rex sole	lard
milk	lemon wedges
flour	melted butter
salt and pepper	

Dip sole in milk, then flour; season with salt and pepper and brown quickly in hot lard about 5 minutes per side. Lift to platter, and place in warm oven. Let stand 15 minutes. Bone by slicing lengthwise along backbone. Lift off filet and remove dark skin. Discard backbone and cut filets into finger-sized pieces. Arrange on plates, pour melted butter over them, garnish with lemon wedges. Serves four.

➤ ## CHICKEN À LA RITZ

2 spring chickens, cut into	3 green onions, chopped fine
serving pieces	1 glass white wine or dry
salt, pepper, flour	sherry
3 oz. butter	2 cups table cream
½ lb. fresh mushrooms, sliced	2 egg yolks

Season the chicken with salt and pepper, and sprinkle with flour. Heat the butter in a saucepan, add the chicken, and sauté until golden. Then add sliced mushrooms, chopped onions and wine. Simmer a few seconds, then add cream. Cook until well done, about 15 minutes. Just before serving, add 2 egg yolks, mixed well with a little cream, to the sauce. DO NOT COOK AFTER EGGS ARE ADDED. Keep in pan of hot water. Serve with wild rice. Serves four.

Place Pigalle ✳

3721 BUCHANAN STREET

moderate

PLACE PIGALLE HAS THE GAY AIR OF A PARISIAN SIDEWALK CAFÉ. Diners along its aisles look out over the streets of Paris—by way of spirited murals. Strolling troubadors provide music. A large wall painting in the main cocktail lounge—a view of the Rue Pigalle as seen from the Place Pigalle—twinkles almost alive. The silhouettes of Toulouse-Lautrec's night revelers cavort and frolic across the screens separating the two main dining rooms. The Gourmet Room resembles an old French wine cellar, the brick walls lined with bottles of champagne and wine barrels.

This carefree continental atmosphere is no accident. Maurice Stergios, one of the hospitable owners, is of French parentage, and spent his growing years in the French-Polynesian paradise of Tahiti, where his father operated the Yacht Club. He came to California in the Thirties to obtain a degree in chemistry from the University of California. During his college days, he worked in the Tahiti Club and in the famous Lucca's, thus undermining in advance a career in petroleum chemistry that was to take him all over the world. A tour of duty in Saudi Arabia did it. In 1953 he returned to San Francisco and opened Place Pigalle with his mother and brother-in-law, themselves experienced restaurateurs. (Today his partner is John Roberge.) When Maurice occasionally steps behind the bar to mix special drinks, he says his background in science helps.

The substantial à la carte menu features escargots, pâté de foie gras (either de la maison or imported from Strasbourg), bula-bula soup (oysters and spinach with a dash of Tahiti), mussels à la marinière, calf's head, oxtails, sweetbreads, and charcoal-broiled, corn-fed Eastern beefsteaks. Honeycomb tripe comes in special earthenware pots, in keeping with its old-world character. Dorothy Stergios, Maurice's wife, told me that Place Pigalle takes care to preserve the ancient methods of preparing this stew, once the delight of fourteenth-century Normandy. For good results, it is important to select the ox hooves and tripe carefully, and to use only the best cognac and dry cider to cook them in. The daily specials include a variety of classic French dishes. You can order chicken chasseur (sautéed with tomatoes, mushrooms, and tarragon), mascotte (with mushrooms, hearts of artichokes, and white wine), sauté bordelaise (with shallots, burgundy wine, and marrow), suprême de chapon (in cream with mushrooms, shallots, asparagus, and croutons), or the reliable coq au vin. There is roast sirloin in a sauce of white wine and mushrooms, beef tenderloin with béarnaise sauce, rack of lamb, bouillabaisse on Fridays, and sweetbreads poulette (in cream with mushrooms, chives, and hollandaise sauce) or financière (braised with cock's combs, sausages, mushrooms, olives and wine). One of the Thursday specialties is civet de lapin, rabbit marinated for several hours in a mixture of cognac and olive oil with onion rings, then simmered gently in red wine. Before serving, the sauce is fortified with the hare's blood, warmed, then dotted with small glazed onions and mushrooms.

If you want something that doesn't appear on the menu, Place Pigalle will gladly cook it up, providing they have the raw materials. The house wines, should you forego the vintage list, are a Napa pinot noir and dry sauterne. After dinner, Place Pigalle recommends their Frenchified version of Irish coffee, with real chantilly.

The Stergioses have given me recipes for breast of chicken, and mussels à la marinière, the choice shell fish which gourmets relish.

BREAST OF CHICKEN, PLACE PIGALLE, SOUS CLOCHE

1 chicken breast	1 cup cream
salt and pepper	1 tbsp. cream sauce
1 tbsp. butter	1 tbsp. sherry wine
6 fresh mushrooms	1 slice toast
1 slice Virginia ham	

After seasoning one chicken breast with salt and pepper, brown gently in butter until lightly colored and not quite cooked. Add mushrooms to the pan, continue cooking until breast is done. Add ham, fry for one-half minute. Add cream, boil for a few seconds. Remove chicken, ham, and mushrooms, and arrange on a triangle of toast. Add cream sauce to pan mixture, blend well; then add sherry wine, mix well. Strain the sauce over chicken, cover with a glass bell, and heat in hot oven for about 3 minutes. Serves one.

MUSSELS À LA MARINIÈRE

50 mussels	mignonette (cracked black
½ cup butter	pepper)
6 shallots, chopped	dash red pepper
¾ cup white wine	½–1 cup white sauce
	½ tsp. chopped chives

Scrub mussels well. Place them in a saucepan with all ingredients except the white sauce. Cover and steam until tender. Drain off liquor and bring to a boil in another saucepan. Thicken according to your taste with white sauce, add chives, correct seasoning. Pour over mussels and serve immediately. Serves four.

✳ Koe's Auberge

1205 STOCKTON STREET

moderate

HAROLD KOE BELIEVES THAT HIS AUBERGE IS THE ONLY REAL French restaurant in this world operated and staffed by Chinese. Mr. Koe, besides being the managing owner, is executive chef. Janie Koe and Marjorie Leong act as maîtres d'hôtel. The menu is French with a few English titles and translations. The small French style bar serves aperitifs, champagne cocktails, cognac or cordials to those lucky enough to find a perch on one of its four stools. As in France, the wine is the thing, and Harold Koe, wine-taster par excellence, keeps one of the largest and best stocked cellars in town. He handles only vintage wines, and the menu offers knowledgeable suggestions about their proper accompaniments.

The intimate dining room—there are fourteen tables altogether, seating no more than thirty-eight at a time—combines a touch of elegance with a dash of informality. Light comes partly from candles, partly from small chandeliers, whose few crystal tear drops flicker as they catch the flames. Rose red drapes and rugs contrast with black tables, and the settings are place mats rather than linens.

Mr. Koe got the idea for this French-Viennese atmosphere when he was in the Austrian capital under the Russian occupation. He built the business from scratch, opening without fanfare in 1954. He has never gone in much for advertising, except in the theatres and opera, but his patrons include a traveling circle of European-international wine-lovers.

Mr. Koe is himself an extensive globetrotter. He has traveled through the Orient, Malaya, South America, Europe, and the South Pacific, collecting recipes wherever he went. Here and there on the menu an Indian curry or a chachlik à la Turque sneaks in among the cuisses de grenouilles and suprêmes de volaille.

Dinner at Koe's consists of soup or salad and entrée. Desserts and beverages come à la carte. There is always a plat du jour, and I can recommend in this category the roast duck with cherries. There are also good veal cutlets and baked scallops in their shells. The pepper steak, top sirloin, and coeur de filet are aged beef from Omaha and Chicago. Koe's blend their own spices and curry. Coffee is also their own blend, and they grind it fresh daily. You can order a café filtre, and thanks to the individual contraptions that perch over your cup, your coffee will be as hot and fresh as anyone could desire. The dessert menu includes marrons glacés and café Liégeois—ice cream topped with glazed chestnuts, and coffee ice cream with liqueur. There is also pineapple with kirsch, cheese, and apple pie with whipped cream.

One of the most attractive dishes at Koe's is beef in Burgundy wine, always served in a handsome copper bucket. Mr. Koe has given us his recipe.

BOEUF BOURGUIGNON

2 lbs. lean stew meat (center-cut chuck), cut in chunks
2 oz. butter
3 medium onions, chopped
2 tbsp. flour
1 cup Burgundy wine
1 cup stock

1 shallot, chopped
salt and pepper
¼ tsp. powdered thyme (or ½ tsp. fresh)
¼ tsp. powdered parsley (or ½ tsp. fresh)
1 bay leaf

Brown meat and onions in butter. When seared, remove meat and onions, stir in flour, add wine, stock, shallot, spices, and herbs, and blend. Place meat and onions in the sauce, simmer three hours. Serves four. Mr. Koe recommends that you serve this stew accompanied by a good Gamay, Beaujolais, Côte du Rhône, or Châteauneuf du Pape.

1121 POLK STREET

moderate

SAN FRANCISCANS HAVE BEEN ENJOYING ALOUETTE'S TRADITIONAL French dishes for some sixty years. Last summer the city's French colony, during the celebration of Bastille Day, elected Alouette's chef to preside officially over all of the gastronomic activities.

The two French gentlemen who now direct the establishment actually met in San Francisco. George LeBrun served with the French Navy, then—during the war—began a club for servicemen in Casablanca. When he came to the United States, he worked for several years at the Waldorf Astoria. Michel Laurent, a Monegasque by birth, but a long-time resident of France, has toured Europe since he was a youngster. When he worked in leading restaurants abroad, he acquired a wide experience in foods, and an enviable background in languages and traditions.

The dining salon over which these gentlemen preside is a warm room, accented with wrought iron, white linens, and pleasant lighting. Although this is a moderately-priced restaurant, you can, and I have, run up quite a bill by dabbling recklessly through the items à la carte. If you order the regular dinner—soup, salad, entrée, ice cream and coffee—you will come off with quite a bargain. You can choose boeuf à la bourguignonne, filet of rex sole in butter, frogs' legs in garlic sauce, capon in Burgundy, or a casserole of calf's sweetbreads financière.

If you are feeling abandoned, however, you can spend as much as the cost of a whole dinner by asking for caviar de la Volga, or Strasbourg pâté. The house pâté, by the way, is half the price and very good. If you choose a fish course, the filet of sole Marguery is poached with shrimps and oysters at Alouette, and the rainbow trout comes dressed with lemon and capers. After this you might try veal kidneys sautéed in wine and mushrooms, the peppered sirloin flamed in cognac, tripe simmered in chablis and tomatoes, in the style of Nice, or a Cornish hen in cherry sauce. The house specialties are coq au vin, duckling à l'orange, and frogs' legs provençale. If you prefer a simple main course, Alouette has a charcoal broiler and can send forth any number of grillades: spring chicken, double-cut French lamb chops, rack of lamb, Chateaubriand. For dessert there are several flaming concoctions, and the proprietors indulge in such niceties as grating the lemon and orange rinds fresh at the table for crêpes suzette. There are also assorted cheeses, baked Alaska, sabayon, baba au rhum, kirsch cake, and crème caramel.

Alouette shares three recipes with us: coq au vin, a Viennese veal specialty, and a dish not on their regular menu, filet of sole véronique.

COQ AU VIN

1 2-lb. disjointed chicken
6 oz. small white onions
6 oz. sliced mushrooms
4 oz. butter
4 oz. shortening
garlic

2 glasses red wine
1 tbsp. flour
¼ cup melted butter
salt and pepper to taste

Roast chicken in 325° oven.

Sauté sliced white onions and mushrooms in the butter and shortening. When the chicken is almost done, drain it and add to the onion and mushroom mixture. Cover and let it cook through. When done, strain the grease, add a minced clove of garlic, and red wine. Simmer until sauce is reduced in half, then add a tbsp. of flour and ¼ cup melted butter. Simmer for a few minutes before serving. Serves three.

➤ ESCALOPE À LA VIENNOISE

4 thin veal cutlets	parsley
salt and pepper	2 hard boiled eggs
bread crumbs	1 lemon
5 tbsp. butter	4 anchovies with capers

Pound the veal cutlets, season, and roll in bread crumbs. Cook them rapidly in butter, then remove to a warm platter. Garnish with parsley, sliced hard boiled eggs, lemon wedges, and anchovies. Squeeze a little lemon juice over all, and top with the brown pan butter. Serves four.

➤ FILET DE SOLE VÉRONIQUE

4 8-oz. pieces of filet of sole	1 cup hollandaise sauce
1 cup white wine	white grapes, peeled and sliced (never use canned)

Poach the filets in the wine for twelve minutes. Drain the fish on a paper towel, then place on an oven-proof platter. Put into warm oven for a few minutes, until any sauce left on the fish is reduced to a few drops. Pour the hollandaise over the fish, add a few peeled, sliced grapes, and put under a hot broiler. Let it brown, but do not broil. Serves four.

✳ *Chez Marguerite*

2330 TAYLOR STREET

moderate

ODDLY, ONE OF SAN FRANCISCO'S MOST PARISIAN RESTAURANTS is the offspring of two non-French proprietors. Herbert M. Emery (who was in the wholesale fabric business) and J. Ross Williams (formerly with the *San Francisco Chronicle*) in fact confess that they have neither one set foot on French soil. But their instincts couldn't be more authentically Gallic, nor their taste in decor, foods, and wine more warmly discriminating. They have scaled

Chez Marguerite to the intimate style of a French bistro, and in further emulation of the French, they constantly delight their patrons with superb cooking.

When these two friends started in business together they decided to keep their establishment cozy. Friends helped with decorations and a charming hodgepodge, antique and otherwise, is the result. Collages ornament the screens. A splendid glassware collection glimmers on the back bar—itself two fireplace mantels salvaged from an old Broadway mansion. The glassware includes such oddities as an Austrian decanter from the Graf Zeppelin or the Hindenberg (Herb can't remember which). This stunner of a container, ruby and brass with a cut crystal top, was once owned by Andrew Mellon. What began as a modest collection of menus has outgrown the wall space originally allotted to it. Now there are stacks of lists from traveling friends and old customers passing through odd parts of the world. Subdued lighting doesn't reveal all the marvels at once, so on each visit a new fascination emerges. The total decorative scheme came off so compellingly that the producers of the television series "Lineup" have used Chez Marguerite as part of their scenery on three different occasions.

Eugene Maissa, the chef, is thoroughly French, and has been working in kitchens since he was a youngster. He was born in Nice, worked in Paris, and managed hotels and restaurants along the French Riviera. Then he and his wife went to São Paolo, Brazil, to open a branch of a well-known Parisian restaurant, La Table du Roy. While presiding over that kitchen, he performed an amusing culinary feat: when the owner requested that he concoct a different potato dish for each meal, he produced a new one every night for three months running. He left Brazil for the kitchen of the Beverly-Hilton in Los Angeles, then came to the Bay Area and took a turn with Trader Vic's. He has been enjoying himself at Chez Marguerite since 1957.

Dinner includes a soupe du jour, salad of mixed greens with French dressing, a choice from a dozen excellent entrées, sherbet, ice cream, or cheese, and coffee. The only à la carte entry is escargots de Bourgogne by the half dozen, served in their shells, dripping gloriously with sweet butter, parsley, garlic and minced shallots.

Everything is well-prepared here, but four items—each with a splendid sauce—call for particular attention. Calf's sweetbreads Parisienne come forth in their casserole in a light wine sauce that does not hide their delicate natural flavor. Boned duckling à l'orange prospers in a rich sweet-and-sour sauce, tangy with gratings of orange peel and sections of mandarin oranges. The classic boeuf bourguignon, a stew of chunky beef, salt pork, pearl onions, and carrots, is served en casserole a whole day after it first begins to bubble in red wine. Another solid dish that takes well to a heavy wine sauce is Belgian hare Bruxelloise, and here is Chef Maissa's recipe:

➤ BELGIAN HARE BRUXELLOISE

4 hares or rabbits, each 2–2½ lbs.	2 leeks, sliced
salt, pepper, 1 tsp. powdered thyme	½ lb. rendered salt pork, cut into finger length strips
2 cloves garlic, minced	½ cup wine vinegar
flour (about 3 tbsp.)	red wine (4 cups or more)
cooking fat (about 4 tbsp.)	½ cube butter
2 onions, sliced	10 pearl onions
	10 mushroom caps

Cut hares into serving pieces. Season with salt, pepper, thyme, and minced garlic. Dredge the hare lightly in flour, then sauté in hot fat until lightly browned. Add onions, leeks, salt pork, wine vinegar, and enough good red wine to cover. Cook over medium flame for ¾ hour, then skim off fat. Add the butter mixed with enough flour to make a medium thick sauce (about 3 tbsp.). Serve hot in individual oval shaped casseroles with a garnish of cooked pearl onions (sauté in butter with a sprinkling of sugar until brown, add a few spoonfuls of red wine and simmer until tender) and mushroom caps (sauté in butter with a clove of garlic). Makes 8–10 servings.

La Bourgogne ❋

IN AN INCREDIBLY SHORT TIME, LA BOURGOGNE HAS BECOME ONE of the best restaurants in San Francisco; it will please the most serious consumer of wine and food. Jean Lapuyade, one of three owners, told me—and it is evident with every bite—that the restaurant is run on the principle that quality in cooking and food can never be replaced by decor; there is nothing that will make a restaurant good except a good chef. This does not mean that the surroundings need be neglected—and they certainly are not here. Champagne and gold satin stripes cover the walls, golden banquettes line them, and blue chairs dot the room. The table is regal with a heavy display of silver. The crystal wine glasses have exquisitely thin stems. But all of this beauty is nothing compared to the food to come.

M. Lapuyade hails from Pau in southwestern France, and was once a fighter for the Free French. He and his partners—James Coulot, a Parisian, and Paul Dufour, from Saumur in the Loire Valley—met in San Francisco only a few years back. They had each had extensive culinary training in France, and decided to go into business together. They opened Le Trianon, at 242 O'Farrell Street, with Jean as maître d'hôtel, Paul turning out filets of sole dieppoise, médaillons de boeuf au Dauphin, and airy soufflés au Grand Marnier from the kitchens, and James delighting the bar patrons with a repertoire that included, besides the standard number of mixes, vermouth cassis and an excellent picon-citron. Diners approved immediately and warmly, and the place is already the scene of what may become a tradition: an annual snail race (with both winners and losers consumed).

After their success with Le Trianon, they decided to open an even more distinguished place, with a character all its own. La

Bourgogne was an instant success, owing largely to the Parisian chef Marcel Perrin's exquisite specialties. He is an expert at such dishes as feuilleté nimois: vol-au-vent type pastries enclosing a pâté compounded of sweetbreads, lamb, veal, cognac, and appropriate spices; fond d'artichaut monselet: fresh artichoke bottom stuffed fittingly with creamy mushrooms and covered over with a slice of pâté de foie gras and truffles; huîtres rochelaise: oysters baked with creamed mushrooms. He serves poached salmon with a cream and white wine sauce, simmers Dover sole from the North Sea in heady Chambertin. If you have ever eaten porcini in Italy or cèpes in France—or gathered boletus edulis in the fields or woods of any country—they are probably your favorite mushrooms. La Bourgogne imports these big brownish beauties from France, and M. Perrin sautés them gently in oil, with just the right amount of garlic.

The menu is filled with tempting dishes of squab, steak, sweetbreads, frogs' legs, veal, lamb kidneys, pheasant. But there are two specialties which are particularly distinguished: selle d'agneau rotie Salardaise, and canard roti à ma façon. The roast saddle of lamb, which serves three or four, takes the whole small part of the loin of lamb; served up in long rare slices, with an accompaniment of cottage-fried potatoes and black truffles cooked together, it makes everything seem right, even with this troubled world. The duck, shunning more traditional orange sauces, is splendidly bathed in bordelaise with a blend of chicken livers. With the possible exception of Peking duck, to which a certain number of my friends and I find ourselves hopelessly addicted, and which is so different as not to be easily compared, this duck beats them all. M. Lapuyade is so proud of it that on the first anniversary of the Peace Corps, he flew to Washington and treated some San Francisco corpsmen stationed there (among whom were several old customers of Le Trianon) to twenty-five San Francisco-prepared portions of it—along with a good assortment of pâté de foie gras, crab, limestone lettuce (carried lovingly in a napkin-covered wicker basket during the whole trip), French bread, pinot noir, and cherries jubilee.

For dessert you can choose, besides the cherries jubilee, from among splendid tarts of fruit, profiteroles in a chocolate sauce, cheeses, meringue glacée, omelettes, soufflés, crêpes suzette, and a number of excellent fruits, fresh and baked. But if you want something unusual, and your dinner has been on the light side, try the pannequet lucquoise. This is a pancake stuffed with purée of marrons and whipped cream, browned under the salamander, then flambéed with kirsch.

M. Lapuyade has generously given me recipes for sole au Chambertin, the duck, and the saddle of lamb.

SOLE AU CHAMBERTIN

The original recipe as prepared at La Bourgogne calls for imported Dover sole and Chambertin wine. You can substitute rex sole and a good California Burgundy.

1 tbsp. butter	½ cup red Burgundy
2 shallots, chopped	½ tbsp. butter kneaded with
salt and pepper	½ tbsp. flour
4 filets of sole	

Spread softened butter in a baking dish that can also be used on the top of the stove. Add shallots, sprinkle with salt and pepper. Lay the filets of sole on top and cover with red Burgundy. Poach in a preheated 350° oven until sauce reduces by two-thirds. Remove from the oven and set over a low flame. Thicken sauce by adding the butter kneaded with flour. Cover, and keep warm until ready to serve. Serves 2 to 4 depending on size of filets.

SUGGESTED ACCOMPANIMENT: small boiled potatoes topped with butter and chopped parsley.

➤ CANARD ROTI À MA FAÇON

duck:

1 4 to 5 lb. duckling	oil
salt and pepper	2 oz. cognac

sauce:

½ lb. butter	8 oz. demi-glace (veal stock)
½ lb. chopped onions (about	1 tbsp. butter
1½ med. size onions)	4 oz. chicken livers
10 ounces red Burgundy	2 oz. chopped shallots (ap-
salt and pepper	proximately 6 to 8 shallots)
bouquet garni (celery, thyme,	2 oz. cognac
parsley, bay leaf, tied to-	1 lump butter
gether)	

Clean, wash, and rub dry the duckling, inside and out. Season the cavity with salt and pepper, rub the skin with oil, and roast in a preheated 500° oven for fifteen minutes, turning often. When well seared, reduce heat to 375° and continue cooking for at least thirty minutes, or until tender. [Tastes differ on the degree of done-ness at which a duck is best. If you like yours very well-done, an-other hour of cooking will not be too long.] During cooking, re-move the fat from the roaster often to avoid frying the duck. When the bird is cooked, remove all fat from pan, pour the cognac over the duck, and flame. Place duck on warm serving platter. [At La Bourgogne, the duck appears on a silver platter, garnished with truffles and Dauphine potatoes.]

SAUCE: While the duckling is cooking, melt ½ lb. butter in a skillet over a low flame. Brown the chopped onions in it, then add the Burgundy, salt, pepper, and small bouquet garni. Keep the flame low and let the sauce reduce. When reduced by about half, add the veal stock, and let simmer.

In another skillet melt 1 tbsp. butter and sauté the chicken livers quickly. It is important not to overcook them. Add the chopped shallots and turn off the flame. Pour cognac over the livers, set ablaze, and flame while moving the skillet back and forth.

Remove the bouquet garni from the first sauce, mix the liver sauce with the Burgundy mixture, and pass through a fine sieve. Pour into the top of a double boiler and add one large lump of butter a little at a time. Mix well with whisk. Taste for seasoning. Keep sauce hot.

To serve, carve the duckling, then pour hot sauce over it. Serves 2 persons in the restaurant, up to 4 persons at home.

[The success of this sauce depends on the quality of your veal stock, the flavor of shallots, and the use of a sieve—no blender. If you make your own stock, the flavor will be superior to any preparations you can buy; if you can't find shallots, don't substitute— it is best to leave them out altogether in this recipe; if you blend mechanically, the texture will suffer.]

ROAST SADDLE OF LAMB SALARDAISE

You need a good butcher for this one. Ask him to cut you a small saddle of lamb without the legs. This is the small loin end of the lamb. He should defat the meat except for a thin top covering. When trimmed, it should weigh between 2½ and 3 lbs.

1 saddle of lamb (trimmed weight 2½ to 3 lbs.)	1 cup dry white wine
salt, pepper, fresh garlic	¼ cup vegetable mirepoix (recipe below)
2 oz. butter, melted	

Set the saddle of lamb in a roasting pan. Season with salt, pepper, and fresh garlic. Tuck the ends under the body of the roast. Baste with melted butter, and set in a preheated 450° oven. Cook for 45 to 55 minutes (rare or medium rare). Remove roast to a warm platter. Eliminate most of the fat from cooking pan, add white wine, deglaze the pan, and place over low flame on top of the stove. Add strained vegetable mirepoix, correct the seasoning, and let sauce reduce until it has a slightly thick consistency. Strain and keep warm. Add juices from the roast when it is sliced. [La Bourgogne serves with cottage-fried potatoes and decorations of sliced truffles.] Slice lamb in thin slabs cut the length of the roast, from the outside edge in to the center bone. Arrange side by side and slightly overlapping on very hot dinner plates, covered with several spoonfuls of gravy, and serve immediately. Serves four.

vegetable mirepoix:

½ small carrot
¼ small onion
½ small stalk celery

1 oz. butter
salt, pinch of thyme, and ½
    small bay leaf

Dice the carrot, onion and celery *very* fine. Cook slowly in the butter [I add the butter from roasting pan when ready to deglaze the pan]. Season with salt, a tiny pinch of powdered thyme, and ½ small bay leaf. Continue cooking until very tender. Strain before using.

✳ *La Petite Auberge*

704-4TH STREET • SAN RAFAEL

expensive

THE REPUTATION OF LA PETITE AUBERGE HAS SPREAD FAR ENOUGH afield—although it has only been operating since 1959—to induce an ensemble of Los Angeles gastronomes to travel to San Rafael, seventeen miles north of San Francisco, just for the occasion of having a meal there. It is no wonder, for this charming French restaurant is one of the Bay Area's choicest spots. Generally the diners clustered around its red-checkered tablecloths are people somewhat closer to home, and the guest list by now includes many of the Bay Area's most (quietly) distinguished citizens.

When it first opened, La Petite Auberge was hardly more than a tiny patio. Although it is now enlarged—and has acquired a bar—the owners have kept it beguilingly small. The heated patio remains at the core, luxuriantly shaded by a lush wisteria, or—should nature fail—by a man-made closure that can seal it off from the elements. In the evenings from about seven on, an accordionist plays nostalgic music ranging from French cabaret songs and gypsy airs to ballads from a marvelous assortment of lands.

Considering something of the background of owner Paul Devaux, this restaurant's happy combination of country vitality and worldly sophistication is no surprise. Starting in his native Vichy, he can tot up a formidable record of culinary experience, including extensive apprenticeship in France, over five years in Bermuda at the Castle Harbor Hotel, a stint at New York's Colony, another at Maxim's in Miami Beach, and—in this area —at Romanoff's and the Ondine in Sausalito. Now he is a United States citizen, who fortunately for us retains all of the skills and tastes of French gastronomy.

Mr. Devaux's able assistant is Parisian Pierre Grigaut, who acts as host at La Petite Auberge. Pierre joined the restaurant when it was remodeled. His training began in hotel school in Paris in 1936, and includes several years with the French Line. When he came to America, he worked first in a French restaurant in Chicago, went on to the Pump Room, then came west to Trader Vic's, where he spent the five years preceding his alliance with Paul.

Although the menu is not gigantic, it offers a splendid assortment, and touches from the haute cuisine that are quite remarkable at the price. Except for a half-dozen specialties, you can have all entrées either à la carte or on the dinner. If you decide on the latter, you will get soup, salad, dessert, and coffee besides your main dish. If you feel more adventurous, you can start with escargots de Bourgogne, a fine pâté from an old country recipe, or crêpes maison—French pancakes stuffed with crab meat. There are several salads, a potage du jour (the last time I ate there it was a first-rate potage germiny, an excellent creamy soup of sorrel and a hint of chervil), onion soup, or vichyssoise. If you want a taste of fish before your main course, split an order with your dinner partner, unless you are in real fighting form. Besides such choices as lobster with sauce suprême, filets of sole, rainbow trout meunière, and coquille Saint-Jacques, there are excellent quenelles, generally of turbot or sole, in a creamy Nantua sauce. This delicate specialty is hard to find elsewhere in the Bay Area.

You can choose next from an assortment of grilled chops, steaks and chickens, stuffed veal cutlets covered with a green olive sauce and mushrooms, kidney sauté, boeuf bourguignon, and tripes à la mode de Caen. There are filets of beef aswim in a Bordelaise sauce dotted with mushrooms, or in a sauce of truffles. One of the steak specialties is Chateaubriand bouquetière, broiled for two. Other classic dishes done up for gourmet couples include whole pheasants garnished with onions, mushrooms, carrots, and potatoes (and served in all the glory of their plumage); canard à l'orange; a casserole of spring chicken bonne femme ("as prepared by the good women of France," reads the menu); and a rack of lamb, trimmed with crunchy bread crumbs, parsley, and an infusion of garlic. With the à la carte orders come potatoes soufflées, served in a basket woven also of potatoes and then baked a handsome brown, perhaps an out-of-season asparagus under a sauce hollandaise, and garnishes such as toasted rounds surmounted with an excellent chopped spinach, and broiled tomato halves sprinkled with basil.

For dessert there are cheeses, tarts, crème caramel, flaming omelette, crêpes suzette, baba au rhum, cherries jubilee. But, if you have had the foresight to put your order in early (the cooking takes half an hour) the best of all is a chocolate or Grand Marnier soufflé. To go with it there is café filtre.

Chef Roger Poli, who hails from southern France in the neighborhood of Marseilles, turns out all sorts of other dishes—specialities appended daily to the regular menu, or on order for private parties. He can stir up a spicy bouillabaisse in the style of his region; or a cassoulet—that husky combination of white beans, pork, mutton, and garlic sausage coaxed gently tender in a casserole; or, for cabbage lovers, he can fix a choucroute alsacienne, a sauerkraut made with pork or ham, and substantial enough to be a whole dish in itself. Another of Chef Poli's delights is quiche lorraine, that classic cheese custard hinting of ham and onions.

Here are three of Roger Poli's recipes.

TRIPES À LA MODE DE CAEN

5 lbs. tripe
¼ lb. fat salt pork, thinly sliced
at least 1 calf's foot
1 onion
½ bunch celery
4 or 5 leeks
6 carrots
1 pt. dry white wine

2 or 3 sprigs of parsley and marjoram
2 bay leaves
a few leaves of thyme
6 cloves
salt and pepper
2 glasses water or veal stock
3 oz. calvados or cognac

Wash tripe in three changes of cold water, then cut in small strips about 2½ inches long and ½ inch wide. Put these in a clay pot with a lid. Add fat salt pork, 3 carrots, and all of the other ingredients and seasonings except the cognac or calvados. Cover tightly (you can seal the lid with a dough of flour and water) and cook for eight hours in a very slow oven—250°. Remove calf's feet and all vegetables, and continue cooking the tripe at 250° for four hours. If it becomes too dry, add wine as needed. One hour before it is finished, add 3 sliced carrots. Cut the calf's feet in small pieces, and add shortly before serving, along with the brandy or calvados. Mix together well, cook long enough to heat through, and serve with boiled potatoes. Serves eight or more.

CUISSES DE GRENOUILLES

24 pairs frogs' legs (medium size)
½ cup milk, or more as needed
½ cup flour, or more as needed
6 oz. butter

1 tbsp. chopped shallots (approximately three cloves)
1 tbsp. chopped parsley
1 tbsp. chopped chives
½ tbsp. minced garlic
salt and pepper
juice of 1 lemon

Dip frogs' legs in milk, then flour, and sauté in 3 oz. butter until brown and cooked through—about ten minutes. Season with salt and pepper to taste. Remove from pan to a warm platter. Discard cooked butter, add 3 oz. fresh butter, and brown. Add herbs, shallots, and garlic, stir a few minutes over the heat, pour over the frogs' legs. Pour the juice of one lemon over all, and serve with boiled new potatoes. Serves six.

PÂTÉ MAISON

1 onion
butter or cooking fat (approximately 1 tbsp.)
1 lb. calf's liver
½ lb. veal steak
½ lb. pork steak
½ lb. fat salt pork

1 tbsp. flour
1 tbsp. salt
½ tbsp. pepper
pinch of thyme
3 oz. cognac
1 slice lard

Slice and brown the onion in the cooking fat or butter. Grind together the meat, fat salt pork, and cooked onion. Put through grinder several times. Add the flour, cognac, and seasonings, and mix together well. Fill a buttered loaf pan with the pâté, and lay 1 slice of lard across the top. Bake in a bainmarie (or put loaf pan in a larger container with enough water to come up one inch) at 350° until the water comes to a boil. Cover the pâté with a lid, plate, or aluminum foil, reduce the temperature to 250°, and bake for two hours. The finished loaf makes approximately 18 servings.

(Roger told me a simple device that will keep the pâté fresh for two or three months under normal refrigeration. Simply melt enough vegetable shortening to cover the surface, pour it on, and refrigerate.)

Chez Léon ✳

124 ELLIS STREET

moderate

IN THE TRADITION OF FRENCH BISTROS, CHEZ LÉON IS SMALL, NOT overly decorated, and provides abundantly good cooking. The prices are in the middle bracket. There is no hard liquor, but you can sip a champagne cocktail, sherry, or vermouth before dinner, and the wine list is ample. If your habit is a martini before you eat, however, the management doesn't mind in the least if you slip into a neighboring bar. They'll gladly fetch you when your table is ready.

Léon Arseguel, the chef, and his charming shy wife, behind the front counter, run the place with loving care. M. Arseguel has cooked for more than thirty-five years, most of them in such gastronomic forts as Paris, Marseilles, Dijon, and Lyon, the Hotel Maraba in Marrakech, Morocco, the Mt. Mansfield Co. ski headquarters in Stowe, Vermont, and—a place that many consider to be this country's best restaurant—Le Pavillon in New York. He has been a Californian for four years, three of them running Chez Léon. Before that he was second chef in command of the Sheraton Palace Kitchens, then head chef of the now defunct Romanoff's.

At Chez Léon the dinner includes hors d'oeuvres or salad, a potage, the entrée with a garnish of two fresh vegetables, rice or potatoes, and a simple dessert with your coffee. There is also an à la carte menu.

If you start with the hors d'oeuvres maison, you will get a handsome assortment of tidbits. The oval plate is decked out with twirls of salami and rolls of marinated tongue, heaped here with spicy red cabbage, there with a generous pile of spiced white beans. Deviled eggs, sparked with coal black caviar, repose in a garden of carved radishes, olives and spiky green onions, all winding artfully around a crock of M. Arseguel's excellent pâté, and an oyster shell brimming over with fish salad in Russian dressing. If you order à la carte, you can choose a large platter of any one of these appetizers, or Nova Scotia salmon, escargots, filet of anchovies, herring in sour cream, and—in season —fresh melon.

Léon's soups are good, steamy and rich, as they should be. His dinner entrées range from the classics like coq au vin, tripes à la mode de Caen, steak au poivre noir (flambéed), and canard à l'orange, to an excellent provincial-style calf's liver, a coquille of sea foods véronique, and pheasant breast in the style of Monte Carlo. He makes a first-rate stroganoff, laced with cream sauce, sour cream and cognac, and a fine saltimbocca: veal slices enclosing Swiss cheese and ham, under a cover of port sauce. There are several good lamb dishes—including rack of lamb for two, if you don't mind the additional half hour this takes to prepare— and grilled steaks, tournedos, and spring chicken, with appropriate sauces. The accompanying vegetables are never dreary.

Desserts, besides crêpes suzette, peaches flambé, and cherries jubilee, include meringues heaped with chantilly, marrons with ice cream and Grand Marnier, peach Melba, and kirsch-soaked pineapple. The crème caramel is excellent, and there are sherbets, ice creams, and assorted cheeses. You can also get café filtre.

➤ CALF'S LIVER PROVENÇALE

1 lb. calf's liver	4 tbsp. bread crumbs
1 to 2 tsp. oil (or enough to grease the bottom of the skillet)	1 tsp. chopped garlic
	2 shallots, chopped fine
4 tbsp. butter	1 tbsp. demi-glace (or very rich brown gravy)

Grease or oil a heavy skillet and put over a very hot flame. Add liver and cook until rare, medium, or well-done according to taste. While the liver is cooking, melt butter in small pan, add all other ingredients except demi-glace, and sauté until golden. Add demi-glace, cook a minute longer, and spread on top of liver. Serves four.

2. FAMILY-STYLE

A CITY that has nurtured since early in its history not only transients but a large number of its own citizens in hotels, boarding houses, and other such homes-away-from-home, encourages from necessity a tradition of home-style cooking which is unpretentious but excellent, and modest in cost. Many of these places have evolved a good way from their original days as pensions, but a few have retained their tables of regular boarders.

In the area of upper Broadway, there are several of these inexpensive family-style places. The city's Basque population has settled hereabouts, and newly arrived immigrants, many on their way to sheep-herding jobs, stay in one of several hotels within a few blocks of each other. Their dining rooms, often open to the public, are plain but good. Among this group, I like the honest upstairs room at the Hotel du Midi at 1362 Powell Street, but you will find Martin's Español and the Hotel de España a bit more dressed up and perhaps more comfortable. They are at 674 and 781 Broadway, respectively.

Just above Broadway and off Columbus, the Italian family-style restaurant La Pantera is going strong. Like most of the places in this category, the food is hearty and comparatively inexpensive, but given a choice, I would prefer the French or Basque dining rooms. La Pantera seems a bit clamorous and rushed. For inexpensive Italian cookery, there are several other more leisurely establishments in this general neighborhood, one of the closest—on Broadway—a very old-timer, Buon Gusto, that serves good lunch, dinner, and cocktails. Another, Jake's, at 673 Union Street, is a chummy place that doesn't take reservations, and is always jammed with old customers, to whom it rightly gives preference. Monday through Friday they serve up a well-cooked home-style lunch (never dinner) that consists of a bottomless serving bowl of soup, French bread, salad, and such entrées as roast beef and chicken alla cacciatore, heaps of green vegetables, and great wedges of salty, garlicky, crusty, oven-browned potatoes. You get a bottle of red wine to wash it all down, and coffee to finish things off. All of this for $1.50! There is no sign over the door, just the number, but you can enter through the adjacent corner bar.

At 846 Jackson Street, between Powell and Stockton, George Firmignac carries on the French restaurant, Ripley's, that his family has owned since 1913. The main floor is devoted to a bar—rather dowdy, in a pleasant sort of way—and the dining room is one flight below. In an anything but pretentious atmosphere, you will get a huge dinner that runs through a salad, assorted appetizers and relishes, soupe du jour, a small entrée (your choice includes filet of sole, chicken in a patty shell, ravioli, chicken livers sautéed in red wine, and tagliarini), a main course of chicken, steak, duck, pork or lamb chops, and various seafoods, cheese or ice cream, and coffee. When the oldtimers come in, there's always a spontaneous songfest.

My favorite establishments of this type—both French—stand almost side by side on upper Broadway. Hotel de France and Des Alpes serve excellent meals, most reasonably priced, and the food you consume is enough to sustain you for days.

Hotel de France ✳

780 BROADWAY

inexpensive

THE FIRST HOTEL DE FRANCE, AN INSTITUTION ALSO FAMOUS IN its day for serving up mountains of excellent food at a very little rate, occupied an elaborate old mansion on California Street. One entered the parlor-turned-bar, then chose between two dining rooms. The smaller of these was the more intimate and elegant, but steady customers preferred to crowd into the larger and noisier room in back. Here they assembled around long tables accented with brimming bowls of fruits, platters of crisp raw vegetables, and the inevitable loaves of crusty French bread. Will Irwin, in his touching requiem of San Francisco, "The City That Was"—a piece written three days after the April, 1906 horrors—recalls the usual scene at Hotel de France:

> Louis, the proprietor, was a Frenchman of the Bas Pyrenees; and his accent was as thick as his peasant soups. The patrons were Frenchmen of the poorer class, or young and poor clerks and journalists who had discovered the delights of his hostelry. The place exhuded (sic) a genial gaiety, of which Louis, throw-

89

ing out familiar jokes to right and left as he mixed salads and carried dishes, was the head and front.

First on the bill of fare was the soup mentioned before—thick and clean and good. Next, one of Louis' three cherubic little sons brought on a course of fish—sole, rock cod, flounders or smelt—with a good French sauce. The third course was meat. This came on en bloc; the waiter dropped in the center of each table a big roast or boiled joint together with a mustard pot and two big dishes of vegetables. Each guest manned the carving knife in turn and helped himself to his satisfaction. After that, Louis, with an air of ceremony, brought on a big bowl of excellent salad which he had mixed himself. For beverage, there stood by each plate a perfectly cylindrical pint glass filled with new, watered claret. The meal closed with "fruit in season"—all that the guest cared to eat. I have saved a startling fact to close the paragraph—the price was fifteen cents!

By the '90's, inflation had edged the price upwards to twenty-five cents, and the Sunday chicken came to ten cents more.[19]

What history lies between that Hotel de France and its present namesake is now forgotten. Claude Berhouet, the current owner-chef, reports that the Broadway quarters opened in 1935. Since then a fire has necessitated some remodeling, but the place retains its rustic, friendly atmosphere. The waitresses are all French-speaking—and so are a good many of the regular patrons, including the famous chef, Lucien Heyraud. Although inflation has pushed the prices a good distance from twenty-five cents, you will pay a very modest sum for an excellent dinner of many courses.

The meal begins with a tureen of soup of a different kind each day. There is an excellent assortment of hors d'oeuvres, a first hot dish, the main course, a salad, dessert and coffee. On Monday, after a stew of ox-tails, you will dine off a roast leg of lamb, Bretonne style, with beans. Tuesday the first dish is a peppy

[19] Will Irwin, *The City That Was*, New York, B. W. Huebsch, 1906, pp. 35–36.

stuffed pimiento with creole sauce, followed by grilled minute steak. Lamb stew jardinière and roast of veal are Wednesday's dishes, sweetbreads and mushrooms in puff shells, and chicken sauté are Thursday's. On Fridays, besides a fine clam chowder, the chef produces buttery rex sole and roast beef. The week end starts with braised beef in Burgundy, and lamb chops, and ends with vol-au-vent à la reine—sweetbreads in pastry shells—and roast stuffed chicken. When you prefer a substitution for any entrée, try the poulet sauté, chasseur—a really distinguished bit of cooking. In my many visits to this restaurant, I have always come away delighted, too well-fed, and not a great deal poorer. M. Berhouet learned about cooking in Lourdes, and for special occasions can produce some Basque specialties. But the regular menu never varies. He has given me his instructions for two fine dishes from his repertoire: Bouchée à la Reine and Boeuf à la Bourguignonne.

BOUCHÉE À LA REINE

stock:

½ gal. water	1 stalk celery
1 carrot	parsley
1 onion	1 stalk fresh thyme
2 leeks	salt and pepper
	1 hen

Put all ingredients in large kettle and simmer 4–6 hours, skimming off the surface fats from time to time. Strain and reserve.

filling:

3 pairs sweetbreads	½ lb. butter
1 carrot	½ cup flour
1 stalk celery	1 glass sherry wine
1 bay leaf	salt and pepper
½ lb. mushrooms, sliced	6 patty shells
2 tbsp. butter	

Parboil sweetbreads with carrot, celery, bay leaf in enough water to cover, for 15 minutes. When cool, trim, and cut into small pieces. Sauté ½ pound sliced mushrooms in 2 tbsp. butter. In a large kettle melt ½ pound butter, add ½ cup flour slowly, blending well, add 2 cups warm stock a little at a time, mixing thoroughly, and cook over low heat for about twenty minutes. Meanwhile, combine sweetbreads and mushrooms, add 1 glass sherry wine, and put in medium oven for five minutes. Add to the stock-roux and cook slowly for ten minutes on top of the stove. Add salt and pepper to taste. Pour into pastry shells. Serves six.

BOEUF À LA BOURGUIGNONNE

4 lbs. round steak, cut into cubes
salt and pepper
½ cup oil
½ cup flour
2 tbsp. oil
1 onion, diced fine
twig parsley
1 clove of garlic
2 cups Burgundy, plus more as needed

2 tbsp. tomato purée
½ bay leaf
thyme
1 cup beef stock (or 1 bouillon cube in 1 cup boiling water)
beef marrow, diced, and poached 3–5 minutes in boiling water

Season steak with salt and pepper, then fry quickly in oil until brown. Sprinkle flour over the meat as you brown it. In a separate pot, put the onion, parsley, garlic with a little oil—about 2 tbsp. When cooked, add 2 cups Burgundy, boil a minute or two, add the meat, mix in tomato purée, bay leaf, a little thyme, beef stock, and wine to cover. Cook for two hours very slowly over a low flame until the gravy is very thick. When almost cooked, add the beef marrow—the more the better. Serves six.

Des Alpes Restaurant ✳

DES ALPES STARTED AS A PENSION JUST AT THE TURN OF THE century, and there is still a long table tucked away in the back for steady boarders and members of the family. Otherwise, the place looks like any other pleasant, modest bistro. Old customers viewed with alarm the redecorating that transformed the premises a few years ago, but the friendly atmosphere still prevails, the food is delightful, and the worriers are relaxing once again over their veal patties and roast beef. And most everyone agrees that the separation of the front bar from the family dining room is an improvement.

The present owners, Catherine and John Bordalampe and Gene Iriartborde, preside over the dining room, bar, and kitchen respectively. All three are French-Basques from Armendarits in the Pyrenees, not far from Bayonne. Chef Gene came to this country to cook at Des Alpes when his cousins, the Bordalampes, purchased the place in 1955. The Bordalampes have been in the United States since 1925. For many years they ran the Hotel Espagnol across the street, and often came as customers to Des Alpes for dinner.

Catherine Bordalampe is rightly proud of her good food, and explains in her energetic way that it tastes fine because they always use pure butter, white wine, lots of mushrooms, and high quality vegetables. In explaining why the Des Alpes soup is so much heartier than the usual, anemic family-style brew, she counts off a rich assortment of vegetables—a veritable marketful—that simmers in the kettle.

The dinner here is large, table d'hôte, the cost moderate. You always start with a soup tureen afloat with all the minerals and vitamins. Then comes another specialty, a cold dressed salad of

93

cooked vegetables, tangy, light, and exceptionally good. Two entrées follow. Tuesday's specials are sweetbreads and roast beef. On Wednesday Gene sometimes cooks meat balls, sometimes beef tongue vinaigrette, and always lamb chops. On Thursdays and Sundays he serves veal patties, tender meat infused with a wine sauce and served in a pastry shell, and follows them on both occasions with a main course of chicken. Friday is fish and steak night, and Saturday means lamb stew followed by roast of beef.

Here is Gene's recipe for the Saturday night stew, as he gave it to me—for 150 portions. If you plan to feed a smaller number, the measurements in parentheses will give you a good main course for four or five.

LAMB STEW

100 lbs. lamb shoulder (5 lbs.)
flour for dredging (2 tbsp.)
20 lbs. carrots (1 lb. or 4 carrots)
10 lbs. potatoes (2 potatoes)
2 lbs. onions (1 small onion)
12 shallots (1 or 2 shallots)
6 cloves garlic (½ clove garlic)
1 qt. white wine (½ cup)
1 qt. meat stock or broth (½ cup)
salt and pepper to taste (same)
1 bunch parsley (1 sprig)

Trim and bone the lamb, chop it into chunks, and put in a hot oven (450°) until brown—this takes 45 minutes to an hour. Remove meat and juices to a large pot. Dredge them with flour and cook over medium heat, stirring until the flour is well mixed. Add carrots and potatoes, chopped coarse, and garlic, onions, and shallots, chopped fine. Add salt and pepper, wine and broth, stir all together, and cook covered over low heat until tender—about 45 minutes. Before serving, sprinkle with chopped parsley.

SWEETBREADS

4 tbsp. butter
1 onion, chopped fine
½ clove garlic, chopped fine
2 tbsp. flour
1 cup white wine for sauce
½ lb. sliced mushrooms

1 lb. sweetbreads
1 cup bouillon or white wine
  for parboiling
salt and pepper
8 toast triangles or 4 vol-au-
  vents

Melt butter, add onion and garlic, chopped fine, and sautée until glossy. Add 2 tbsp. flour, a little at a time, blending well to make a smooth sauce. Add wine and cook until medium thick. Add mushrooms, cover, and cook over low heat 10 minutes. Parboil sweetbreads 15 minutes in bouillon or white wine, drain, trim, and slice. When sauce is ready, add sweetbreads and salt and pepper to taste, and cook just long enough to heat through. Serve over toast triangles or fill vol-au-vents. Serves four.

3. CHINATOWN

THE story of San Francisco's Chinatown describes at once a community that has been the most exotic, overcrowded, tumultuous, dangerous, and—qualities generally overlooked—law-abiding and industrious in the city.

Historical accounts are at variance, but it is certain that at least one Chinese reached these shores in 1847, and a few more the year following. Within four years there was a Chinese population in California of 20,000. The first attraction was the gold mines, but many turned to the city to establish such services as laundries (one report has it that 1,000 emerged in the 20 years after 1851, when Wah Lee opened the first on a corner of Washington and Grant), and to provide the growing general population with domestic help. Besides these employments, over 10,000 Chinese laborers worked during the '60's at building the Central Pacific Railroad, and, once that monumental job was finished, at reclaiming, and subsequently farming, vast territories of marshland. Many early Chinese immigrants found work in factories, particularly those manufacturing shoes. After several years, the Chinese seemed to congregate in one locale, and accounts estimate that by the '80's well over 30,000 inhabited the dozen or so blocks of Chinatown that fed into the main artery, Dupont Street. A like number of Chinese were dispersed throughout the rest of the state. Despite a variety of agonizing and discriminatory immigration laws, and the harassment of frequent fires—two of which leveled the settlement almost completely— the Chinese citizenry remained, made its way in an often punitive and hostile environment, and contributed the enrichments of its culture and its heritage to a city that is now particularly proud to claim it.

Although the majority of Chinese were hard working, touchingly loyal, and in possession of an admirable endurance, there was a thriving criminal element in their midst, whose exploits and adventures lent a horror—and a good deal of macabre color —to the developing community. Those offenders prospered, one should hasten to point out, only through the protection and connivance of public officials—as graft-ridden a municipal family as has ever inhabited a city hall. There were dens of gambling and prostitution, and a flourishing traffic in opium and slaves. There were also a number of synthetic settings displaying "evils" for the also-flourishing tourist trade.

The Tongs were the base of the Chinese underworld. A peculiarly American institution, they developed their own code of behavior, which included the employment of thugs, salaried murderers, and the waging of vengeful and bloody wars. Hatchets and knives were the trademarks of these mutual benefit associations (a misnomer, even within the framework of their perverse ethic). The Tongs flourished well into the 1920's.

The Six Companies, which exist today, were associations representing the six districts of China, whose purpose was the arbitration of various disputes: financial, personal, or family disagreements, trade arguments, and the like. These companies were, like a governing agent, supreme in all matters commercial. They arranged to import workers and establish them in jobs, for which service they were paid back their investment with interest—and some say, with continuing contributions. They have always attempted to keep vice out of Chinatown.

In modern times, the community has become entirely respectable, and although still overcrowded, it has come a long way from the days when hundreds of families lived together in two tremendous cellars beneath, and accessible only by ladder from, Washington Street and Bartlett Alley. In some respects, old timers feel, it has come too far, blending more and more chameleon-like with the city that surrounds it. Its Chinese telephone exchange, a feature since early days, has closed down. The great winding dragon still parades through the streets on New Year's and some other festivals, but the din of accompanying firecrackers is a thing of the past. The pot of tea, once on every shop counter to refresh all who entered, is now confined to the tearoom or restaurant. Waiters seldom scurry through alleys balancing trays of food on their heads; or trundle buckets of steamy morsels up several flights to hungry families indulging in the custom, that lasted well into the '30's, of having their meals sent home from a favorite restaurant. The traditional painted signs have changed to a nightmare of neon, flashing and garish, far from their original calligraphic beauty, and ignorant, in their electric modernity, that writing was a fine art in old China. Chemists' shops are giving way to modern pharmacies; tabashir, lotus kernels, and wolf's bane to multiple vitamins, estrogen, and phenobarbital. And the joss houses are more for tourists than worship. Restaurants have forsaken in their names the poetic character of their forerunners. There are no more such designations as Charles Caldwell Dobie celebrates in "San Francisco's Chinatown": no "Fragrant Almond Chamber," or "Chamber of the Odors of Different Lands"; no "Garden of the Golden Valley," or "Balcony of Joy and Delight." Vanished is another scene from Dobie's youth, "All of the restaurants had divans where one could recline and take a long pull at an opium pipe during the progress of a banquet." [20] But in spite of the encroachments made by progress, Chinatown retains a mystery and a fascination, an atmosphere at once foreign and antique. And its culinary skills, inherited, practiced, and refined over years of civilization, make a Chinatown meal a splendid adventure.

The Chinese for centuries employed the delights of the dinner and banquet table in the entertainment of their friends, and in the celebration of affairs of importance. Lin Yutang says, "If there is anything we are serious about, it is neither religion nor learning, but food. We openly acclaim eating as one of the few joys of this human life. This question of attitude is very important, for unless we are honest about it we will never be able to lift eating and cooking into an art." [21]

It was in this spirit that banquets in times past included over a hundred courses—the tradition calling for a main course for each guest. And what a clutter it was by the end of the meal, since according to the niceties of Chinese etiquette, one doesn't hurry the guests by clearing away the dishes! Dobie recollects that even the ordinary Chinese menu used to offer such riches

[20] Charles Caldwell Dobie, *San Francisco's Chinatown*, London–New York, D. Appleton-Century Company, Inc., 1936, pp. 305, 252.

[21] Lin Yutang, *My Country and My People*, New York, The John Day Company, Inc., 1939, p. 337.

as "stewed ortolans, a dish called Taranaki fingers contrived from the fruit of a New Zealand tree, fish brains, Chinese quail, reindeer sinews, scorpion's eggs, and stewed moss." [22] For those with less exotic tastes there was chop suey, a San Francisco invention, according to some accounts. At any rate this dish appeared almost simultaneously on the West Coast and in New York during the '90's, and San Franciscans yearning to try it flocked to Hang Far Low Restaurant, the undisputed king of chop suey makers in these parts.

Chinatown is, at least culinarily, Cantonese, which in practical terms accounts for the number of tea houses, and the versatility of its menu. The average citizen in the south and west of China eats two substantial meals, filling in with tea and snacks. Buwei Yang Chao tells us, in her informative and charming cookbook, that some of the most respected Cantonese restaurants owe their fame much more to their midday teas than to their excellent dinners.[23] The Chinese eat three kinds of meals: the tea, snack, or light meal; the family-style meal where the food is served all at once in large common utensils; and the more elaborate banquet in a series of courses.

When you eat in a tea house, you can choose a light meal of meat-, fish-, or vegetable-stuffed pastries, or a one-dish concoction of noodles, vegetables, and meat. The menu generally contains additional dishes—pickled mustard greens, fried chicken wings, abalone, braised beef ligament—depending on the proprietor's inclination. The tea with assorted delicacies, Dim-Sum, usually comes on a tray and you select those items that look most appealing. When you have finished your meal, the waiter arrives at your bill by totting up the number of empty dishes. But even hearty eaters can't run up much of a total.

Probably the best known tea house is down a little alley off Sacramento Street, next to the Chinese playground. The Hang

[22] *San Francisco's Chinatown*, p. 263.

[23] Buwei Yang Chao, *How to Cook and Eat in Chinese*, New York, The John Day Company, Inc., 1945, p. 4.

Ah Tea Room, at 1 Hang Ah Street (also known as Pagoda Alley, after the structure in the neighboring play yard) is open every day but Monday from 11 in the morning until 3:30 in the afternoon. Here you can either get an already-assembled plate lunch that includes a half-dozen items; order directly from an à la carte menu; or select from the tray service. There are a number of sweets, including the favorite custard tarts and lotus buns.

At the corner of Powell and Broadway, the Yank Sing Tea House opens its doors from 10 a.m. until 5 p.m., except on Fridays. This is a one-family endeavor, and thoroughly successful. Its menu includes an item or two from the cuisine of north China, and its devotees think its shrimp rolls are the best in town. Its atmosphere is completely plain.

The Songhay Tea House, at 650 Jackson Street, opens every day but Monday, serves Dim-Sum from 10 a.m. until mid-afternoon, and dinner until 10 p.m. Complete meals here are family-style, substantial, and inexpensive.

At a few restaurants—like Sam Wo and Sai-Yon, discussed in detail below—you can get a snack at any hour of the night.

In a discussion of regional differences in cooking, Mrs. Chao remarks that in Canton "restaurants are perhaps the most versatile of all and excel in all lines. They also excel in cooking materials for their original flavor with little adornment, such as slow-cooked chicken, paper-sealed mushrooms, etc." [24] In San Francisco, in spite of the predominance of Cantonese, specialties from other areas find their way onto many menus—Peking duck being the most immediate example—because many dishes, regardless of their place of origin, become national favorites.

The main exception to Cantonese cuisine in San Francisco is a comparatively new restaurant, The Mandarin, at 2209 Polk Street, outside of Chinatown. This establishment specializes in the cooking of northern China, with such rare procedures—in San Francisco, at least—as that of the Mongolian chafing pot. This vessel, warmed by a charcoal fire and a central chimney,

[24] *How to Cook and Eat in Chinese*, p. 8.

contains a substantial chicken broth, enriched by successive dunkings of thinly sliced chicken, beef, pork, shrimp, vegetables, bean curd, and rice noodles. By the time those morsels have cooked in it, the broth is a rich brew. The Mandarin believes that it is the first and only Chinese establishment in this country to present beggar's chicken—a finely flavored bird bundled in clay and baked. Prawns à la Szechwan are sautéed with a special hot sauce, duck is smoked whole in tea leaves, or roasted Mandarin style. There are sweet and sour meatballs, and Chinese cabbage in a creamy white sauce. The carp in a sweet and sour sauce, full of such delectables as lichee nuts, is outstanding. Pepper chicken is characteristic of the spicy cooking from the Szechwan area. There is an unusual dessert here of fried apples or bananas in a candy-coating. Prepared in chunky pieces, they come piping hot in a flowing caramel sauce. You pick up a piece with your chopsticks and plunge it for an instant into a bowl of ice water. The candy-coating hardens, the fruit stays hot, and the result is altogether delicious. The Mandarin offers a substantial choice of à la carte dishes, three family-style dinners, and a banquet menu. Its prices are comparable to those of the most expensive restaurants in Chinatown.

In general, when you order in a Chinese restaurant, unless you have a large group, or have made special arrangements for particular banquet foods, your meal will be served more or less family style. In China you would get all the food at the same serving, dipping up a chopstick full of this, then a chopstick full of that, with only your own bowl of rice. Even the soup would be served along with the other foods, rather than eaten as a separate course. Here you will probably receive your soup first, then the pedestals containing all the other dishes you have ordered. In general, you should order a main dish for each person, plus one extra, as well as a soup and rice. If you increase the size of your party beyond eight or ten, you may want to double up on some orders, instead of adding further variety to your meal.

708 GRANT AVENUE

expensive

JOHNNY KAN OPENED HIS DE LUXE GRANT AVENUE RESTAURANT in 1953, and has made it into one of Chinatown's best. The cooking and service are always superb, the atmosphere decorous, and a number of touches—like the clearly descriptive menu, and the perfumed towels Hong-Kong style at the end of the meal —a comfort and joy. Besides introducing these and other widely-imitated niceties to Chinatown, Mr. Kan has established the lazy susan as an appropriate device for serving Chinese food. His latest enterprise is an excellent cookbook, "Eight Immortal Flavors."

One flight above the handsome main dining room—itself a story above street level—is an unusual salon for private parties. It houses a permanent exhibit of watercolors depicting the history of the Chinese in the United States. Kan named it Gum Shan (Golden Hills) Room, since this Chinese term has been synonymous with United States ever since the Chinese mined gold in the hills of the Mother Lode. Mr. Kan is one of the leading civic spirits in Chinatown, and proud of the accomplishments of his forebears. He commissioned a Chinese-American artist, Jake Lee, to decorate the Gum Shan Room, and Mr. Lee put in a year of historical research for the job. His paintings show the first immigrants disembarking in 1849, Chinese miners in the gold fields, lantern-making in San Francisco, railroad workers laboring on the first transcontinental track, and the once-famous China Camp shrimp fishery. They also depict some less well-known aspects of Chinese-American cultural history: Chinese shoemakers in Massachusetts in the 1870's, vineyard workers in Sonoma county, San Francisco cigar-making, an 1862 view of the Chinese Opera House, and the champion Chinese fire-hose team of Deadwood, South Dakota, 1888.

Kan's menu is virtually an epitome of San Francisco Chinese cooking. There is a wondrous array of soups—mushroom, won ton, delicate sea weed (a favorite of mine), bird's nest, shark's fin, abalone, and—in season—mustard green. As for vegetables, snow peas, mushrooms—both black and white—broccoli, long beans, onions, bitter melon, bamboo shoots, water chestnuts, bean sprouts, wood ears, celery, and a whole gardenful of greens, tumble together in various combinations sometimes with the addition of sautéed slices of beef or pork, sometimes mixed with chicken, or prawns, or simmered in oyster or black bean sauce. There are a number of curries—tomato beef, chicken, prawn, and rock cod, and—when it is in season—crab, San Francisco variety, and lobster. There are tangy meat dishes of pork, spareribs, ginger beef, or—my favorite—beef in oyster sauce. Chicken comes with almonds, sesame seeds or cashews; and chicken wings fry in parsley butter. An unusual dish consists of thin slices of imported abalone meat over Chinese ravioli, the whole soaking up a rich oyster sauce. The menu offers several rice and noodle dishes, but, because chow mein takes a good deal of last-minute preparation, these dishes are reserved for the lunch hour or for after 10 in the evening.

If you get together a group of eight or more friends, and give two days' advance notice, Johnny will prepare you an elegant nine course banquet. When it is in season, you can start with Doong Gwa Joong—chicken broth studded with diced chicken, bamboo shoots, mushrooms, peas, and lotus seeds, and steamed for several hours in a whole wintermelon. Each serving contains succulent scoops of melon in the rich chunky broth. The other courses range from sweet and sour pork with pineapple, to lobsters cooked with vegetables, and include two chicken specialties, one with vegetables and roasted walnut halves, the other marinated in spices, wrapped in parchment, and deep fried. The masterpiece is Peking duck—Kwa Law Opp. To prepare this dish, Kan's rubs a fat duck with honey, wheat syrup and seasonings, then barbecues it until its brown skin crinkles. It is served with condiments and steamed nine-layer buns in which you can sandwich the crackling skin. There are gourmet vegetables sautéed with beef tenderloin and laced with crisp long rice; fried rice tossed with shrimps, peas, pork, onions, and lettuce shreds; and for dessert, tea cakes and icy lichee nuts, with a choice of oolong or jasmine tea.

Kan's will prepare any number of specialties if given notice in advance. Besides wintermelon soup, which feeds from four to ten diners, depending on the size of the melon, they prepare such delicacies as whole rock cod in any one of three ways: steamed in soy and peanut oil; simmered with barbecued pork, black mushrooms, green onions, bamboo shoots, water chestnuts, Mandarin orange rind, and Chinese dates; or infused with a sweet and sour sauce bubbling with peppers, onions, tomatoes, and celery. Canton lobster, also an advance-order delicacy, is available only when lobster is in season. Kan's prepares it by combining the lobster meat with mushrooms, pork, bamboo shoots and water chestnuts, stuffing the mix back in the shell, and steaming it thoroughly. Another fanciful dish is sautéed smoked oysters with a combination of meat, vegetables, bamboo shoots, and water chestnuts.

There are a number of complicated squab, duck, and chicken dishes, which also need extra notice to prepare. Kan's does a fine whole boned duck, braised, then steamed in a spicy sauce (Sai Woh Opp). A variety of stuffings improve the humble chicken. An order of Naw Mai Gai, chicken plump with a glutinous rice, sausage, ham, and mushrooms, will feed three or four. Both squab and chicken come filled with bird's nest, and steamed en casserole in a good broth. Another exceptional dish is squab Chung Kwong, first steamed, then deep fried. Perhaps one of the most delicious of all fowl recipes is gold coin chicken, alternate chunks of chicken meat, and squares of ham and pork barbecued together, and served on skewers with delicate steamed buns.

Kan's other special order dishes include those 1,000-year black preserved eggs (really 100 days old), served in thin slices with pickled scallions, but not recommended unless you are proceeding in the interests of experiment. Johnny Kan says that it takes a bit of educating before one's palate readily accommodates them, and maybe a little more time before you can really look on them as a delicacy. 1,000 years?

Although Kan's must be considered deluxe among Chinatown restaurants, on a city-wide basis its meals are still only moderately expensive.

Here are two fine recipes from Johnny Kan's cookbook.[25]

⤳ CHICKEN SMOTHERED IN ROCK SALT

(Yim Gai)

One 5 pound dressed roaster-sized chicken (must be fresh, wet picked)
½ tsp. Chinese rose liqueur or any brand of gin
1 cup water
1 tsp. minced ginger root

2 tsp. almond salt (if available)
½ tsp. chopped Chinese parsley (optional)
1 green onion, flattened
10 pounds rock salt

Hang chicken beforehand in cool place to drain, and wipe dry with absorbent toweling. Combine rose liqueur or gin, water, ginger root, almond salt, parsley, and green onion. Tie neck of chicken with string and fill cavity with the above marinade. Sew up tightly all openings of the bird so that no liquid will leak out. In a huge pot, place 10 lbs. rock salt. At high heat, stir and mix rock salt until red hot. Thirty or more minutes should suffice. Make a deep impression in the center, place chicken in it, making sure there is at least 2 inches of salt "bedding" underneath. Cover pot tightly, cook over low heat 30 minutes, turn off heat and let stand another 30 minutes. Remove chicken from pot, cut the strings and drain the cavity marinade into a pot. Keep it hot over a low fire until ready to place in a gravy boat. Cut and serve chicken. Serves four.

[25] *Eight Immortal Flavors*, to be published by Howell-North Books, Berkeley, California. Used by permission.

PINEAPPLE CHICKEN WINGS SWEET AND SOUR ⊰
(Bo Law Teem Seen Gai Yik)

12 large chicken wings
2 beaten eggs
½ cup cornstarch
¼ tsp. salt
dash of pepper
vegetable oil
1 cup vinegar

1 tbsp. catsup
1 tsp. soy sauce
¼ cup pineapple juice
3 tbsp. sugar
pinch of salt
1 cup pineapple chunks

Clean and dry chicken wings, dip in beaten eggs. In a large heavy paper bag place cornstarch, salt, and pepper. Drop egg-coated chicken wings into bag, shake well until completely coated. In a large deep skillet place 2 inches vegetable oil heated to boiling point. Deep fry chicken wings until golden brown. Drain on absorbent toweling. Pour off oil from skillet except 1 tablespoon. Keep skillet hot. Mix well and pour into skillet: vinegar, catsup, soy sauce, pineapple juice, sugar, and a pinch of salt. Cook at high heat to boiling point, then thicken with cornstarch paste until medium thick. Add pineapple chunks and chicken wings. Toss and mix thoroughly for 5 minutes at high heat or until wings are heated through. Serves four.

Imperial Palace ✳
919 GRANT AVENUE

expensive

IMPERIAL PALACE IS ONE OF THE NEWER LUXURY RESTAURANTS. The trio of owners, friends of long standing, include Joe Yuey, an art connoisseur, Y. C. Yu, a literary scholar, and Kee Joon, an experienced restaurateur who long ago also did a bit of professional photography. Mr. Yuey, a member of the American Society of Asian Art, and a close friend of philanthropist Avery Brundage (the collector who gave his fabulous oriental collection to the city of San Francisco) has his own rather extraordinary treasury of Asian Art. At present the restaurant houses two cases where a few pieces are exhibited at a time. Every few months the miniature museum changes its show. Eventually, the Imperial Palace hopes to exhibit the Yuey collection in its own gallery. In June of 1960, during the week preceding the opening of the restaurant, the Imperial Palace held a three-day exhibition of the full collection. More than 15,000 art lovers came to view it.

Mr. Joon is responsible, except for some technical architectural details, for the fundamental design and interior decor of the handsome new restaurant. I like his choice of fixtures. Overhead white globes glimmer through a cover of varicolored glass strips, in a modern version of the oriental paper lantern. The entrance doors are the highest in Chinatown and lend a proper majesty to the scene. The most striking feature is the wall between bar and entry, a partition inlaid with six hand-cut crystal panels of great beauty. They came originally from Peking and were once part of the decor of Hang Far Low, one of the first Chinese restaurants in San Francisco.

Mr. Joon tells me that according to an old Chinese saying, Soochow is the place to be born because the people are so fair and the women so beautiful; Canton is the place to eat, because the food is the best of all of China; and Laochow is the place to die, since there is the best wood for coffins. Since we are too late for the first, and not yet considering the last, we will have to concentrate on the food of Canton—which we can at least enjoy transplanted to these shores. Mr. Joon also tells me that during ancient days it was the custom for the people to search out the best chef in all of China to become cook to the ruler of the land. Invariably the winner was a Cantonese—and the subject who discovered him was highly rewarded.

The variety of Chinese cuisine is so vast as to defy acquaintance, but a good number of rare and special dishes await your order at Imperial Palace. (Go lightly on the hot hors d'oeuvres in the bar!). You can order an excellent dinner of several courses, or make up your own menu from the easy-to-read list, with adequate descriptions of whatever might otherwise be mysterious. To start with, the fried won ton are especially good here. Spareribs are marinated in honey, wine, and plum sauce before barbecueing, and golden chicken wings are fried light and crisp. Another good appetizer is the shrimp puffs—won ton filled with pork, mushrooms and shrimp finely minced. The soup course provides a choice from several broths of the simpler home-style variety, and from more elaborate simmerings in the banquet style. Imperial Palace serves, with twenty-four hours' advance notice, a ginseng root soup, an ancient broth known for its flavor and for its health-giving qualities. The good herb in company with a fine whole chicken steams for ten hours to produce this broth.

Among the Imperial specials, beef Imperial, fresh ginger root oysters, and the sweet and sour lichee chicken are all first-rate. If you yearn for something a bit more unusual, you might try the bird's nest soup, three-kingdom eggs, roast squab stuffed with sweet rice, or the excellent five willows rock cod—deep-fried chunks of cod dressed with five different preserved fruits shredded like willows, then joined by a sweet and sour sauce. Lobster Kwangtung—sautéed with bamboo shoots, snow peas, water chestnuts, and Chinese mushrooms—is another good bet. Tossed chicken Imperial—a whole chicken fried, shredded, jumbled with seasonings, almonds, scallions, and Chinese parsley, and served still warm—is certainly as good as any of the two hundred or more ways that the Chinese can cook a chicken.

By special arrangement, Imperial Palace will produce Cantonese-style banquets ranging in price from $40 to $200, consisting of ten or a dozen courses, not all of which are familiar to Western palates, and taking four or five hours to consume. If you plan such a feast with Mr. Joon, he may suggest that you start with Lonpon, or Phoenix-Dragon Plate, a cold hors d'oeuvre in which smoked tongue, boiled beef with Chinese spices, smoked chicken breast, 1,000-year eggs, large prawns, Chinese smoked ham and sliced Chinese steamed eggs of different colors are elaborately arranged to emerge as a glorious butterfly, a splendid peacock, or a handsome fish. This edible decoration is followed by hot hors d'oeuvres, including such delicate goodies as sautéed little bay shrimp, or chicken with abalone.

The more important dishes follow: rare ($300 a pound) mushrooms—found sprouting up just as the snow melts—a very crispy delicacy; the marrow of young bamboo; chicken stuffed with sweet rice; abalone, small, tender, imported from China, soaked and simmered in oyster sauce, then covered with a sprinkling of shrimp and caviar; squab steamed in the juice and grated peel of fresh lemons; stuffed whole fresh lobster—the filling of lobster meat, water chestnuts, and prawns beaten for a long time until it is remarkably light; bon chee, sautéed whole pieces of shark's fin steamed for two days to tenderize it. You might have crab legs prepared with Chinese cabbage: the heart of the cabbage hangs for a week to age like a steak; then the cook deep fries it whole, lays it on a plate, covers it with steaming chicken broth which it soaks up until tender; creamed crab legs go over the top, and the dish is finished off with a sprinkling of Chinese ham. The real masterpiece—and a dish that no other restaurant in the country makes—is this recipe for duck: the chef bones the duck, lays it flat, seasons it with a variety of spices, and steams it until tender; then he deep fries it until brown, and barbecues it until the skin is crispy. The sauce, poured over the top, is sweet and sour, based on pure orange juice.

After all these riches, a good soup is in order—a steamed whole wintermelon, a soup of rare mushrooms, or perhaps a broth with bird's nest. Dessert might be Imperial Delight, an almond-flavored junket-like pudding.

Mr. Joon has most generously supplied three recipes—of a simpler nature—that are among the specialties of his restaurant.

BEEF IMPERIAL

1½ lb. sirloin of beef
1 5-oz. can bamboo shoots
1 3-oz. can water chestnuts
½ lb. snow peas
½ lb. mushrooms
1 small stalk celery
2 small onions

3 tbsp. peanut oil
1 tbsp. soy sauce, or more
salt and pepper
½ tbsp. sugar
1 tbsp. cornstarch
2 tbsp. cold water

Cut the beef against the grain into very fine slices no more than two or three inches across. Drain bamboo shoots and water chestnuts, and cut the first into slivers, the second into slices. Trim the end of the snow peas and cut each piece once diagonally. Slice the mushrooms vertically through the stem in thin pieces. Cut the celery in small diagonal sections, discarding the leaves. Dice the onions into small pieces. Heat peanut oil very hot in a heavy skillet. Add meat, and toss-cook a minute or two. Add vegetables and continue to toss-cook over high heat two minutes. Season with soy sauce, light salt, pepper, and sugar; add cornstarch pre-mixed with water until smooth. Mix, cover, and cook over lowered flame two minutes.

THREE KINGDOM EGGS

2 1,000-year eggs (preserved eggs, in reality between 30–100 days old)
2 preserved salt eggs
2 fresh eggs

½ cup cold water
salt and pepper
2 green onions, chopped fine
1 tbsp. oyster sauce

Cut the 1,000-year eggs, and the preserved salt eggs in dice shape. Whip the fresh eggs together with cold water, add light salt and pepper, mix in the diced eggs. Put the mixture into a deep bowl set in a larger pan of water. Cover the pan and steam over a moderate flame until the center is firm (about 30 minutes). Garnish with chopped green onions and oyster sauce.

➤ FRESH GINGER ROOT OYSTERS

1 jar fresh oysters
2 tbsp. peanut oil
3 green onions, sliced

2 oz. fresh ginger roots, in fine slices
2 tbsp. soy sauce
salt and pepper

Poach oysters a few minutes in boiling water until plump. Drain as dry as possible. Heat oil in skillet until very hot, add oysters, sliced green onions, ginger roots, soy sauce, light salt, and pepper. Cook a few minutes, stirring often to avoid sticking.

✳ *Tao Tao*

675 JACKSON STREET

moderate

TAO TAO IS NEITHER DELUXE NOR ONE OF THOSE FAMILY-STYLE places of a more homey nature, but rather takes on some qualities of each. Its cooking is excellent, its menu substantial, its decor friendly, and its prices moderate.

Tao Tao houses on its first and second floors a permanent exhibit of thirty-three photographs of old-time Chinatown that are probably the best of their kind. Arnold Genthe's scenes reach into the interior of Chinatown at the turn of the century, to find the grace and beauty of its people, to record the exoticism of their braided hair, their embroideries, their painted fans, still-lifes of simple baskets, a clutter of bottles, a profusion of lilies in bloom, the porcelain faces of a family, the texture of silk, incense spiralling from a burner.

In the 1890's, Genthe, trained in Berlin in classical philology, took a position as tutor to the son of a German nobleman then living in California. In order to illustrate his letters home, Genthe took to the camera. Although until that time he had never used the machine, he found it intriguing and his results were remarkable. His tutoring job completed, he set up a studio in Sutter Street, and because his camera technique was meticulous, he was within a few years time the great portrait photographer of the area. His clients were mainly social personalities, but theatrical celebrities and the literati came to pose before his camera as well.

The city around him fascinated him, and he did a series of photographic studies of its quarters and its people. He stalked the byways of Chinatown with his small black box camera, and the hundreds of resulting pictures eventually formed the basis of a book, *Pictures of Old Chinatown*, for which Will Irwin, a prominent writer of the time, wrote the commentaries. The original collection of prints and negatives were his only possessions not totally destroyed in the 1906 fire. Irwin, realizing their value, had persuaded him to contain them in an underground vault. In 1913, these documents came to life as the basis of the book. Originals now owned by Mills College, the California Historical Society, and a few private sources, were the basis for the Tao Tao enlargements.

You will find, once you have toured the gallery, that a good dinner awaits you. The menu gives both the Chinese and English designation for à la carte items, but from there on, you're on your own—no descriptive paragraph follows to tell you that almond duck is steamed with herbs and condiments, boned, pressed with flour made from water chestnuts, fried until brown and crispy, smothered in a tangy sweet and sour sauce, and finally, sprinkled with crunchy chopped almonds. If you are unfamiliar with Chinese cuisine, Tao Tao helps you out by setting up several dinners—for from one to six persons—that will allow you to sample a selection of good things. The dinner for one starts with won ton soup, and includes fried prawns, mushroom chicken, fried rice, tea and cookies. A group of six will get, besides soup, spring rolls—fried stuffed pastries of crisp, thin dough (named because they date from the old New Year's celebration, once a springtime event); chunks of lobster in the shell simmered in black bean sauce; barbecued pork tossed with mushrooms and water chestnuts; sweet and sour pork; So See Gai, the most elaborate chicken dish in the house; fried rice; cookies and tea.

If you prefer, you can make up your own meal, or ask the waiter to help with your selection. Some dishes particularly worth trying are the abalone soup, paper-wrapped chicken, prawns with fresh sweet peas (seasonal), fried squab, and fried oysters. The chow yuke is especially good with water chestnuts. With advance notice, you can order up all of the usual banquet delicacies, from shark's fins to wintermelon soup.

DEEP FRIED SQUAB

(Sang Jow Bok Opp)

2 young squab	1 cup water chestnut flour
2 tsp. soy sauce	(see below)
1 tsp. salt	2 to 3 beaten eggs
½ tsp. ground pepper	1 qt. vegetable oil
½ tsp. minced garlic	

Cut squabs into approximately 1½-inch pieces. In a large mixing bowl, combine soy, salt, pepper, garlic, flour, and two eggs to form a batter. If batter is too stiff, mix in a third egg. Add pieces of squab and mix until each piece is well coated with batter. Heat oil to a racing boil in a large kettle. Add the squab pieces and fry over high heat for fifteen minutes. Remove with a strainer, and drain, before serving, on absorbent toweling. Serves four.

NOTE: The coating is rather bland and the finished squab improves greatly by dunking in a nippy sauce. Suggestion: mix half prepared mustard, half ketchup, several dashes of Worcestershire sauce, and serve in individual bowls.

Water chestnut flour (sometimes called water chestnut powder) is hard to obtain, expensive, and makes a rather heavy batter. Its virtue is the unmatched crispness which it contributes. My own preference is to mix half all-purpose flour with half water chestnut flour. If you can't obtain it at all, use all-purpose flour by itself.

CHINESE BARBECUED PORK

(Char Siew)

½ cup soy sauce
½ cup granulated sugar
½ tsp. garlic powder
2 tbsp. ketchup
½ tsp. monosodium glutamate

¼ tsp. salt
1 lb. pork tenderloin (see below) in two strips
toasted sesame seeds

Combine soy, sugar, garlic powder, ketchup, monosodium glutamate, and salt in a mixing bowl. Add pork strips and marinate for at least three hours, turning every hour or so. Drain pork. Broil at 425° for twenty minutes or more, depending on the thickness of the meat. It must be thoroughly cooked. Turn every ten minutes to brown evenly. Slice into ¼-inch pieces, arrange them overlapping on a platter, and sprinkle with toasted sesame seeds. Dipping sauce of hot mustard and soy is optional. Serves four (if you are eating Chinese style, and have other dishes besides).

NOTE: Pork tenderloins are often unobtainable. If your butcher looks at you with a mixture of chagrin and mirth, just ask him for pork shoulder instead. It works almost as well. Toast sesame seeds in a flat pan in the oven or over the flame—with a little oil, if you like—until they take on a nice golden color.

✳ *Sai-Yon*

641 JACKSON STREET

inexpensive

SAI-YON IS A CHINESE FAMILY-STYLE RESTAURANT. IT SERVES A number of special dishes which attract a clientele from as far afield as Stockton and Sacramento. Some Westerners have come here so often that they have adopted chopsticks; and some Chinese represent the third generation of their families who are Sai-Yon regulars. Many customers take food out; some even send taxis for their dinner. There are a few American dishes on the menu, but don't let that throw you off; this is one of China-town's best places, and the Chinese food is authentically Chinese. The chefs here can prepare just about any home-style dish that you have a yen for, whether or not it appears on the menu. Just ask the waiter to have the chef cook it up.

The restaurant has been going strong since 1922. The present owner, Mrs. Helen Jung, has been in charge for more than half of that time. It is one of the few restaurants in the city that stays open all night, with a special after-eight menu. The prices are very reasonable, and the service is good, and quick.

Not long ago, the restaurant underwent a complete renovation. The setting is now contemporary Chinese, and the new stainless steel kitchen has been enlarged to a seven-wok capacity. A modern addition of which I thoroughly approve is a tier of automatic radiation shelves which keep the plates always warm.

Two of the best family-style dishes are the rice noodles—large lasagne-like bands—mixed with pork, greens, and other com-binations in or out of soup; and the casserole of rice cooked with beef, chicken, Chinese sausage, squab, or whatever else you prefer. This dish is a meal in itself, and makes an excellent order for a single person. You will see many Chinese eating jello here for dessert, but with a difference. The Chinese version is a

116

tasteless gelatin whose flavor comes from syrups poured over it. There is a special dinner—it changes every day—and daily and seasonal specialties, so it is good to ask your waiter what he recommends that day.

The late evening menu offers chuk, or jook, a rice gruel that you can order with meat or chicken; green bean soup, a sweetish porridge that the Chinese find soothing; egg tea, brewed with a whole egg in it; and the real delicacy, fresh water snails sautéed in a curry sauce, or cooked in their shells with red peppers, black bean sauce, garlic, and small green chili peppers. It's these escargots that bring the people down from Sacramento, I'm sure. They are fragrant, hot, and altogether delicious. The approved implement for getting them out of their shells is a wooden toothpick.

The last time I lunched here with a group of friends, Mrs. Jung suggested the menu. First course was matrimony soup, green leaves of a slightly pungent, spinachy flavor, swimming in a fine chicken broth with bitlets of pork, bean curd, and cloud-like noodles (formed by dropping beaten eggs into the hot broth). Then followed a dish of peppery snails—you could smell them cooking; their sharp garlic odor teased us all the way from the kitchen. After that came long string beans—available only in the summer months—cooked with shrimp and onions; and salted eggs steamed with pork in an excellent custard. (The eggs are duck eggs soaked for five or six weeks in salt water, then added to whatever recipe calls for them.) The pièce de resistance was a whole rock cod steamed in oil and a light soy sauce, together with Chinese parsley, ginger root, and green onions sliced thin the long way. If you don't like bones, you can request this dish in filleted form. Sai-Yon also cooks rock cod in an excellent sweet and sour sauce. Mrs. Jung has given me instructions for preparing the whole steamed rock cod, but first I should pass on some of her comments about the dish. The timing in steam-cooking fish is most important, but you can easily master the secret after a few experiments with different utensils. At Sai-Yon the fish cooks on a trivet in a regular steamer, but you can adapt any vessel large enough to accommodate the fish, and any type of rack to hold it above the water. If you have no cover, foil makes an acceptable substitute. Steam cooking preserves the natural flavor of the fish, and this recipe, which calls for only hot oil and soy sauce—ingredients that complement but do not disguise it—is what the Cantonese call "Wot, Ching-teem" or "smooth, pure-sweet." Mrs. Jung says that when your fish is cooked, you will appreciate the flaky meat most fully if you spoon some of the soy sauce and oil from the platter over each bit—and be sure to get some slivers of green onion with each mouthful, for they give it zing.

JING SHEK BON

(Steamed Rock Cod)

1 fresh black rock cod (2 to 2½ lbs.) dressed, with the head left on
1 tsp. shredded fresh ginger root
½ tsp. salt

1 whole green onion
¼ cup vegetable oil
¼ cup light soy sauce
1 green onion shredded fine (white section)
a few leaves of Chinese parsley

Place fish on a thin platter, and spread the shredded ginger root and salt evenly over it. Place the whole green onion on top. When the water in the steamer is boiling rapidly, place platter on the rack or trivet in the steamer, cover, and steam for about twenty-five minutes. Test with a fork. Fish should be removed as soon as it is done, or it will overcook. While the fish is steaming, heat the vegetable oil. When the fish is done and ready for the table, discard the whole green onion and pour the hot vegetable oil and soy sauce over fish. Garnish with the shredded green onion and Chinese parsley, and serve steaming hot with fried or steamed rice. Serves two or three.

Sun Hung Heung ✳

744 WASHINGTON STREET

inexpensive

SUN HUNG HEUNG RESTAURANT IS AN OLD ONE, HAVING OPERATED in the same location since 1919. Most of the original founders have passed on, but the present company manager, Yun Wong, has been there since the beginning. His son Leonard is now chef as well as assistant manager, and learned to cook by apprenticing in the restaurant for ten years. He isn't the only chef to graduate from its kitchens: many cooks fresh from China train at Sun Hung Heung before going on to work in other San Francisco restaurants. Leonard estimates that at least twenty cooks have apprenticed in these kitchens.

The older generation named the restaurant Sun Hung Heung Jow Low, after a Chinese village renowned for its celebration of food, drink, and having a good time. Jow Low means a house where whiskey is served. In the interests of modernity, this part of the name has been dropped, but not the pleasures originally implied. Sun Hung Heung has made other changes in the interests of the times, but it retains a number of gratifying traits belonging to more colorful days. The modern decor—red booths, black tables—simple and pleasant enough, is enriched by a rare teakwood screen brought from Hong Kong by the senior Wongs. In keeping with this double personality, the juke box in the back of the bar has both Chinese and American records. At the back table waiters sit with mounds of dough and filling for making won ton. They stab and jab with chopsticks, pinch and seal with fingers, moving so swiftly and rhythmically that in an incredibly short time there rises a mountain of finished won ton— one of the very good things to eat here.

CHINATOWN

The gentleman at the front desk does his accounts on an abacus, the discs clicking gently and pleasantly as they glide. But there is also an adding machine on the premises nowadays, Leonard tells me. All of the records are still kept in Chinese, and the bookkeeper's pages are classics in the art of calligraphy. I understand that in the past some Western artists have come to study these masterful brushstrokes, but no one at Sun Hung Heung seems to recall whether this is so.

For the many Chinese patrons, the restaurant mimeographs a daily menu in Chinese attached to the regular list. Your waiter will help you out if you don't read the characters and are interested in some of the daily specials. These include such excellent dishes as crab in black bean sauce or prawns fried with bacon. Another exceptional dish is a plateful of these jumbo prawns fried in their shells with slivered scallions. Although the crusty golden shells are not supposed to be consumed as part of this dish, they are good enough to eat.

Other specialties from the à la carte menu include chicken wrapped in paper (Leonard has given me the recipe for this one); chicken salad—chicken steamed, sliced, then fried with sesame, oil, salt, wine, parsley, green onions, and soy sauce; Gum Chin Gai—thin slices of sautéed chicken, and pieces of Virginia ham alternating on a skewer with fat pork seasoned in sugar, then cooked for about a half hour in a roaster over a moderate flame; and Suey Gow—a large scale won ton stuffed with a mixture of chopped pork, shrimp, mushrooms, water chestnuts, bamboo shoots, green onions, and green vegetables. Originally, in Hong Kong, the dough for Suey Gow was made of fish meal and flour, but in Chinatown it is all flour. A humble dish that I have seen many an old Chinese make a feast of at Sun Hung Heung is soup cooked with chicken feet; the feet are plump, tender, and delicious, having taken on all of that rich broth. Another well-prepared and delectable dish here is black mushrooms with oyster sauce.

There are modestly priced course dinners on the menu for varying numbers of eaters. Banquet style service is available on advance order.

Here are two recipes from chef Leonard Wong.

CHICKEN WRAPPED IN PAPER

1 chicken or capon, 4–5 lbs.
3 cloves garlic
1 tsp. grated ginger root
2 green onions
½ bunch Chinese parsley
1 tbsp. sugar
1 tsp. soy sauce
3 tbsp. ketchup or barbecue sauce

2 tbsp. oil—vegetable or peanut
2 tbsp. cornstarch
Salt and pepper
1 pkg. 6″ x 6″ squares of cooking parchment (or oiled brown butcher paper)
kettle of fat for deep frying

Bone chicken, and chop into little chunks. Chop the garlic, ginger root, green onions, and parsley into fine pieces. Mix all remaining ingredients together, add chicken and chopped seasonings, then wrap in squares of cooking parchment. (Lay the paper with a corner point at the top, bottom, and each side. Spoon a small amount of the mixture in the middle. Fold the bottom up over it, the point coming to about 1½ inches below the top corner. Fold the left side over, the point coming three inches from the right corner; then the right side over, the same distance. You should now have a rectangle of about four inches by three, with a triangular piece across the top. Fold the rectangle exactly in half, its bottom coming to the base of the triangular flap. Tuck the flap into this piece.) Heat the fat to 350° and deep fry the chicken envelopes for about ten minutes. Serve in the paper, and they will stay warm until you open them to eat. Serves four or six. (Makes approximately 2 doz. packages.)

➤ GA MIN YUNG

(vegetable dish)

3 stalks asparagus	2 or more tbsp. oil
2 pieces celery without leaves (preferably heart)	a few drops soy sauce
	a few pinches of sugar
¼ lb. dried black mushrooms (soak at least an hour in cold water)	salt
	1 tbsp. cornstarch
	¼ lb. rice noodles
10 pods sweet sugar peas	kettle of fat for deep frying
¼ lb. beef	

Slice the asparagus, celery, black mushrooms, pea pods, and beef into very fine strips. Sauté the beef in 2 tbsp. oil, with the soy sauce, sugar, salt, and cornstarch. Mix all the vegetables together. Move beef to the side of pan or wok, and sauté the vegetables over a brisk flame, adding a little oil if necessary. After a minute or two of cooking, mix in the beef, and continue cooking, stirring vigorously until it is finished. It should be more or less dry when it is finished, and the vegetables should still be crisp. Serve with rice noodles over the top. Serves two.

NOODLES: Heat oil in kettle to 400°; drop in rice noodles, and deep fry until lightly browned. Drain.

❋ *Nam Yuen*

740 WASHINGTON STREET

inexpensive

NAM YUEN IS TEN YEARS OLD, BUT HAS THE REPUTATION FOR reliability and good food that is usually reserved for old-timers. Four partners run the establishment: Alphonse Chan and Don Mar, who alternate as host, Chow Wing Tong, who acts as day chef, and Quan Tong, who is night chef. Several years ago, Quan Tong returned to Hong Kong for several months to work in one of the big restaurants for additional training. Mr. Chan comes from a thoroughly restaurant-minded family: his father ran a hotel-restaurant in Hong Kong; a brother directed two Hong Kong restaurants; a sister runs a restaurant in Australia; and number three brother has recently established a Chinese restaurant in Frankfurt, Germany.

Nam Yuen was recently redecorated, and now boasts two modern dining rooms, a handsome bar, a banquet room, and an impressive kitchen. The dining room which you enter first has an informal atmosphere with a series of banquettes against the walls; the second is a bit fancier, with handsome lanterns and a number of Chinese paintings. The banquet room, with the use of a set of movable partitions, permits arrangements that will accommodate from ten to one hundred and twenty celebrants at a time. But the room which I found most noteworthy of all is the kitchen. Along one wall for the length of the room extends a special range with several woks set into it; down the center an island provides cutting and chopping surfaces, containers for food storage, and in tiers above, an assortment of pedestals and serving dishes. A special tank off to one side holds a number of fresh water fish, blissfully unaware that they are about to be cooked to order. The room is a-bustle with fifteen cooks: two do nothing but chop vegetables, their cleavers making mince of cabbage, celery, Bok Choy, peppers, onions—whatever is needed —in a matter of seconds. Another cleans fish for the steamer; and one watches over the rice. Here a cook is boiling noodles, there a man scoops stock from the master kettle, adds chopped mustard greens, simmers them a few minutes, and finishes the soup off with a sprinkle of finely sliced ham. Three cooks are busy just assembling orders.

The fact that every order is individually cooked is one of the factors which makes the Chinese cuisine so exceptional. That, and the assurance that ingredients are—if not a thousand years old—fresh from the morning market. At Nam Yuen, for instance, the daily supply of fresh vegetables comes direct from the farm—or rather, several farms in nearby Hayward and San Leandro.

The menu suggests a very moderately priced family dinner, or, at slightly higher cost, a special gourmet dinner chosen for you by the chef. There is a daily menu published in Chinese, and your waiter will help you select dishes from it if you desire. Otherwise, there is a good assortment of à la carte items: shark's fin soup, jasmine blossom eggs, lobster balls, curried cracked crab, Tze Jup spareribs, chicken with black and white mushrooms, walnut squab, and a variety of chow mein, noodle, won ton, and rice dishes for late snacks.

Among the specialties that you should try are the clams with a garlic and wine sauce, oysters in ginger and onion sauce, spareribs cooked in black bean sauce, fresh squid with assorted vegetables, steamed sand dabs, pork tripe with a very special, highly seasoned sauce, and stuffed chicken wings—boned, filled with a mixture of chicken, shrimp, and mushrooms, and deep fried.

Alphonse Chan has given me two excellent recipes, with instructions for cooking them as the Nam Yuen chefs do. If you prefer a more standard procedure for the oyster sauce beef, follow the alternate method suggested after the recipe.

OYSTER SAUCE BEEF

for each portion:

½ lb. sliced flank steak of beef	1 dash of sugar
	1 cup hot oil
1 tsp. soy sauce	1 tbsp. bottled oyster sauce

The beef should be sliced very thin and against the grain. Marinate the slices in the soy sauce and sugar for about three minutes. Put the meat in a very large ladle-strainer, heat the oil very hot, and pour over the beef until it is about half cooked. Drain all the oil from the meat and put beef in a hot frying pan without grease. Add oyster sauce, cook rapidly for 1 to 1½ minutes, and serve immediately.

alternate method:

Heat 2 tbsp. oil in skillet, cook and stir marinated beef about four minutes over high flame, pour off any excess oil, add sauce, cook rapidly for 1 to 1½ minutes, and serve immediately.

ASPARAGUS BEEF

for each portion:

4 oz. sliced flank steak of beef
1 or more tsp. oil
½ lb. asparagus, sliced on the diagonal

¼ cup water, or enough to moisten asparagus in pan
1 tsp. salted black bean sauce (bottled; or mash packaged black beans with water)

for gravy:

⅛ cup water

⅓ tsp. cornstarch

Slice beef thinly against the grain. Place oil in wok or skillet over high heat, add asparagus, and toss continuously for a few minutes. Lower fire, add small quantity of water, cover pan, and cook for about three minutes. Push the asparagus to one side, move that side of the pan off the fire, add a little more oil to the center of the pan, and raise flame. Add beef and black bean sauce. Cook briskly for about four minutes, then stir in asparagus, and continue cooking another minute. Mix the water and cornstarch, add to the pan gravy, blend well, and serve at once.

Sam Wo ✳

813 WASHINGTON STREET

very inexpensive

PEOPLE WHO ARE SEEKING COLOR WILL FIND A RAINBOWFUL HERE. Sam Wo is a unique San Francisco institution, a spot to which all but ladies with the most delicate sensibilities and a penchant for compulsive housekeeping should certainly repair. Technically this smallest of all restaurants is known as a jook (or chuk) house, because it specializes in a rice gruel of that name. It has probably the least expensive good food in the city. You can still eat a substantial meal here for under a dollar. Portions are so large that one bowl of jook is a meal in itself.

The establishment is over fifty years old, and the name means "three in peace," a reference to the partners who started the business. Lee Chong, or Ho Suey, as he is more often called, was one of the founding fathers, and is now well into his seventies. He has a grin that shows off some fancy dentistry, a wizened narrow face peeking above a pointed grey beard, and he makes the best Chinese crullers around. These holeless doughnuts first introduced to Chinatown at Sam Wo, are a special on Fridays, Saturdays, and holidays, when crowds still line up around half-past four in the afternoon to buy them up. Besides being a doughnut maker extraordinary, Ho Suey is Dragon Master of Chinatown, who teaches the young boys about the ceremonial winding dragon that characterizes the great festivals of the Chinese community. This venerable gentleman is also something of a linguist, being fluent in both Filippino and Japanese.

Sam Wo occupies quarters about the size of a small railroad car turned on end. The downstairs is both entry and kitchen, and here you can watch old Ho Suey kneading up a cloudlike batch of the lightest cruller dough imaginable. A narrow staircase juts precipitously up to the second—and again to the third—floor. On these upper levels, a few tables line each side of the skinny room, the aisle space just large enough to pass through. At the front, windows overhang bustling Washington Street. Cuspidors dot the floors, and waiters sing their orders down the dumb-waiter shaft. After 5:30 a.m., there are no waiters on duty, and hungry patrons who serve themselves eat standing on the first floor by the kitchen. Another restriction goes into effect at half-past one in the morning: after that hour, no fried food is served.

Edsel Ford Fung, certainly the liveliest waiter in all the city, is a cross between Chum Fun of Dragon Lady fame, and Jack Benny. He makes jokes about everything, maintains a constant wide grin, and jumps about the premises like a jack-in-the-box. He told me that the doughnuts sell like hot cakes. He characterizes the Sam Wo menu as "no rice, no chop suey, no won ton, but oodles of noodles." He is the son of one of the original partners—not silent, I'm sure—who has now retired. He will help you select a good lunch, dinner, or snack, and will encourage you to try out some of the things which may be new to your palate. On one occasion, when I had had more than enough to eat, he insisted that I try just one other delicacy. When I hesitated, he hopped to the kitchen, brought back a nibble-sized portion, picked it up with a pair of chopsticks, dunked it in a dish of sauce, and one-two-three plunked it in my appreciative mouth. I hadn't been reluctant enough.

Edsel tells me that in the old days they used to make Yoan during the two weeks before Christmas. Yoan are sweet-rice dumplings served with sliced turnips combined with chicken, duck, pork, beef, ham, shrimp, tripe, and all sorts of other protein. They also used to cook up Chinese jello as a regular item, but it takes too much work, so they have dropped it from the menu. They do, however, still make marvelous rice noodles on the premises, and serve these big, wide ribbons in soups, soft fried, or boiled. The soup form comes with roast pork, beef, beef stew, chicken, duck, or curry. The soft fried noodles are cooked with chow yuke (bean sprouts or mustard greens with roast beef or pork). If you come in early enough, there will be rice noodle rolls, which you can dunk in small saucers of oyster sauce. (Edsel recommends that you dunk the Chinese doughnuts in oyster sauce, too.) If you come in late enough—after 7 p.m.— you can have jook, a thick rice soup. Jook (also called Congee) comes in nearly a dozen varieties—mixed with raw beef, shredded duck or chicken, small shrimp, shredded pork, razor slices of beef, pork meat balls, or with giblets, tripe and liver (called "mixed soup"). In combination with chunks of beef, pig's liver, pork tripe and giblets it is called beef stew soup—"authentic and exotic," Edsel chimes in. Without the addition of gruel, this stew comes as a side order.

If you want to eat in style, the chef will cook up a rice noodle roll with oyster sauce and sesame seeds, a "super deluxe special," in the words of you know who. Another specialty is raw fish salad, much less daring than it sounds, and for which the Sam Wo recipe follows. This is one of the few Chinatown establishments that brews egg tea, a sweet, thick dessert tea, a little like hot chocolate, with an egg, raw, medium, or hard boiled, plopped in the middle of it. Edsel is all for the raw egg, which looks less raw when you stir up the syrupy brew. There is also herb tea, supposedly good for what ails you, but this black drink is not to my taste, cure what it may.

There is an assortment of chow mein listed on the menu—with sprouts, greens, or tomatoes, and pork or beef; or you can order any other combination of fried noodles—with chicken, shrimp, or curry, for instance. There are excellent fried shrimp, and also egg foo yung.

If a party of four comes in and leaves it up to Edsel to order for them, their dinner will start with duck or chicken soup (rice base), and include a medium fish salad, fried shrimps, rice noodle roll (if there is any left), soft fried noodles with cooked greens, and tomato beef. And maybe some egg tea.

If you try this recipe for raw fish salad, it is necessary to use the very freshest fish and to clean it meticulously.

MARINATED RAW FISH SALAD ≺

1 lb. of any of the following:
  cod, salmon, hardhead
  (steelhead trout), smelt
  (grunion or jacksmelt)
¼ tsp. cinnamon
pinch of salt, black pepper
2 tbsp. sugar
1 tsp. sesame oil
¼ cup oil for marinating
  (Sam Wo uses the oil from
  frying doughnuts)

1 tbsp. each: pickled onions
  or Japanese scallions, preserved sweet cucumbers, preserved red ginger, preserved
  sweet and sour yellow ginger
  (hot), and fresh chopped
  broad-leaf parsley
juice of one lemon
¼ lb. rice noodles
oil for deep frying the noodles
2 tbsp. sesame seeds, toasted

Skin fish, remove bones, cut into very thin slivers. Mix together cinnamon, salt, pepper, sugar, sesame oil, and marinating oil, and pour over fish slices. Toss well together, marinate ten minutes. Drain the fish, spread it out thin on a plate, put all vegetables, diced, over the top, add the lemon juice. Deep fry the noodles, and add along with sesame seeds just before serving, so they don't get soggy. Serves two.

NOTE: If you are not up to raw fish, cold, boiled fish can be used, though Edsel would point out with some measure of disappointment that this was neither authentic nor exotic.

4. OLD-STYLE SAN FRANCISCO

As a group, San Francisco restaurants are showing the despoilment of Interior Decoration and the ravages of Expense Account thinking. Lighting has been designed practically out of existence. It is not considered chic if you can see as far as the menu. One of my friends has taken to carrying a small purse flashlight when she goes out to dinner; another steadfastly made his way recently through one of the town's most complicated lists with the aid of half a packet of matches. Redwood and Roman brick have become as much of a cliché as the baked potato with sour cream and chives. Excellence of service is giving way to ineptitude and familiarity. The new decor includes costumes and sets outrageous enough to appear in MGM's latest technicolor extravaganza. A catering manager of one of the town's plushiest hostelries told the press, in a recent interview, that people go for food, drink, and accommodations that are ostentatiously overpriced, prefer packaging to quality, and that, in short, in his domain any commodity with a tariff that appears reasonable to a sane eye goes a-begging.

I do not imply a blanket condemnation of either the baked potato with sour cream or the interior designer with Roman brick. I devour a well-dressed Idaho on occasion, and applaud good design, handsome materials, and truly elegant settings. But I do deplore the growing departure from honest values, and the increasing confusion of what comes first. I am old-fashioned enough to think that the food and drink in a restaurant should be primary; that the decor—and I don't eliminate grandeur—should provide a setting in which to enjoy the meal, not overpower it. In my book, a waiter wears a black suit and white linen, and he fillets a fish, carves up a duck, and flames a kidney with skill and a regard for aesthetics.

A number of San Francisco restaurants embody these antique attitudes, and they are less anachronistic, somehow, than the slick newcomers with their modern lighting, piano bars, piped music, and other signs of our times. Whether they have chandeliers, or sawdust on the floor, they have all emerged with a glow and patina that is the antithesis of neon and veneer. Jack's, already described under French restaurants above, should certainly be included in this group. So should Panelli's (see Continental restaurants) and Lambro's (again see Continental Style). Part of the quality of these places derives from the fact that they are downtown, open for lunch, and cater to a group of business and professional men who value honest drinks, good food, unobtrusive service, and familiar surroundings. The same unpretentiously high quality carries through to the evening. In all of these places expansiveness and pleasure will overtake you. In a way, this contribution to your feeling of well-being is the most typical characteristic of old San Francisco restaurants.

✳︎ *Bardelli's*

243 O'FARRELL STREET

moderate

BARDELLI'S RETAINS A GOOD BIT OF THE GRACIOUSNESS OF OLD San Francisco. The bar is ample, the ceiling high enough to accommodate crystal chandeliers with nonchalance, and there is in the dining room a snow of white linen and sparkle of silver. The enclosure of the vestibule is one of the few remaining stained glass masterpieces extant: a peacock that struts through a cascading fountain in the midst of a garden of peonies, clematis, daphne, and hollyhocks.

The first restaurant on this spot was an oyster house built just after the 1906 fire by the team of Darbee and Immel. Five years later, Charles and Jack Tollini took over the property, calling their restaurant Chas. Fashion Grill, a name still etched in the front glass. Charles Bardelli, well known as a chef in Milan, New York and San Francisco, took over in 1949. When bearded Sig. Bardelli retired, his son-in-law, Stuart Adams, with partner Louis Meyer, took over the supervision of the restaurant. Their warm greeting is the first of many nice things you will encounter here.

The moderately priced menu features continental style food, with the emphasis on Italian dishes. A complete dinner includes hors d'oeuvres, soup (minestrone, French onion, or consommé), a tossed green salad, lasagne, a wide range of entrées, cheese or ice cream, and coffee. Here you will find Chicken Raphael Weill or Jerusalem, lobster thermidor, rex sole in white wine sauce, broiled deviled breast of turkey, veal scaloppine with marsala, or sautéed filet of beef tips. Besides these specialties, there is broiled tripe with green peppers, and jumbo squab, brown and juicy in a casserole, or broiled crisp and gold. Sweetbreads, chicken livers and mushrooms are sautéed or toasted en brochette; calf's liver comes with bacon; chicken with mushrooms and Madeira. Abalone steaks are prepared here under a gentle cover of butter, and half lobsters are wonderful in broiled simplicity. There is an especially delicious crab dish—plump legs sauced with a marrow bordelaise mixture, and served piping hot sous cloche.

For diners who want less than a full dinner, there are a number of excellent platters, which come with tossed salad, potatoes, vegetable, and coffee, and include top sirloin or New York steak charred over the coals, prawns deep-fried and served with tartare sauce, and paillard à la marchand de vin—beef in a red wine sauce spiked with shallots—the recipe for which follows. There is always good roast beef.

Service from the à la carte menu includes a sturdy list of grillades—steaks, chops, chicken, squab, liver; entrées from the dinner, plus such excellent additions as calf's brains in a brown butter and caper sauce (as delicate a dish as I've eaten), veal parmigiana, chicken risotto alla milanese, and rack of lamb for two. There are several fine fish dishes, including crab Mornay, curried, or deviled au gratin, and deep fried English sole. To start with, there are always fresh chopped chicken livers and smoked Nova Scotia salmon, and—when they are in season— Olympia oysters. The dessert specialty is flaming Jerusalem pancakes—delicious cinnamon crêpes enclosing apples, orange rind, and almonds, and doused in orange juice, anisette, and brandy. If you prefer, Bardelli's will set a torch to plain old crêpes suzette, cherries jubilee, or baked Alaska. There is also a good selection of cheeses.

OLD-STYLE SAN FRANCISCO

"Stu" Adams has given me two recipes for specialties of the house.

CHICKEN JERUSALEM

2 lb. chicken, disjointed
flour
4 tbsp. melted butter
salt, white pepper, nutmeg
¼ lb. sliced (or button) mushrooms

6 artichoke bottoms, quartered
1 cup sherry wine
1 pint cream, heated
chopped chives and parsley

Roll pieces of chicken in flour, and poach in melted butter until chicken is *lightly* browned. Season with salt, pepper, and nutmeg; add sliced mushrooms and quartered artichoke bottoms. Pour sherry over all. Cover skillet and simmer about fifteen minutes, or until chicken is tender. The wine should be almost evaporated. Add one pint of warm cream, stir well, and add finely chopped parsley and chives. (Entire cooking time should be about 35 minutes.) Serves four.

PAILLARD À LA MARCHAND DE VIN

1 lb. beef sirloin
flour
2 tbsp. butter
salt and pepper

2 shallots, chopped
½ clove garlic, chopped
1 glass red Burgundy

Cut meat into four thin slices, and pound flat. Coat with flour, then brown in butter over a hot fire. When both sides are well colored, season with salt and pepper, and remove to a warm platter. Add chopped shallots and garlic to the pan, cook a few minutes; deglaze the pan with the red Burgundy, and continue cooking until the sauce reduces to one-third. Pour over the beef and serve immediately. Serves two.

The Fly Trap ✳

WHEN THE FLY TRAP OPENED IN 1883 IN THE TRIANGLE OF Sutter, Market and Sansome streets, its owner Louis Besozzi named it—in the style of those times—Louis' Fashion. In 1898 Navy boys, home from the Philippine War, flocked through its two entrances, one on Market, the other on Sutter, and, as sailors do, rechristened the premises. In this case the name stuck like flies to fly paper, which is what gave them the idea in the first place. In those sprayless days, restaurants were festooned with the stuff—as a sanitary measure. Louis retired a year before the great fire, and Domenico Tollini, still active in the business to-day, took over the restaurant. The fire wiped the place out, but Domenico reopened in temporary quarters on Golden Gate between Larkin and Polk. He stayed there until February 9, 1909, when, as he clearly recalls as though fifty-odd years had not passed in the meantime, he moved to the present location. At that point, since everyone happily called the place the Fly Trap anyway, the name became official. Domenico remembers that in the old days the Fly Trap served soup, salad, entrée, po-tato, dessert, and coffee for a quarter.

You enter this fine old place through the original doors, into a simple room whose decor hasn't changed much over the years. There is dark wood paneling, with some fresh green paint above it, punctuated only by the curve of old coat hooks, and a few potted snake plants. There is a second floor above. Today there are three working partners: Domenico, Charlie Bodio, and chef Ernesto Cafferata. There is no specialità della casa, Domenico tells me, but the emphasis is on good cooking. The food *is* excellent, and the prices moderate besides. The menu remains fairly constant, because when they change the bill of fare, old customers complain.

There is one specialty of a sort, and that is game cookery—if you supply the game. Chef Ernesto is skilled with a duck press, but equally talented when it comes to bringing out the flavor of deer and fish. If you yearn for the taste of wild duck or pheasant, or a good hunk of striped bass, bring one along to the Fly Trap.

The menu here includes a number of San Francisco favorites: celery Victor, Hangtown fry (made with Eastern oysters), filet of petrale, sand dabs and rex sole, spring salmon, and fresh crab. It ranges through variety cuts, including an excellent kidney sauté (the recipe follows), beef tongue served with creamed spinach, brains, scrambled, and fried Spanish or Milanese style, broiled or sautéed sweetbreads and chicken livers, tripe cooked Spanish style with rice, and a marvelous calf's liver steak, smothered in onions, or garnished with bacon. You can get good, honest, unadorned dishes, such as roast of turkey with cranberries, pork chops and applesauce, hamburger steak, or chicken croquettes. There are excellent broiled steaks, chops, and chicken, as well as wiener schnitzel with egg, and breaded veal cutlets. The Italian background of the owners shows on the menu with such dishes as Italian bean salad, prosciutto, spaghetti, tagliarini, risotto, homemade ravioli, scaloppine of veal, Milanese style, and chicken cacciatore.

There are regular or deluxe dinners that start with relishes, salad, and soup, and include paste, a substantial entrée with potatoes and vegetable, dessert and beverage. For light eaters, there are sandwiches, vegetable plates, platters of cold roast beef or ham with potato salad, a variety of omelettes, and a fine assortment of salads—imported mackerel, anchovies, romaine, avocado stuffed with shrimp or crab, asparagus with mayonnaise.

Here are three recipes from Ernesto Cafferata's kitchen. His scaloppine recipe is simple, but Ernesto says that the minute you add anything else to it, you are beginning to make a veal stew, and veal stew isn't scaloppine. He also told me that he believes

—contrary to many modern chefs and cookbooks—that kidneys should never be blanched or soaked, because they lose all their flavor.

SCALOPPINE ALLA MILANESE ≺

2 lb. veal loin, cut into very thin pieces, about 2 inches square
2 eggs, beaten
flour

2 tbsp. butter
1 tbsp. oil
2 oz. sherry or Marsala
salt, pepper
juice of 1 lemon

Pound the veal pieces flat with a heavy mallet. Dip them in egg, then flour. Heat the butter and oil until it just starts to color, add the veal, and fry—about three minutes on each side, or until golden brown. Add sherry or Marsala, and salt and pepper to taste. Heat through. Pour lemon juice over all, and serve immediately. Serves four.

KIDNEY SAUTÉ, MADEIRA SAUCE ≺

2 lbs. beef kidneys
2 tbsp. oil
2 oz. salt pork, diced
4 green onions, chopped
1 tsp. garlic salt
1 pint espagnole sauce

½ lb. sliced mushrooms
½ fresh or 1 dry bay leaf
4 oz. Madeira (sherry can be substituted)
salt and pepper to taste

Remove all muscles, fat, and fibers from the kidneys. Slice very fine. Sauté in hot oil over high flame to seal in all the juices and flavor as fast as possible. Lower heat, add chunks of salt pork, chopped green onion, and garlic salt, and cook until kidneys are well browned. Add rich espagnole sauce (or brown stock and one or two tbsp. tomato purée thickened with a little flour). When mixed in, add mushrooms, bay leaf, Madeira, and salt and pepper. Be careful not to oversalt. Cook all together for at least ½ hour, or until tender. Serves four.

[I find that this one improves with age, so I make it early and let it sit in its juice for a few hours before serving.]

➤ CREAMED SPINACH

3 lbs. spinach	3 tbsp. flour
two or three leaves Swiss chard	salt, pepper, nutmeg
3 tbsp. butter	1 cup hot milk

Wash spinach, drain, and put one half in a large skillet without water. Cover, and cook over a low flame until wilted—about five minutes; turn the spinach, cover, and cook a few minutes longer. Purée in a blender, or chop as fine as possible. Repeat with remaining spinach and chard. Melt butter, add flour, salt, pepper, and a grating of fresh nutmeg; stir until smooth. Add hot milk, a little at a time, and continue cooking until thick and creamy, and flour is thoroughly cooked—at least ten minutes over very low heat. Add the chopped spinach and chard, mix well, and heat to bubbling. Serves eight.

* *Tadich Grill*

THE ORIGINAL COLD DAY RESTAURANT

545 CLAY STEET

moderate

TADICH GRILL, WHICH DATES BACK TO 1849, IS AMONG THE ONE hundred oldest enterprises in the state. It bustles with an energy and authority that derive from long experience, and even the size of its portions recalls days when appetites were more capacious. It serves seafood—a good three dozen different entrées —steaks, and chops, and a few special dishes. The cooking is always hearty and tasty, and often distinguished.

Since the 1880's, Tadich Grill has been known also as the "Cold Day." A vigorous politician named Alexander Badlam once announced his victory after a heated political battle with the words, "It's a cold day when I get left." Because he and his cronies frequented Tadich's, the remark became associated with the grill, and soon everyone was referring to it as the "Cold Day."

For as long as any one can remember, Mr. Joseph Granat, who died recently, came every day by taxi from his jewelry store on Mission and 20th streets, to have his midday meal here. Sometimes his cab fare added up to more than his restaurant bill. One afternoon when the Giants were in town, such crowds headed for the game that no taxis were available, and he had to hire a limousine to take him back. When he couldn't make it—a rare occasion, indeed—he phoned Tadich's so that they wouldn't worry about him.

Tadich Grill nestles unobtrusively on a corner of Clay and Leidesdorff streets. Its highly polished brass doors invite you into a place of obvious character. A large bar-counter runs the length of the restaurant, and white-clothed tables fill the remaining space. There are a series of private booths along one wall, with movable partitions that allow them to accommodate a good-sized party. The small kitchen at the rear is open, and you can see everything from the sawdust on the floor to the cooks scurrying among their pots and casseroles.

The place is run by Louis Buich along with partners Joseph Shurko and Joseph Martlick, Slavonians all. Many of the recipes are old Buich family favorites; some are the invention of brother Mitch, who, before he left the firm had been with Tadich's for fifty-five years—most of it in the kitchen.

The menu is all à la carte, and the prices are most reasonable. There are several excellent salads, most of them bulging with shrimp, crab, or prawns, a delicious clam chowder, for which we have the Buich family recipe, and a good clam broth.

The specialty of the house is fish and shellfish: broiled, baked, steamed, or fried, as well as boiled or curried. There are endless combinations of seafood that bubble together in cheese sauces, wine and mushrooms, peppers and tomatoes creole style, or creamy smooth sauces à la Newburg. The crab sauté and deviled crab are both excellent, the crab and prawns à la Monza one of the house favorites. Sea bass and crab meat heaped on rice dressed with saffron sauce is a good dish for hearty eaters, peppery oyster and crab creole is a bit unusual, and salmon and crab cooked together à la Newburg is rich—but delicious. Broiled brook trout aswim in butter sauce is a light and delicate dish, or if you prefer something heartier, try the smoky steamed finnan haddie. There is a Hangtown fry made with Olympia oysters, or if you want your seafood pure, these small delicacies come fried gold and crusty without any eggs. This is a good place to try out abalone steaks, browned lightly and accompanied by a good tartare sauce.

From the charcoal broiler come a variety of cuts of choice beef, half spring chickens, lamb and pork chops. There are omelettes, and fresh jumbo asparagus when it is available from the market. Sometimes there are homemade fish cakes with rice and a sturdy mushroom sauce, sometimes fisherman's style bouillabaisse, baked ravioli, or risotto. Sweetbreads and calf's liver are usually on the menu.

There are daily specials: Monday and Saturday, roast prime ribs of beef; Tuesday baked shoulder of lamb; Wednesday roasted rack of lamb; Thursday roast sirloin of beef; and Friday, the regular assortment of fish.

If you can manage dessert after one of Tadich's substantial main courses, there are pies, ice cream and sherbet, rice pudding, good baked apples, fresh or preserved fruit, and a cheese or two.

The Buich family has given me two excellent recipes, one of which is a sauce in which to bake fish that they first concocted in 1910 and have been making ever since.

CONEY ISLAND CLAM CHOWDER

1 lb. or more canned or fresh clams
4 oz. bacon fat, or 2 oz. butter and 2 oz. oil
2 onions, chopped
1 clove garlic, minced
1 bell pepper, seeded and chopped
leaves from 2 or 3 stalks of celery, chopped

1 tbsp. minced parsley
pinch of curry
½ qt. solid pack tomatoes
1 qt. clam juice
1 qt. water
2 potatoes, diced fine
¼ tsp. pepper
salt to taste

Steam raw clams with a few drops of water until their shells open. Reserve the juices, and chop the clam meat coarsely. If you use canned clams, drain, saving the liquor, and chop coarsely. Set aside. In a large kettle heat the bacon fat or butter and oil. Add the chopped onions, garlic, pepper, celery leaves, parsley, and curry, and sauté until glossy and golden. Add the solid pack tomatoes, 1 qt. clam juice, reserved clam liquor, with enough water added to make 1 qt., and diced potatoes. Cook one and a half hours over a low fire. Add the chopped clams, pepper, salt to taste, and simmer for 20 minutes. Serves six.

FISHERMAN'S SAUCE

3 oz. olive oil
2 or 3 leeks, well washed, and chopped very fine (use both white and green parts)
1 bunch green onions, chopped fine

1 qt. solid pack tomatoes, squeezed, or well broken up
salt and pepper
½ cup chicken or beef broth
about 3 lbs. of halibut, sea bass, striped bass, or similar fish, whole or in slices

Heat oil very hot, and braise the chopped leeks and onions until well cooked. Add the tomatoes, and salt and pepper to taste. Cook two hours over a slow fire, stirring occasionally. Add broth (water can be substituted) and simmer a few minutes more. Yield: enough sauce for six portions.

to bake fish with sauce:

Heat oven to 400°. Cover bottom of baking dish with sauce, place fish on top. Score the center of a whole fish so that it will absorb the juices. Cook about ten minutes to the pound, up to about 40 minutes altogether. Cook slices about ten to fifteen minutes. It is important to judge according to type and size of fish. Test for doneness with a fork. When done, meat should be moist but flaky. Add remaining sauce over the top, and return to the oven for five minutes, or until heated through. Serves six.

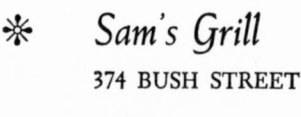

✳ Sam's Grill

374 BUSH STREET

moderate

ORIGINALLY SAM'S GRILL WAS ONE OF THOSE RESTAURANTS SPEcializing in seafood in the old California Market. Since its beginning in 1867, its ownership and location have changed from time to time, but it has always kept the same specialty, and has never departed from its San Francisco traditionalism: it remains a genuine eating-place. The tone of the decor is old-fashioned, the food is good, and there are always stacks of sour dough French bread with plenty of butter. Most of the patrons are San Franciscans, some of whom claim that their families have been eating at Sam's for a couple of generations.

The present ownership dates from 1937. Frank and Walter Seput are in charge, having taken over after their father. Chef Harry Gough has been at his business since 1921. He has worked all over the world—from Shepheard's Hotel in Egypt to the Waldorf Astoria in New York—but he has always come home to San Francisco. He studied cooking in France and Boston, and when he was young, worked under several famous chefs. To get such positions he had to take very modest wages, but he felt that it was worth it to be able to learn from the masters. One of his most important lessons was that you can't cut corners and expect the same results as are achieved through patience and attention; another, that you must always use the best quality ingredients. These days he is hired by various food companies to invent recipes using their products, and his by-line appears over articles in the *National Restaurant Magazine*. But best of all, he likes his work in Sam's small and friendly kitchen.

The menu is entirely à la carte, and the specialty is still seafood. The clam chowder and turtle soup are both excellent, and there is a fine variety of salads, with or without shellfish. Celery root (with) makes a particularly tasty dish, and romaine and red beans (without) is another fine combination. Sam's special salad is based on boiled celery hearts, tomatoes and chunks of avocado, to which they add the shellfish of your choice. There is also celery Victor and hearts of artichokes covered with anchovies.

The oyster, as in the old days, comes in a dozen tempting forms: plain or Hangtown fried, or raw on the plate or the half-shell, in roasts—pan, pepper, or fancy—in stews, in omelettes, and in cocktails. Other delicacies are rex sole à la Sam (boned filets served with meunière sauce), charcoal broiled petrale (large round-nose sole, filleted and broiled, and surely one of the most delicious of all fish), and clams Elizabeth (baked on the half-shell bubbling in sherry, lemon juice, and Parmesan cheese).

143

Deviled crab is particularly good here, and is probably the largest-selling dish on the menu, but you can order crab in as many variations as oyster. There is fresh cracked crab, a variety of salads including Louis, crab creamed and baked with shirred eggs, curried with rice, or melting in a Newburg sauce. You can order whole crab legs fried and served up with a piquant tartare sauce. If you feel like a spicy dish, creole-cooked crab is a good one. You can also get crab baked au gratin, or gently creamed with noodles.

The menu is filled with other fine fish and shellfish dishes, including all manner of creatures broiled, baked, or fried, and masterpieces like filet of sole à la Marguery. Although the emphasis is on seafood, there are delicious omelettes made with chicken livers, artichokes, and mushrooms. There is often a steaming Hungarian goulash. Macaroni are baked with chicken livers, and fresh mushrooms are sautéed juicy and brown, and served up on toast. You will find asparagus alla Milanese, veal cutlets and tagliarini rich with mushroom sauce, and excellent lamb kidneys, sweetbreads or calf's liver, each broiled and served with a garnish of crisp bacon. There are charcoal broiled steaks, chops and chicken, and sautés of veal, mushrooms, sweetbreads, or chicken, all rich with butter, cream, herbs, sherry, or dry white wine.

To go along with these entrées, zucchini, eggplant, sautéed celery root, hearts of artichokes, creamed spinach, and a variety of seasonable vegetables are all cooked with imagination. Sam's desserts include cheeses, pastries, pies, and ice cream, excellent baked pears or apples with cream, sabayon, and French pancakes with lemon and sugar or jelly, or—the house specialty—doused with anisette.

Chef Gough has given me the instructions for two of Sam's specials.

DEVILED CRAB À LA SAM

4 stalks celery, without leaves
2 medium onions
1 large green pepper
1½ cups vegetable oil
2 cups flour
1½ qts. milk, scalded
3 heaping tbsp. Coleman's dry
mustard

2 tbsp. Lea and Perrins sauce
dash of tabasco sauce
½ cup sherry wine
2½ lbs. fresh crab meat
butter
Parmesan cheese, grated

Chop celery, onions, and green pepper fine. Cook slowly in oil until soft. Add flour to make roux, sprinkling in a little at a time, and blending smooth. Add scalding milk slowly, blending well, and cook for several minutes until thick and smooth. Add dry mustard, Lea and Perrins sauce, tabasco, sherry, and crab. Bring to a boil, then remove from fire immediately. Cool by pouring into a shallow pan. When cool, place in casseroles, dot with butter, cover generously with Parmesan cheese, and bake at 400° for ten minutes, or until golden brown and bubbly. Serves eight.

CLAMS ELIZABETH

1 doz. med. clams
1 tbsp. chives or scallions,
chopped fine
2 tbsp. fine bread crumbs
1 tbsp. grated Parmesan
cheese

juice of 1 lemon
2 tbsp. melted butter
2 oz. sherry wine
paprika

Use any clams in season. Open, leaving the clam in one half of the shell. Reserve the juice. Place the clams in a shallow baking dish. Pour a small amount of juice on each clam, and sprinkle with chives or scallions. Mix bread crumbs and Parmesan cheese, and sprinkle lightly over each clam. Pour the lemon juice, then the butter over all, and add the sherry wine around the edge. Cover lightly with paprika and bake in a hot oven (400°) for twenty minutes, or until brown. Makes one portion.

NOTE: Sam's makes its breadcrumbs by sieving crustless dry, white bread.

5. ELEGANT

SAN FRANCISCO's taste for elegance started with the lush prosperity of the Gold Rush, and has been continuously supported —more lately by its being the financial center of the West and its having strong social and cultural ties with the continent. It handily supports a goodly number of deluxe restaurants. Many

146

of these are, for convenience, classified in this book by the type of cuisine they offer. Certainly Ondine and La Bourgogne must be classed as elegant, as must Fleur de Lys, Doros, Paoli's, Oreste's, and Fior d'Italia. But the restaurants that follow have a special reputation, and deserve a section for themselves.

Probably the most expensive place in town is Alexis. Alexis Merab has created a stage set atop Nob Hill that leans heavily on the exoticisms of the Middle East. The menu couples Caucasian shashlik, Iranian caviar, and chicken à la Kiev with a respectable representation of French delicacies. The list of wines —and it is probably the best in the city—is formidable, and the prices for them often staggering. But I have never dined here when the dinner wasn't good. There is a cocktail lounge downstairs, and a good amount of gypsy music. Owner Alexis thoroughly enjoys the lush Byzantine splendor of his new restaurant (he had to move recently from a nearby building which was being razed for apartments). He has been quoted as saying that he created the restaurant for his own satisfaction—that the public could have the rest rooms. His architect, whom Alexis proudly described as a madman and leading Middle Eastern designer, flung himself easily into the mood of things, apparently communed with some of the statues that serve as room dividers between bar and dining room, and according to one report, grandiosely had a wall torn down that he had just ordered put up, because of a sudden change of ideas. Merab himself is a former movie actor. If he doesn't look familiar, it is only because he starred in silent Russian movies. He arrived in San Francisco in 1947, via Shanghai, and became a citizen in the early Fifties. His mother, a Russian gynecologist, recently made her first visit to this country, with the help of San Francisco's mayor George Christopher, who interceded with Khrushchev to obtain the necessary visas. If you are out for an evening, don't care what you spend, or how long you may have to wait for a table, you will have a good time at Alexis—providing he lets you in.

✳ *Trader Vic's*

20 COSMO PLACE

expensive

TRADER VIC'S IS A MARVELOUS PLACE. OWNER VIC BERGERON'S INstincts about food and drink—booze, he would prefer to call it —are as sure as the bees' about nectar: he knows how to adapt the best qualities of an exotic dish for palates that might find it strange in its native form; he is particularly good at combining spices and seasonings; and he probably knows more about rum than anybody else you'll ever hear of. This salty but elegant gentleman has flair and showmanship, and no room for nonsense, and these are precisely the qualities of his restaurant.

Vic is a native San Franciscan, but he and his peg leg have traveled extensively. He knows particularly the islands of the South Pacific and Hawaii, and the Polynesian motif of his restaurant succeeds in transferring their atmosphere of relaxed frolic into our hurried and complex city.

Food has always been a Presence in Vic's life. His family owned a grocery store; his father was a good cook, beyond the ordinary. The first Trader Vic's opened in Oakland in 1934, and it is still the best restaurant in the East Bay. Vic opened the San Francisco place in 1951, in exactly the same tradition, but with seats for one hundred more customers. He operates for other owners ten restaurants bearing his name. Plans are in the works for a London one, and Australia and Rome are under consideration. Prince Rainier of Monaco has invited Vic to consider a Monte Carlo location, and Vic has been toying with the idea of a really dazzling Mexican restaurant—in San Francisco. As Herb Caen said, it's "a long, long way from 65th and San Pablo in Oakland, where the Trader got started with a beer parlor called Hinky-Dink's."

Trader Vic's decor is a melange of outriggers, grass matting, giant clam shells, anchors, nets, coils of rope, and shrunken heads, real ones, that are discreetly placed in the outer entry. Characteristic of Vic's are drinks served in fantastic containers, afloat with gardenias, set down in the middle of the table, and sipped by the whole party from straws that must be a good three feet long. There are no finger bowls here, I'm sure on the theory that if it comes in a bowl, the customers will polish it off, but there are perfumed hot towels instead. Other niceties, elegances that have some meaning to them, are the twists of cheese-cloth that enclose each lemon wedge so that you never have to cope with lemon seeds in your oysters, and the olive, onion, and lemon peel on an ice-filled extra glass that accompanies every martini.

For a couple of dozen years Vic has used Chinese smoke ovens extensively and the results are unique and wonderful. The ovens are big pot-bellied containers into which the fish, meat or poultry to be cooked is hung from above. Heat from fires of white oak is let in at the bottom.

The menu is a combination of Chinese, Javanese, and Tahitian dishes (often embellished or changed to accommodate Western tastes), curries, French dishes, and excellent barbecued meats. Everything is à la carte on the large list, and justly expensive. The waiters are expert, and if you ask their advice, most helpful in planning your meal.

To begin with there are all kinds of nibbly hors d'oeuvres, like barbecued spareribs, stuffed shrimp, clam rolls, curry puffs, and chicken livers (these are sometimes combined with water chestnuts and bacon, and called rumaki—the recipe for which follows) kept deliciously hot over little burners on your table. Along with a drink, these tidbits help to assuage the inevitable hunger pangs as you read through the rest of the menu. There are traditional appetizers: prawns, oysters, pâté de foie gras de Strasbourg, caviar with blinis and sour cream, cracked fresh crab in season; or an excellent lobster mousse, crêpes with crab, and delicious smoked sturgeon. There are some interesting soups, starting with Trader Vic's own good chicken broth afloat with egg shreds, green onion slices, and dice of potatoes. Turtle soup, clear or Boula Boula style, is sturdy and nourishing, and there is an ambrosial purée of spinach and oysters—Bongo Bongo, by name (the recipe is given below)—as well as cold borscht, Tahitian onion soup, Chinese egg noodle, and consommés, hot or jellied.

After hors d'oeuvres, you must decide whether to eat Chinese style, or pick one of Trader Vic's barbecued, curried, or other special dishes—though some of these latter entrées combine well with the Chinese menu. There are about two dozen Chinese dishes ranging from won ton in a sweet and sour sauce to lobster Cantonese, and including some marvelous mixings of chicken, duck, pork, beef, shrimp, or abalone with crisp greens, slivers of mushrooms, bites of water chestnuts, almonds, sesame seeds, and delicate seasonings. There are also buttered golden noodles speckled with toasted sesame seeds, or fried noodles and Chinese vegetables in chicken broth. The thing to do is order several different dishes, depending on the number in your party.

There are hot curries, mild cream curries, and a special Cantonese curry for lobster, crab, and shrimp dishes. With these come an assortment of sambals, including Trader Vic's own delicious chutney. Chicken-in-a-Coconut has a gentle curried flavor that easily fits in with many of the dishes on the menu, and you should order at least one portion for everyone to sample. It is too good to miss.

Among the entrées is a varied selection of fish dishes, but if your mood is expansive many are suitable as a first course. There are ceremonious oysters flambé; or San Juan style layered over with devilled crab and grilled; curried oysters with steamed rice; fried oysters with mustard sauce; baked Florentine oysters bursting through a cover of spinach and cheese sauce; or broiled oysters—big ones from nearby Tomales Bay—strung on a skewer with bacon and mushrooms, or lazing in their shells with slices of bacon, a sprinkling of shallots, and a dusting of paprika. There are a number of delicious sole dishes; salmon barbecued or poached and served with a caviar sauce; Hawaiian Mahi Mahi; pan-broiled mountain trout; lobster, stuffed, broiled, or in the form of a mousse; abalone; soft shell crabs; and—my very favorite—paké crab. When crab is in season—and this is the only time you will find this dish on the menu—I never eat at Trader Vic's without having some. Winey, dripping morsels of crab are served in a large abalone shell. Since you will be carefully aproned and bibbed before the attack begins, and coddled with perfumed hot towels when it ends, there is no reason short of allergy not to know this delight.

Vic treats kidneys, sweetbreads, and chicken livers with a knowledgeable respect, and such dishes as noisettes of lamb, veal à la Cordon Bleu, or plain old chopped sirloin, with proper authority. A steaming truffled chicken with its broth is perfect for light eaters, and beef enthusiasts who are tired of chateaubriand will be pleased by the pyramid of beef, the butterfly steak, or paper-thin strips of filet ablaze in a mustard sauce. But the roasts that issue from the Chinese ovens are perhaps the most delicious of all: glazed and dripping pheasant-chickens, squabs, and rock Cornish game hens, skewered cubes of marinated beef decorated with pineapple wedges, triple lamb chops, double steaks, whole filets of beef, Indonesian lamb so succulent that you can hardly keep from chomping the bones, and Lucullan whole suckling pigs (these ordered a week in advance for large parties of fifteen or more).

There are good vegetables including baby carrots, new peas, artichoke bottoms filled with creamy spinach, and a whole assortment cooked Chinese style. Salads range from hearts of palm and limestone lettuce to a julienne of endive with water cress.

ELEGANT

There are icy perfumed fruits to refresh you at the end: fresh pineapple, giant stemmed strawberries, mangoes, melons, and papaya. Some of these combine well with ice cream or a splash of curaçao. There are traditional banana fritters, or peesang goreng Javanese (with guava sauce). There are delicious baked nectarines, cheese cake lush with raspberry or blueberry trimming, and an exotic array of ice creams with such flavors as ginger tea, coconut honey, rum, kona coffee and tangerine. Trader Vic has concocted a number of unusual desserts and here are his recipes for two of them:

TRADER VIC'S ICE CREAM

per serving:

1 oz. Trader Vic's flaming brandy (or other good brandy)

1 tbsp. chopped preserved kumquats
1 scoop coconut ice cream
shredded coconut

Warm brandy and kumquats slightly in a chafing dish or pyrex pot with a handle, and set aflame. Spoon the mixture over the ice cream and top with shredded coconut.

TAHITIAN ICE CREAM

per serving:

¾ oz. Trader Vic's flaming rum (or other good light rum)
¼ oz. dark Jamaica rum

1 tbsp. pineapple and apricot preserves
1 rhum baba (these come canned)
1 scoop coconut ice cream

Warm rum and preserves slightly in a chafing dish or pyrex pot with handle, and set aflame. Scoop ice cream on rhum baba, then spoon the flaming rum mixture over.

152

Here is Trader Vic's excellent recipe for rumaki, especially good fare for cocktail parties.

RUMAKI   ◁

4 cups soya sauce	1 small piece ginger root
2 cups chicken broth	2 lbs. chicken livers
2 tbsp. sugar	about ½ lb. bacon
2 bay leaves	1 small can water chestnuts
1 small piece stick cinnamon	fat for deep frying
1 clove garlic	

Combine soy, chicken broth, sugar, bay leaves, stick cinnamon, garlic, and ginger root in a large saucepan or kettle, and bring to a boil. Simmer over a slow fire for five minutes. Simmer fresh chicken livers in this sauce for about ten minutes, then let cool. Cut chicken livers into slices, water chestnuts into thirds, bacon strips into two or three pieces. Wrap a piece of bacon around a piece of cooked chicken liver and one third of a water chestnut. Secure with a tooth pick. Fry in deep hot fat until the bacon is crisp. Drain on absorbent paper and serve immediately.

BONGO BONGO SOUP   ◁

1 pt. milk	1½ tsp. Trader Vic's Mai Kai
¼ pt. half and half (milk and cream)	(or ajinomoto, or any MSG flavoring powder)
1 9½ oz. can oyster purée or equivalent purée of fresh oyster	1 dash garlic salt
	1 tsp. A-1 sauce
	salt and pepper to taste
¼ cup puréed spinach (Vic says Gerber's baby food is okay)	2 tbsp. butter
	2 tbsp. cornstarch
	½ pt. whipping cream

Heat milk and half and half; add oyster purée and spinach; add seasonings and butter. Bring to simmering point, but do not let boil. Thicken with cornstarch mixed with a little cold water. Simmer several minutes to allow cornstarch to cook through. Put into oven-proof casserole, or individual casseroles, top with cream, whipped, and slip under the broiler to glaze until golden brown. Serves four.

➤ TRADER VIC'S JAVANESE SATÉ

1 tsp. Trader Vic's Saté Spice (obtainable from fancy food shops, Trader Vic's restaurants, or by mail order from Trader Vic's Food Products, Inc., 2809 San Pablo Ave., Berkeley 2, California)

1 large onion, finely chopped
¼ tsp. finely chopped garlic
1½ tsp. salt.
juice of 1 large lemon
1 tsp. honey
1½ lbs. beef, veal, lamb, or pork

Combine seasonings, onion and garlic with lemon juice and honey. Cut meat into 1½ inch cubes, and add to marinade in a large dish or earthen crock. Mix well to coat all meat, and marinate for at least ten minutes, better a couple of hours. Thread pieces of meat on bamboo or metal skewers, allowing pieces of onion and garlic particles to adhere to meat. Barbecue over open fire or charcoal, or broil in oven until tender. Serves three.

➤ BARBECUED SQUAB

Brush whole squabs inside and out with soya sauce, and barbecue or roast in oven for twenty to twenty-five minutes. Baste occasionally with a mixture of soya sauce and melted butter. Squab can be tested for doneness with fork in thigh. (The soya sauce and butter makes the skin deliciously crisp.) One squab per portion.

✳ *Ernie's*

847 MONTGOMERY STREET

expensive

THE MAHOGANY AND STAINED GLASS DOORS OF ERNIE'S OPEN ONTO a vision of late nineteenth-century San Francisco. Originally it was the lusty Frisco Dance Hall that perished in the quake and fire. Rebuilt by an Italian-American family in 1907 as the European Hotel, it took on a somewhat less boisterous character. During World War I it changed names again, this time to become the Il Trovatore Hotel. Early in the Thirties a beloved North Beach character named Ernie Carlesso took over, and after a few years attached his name to it. At that time—1939— he took on a new partner, Ambrose Gotti, and together they continued to dispense seven-course Italian dinners, wine included, in an atmosphere heavy with gay checkered tablecloths and sawdust floors. In 1946 Ernie died. Within a year Ambrose retired, giving over the successful establishment to his sons Victor, then 25, and Roland, 23, who were told firmly that they could sink or swim. For four months, everything went swimmingly. Then aged chef Hugo Carisimo died and the business almost died with him. A comparable chef seemed impossible to find, and old customers began drifting away.

The Gottis decided it was time to do something drastic. Victor hit upon the idea of redoing the premises in an authentically grand manner, and enticing a top chef by offering him a partnership in the business. They haunted antique shops on Divisadero, second-hand bazaars on McAllister Street, and frequented the auction rooms all over town. They tore up the linoleum from the restaurant floor and replaced it with lush red velvet carpeting. The walls became late-Victorian with wainscoting of mahogany and embossed crimson paper. From Pacific Heights mansions came brass candelabra; from the estates of William Sharon the Comstock King, and Claus Spreckels the Sugar Baron came chandeliers to hang in splendor from overhead mahogany beams. Massive sideboards, elaborate gold-leaf floor-to-ceiling mirrors, cut-glass hurricane lamps, famed Charles Dana Gibson sketches of Victorians at dinner, and a singular mahogany bar—an extravagance of leaded glass, mirrors, and fluted columns that came around the Horn by clipper ship—all these, and other period pieces turned Ernie's into an authentic replica of San Francisco's Golden Age.

Mario DeFenzi, a superb chef, joined the Gottis and took over the supervision of kitchens and dining room. Old customers came back, new ones quickly followed, and Ernie's became a cherished institution. Neither fame, nor increasing luxury, nor the eminence of its regular patrons has tempted the owners to alter their splendid sense of hospitality to all comers. Nor can they be persuaded to crowd their premises or hurry their guests. Thus, to insure yourself a table, it is wise to make reservations well in advance.

There have been several additions to the redecorated premises. The Ambrosia Room, named after Gotti Senior, is an upstairs lounge and dining room with an Italian marble fireplace and a number of oil paintings well in keeping with the original decor. The latest additions are the Elysian Room, furnished largely from the 1860 C. C. Rohlff Mansion on Russian Hill; the Bacchus Cellar, an old-world private dining area and wine room for small groups; and a completely new kitchen, likely one of the finest installations of its kind in the west. If you have seen the Alfred Hitchcock thriller "Vertigo," or the movie "The High and the Mighty," you have seen Ernie's, for it has been depicted in both. Both Victor and Roland had walk-on parts in "Vertigo."

The cuisine is largely French-Italian. The Gotti brothers have on different occasions spent several months touring the best restaurants of Europe and New York for fresh ideas. The last trip included touring the great wine-growing areas of France, Germany, and Italy with Alexis Lichine to pick wines for Ernie's cellars (among the best in the city).

Ernie's is famous for its style of dinner—often referred to as San Francisco-style—which always starts with several platters of hors d'oeuvres: iced cracked crab in season, prawns when not, imported peperoncini, ceci beans vinaigrette, Italian salami, marinated tongue, hearts of celery, jumbo olives, fresh radishes. After this comes soup, perhaps a choice of onion or cream of

germiny, or at slightly extra cost, tortellini alla romana. There
are double cut lamb chops, various broiled steaks, tenderloin of
beef en brochette with wild rice and a dark sauce chasseur—long
an Ernie's favorite—filet of rex sole, bonne femme or meunière, grenadins of beef with béarnaise sauce, chicken sautéed, or
boned and stuffed with wild rice, then roasted in the winey style
of Burgundy, frogs' legs, sweetbreads, or veal medaillons, all in
splendid and appropriate sauces. (Maxim's sent one of their
sauciers from Paris to give a three-week seminar for Ernie's
chefs—another result of the Gottis' European treks.) Afterwards there are banana fritters, fried cream, ices, and delicious
coffee.

If you order à la carte, you can satisfy any cravings you may
have for melon with prosciutto, Olympia oysters, Bay shrimp,
or pâté with truffles. There are excellent salads: crunchy hearts
of romaine, tender leaves of limestone lettuce, spikes of Belgian
endive and subtle hearts of palm doused with Roquefort or
French dressing. You can have your rings of tortellini floating
in broth, or select a cold, soothing vichyssoise. Ernie's quenelles
are worth a try. They are expertly made of sea bass and baked
in a sauce Nantua.

When you come to the entrée you can order, if there are four
of you, a most beautiful steak, a hobo New York cut sirloin gros
sel, banked with garden vegetables and as appealing to the eye
as to the appetite. One of Ernie's best dishes, in my estimation,
is hen à l'orange, cooked up for two. There is saddle of lamb
Marie Louise, a whole brown roasted loin, hinting of onions and
herbs, and richly covered with a dark Marsala sauce, all of this
planked among quartered artichoke hearts, button mushrooms,
sautéed new potatoes, grilled tomatoes, and braised celery sparkling with a glaze of Parmesan cheese. Ernie's is adept at cooking tournedos de boeuf à la Rossini, an old standby of many
good restaurants, but not always prepared with such success.
Here the center of the filet is larded, then cut into four equal

steaks. Each piece is tied around with lard, lightly floured top and bottom, and sautéed to taste. The tournedos, lard removed, come to the table resting on a large crouton, and covered with a slice of pâté de foie gras, a slice of truffle, a large mushroom cap, and a dollop of brown sauce accented with Madeira and chopped truffles. Dinner ends with fruit, cheese, ices, or some sweet extravagance, and a silver pot of very hot coffee. If you are like me, you may not always have room for more than the coffee.

Victor Gotti has most generously given me the recipes for four of Ernie's entrées, each one a specialty of the house.

➤ CHICKEN CYNTHIA À LA CHAMPAGNE

2 chickens (approx. 2¼ lbs. each)
salt
flour
1 tbsp. butter
1 tbsp. oil
1 oz. curaçao
6 oz. dry champagne
1 cup consommé or bouillon
1 tbsp. butter
1 cup sliced mushrooms
½ cup heavy whipping cream
1 orange, peeled and separated into wedges
1 cup skinless and seedless grapes

Disjoint chickens. Set wings and legs aside for another purpose and bone remaining parts [or ask your butcher to do it for you]. Salt and flour the chicken. Sauté in butter and oil for ten minutes on each side. Remove from frying pan to baking dish and continue browning for twenty minutes in a 350° oven. Remove the fat from the dish, pour on curaçao and champagne [California Pinot Chardonnay can be substituted for the champagne]. Cover with bouillon or consommé and let chicken simmer on top of the stove until tender, approximately twenty minutes. Add sliced mushrooms which have been sautéed in 1 tbsp. butter. Then add heavy cream. Serve in a chafing dish, garnished with orange wedges and skinless, seedless grapes. Serves four.

BREAST OF CAPON PAPILLOTTE À LA PAILLARD ◄

4 large breasts of chicken (10
  oz. meat per person)
6 oz. pâté de foie gras
salt and pepper
flour for dredging
butter and oil
½ lb. small mushrooms
½ lb. cooked baby carrots

4 large mushroom caps
4 large sheets greaseproof
  paper (parchment or Kraft)
1 cup Marsala
2 cups demi-glace (or good
  brown stock)
1 truffle

Salt and pepper the chicken breasts. Divide the pâté in four equal parts and spread on the meaty side of the breasts. Dredge with flour, and sauté *slowly* in half butter and half oil for approximately fifteen minutes on each side. In the meantime, sauté small mushrooms and carrots together in butter. Reserve, but keep warm. Sauté the mushroom caps and keep warm. When the breasts are ready, remove them from the pan. Dip greaseproof paper in oil [or brush on oil liberally with a butter brush]. Place breasts on paper. Remove oil and butter from pan and deglaze with Marsala. Then add demi-glace, salt and pepper to taste. Garnish with small mushrooms and carrots separately for each breast. Add slice of truffle to each and julienne remainder of truffle to decorate. Top with sautéed mushroom caps. Spread each breast with 1½ tsp. of gravy. Fold paper to form papillotte (see below) and one minute before serving place in a hot oven. Parchment paper will pop when ready to serve. If you use Kraft paper (which will not burst) heat through for a minute or two. Serve remainder of gravy in a side dish. [To fold paper, lay sheet with one point up, one down, and one to each side. Place chicken in lower center. Fold up bottom point over chicken, then fold in each side, one at a time. Fold bottom up and over towards top leaving enough top paper to make a flap. Tuck flap in bottom half.] Serves four.

➤ ENTRECOTE DE BOEUF LUCIUS BEEBE
AU POIVRE

4 sirloin steaks (16 oz. each) without bone	whole black peppers
salt	2 tsp. butter
Worcestershire sauce	1 tsp. chopped shallot
mustard	2 shots cognac
	sauce diable (see recipe below)

Pound each steak flat to form an entrecote. Salt and cover with Worcestershire sauce and mustard, spreading on with a brush. Crush peppers in a mill of the largest (coarsest) grind, and sprinkle a little over the meat. Sauté in 1 tsp. butter over a moderate flame until cooked according to taste. On a flat chafing dish, melt 1 tsp. butter and sauté the chopped shallot in it. Add the prepared steak and heat through. Pour cognac over the steak and set it afire. Rotate the steak while flaming. When the flames cease, pour on enough sauce diable to cover, and serve piping hot. Serves four.

sauce diable:

2 tbsp. shallots	1 cup brown sauce
6 peppercorns	1 tsp. Worcestershire sauce
3 oz. dry white wine	salt to taste

Mince shallots and crush peppercorns very fine. Cook with the wine until it reduces to a thick sauce. Add the brown sauce and Worcestershire, adjust seasoning, and simmer gently over a low flame. Strain before using. Makes one cup.

➤ RACK OF LAMB BOUQUETIÈRE

2 racks of lamb (approx. 1½ lbs. each, when fully trimmed)	1 tsp. thyme
salt and pepper	1 laurel leaf
1 whole onion, sliced	1 cup white wine
	1 cup brown sauce

vegetables:

butter	4 cooked artichoke bottoms
½ cup cooked baby carrots	1 cup cooked new potatoes
1 tbsp. cooked peas	2 tomatoes
1 tbsp. cooked green beans, diced	water cress

Salt and pepper the lamb and roast in 400°–450° oven for approximately twenty-five to thirty minutes, depending on how well done you want it. Add sliced onion, thyme, and laurel to meat and roast for five minutes more. Remove meat from oven, discard onions and laurel, and drain fat from pan. Deglaze pan with white wine, add brown sauce, let simmer for five minutes. Drain the sauce. Use a little sauce to glaze the rack of lamb and serve the rest on the side. Put rack on serving tray and garnish with the prepared (see below) artichoke bottoms, potatoes, and tomatoes alternately around the rack. Add bouquet of water cress here and there for color.

To prepare the vegetable garnishes, sauté each vegetable separately in butter while the lamb is roasting. Put the smaller vegetables inside the artichoke bottoms. Grill the tomatoes in halves. Serves four.

The Blue Fox ✳

659 MERCHANT STREET

expensive

THE BLUE FOX HAS COME A LONG WAY SINCE IT STARTED IN THE Twenties as an unobtrusive place with an open patio at its entrance and a name that nobody remembers. Far better known was its next door Merchant Street neighbor, Billy Lyon's Saloon and Bail Bond House, which was crowded with characters from the underworld, only slightly less colorful figures from the Hall of Justice across the way, wandering bands of gypsies, boxing personalities, including James J. Jeffries, and on later occasions even "Baby Face" Nelson.

In the Thirties, the restaurant acquired its present name— after a brief interval as the Philosopher's Inn—and a Bohemian character which it has since lost. It was then run by three partners: Mario Picolli, whose duties alternated between playing chef in the kitchen and guitar in the barroom; Tony Barbieri, once an opera singer in Italy, a bartender in Paris, and both at the Blue Fox; and Joe Pinoni, fresh from managing a hotel and restaurant in Mexico. In those days, you entered from the dingy alley through an iron gate that led into a patio fresh with plants and flowers. Guests came for the frogs' legs, lobster thermidor, lamb sweetbreads poulette, boneless squab stuffed with wild rice—and the music of Mario and Tony.

When Mario Mondin purchased the place twenty years ago, it showed the ravages of the depression, but over the years he and Piero Fassio, a partner who came in a bit later, transformed the Blue Fox into an aristocrat among restaurants, a favorite haunt of society folk and visiting movie stars. Even the ladies' room now boasts Italian marble on its counters, French porcelain washbowls inlaid with gold and filled from twenty-four-carat swan fixtures, a pink terrazzo floor, pink and silver wallpaper (handmade), French gold and crystal doorknobs, an imported bench covered in cerise Italian silk, and a guardian four-foot mermaid decked out in sea shells, white coral, pearls, and sparkling rhinestones. I have it on good authority that the wall paper in the men's room also has that handmade touch.

The neighborhood is a cradle of the city's history. In the 1830's a plot of land nearby the present Blue Fox provided villager Candelario Miramontes with potatoes; by the next decade it was the civic and "cultural" center of the community. Mid-nineteenth century Portsmouth Plaza—a half-block distant from the Blue Fox—was then almost at the water's edge, and there, early one July morning in 1846, sailors from the U.S.S. *Portsmouth* under the command of Captain John B. Montgomery ran up the first American flag. Captain Montgomery's troops found quarters on the northwest corner of the square in the old adobe custom house that later contained the principal government offices, and provided on its south porch the beam from which the Vigilance Committee of 1851 dangled thief John Jenkins by his neck. The Plaza also housed the city's first hotel, first schoolhouse, and first theatre. The schoolhouse took on besides, the functions of jailhouse, court, town hall, and church.

By the height of the Gold Rush, the square was most famous for its numerous bawdy saloons and gambling houses—the El Dorado (which started in a tent, but soon gave up canvas for a more elegant setting, an orchestra, and fashionable nude paintings), the Parker House, and Dennison's Exchange Saloon. In good weather dice and card players turned the square itself into a casino, while on its western face the Rev. William Taylor preached daily from his front steps against the evils of gaming. When the first cable car made its pioneer run, marveling onlookers gathered at its terminus at the corner of the plaza. Robert Louis Stevenson sunned himself here in 1879, and the Pony Express ended its run less than a block from the Blue Fox's quarters.

The Jenny Lind Theatre and Maguire's Opera House fronted on the plaza, and the city's first play was performed there in 1850 in Washington Hall—a building which later became one of the city's swankiest houses of prostitution. In due course the governors established a city hall on the very same site. The original buildings were eventually razed to make way for a Hall of Justice, which, rebuilt after the quake and fire, functioned there until 1961. For years the Blue Fox took pride in pointing out that its fashionable entry was in the dimly lit alley just across from the city morgue. When its strange neighbor moved, along with the city's courts, records, police department, and assorted prisoners, the restaurant tendered it a sumptuous farewell feast. In the spirit of a wake, along with funeral music, the departing neighbors ate luncheon delicacies spread straight down the middle of Merchant Street. This was true to neighborhood tradition of fetes for the departed: in 1859, thirty thousand people had gathered in the plaza to hear Colonel E. D. Baker's oration over the body of Senator David Broderick, who had lost his life in a celebrated duel.

The Blue Fox's chef is Tony Penado, a sweet and gentle man, who was born for his métier. He discovered that he liked to cook when he was a youngster, and he taught himself, prescribing a course that included an exhaustive study of all the authoritative books he could get his hands on. He is the kind of person with whom it is a pleasure to discuss food; he speaks of it with all the love and learning of a true scholar.

The Blue Fox's regular dinner offers an extraordinarily good sampling of the restaurant's dishes, including hors d'oeuvres, cracked crab when it's in season, soup or paste, entrées, dessert and coffee. If you order à la carte, you will have a selection of additional continental dishes, including particularly good pastes and other Italian specialties. The Blue Fox makes roasted red peppers, a dish I can never resist. The peppers, roasted and peeled, are served in oil and vinegar, speckled with fresh ground black pepper, and mingled gently with the fresh tang of garlic. Scampi alla Livornese is another specialty; the delicate scampi are cooked in a thin velouté, then finished with the addition of lemon, wine, and butter. Vitello tonnato, a dish not offered by many establishments, is an appetizer of lean veal round, molded into sausage form, wrapped in cheesecloth, boiled tender in vinegar and herbs and topped with a sauce of tuna.

Among the pastes are excellent gnocchi verdi, green lasagne with a rich Bolognese sauce, and fine, creamy tortellini, the recipe for which Tony has given me.

Among the entrées of which the Blue Fox is most proud are cotoletta imbottita alla palatina, recipe below, filet of pompano farci en papillote, stuffed boneless roulade of capon, and fagianino alla creta. The pompano, brought in from Florida waters, is skinned, split, and pounded flat, before being rolled around a seafood pâté of generous quality. Tony makes it by poaching filet of turbot in white wine, and adding it, strained, to a roux of butter, shallots, and the poaching liquor. When this sauce is reduced to almost pâté consistency, he spikes it with sherry, nutmeg, and lemon juice, and adds a portion of chopped spinach, another of crabmeat, and a crowning glory of shrimp. After the filling cools, he uses about three ounces for each filet and bakes it for a quarter-hour in oiled brown butcher paper, moistening each serving with half béchamel, half chicken velouté, and anointing it lightly with sauterne, sherry, and a dash of mace.

The capon breast is boned and stuffed with a pâté of veal and chicken, bolstered with sherry, almonds, Parmesan cheese, and nutmeg. Then it is dressed with a fine glaze, which Tony makes on a base of brown chicken sauce. First he adds lemon juice and sherry, reduces it, and beats in soft butter until it is light tan and fluffy. Madeira, port, cherry juice, and a further reduction bring the glaze to perfection.

The pheasant baked in clay is a rather ceremonious adaptation of a dish that Fassio's sister told him she ate in upper Piedmont, in a Turin dining spot with the unlikely name of The Japanese Restaurant. Mario and Fassio had a bird flown—by airplane, that is—to San Francisco. After experimenting with baking temperatures and variations on the seasonings, they produced what is now one of the house specialties. Although pheasant baked in clay may have been new to San Franciscans, game and meat baked in similar fashion were enjoyed by the American Indians and the ancient Romans. Baking in this fashion retains all of the juice, and the bird stays hot for two hours after it has been removed from the oven. The Blue Fox uses pheasants weighing about one pound, but if you have some spare clay on the premises and feel like trying this, there is no reason why Cornish game hens, partridges, larger pheasants, or even small hen turkeys should not be cooked in this manner.

The Blue Fox recipe for the one pounder starts with a stuffing of wild rice, steamed slowly until it is half cooked. Three or four white Italian truffles go into the bird along with the rice, and over it butter and a center cut—preferably with a little fat—of thinly sliced prosciutto. The clay coating goes on over a lining of foil. Ceramic clay, available from ceramic equipment supply houses in five pound bags for around one dollar, is perfect for this recipe. The baking time is one hour and 25 minutes at 350°. The Blue Fox serves a thick sauce along with their fagianino alla creta, based on a good pheasant stock, liberally seasoned with celery, onions, sage, rosemary, and generous additions of red and white wine. If you want to do this strictly according to Blue Fox procedures, you must wheel the finished product to the table on a cart, and break the clay with a resolute tap from a silver mallet.

Here is Tony's recipe for cutlet of veal Palatina (named in honor of the Blue Fox's new and most elegant Palatine Room), and his instructions for preparing Venetian tortellini.

➤   COTOLETTA IMBOTTITA ALLA PALATINA

10 oz. lean veal round, cut into four slices, 3 inches by 2 inches	a paste of: 2 oz. grated Parmesan cheese, 1 tbsp. soft butter, ½ beaten egg
2 oz. prosciutto, or two slices cooked ham	flour for dredging
2 slices Monterey Jack cheese	batter of: 1½ beaten eggs, plus ½ cup flour
	¼ cup cooking oil

sauce:

1 oz. butter	1 tsp. chopped parsley
2 dashes lemon juice	

Place veal slices on pounding surface, cover with heavy waxed paper, and flatten with cleaver until ⅛ inch thick. On each of two slices of veal, place one slice of ham or half the prosciutto, and one slice of Jack cheese. On the other two slices of veal, spread the paste of Parmesan cheese, butter and egg. Turn these over on top of the first two slices, making two sandwich-cutlets. Press firmly with hand; trim rough edges to form an even cutlet, place in refrigerator until chilled. When ready to cook, dip in flour, then in egg batter. Fry in oil heated to 350°, until brown on both sides.

SAUCE: Brown the butter, add the lemon juice and chopped parsley. Pour over the cutlet. Serve piping hot. Serves two.

TORTELLINI ALLA VENEZIANA

Tortellini are half moons of pasta stuffed with a veal-chicken pâté (as well as several variations) and formed into circlets. The Blue Fox has the advantage of being able to obtain first-rate freshly made tortellini from a nearby pasta maker. The same should be true for all of us near large Italian neighborhoods. In other localities there are excellent frozen tortellini, some of which I have tried with great success. I have also made my own, an arduous but rewarding labor. This recipe starts with tortellini in hand—or at least on hand—but whether purchased or homemade is up to you. One pound of tortellini—about fourteen dozen very small circlets—will feed from four to six persons amply. If you serve this dish as the Blue Fox does, before the main course, you will want to use one or two dozen tortellini for each portion.

1 lb. tortellini	2 oz. butter
6 cups chicken broth	3 oz. or more grated Parmesan
1 pt. or more half and half (milk and cream)	cheese

Boil tortellini in chicken broth, until tender but still "chewy" —eight to ten minutes if fresh, twenty to twenty-five minutes if frozen. Cool in the broth, then drain.

SAUCE: In a saucepan combine half and half with butter. Bring to a boil, add tortellini, and simmer three minutes. Add the grated Parmesan cheese, and gently shake the pan until the sauce thickens. If you desire a thicker sauce, add more cheese; if you prefer it creamier, add more half and half. Makes four to six large portions.

Elegant Settings for Lunch

Not every good restaurant serves lunch, but in San Francisco many excellent ones do, for the city especially enjoys dining at noon. You can't find better food or more congenial luncheon atmosphere than in the old-style restaurants, the grills, and the fish houses. Most of the Chinese places and a number of the Japanese welcome noon-time clientele, as do a scattering of French and Italian restaurants. Trader Vic's dispenses great hamburgers filled with chutney, or a harvest of tropical fruits for ladies who insist on salad at midday. But there are three places with a very special luncheon tradition. They give an attention to menu, setting, and detail that has overtones of more glorious days. They are El Prado in the Plaza Hotel, the Redwood Room in the Clift, and—a place that recalls the most exciting years of the city's history—the Garden Court of the Palace Hotel.

El Prado ✳

UNION SQUARE (POST NEAR STOCKTON)

expensive

EL PRADO'S CHEF DE CUISINE, THEODORE POUMIROU, HAS MANAGED its large kitchens from an impressive crow's nest of an office with view—in this case of the cooks below—for more than a dozen years. He has worked at the art of haute cuisine in San Francisco for thirty-five years, serving the patrons of the St. Francis and Sir Francis Drake Hotels, and the members of the Pacific Union Club and the Family Club. His training was in the classic French tradition. Born in Pau in the south of France, he was trained in the country of his birth, and before settling down in San Francisco, he worked in New York and Philadelphia. He has won a prize in a nationwide contest among chefs for creating a new sandwich, the Gourmet's Delight, and its recipe is among the many that he has so generously given me.

When you enter El Prado you find white linen, rich wood, a fine old bar, attentive service, and a menu that ranges wonderfully through buckwheat crêpes topped with dollops of sour cream and Romanoff caviar, Bombay curry, homemade enchiladas, chopped raw steak Tartare fashion, bouillabaisse Marseillaise, beef Stroganoff, minestrone alla milanese, and roast tom turkey with giblet gravy and cranberry sauce (and good!).

To begin, there are celery stalks à la Victor, or brimming with blue cheese, fine thin slices of Nova Scotia smoked salmon, marinated herring tidbits in cream, Olympia or blue point oysters, and a variety of other seafood in cocktails or bedded down on ice. There are fine soups—French onion, Boston clam chowder, leek and potato. The salads are things of beauty—artful heapings of crab legs, red chunks of lobster, curls of anchovies resting on hearts of romaine lettuce or halved avocados. There are Caesar salads, crab Louis, and pineapples stuffed with fruits. El Prado is one of the few places with a variety of sandwiches on its noon day menu (many places have none). Besides Theodore's prizewinner, there is an El Prado Special—baked sugar cured ham, roast turkey and coleslaw on Russian rye; there are Denver, tuna, ham, Swiss cheese, club, and half a dozen hot sandwiches.

Main courses include tender omelettes, and juicy slabs of roast prime ribs of beef. Theodore dresses up filet of sole with crab legs, lobster, shrimps, and mushrooms; or bakes it richly à la Marguery. He stuffs scaloppine of veal, smothers them with mushroom sauce, and sends the dish forth with a batch of buttery egg noodles to soak up the juices. One of his most delicious dishes is stuffed artichoke bottoms, these laced with creamed crab meat, mushroom slivers, and sherry wine, and served with an accompanying rice alla milanese. His bouillabaisse, remarkable considering that you are sitting in mid-town San Francisco, and not on the sandy edge of the Mediterranean sea, is an aromatic fish stew with real Marseillaise overtones. When the waiter ladles it hot from the copper tureen, you find crab legs, lobster, and curlicues of prawns, clams, rock cod, and great chunks of sea bass, all afloat in a steaming broth, pungent with wine, garlic, and saffron.

The dessert cart is unfortunately bewitching; this is no place to come if you are weak-willed and dieting. French pastries abound, and cheesecake, strawberry strips, apple and lemon meringue pies vie temptingly with praline, rum, Black Forest-cherry, and nesselrode layer cakes. There are always fine French pancakes, petit coeur à la crème, baba au rhum flambé, and cherries jubilee or crêpes suzette. There are parfaits, snowballs, and sundaes, fresh fruits in season, and a half dozen good imported cheeses, as well as Monterey Jack.

Here are a number of El Prado recipes.

GOURMET'S DELIGHT SANDWICH

2 slices white bread
2 pats butter
1 2-oz. slice baked ham
3 1-oz. slices dill pickle
1 tbsp. sour cream
½ tsp. horseradish
dash Lea and Perrins Worcestershire sauce
1 slice—2 oz.—of cooked white meat of turkey
1 2-oz. slice American cheese

Butter the bread, and on one piece place the ham, the dill pickle slices cut the thickness of fifty-cent pieces, the sour cream combined with the horseradish and Worcestershire sauce, the slice of turkey,

171

and the second slice of bread. Trim the edges, place the cheese on top, put in a hot oven or under the broiler until the cheese is soft but not melted. Serves one.

[El Prado serves the sandwich covered with a creamed mushroom sauce to which Theodore adds shallots, sherry wine, and grated Parmesan cheese. The whole is placed under the broiler until it browns lightly.]

➤ THEODORE'S STEAK SANDWICH

6 skirt steaks or top round
   steaks, 4 oz. each
salt
fresh ground pepper
6 good quality hamburger
   buns
2 tbsp. cooking oil

3 oz. butter
1 bunch scallions, chopped
2 tsp. Lea and Perrins
   Worcestershire sauce
1 tsp. prepared mustard
1 tbsp. chopped fresh parsley

Pass the steaks through the tenderizer machine twice (or ask your butcher to prepare them for you). Season the meat with salt and pepper. Split the buns, place them on a pastry pan in a hot oven or under the broiler until they are a light brown. Heat a skillet or frying pan very hot. Add the oil, then the steaks. Fry for about one half minute on each side. Remove and place on the half buns. Discard the oil, add the butter, then scallions to the skillet. Fry for a minute, add the Worcestershire sauce, mustard and parsley, pour over the steaks, and cover with the other half of the bun. Garnish with wedges of tomato, dill pickles and olives. Serves six.

➤ ROAST LONG ISLAND DUCKLING AU CERISES

1 4 lb. duckling
1 carrot, cut into large pieces
1 stalk celery, cut into large
   pieces
1 onion, cut into large pieces
1 cup stock

2 oz. brandy
1 cup pitted black bing cherries with their juice
2 tsp. arrowroot or cornstarch
   mixed with a little brandy

Add rough cut vegetables to duckling and roast until tender. [The time will vary considerably according to your taste, but most people will want to cook it for at least an hour and a half at 350°.]

When finished, remove the duck and keep warm. Skim the fat off the gravy, add stock, correct seasoning, and strain into a small pot. Add brandy, black cherries and juice. Thicken with cornstarch or arrowroot mixed with brandy, and cook through a few minutes. Carve the duck, pour some gravy over the slices, and serve the rest on the side. Serves four.

[Theodore serves this dish with special sweet potatoes, cooked and mashed, rolled into balls, and deep fried. When served they are glazed with currant jelly blended with maple syrup.]

DANISH LOBSTERS

8 to 10 Danish lobsters
  (scampi) or jumbo prawns
salt and pepper
¼ cup olive oil
1 cup bread crumbs

melted butter or oil
2 cups cooked rice pilaf (or
  wild rice)
1 cup béarnaise sauce
4 large broiled mushroom caps

[Danish lobsters, or scampi, are a hard commodity for the average housewife to find, and are very expensive besides. Jumbo prawns, though not so delicate, are a perfectly agreeable substitute in this recipe.]

Shell eight or ten Danish lobsters. Season with salt and pepper. Roll in olive oil, then in fresh bread crumbs. Thread whole on a skewer and sprinkle with a little butter or oil. Broil on a hot broiler ten to twelve minutes. Serve on rice pilaf. [I prefer the flavor of wild rice with this dish.] Pour béarnaise sauce over the top, and serve with broiled mushrooms on the side. Serves two.

PETIT COEUR À LA CRÈME

3 8-oz. pkgs. Philadelphia
  cream cheese

1 pint sour cream
3 tbsp. granulated sugar

sauce:

1 small pkg. cream cheese
⅓ cup sour cream

½ tbsp. sugar
⅓ cup sweet cream

Soften the cheese and pass through a sieve. Add sour cream and sugar. Blend ingredients carefully before placing in individual heart-shaped molds lined with cheesecloth, and let set in the refrigerator over night. Make the sauce by following the first two steps. When well blended, thin to desired consistency with sweet cream. The dessert, when unmolded, can be used with whatever fresh fruit is in season. Fresh strawberries, peaches and apricots are most popular. French Bar-le-Duc—currant jelly—is a good substitute when fruits are not available. Serves eight.

✳ *The Redwood Room*

CLIFT HOTEL, GEARY STREET AT TAYLOR

expensive

THE REDWOOD ROOM PRESERVES A LUXURY OF DETAIL THAT IS common to few places these days. Its intelligent management can be credited with such rareties as serving at the end of each meal cookies and mints from a white spun sugar basket light-heartedly entwined with pink and green confectionery roses and sprigs of lily of the valley. The restaurant borrows some of its tone from the Clift Hotel which houses it, and among whose own notable features is a ban on conventions—thus assuring its guests a maximum of peace and quiet.

Lest you think this is a dull spot, be reassured at once. Restful, indeed, but alertly in the center of the city—just two blocks from Union Square, a half-block from the Airline Terminal, and side by side with San Francisco's two leading legitimate theatres, the Curran and the Geary, which provide it with any number of distinguished clients.

It is the favorite lunch spot of several celebrated San Franciscans who assemble at a reserved Round Table for animated conversation over dishes that are meticulously prepared and faultlessly served: the likes of Harold Zellerbach, chairman of the paper company, Grover Magnin, an emeritus president of I. Magnin and Company, Harry Ross, San Francisco Controller, various impressarios of the theatre, the mayor, and occasionally —when he's in town—a justice of the supreme court.

The Redwood Room itself was designed by Albert Lansburgh, the architect of the San Francisco Opera House. It has dignified and lofty proportions, and takes its name from the variety of highly polished redwoods that adorn it. Its walls are lined with smooth blocks of curly redwood, and the bar is of rare solid burl. Against the dark woods, the ceiling is of striking silver leaf, and the adjoining French Room a contrasting ivory tone, accented by crimson chairs in deepest black frames. Tables are spaced at generous intervals, allowing room for the traffic of carts and the flourishes of waiters, and providing a feeling of privacy for each of its dining parties.

The most distinguishing features of the room are its extensive cart service and buffets, appointments that Mr. Odell, the owner-manager, installed because he so enjoyed them in his European travels. There are always three roast beef carts, another providing roast stuffed turkey, and one featuring the special dish of that day—Irish stew on Tuesdays, Yankee pot roast jardinière with potato pancakes on Wednesdays, curried spring lamb madras with rice pilaf on Thursdays, lobster thermidor on Fridays. There is an oyster cart, and a cheese cart with one of San Francisco's best assortments of imports. The dessert cart is lavishly arrayed with such enticements as French pastries that are baked on the premises daily, along with all the bread and rolls, by two resident pastry chefs. But certainly the most beautiful of all is the cart with racks of glasses and snifters appropriate to each of the liqueurs and brandies it transports.

The Redwood Room is notable for fresh vegetables early in their season, and fruits of quality long before one expects them. An unusual favorite during the berry season is stewed strawberry-rhubarb. The house wines—a mountain sauterne, a rosé, and a Burgundy—are products of a distinguished California vintner, Louis Martini, bottled by him especially for the Redwood Room.

ELEGANT

The cracked crab is superbly prepared here. The kitchens purchase the ugly fellows alive and cook them fresh daily. If crabs are not available still kicking, they don't make their appearance on the Redwood Room menu. A procedure that most guests know nothing about, but enjoy the results of, pertains to the daily fresh fish dishes. The fishermen who supply the Redwood Room radio in at about eight a.m. to report on their catch that morning, and the chef plans his menu accordingly.

The menu is à la carte and the same for lunch and dinner. It offers cocktails and appetizers—seafoods, fruits, vegetables, juices—soups by the bowl or tureen; salads: green goddess with shrimp, crab or chicken; halekulani: half a fresh pineapple with papaya, bananas, prunes and cottage cheese; chef's salad: turkey, ham, tongue and Swiss cheese tossed among greens; and a variety of seafood combinations; sandwiches: smoked salmon with or without cream cheese on Russian rye with potato salad and cucumbers in sour cream; hot roast prime rib with mashed potatoes; thick corned beef with Swiss cheese, coleslaw, tomatoes, and dill pickle; and other equally nourishing meals on bread. There is a cold buffet; grillades: steaks, chops, chicken, calf's liver, genuinely broiled over charcoal; and besides the cart service, a number of other entrées that range from Spanish omelette to Grand Central Station oyster stew.

The chef has given me his recipes for two favorite Redwood Room specials, lobster thermidor and crêpes suzette.

➤ LOBSTER THERMIDOR

1 boiled lobster	1 tsp. dry mustard
2 shallots	2 cups cream
1 sprig parsley	2 oz. fresh butter
1 sprig tarragon	1 tbsp. hollandaise
6 small mushrooms, diced	1 tbsp. whipped cream
1 tbsp. butter	

Cut the lobster in two lengthwise; remove the meat from the shell and cut in squares. Then make a sauce as follows:

Chop the shallots, parsley, and tarragon. Sauté along with the diced mushrooms in 1 tbsp. butter until clear but not brown. Add the dry mustard, two cups of cream, and two ounces of fresh butter. Reduce. Put some of the sauce in the bottom of the shells, place the lobster chunks in the sauce, then pour the remainder over the top. Glaze with hollandaise and whipped cream, mixed, under the broiler—or salamander, if you should be antiquarian enough to have one—until brown. Serves one or two.

CRÊPES SUZETTE

This showy dessert makes its most attractive presentation in a chafing dish, but it will taste every bit as good—should you lack a long-handled crêpes suzette platter and its customary flaming stand—conjured up in a large frying pan over the range.

16 crêpes about five inches in diameter (thin to a transparency)	2 oranges
	1½ lemons
	4 oz. brandy
12 pats sweet butter	2 oz. Cointreau
8 cubes domino sugar	

After the flame has been lit under crêpes suzette platter and the platter has become warm, put in the butter to melt. Rub four cubes of the domino sugar on the skin of one of the oranges to extract the oil. Rub the other four cubes on the whole lemon to absorb its essence. Place the prepared sugar cubes in crêpes suzette platter and squeeze the juice of the second orange and the half lemon over them. Add two ounces of the brandy and one ounce of the Cointreau. Cook about ten minutes, stirring so that the sugar dissolves completely.

Take the crêpes, one at a time, and turn them over in the sauce, then fold in halves, and fold once again so that the final shape is a triangle.

After basting the crêpes with sauce, pour over them the balance of brandy (2 ounces), and flame. Add the remainder of Cointreau (1 ounce), and baste again. Have four plates as hot as possible, and place four crêpes on each. Ladle a small amount of the remaining sauce over each serving. Serve with dessert fork and teaspoon. Serves four.

➤ PANCAKES

The Redwood Room recipe can be used with any variety of sweetened crêpes, but in case you don't have a favorite, here is a simple and easy recipe:

1 cup flour	½ cup cream
3 tbsp. sugar	1½ oz. rum
¼ tsp. salt	grated lemon and orange peel
3 eggs	to taste
½ cup milk	butter

Sift the dry ingredients in a large bowl. Add the eggs and whip lightly. Blend in the milk and cream, a little at a time, but do not overmix. Stir just enough to mix through smoothly. Add rum and grated lemon and orange peel. Brush a heated five-inch skillet with butter, pour in a measured amount of batter—just enough to coat the bottom—and swirl the pan quickly until the batter makes a thin even layer. Cook over medium high heat until the center begins to puff and the edges are noticeably brown. Flip over with a spatula and cook just long enough to cook through. The cooking should take no more than a minute or two. Reserve on a platter until ready to use. Continue, using the same measure for uniformity, until batter is used up. Makes about twenty-eight crêpes, of which four are a minimum portion.

※ *The Garden Court of the Palace Hotel*
NEW MONTGOMERY AT MARKET

expensive

IF ANY ONE PLACE IN SAN FRANCISCO CAN BE SAID TO REFLECT the city's history, it must certainly be the magnificent Palace Hotel. Its Garden Court, a wonder of space and color and luxury,

1. *Broadway, with Hotel de France and a cluster of other restaurants, the Bay Bridge in the background.*

2. Above: *The Garden Court of the Palace Hotel, an elegant setting for lunch.*

3. Left: *Ernie's, Montgomery Street, where red velvet, mahogany and cut glass are the background for "San Francisco-style" dinners.*

Two views of Fisherman's Wharf:

4. Left: *Fisherman's Grotto in the evening.*

5. Below: *Tarantino's as seen from the water.*

6. Above: *Pizza tossing, a typical scene in Italian restaurants.*

7. Upper Left: *Tao-Tao and other Chinese restaurants on Jackson Street, with a view of the Bay Bridge.*

8. Left: *Chinese delicacies as served at Kan's, Grant Avenue.*

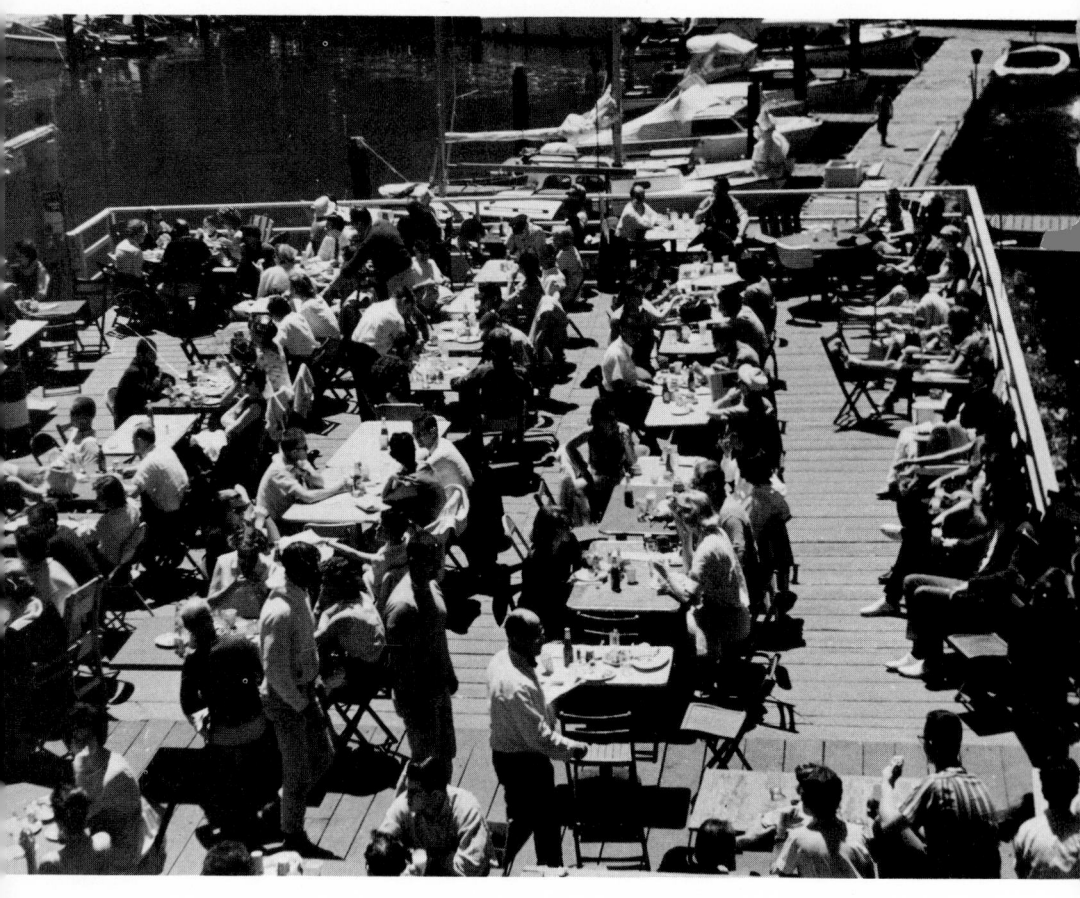

9. *Outdoor dining on the sun deck at Sam's Anchor Café, Tiburon.*

recalls the extravagance of an era when opulence was a commonplace. The hotel's acquisition in 1954 by the Sheraton chain frankly caused nervous rashes in a coterie of San Franciscans whose concern it was to preserve uniqueness in a city that has grown famous on it. The press, aided and abetted by what can most generously be called a complete lack of sensitivity to its new property on the part of the Sheraton hierarchy, voiced the city's outraged suspicions. Herb Caen wryly wondered whether the Palace would be "Sheratonized"; rumors spread wildly that the Garden Court would be ruined, modernized, that margarine might replace butter, and that—God forbid—the club sandwich would surely become the lunch hour staple. The Sheraton people, after a generous period of bumbling, inadvertently exaggerated by cost analysts and other experts on proper management, began to develop a rash of their own. Like most innkeepers, they wanted—and needed—to be loved. They began to catch on to the kind of wooing San Francisco would respond to, or better yet, to the fact that there already existed a love affair of long standing between the city and its radiant hotel, and that the way to preserve the relationship was to keep the principals as unchanged in their traditions as possible. Announcements assured the city that everything would stay just the way it was; and should future changes be necessary, the management promised, they would preserve the spirit of the original. When the furor had somewhat abated, they went ahead with their plans to renovate the Garden Court—but strictly along traditional lines.

Before the 1906 fire, the court served as the hotel's grand entry. As the Palm Court, it first took on its role as a dining salon following the 1909 rebuilding. It changed its palms for flower boxes and its name to Garden Court only in 1942. The Sheraton refurbishing, to an almost audible San Francisco sigh of relief, restored the palms—though not the name—repainted and regilded the entire court as it had been in 1909, replaced the wall-to-wall carpeting and coverings on the chairs, and in short, bolstered and accentuated the prevailing elegance. The Court's dazzling setting is most appropriate for the annual dinner heralding the opening of the opera season. The yearly Debutante Cotillion waltzes through it, and the Mardi Gras and Black and White Symphony Balls both fill it with their revelers. More recently, the Garden Court has taken on the evening role of a theatre-restaurant, reviving an old city tradition from the Nineties. Nightly, dinner guests arrive at six, conclude their meals by 8:30 curtain time, then partake of an evening of legitimate theatre. Top professionals perform musical comedies in-the-round, on a stage raised up in the center of the court.

The Palace Hotel first opened in October of 1875, and was instantly heralded as one of the world's great hostelries. Just two months earlier, its originator, William Chapman Ralston, had died of drowning one day after the collapse of his Bank of California, the largest finance house in the West. He had amassed such a fortune since his arrival in 1853 as a New York steamship agent that he owned fabulous estates, and became the backer of a number of enterprises designed to release the West from its dependence on foreign manufacture. His vision was flamboyant, his production dramatic. His plans for the Palace showed no lack of either of these qualities.

The building was massive and substantial, designed only after its architect, John P. Gaynor, had studied the great Eastern hotels of this country, and the noble style of Viennese palaces. Foundations and walls, basements and sub-basements, were all of gargantuan construction. Columns of nearly seven hundred bay windows jutted from its exterior; Harold Kirker says, in *California's Architectural Frontier*, that the project "covered nearly two and one-half acres and required twenty-six million bricks and forty thousand square feet of paving." [26]

Besides relying on the most extravagant materials—among them rare woods, imported marbles, and Irish linens—the hotel

[26] Harold Kirker, *California's Architectural Frontier*, San Marino, California, The Huntington Library, 1960, p. 95.

was wired up with the most recent electrical devices, including clocks, and numerous contrivances designed for fire protection and to extend the comfort of its guests. It had its own well and reservoirs of water. The furnishings came largely from West Coast factories, not a few of which Ralston put in business to provide the necessaries for his hotel. But the rugs were commanded from French weavers, or ordered from the New York establishment of W. and J. Sloane, which solely for the purpose of supplying this order opened a San Francisco branch that is still thriving today.

Lewis and Hall, in their biography of the Hotel, *Bonanza Inn*,[27] describe some of the equipment:

> Of dishes there were enough to supply an army, although they were not of army quality: 9,000 plates, 8,800 "side" and 8,000 "vegetable" dishes, 4,000 cups and saucers. These had been made, on special order, by C. F. Haviland, France.

Long before the turn of the century, the Palace had set in a stock of Gold Service that misered all others. It is still in use. Settings for one hundred, including plateware, Bavarian china, glassware, and flatware, come out of the special storage rooms about a dozen times a year for events of importance. Along with them are the odds and ends of pre-earthquake dining: tabasco and horse-radish holders, consommé standards, containers for Bar-le-Duc, cigar lighters, and stands for quill toothpicks.

The kitchens, chefs, waiters, and other personnel outdid in sheer size and number any other establishment in the United States. At one time there were thirty bartenders alone. By the end of the last century, the Palace Grill Room was the most revered restaurant in the West—and the unofficial state capital: it is said that more state business was conducted over its bar than ever in the halls at Sacramento. The Grill Room, Frenchified with trappings of gold and white, enormous mirrors, and the

[27] Lewis and Hall, *Bonanza Inn*, p. 29.

blazing light of an uncountable number of bulbs, was the apogee of splendid and gaudy salons in a city that had more of them than it could handily count up.

But the highlight of the entire extravaganza was the Grand Court. Through the arched Montgomery Street entry, horse-drawn carriages clattered in, literally driving their passengers right off the street and into the hotel. Eventually, because of the echo-chamber effect on the seven floors of guest rooms which lined this giant well, through traffic was abandoned. But the glass-domed, pillared courtyard, illuminated by hundreds of gas flares, and heated, Kirker informs us, "by huge braziers of polished bronze," could contain fantastic receptions in its vast reaches, including one for General Grant during which he was serenaded by a choir of five hundred.[28]

In the early days, it was the tradition during Christmas to erect a giant fir in the middle of the Court. It reached the peak of its splendor in 1896, when after forty-eight hours of electrical embroidering by a substantial crew, the tree shot spectacularly ablaze with hundreds of colored lights. Alas, the Christmas tree tradition died in the fire; in its place there is now a Christmas Carol luncheon.

The Palace has always been associated with celebrities. A group of prominent attorneys, judges and newspaper publishers has been lunching together at the Cabinet Table in the Court for fifty years or more. United States Presidents who have slept at the Palace include Hayes, Harrison, McKinley, Theodore Roosevelt, Taft, Truman, Eisenhower, and John F. Kennedy. Woodrow Wilson gave a famous League of Nations speech here. Dom Pedro II, Emperor of Brazil, was the first of many royal guests; Paderewski and Caruso, John D. Rockefeller and Rudyard Kipling, Nikita Khrushchev and Madame Chiang Kai-shek are a few of the other notable personalities to visit the Palace.

[28] Kirker, *California's Architectural Frontier*, pp. 95–6.

Ralston was, of course, the first great name allied with the establishment. His interest was taken up, on his premature demise, by the Nevada Senator, William Sharon, whose heirs carried on after him. His granddaughter, Mrs. William B. Johnson, sold the hotel to the Sheraton chain in 1958. The first chef, Jules Harder, was a recognized authority on gustatory mores, whose range of epicurean offerings trained those of his guests who were naïve in matters of the table while it satisfied the most sophisticated. Fred Mergenthaler, who succeeded Harder, had learned to cook in Paris, and had served various royal families in Europe with marked success. While he and Harder before him had been busy educating nouveau riche Californians to the fine art of dining, visitors from abroad were in their turn becoming acquainted with the gourmet qualities of California foods. The fame of California's wild duck, pheasant, and quail, venison and bear steaks, rainbow trout, sand dabs and Pacific oysters (chef Ernest Arbogast put the oyster omelette on the menu) spread throughout the gastronomic world. John C. Kirkpatrick will long be remembered for the splendid dish of oysters, bacon and catsup served up bubbling on the half shell, that was named in his honor. When he managed the hotel, this gourmet earned $30,000 a year, and he would gladly have spent his entire stipend on food. In more recent years, under the discriminating management of Edmond Reider, the great chief Lucien Heyraud supervised the kitchens. The newest chef of all is Swiss Walter Frëy, who comes highly recommended as the chief commandment of the Sheraton Kitchen Empire. His direction is able, but headquarters doesn't allow for the menu luxuries of more glorious days. The hotel's best known and most loved personality is Adolph Steinhoff, who has been greeting guests in the dining rooms since 1917.

The hotel has several bars and dining areas now, besides the magnificent Court. There is the Tudor Room, in a "mood" setting that features dimmed lighting, nine-foot murals of Henry

VIII and his sextet of wives, a buffet lunch, Black Angus beef, and dinner-dancing. In another context altogether—no females, wifely or otherwise, permitted—is the Pied Piper Men's Bar. Esquire not long ago named it—with the Ritz in Paris and the Raffles in Singapore—one of the seven most famous bars in the world. Having never been allowed entry, I can only take their word that its reputation is deserved. Hearsay has it that, besides beverages that are beyond reproach—and a dignified luncheon service—the bar boasts a large and costly painting by Maxfield Parrish, commissioned by the Sharon family when they rebuilt in 1909, of the Pied Piper of Hamelin. When the bar stood fast in 1915 and refused to join others that were forced to lower prices—the Palace preferred to keep a place for those who still liked the grand feeling of paying a quarter a drink—the press acclaimed it; when the management finally capitulated and lowered the tab, the press lamented the passing of the "last two-bit bar on the coast," sourly commenting, "one can now step up to the Palace bar and purchase a whiskey for twenty cents." The most quietly agreeable and fashionable rendezvous in the building—and there are some who might say, in the city—is the Happy Valley Bar. The Sheraton clan can't seem to make up its mind whether to serve lunch there or not, but when they're in a positive mood, it is a delightful hideaway, uncrowded, almost noiseless, and with a surrounding comfort of old-time authenticity, although the room itself has been open only thirty years. In its early days it was a ladies' lounge, gentlemen admitted only when in the company of. For its first ten years there was evening entertainment by zither players and other such accommodating bar fixtures. Happy Valley was the name of the gold miners' camp which became the site of the present hotel.

The Garden Court menu is simpler than in greater days, but it still offers a variety of delicacies—a pastiche of European recipes, imported goodies, and local fare. The Court is, of course, the place where many innovations first found favor, then fame. The Palace introduced artichokes as an important item on its menu; Chef Arbogast invented for Col. Kirkpatrick, besides his famous oyster dish, a peppy breakfast of eggs and tomatoes. Green goddess dressing originated here, and the popularity of strawberries Romanoff owes no little to its early place on the Palace menu. Today you can command iced caviar, avocado gourmet, escargots, melon and ham, pâté, oysters—Kirkpatrick, of course, and Olympia, blue points, or stewed. You will find cioppino, vichyssoise, and the less familiar cream Sénégalaise: egg yolks, thick cream, and a hint of curry enriching an already rich chicken consommé, served very well iced. Shirred eggs with lamb kidneys Meyerbeer was good the last time I lunched at the Palace. There are eggs benedict, chicken liver omelettes, and a good assortment of fish: sole, lobster, abalone, trout, poached salmon with hollandaise, and swordfish steaks broiled with a fillip of anchovy butter. The cold buffet includes steak tartare, there are a number of standard grilled entrées, and there are assorted salads including the original Palace Court Salad: a mound of either tuna, prawns, shrimp, chicken, or crab pyramided atop an artichoke base and a slice of tomato, skirted with lettuce ruffles and chopped egg, and accompanied by a boat of thousand island dressing.

There are always special dishes likely to enliven any doldrums of appetite or taste: minced calf's liver lyonnaise with hashed brown potatoes and summer squash; Swedish meatballs poached in white wine sauce with capers, mousseline potatoes, and beans panache; Westphalian style ham on French bread with asparagus and tomato; veal paillard flambé; medaillon of sweetbreads on Virginia ham with sauce madeira and fresh green peas; roast duckling with black bing cherries and wild rice; and beef stroganoff with egg noodles.

The ice creams and baked goods are made on the premises, and the array of pastries on the dessert table is satisfyingly deluxe.

Here are a number of recipes passed on to me by chef Walter Frëy.

➤
BÉARNAISE SAUCE

2 shallots, chopped
1 tbsp. black pepper
3 tarragon stems (chopped)
  (save leaves)
¼ cup tarragon vinegar
5 egg yolks
½ egg-shell of water

1 lb. butter, melted
1 tbsp. meat glace
salt
cayenne pepper
lemon juice (optional), to
  taste

Put the shallots, crushed black pepper, tarragon stems, and vinegar in the top of a double boiler, and braise until practically dry. Gradually add egg yolks, beaten, and one-half egg-shell of water. Beat over just warm water with wire whip until fluffy and thickened in the manner of a meringue. (If water is too hot the mixture will curdle.) Remove from double boiler, add the melted butter very slowly, a little at a time. Add the meat glace. [This can be omitted if you don't have any on hand.] Mix thoroughly, strain through cheesecloth or a fine sieve. Season with salt, cayenne, and lemon juice, and add the reserved tarragon leaves, chopped.

[This sauce is notable for its tendency to curdle; the trick is patience, and a low flame. An even trickier trick is to use a blender, a guarantee against failure. Follow above directions until just before adding butter. Put the sauce into blender, and there allow it to cool. Add all other seasonings except the chopped tarragon leaves. Add cooled melted butter a little at a time, blending in well on high speed. After all of the butter has been added, the sauce will be the correct thickness. Add chopped tarragon leaves, stir, and serve.] Serves at least eight.

➤
VEAL CUTLET À LA OSCAR

5 oz. veal cutlet
salt and pepper
flour
butter and oil for frying

4 spears cooked asparagus
4 crab legs, breaded and
  sautéed
½ cup béarnaise sauce

Season the cutlet, dip it in flour, sauté it in oil and butter until golden. Remove to a hot dish. Put the four spears of cooked asparagus on top, crisscrossing the four sautéed crab legs. Cover with béarnaise sauce. Serves one.

BAKED CHICKEN SUPRÊME ◅

4 broilers, quartered	10 oz. flour
12 oz. shortening	1 qt. tomato juice
1 clove garlic	1 pt. sour cream
4 oz. sliced onion	2 oz. grated Parmesan cheese
2 tsp. salt	

Brown chicken in shortening. When well colored, remove and place in casserole. Pour off all but 1 tbsp. of the chicken drippings, and cook in it the onion and garlic (mashed) until transparent. Blend in salt and flour. Add tomato juice, stirring constantly, and heat to boiling. Remove from heat. Add sour cream gradually, stirring vigorously. Blend in Parmesan cheese. Pour over chicken in baking dish. Cover and bake in a slow oven (325°) about forty-five minutes. Serves eight.

NOTE: This should be served over rice or paste since the sauce is more than generous in quantity.

VEAL CUTLET SAUTÉ WITH WHITE WINE AND ◅ FINE HERBS

8 6-oz. cutlets	2 cloves garlic
2 tbsp. butter	2 bay leaves
6 scallions	1 cup white wine
1 tsp. fresh tarragon (or ½ tsp. dried)	1 cup stock
	salt, pepper
2 tbsp. parsley	8 tbsp. chopped chives

Brown cutlets in butter in a sauteuse or deep skillet. When golden on both sides, add scallions, tarragon, and parsley, all chopped fine, and garlic cloves, and bay leaves. Add white wine, stock, and salt and pepper. Cover and simmer for about 35 minutes. Then cover each cutlet with a tbsp. chopped chives and cook uncovered for ten minutes more. Discard the garlic and bay leaves, skim off any fat, and serve. Serves eight.

BÛCHE DE NOËL (YULE LOG)

filling:

10 oz. semisweet chocolate pieces

scant ½ cup sugar

½ cup water

10 eggs, separated

1½ tbsp. vanilla

roll:

1 cup cake flour

¾ cup cocoa

½ tsp. salt

1½ tsp. baking powder

8 eggs, separated

1½ cups sugar

2 tsp. vanilla

confectioner's sugar

mocha-butter icing:

½ lb. butter

1 cup confectioner's sugar

4 tbsp. cocoa

1 tbsp. instant coffee

salt

3 tbsp. cream

FILLING: Melt chocolate with sugar and water in double boiler. Stir until smooth. Remove from heat and cool. Beat egg yolks until thick, add to sugar-chocolate mixture, then add vanilla. Beat egg whites until stiff, then fold into mixture. Chill to spreading consistency (3 to 4 hours). [In my refrigerator, this comes out pretty runny, but the flavor is great. I use what I need to spread on the cake, save the rest to spoon over each cut piece.]

ROLL: Sift together three times, flour, cocoa, salt and baking powder. Beat egg whites until they form soft peaks. Fold in sugar, 1 tbsp. at a time. Beat egg yolks until thick. Add vanilla. Fold in egg whites. Fold in sifted dry ingredients. Grease two 15½ x 10½ x 1 inch pans, then line with greased wax paper. Spread batter evenly and bake in a 400° oven thirteen minutes. Turn out on a towel sprinkled with confectioner's sugar. Quickly cut off any crisp edges, and roll up and cool. When cool, unroll, spread with filling, roll up again. Chill several hours or overnight. Frost with mocha-butter icing to resemble log, first putting both pieces together to look like a continuous piece.

ICING: Cream butter, gradually add sugar, cocoa, instant coffee, salt and enough cream to required spreading consistency. Serves sixteen. [Marvelous as a birthday cake with one long row of candles.]

6. OFF-BEAT PLACES

EVER since real Bohemians settled in the city, there have been places to feed them—places that supplied hearty, often quite unusual food, a good flow of wine, low prices, and an atmosphere that was affable, warm, and just the least bit exotic. Early restaurants that pleased the artists, writers, and other less well-to-do bon vivants included Sanguinetti's—a place where, in an uproar of music and laughter, revelers consumed table d'hôte dinners and abundant quantities of cheap red wine; and a number of other similar eateries: Coppa's, Buon Gusto, Gianduja, Campi's, Fior d'Italia, the Fly Trap, the Iron Pot, the St. Germain, the Cosmos, Lombardi's. Luna's dished up the best Mexican food, but a similar place with even more color was hidden in an alleyway back of the old jailhouse off Broadway. Maria and Felipe ran it, and Clarence E. Edwords in *Bohemian San Francisco* describes the courage that was needed to partake of a meal there:

> Chattering monkeys and parrots were hanging around the kitchen, peering into pots and fingering viands. . . . One could go to this place just on the theory that one is willing to try anything once, but aside from its picturesque old couple, and its Dantesque appearance, it offered nothing to induce a return unless it was to entertain a friend.[29]

Bonnini's Barn, in Washington Street, was for all purposes like a barn; piles of hay, harnesses, hoes, pitchforks, crude lanterns, and cruder chairs and tables persuaded the diner that he was in the most bucolic of settings. In later years, under new ownership, the place became the Manger. Downstairs there were booths and a cozy fireplace; upstairs the kitchen, a number of stuffed fowl perched about, garlands of drying peppers, and of course a manger or two. The food was still delicious. Now the Owl 'N Turtle has taken over the premises, removed all signs of the barnyard, substituted pecky cedar walls, a good amount of polished copper, and serves generally excellent food, of the deluxe variety.

The spirit of individuality generated a number of places that tried the same extremes of decor to entice the dining crowds. But some of them were stronger on atmosphere than cooking. Perhaps the strangest place ever to open in San Francisco was Bab's, designed in emulation, Edwords tells us, of the Parisian Cabaret de la Mort. One's table was a coffin, and the lighting came from clammy green candles whose holders were skulls.

A less garish masterpiece of decorating was a spot called The Backyard. The interior was done up like an ordinary backyard,

---

[29] Clarence E. Edwords, *Bohemian San Francisco*, San Francisco, Paul Elder and Company, 1914, p. 30.

but what lent interest were the scenes silhouetted in the windows of the "neighborhood," and the racy assortment of clothes on the line "next door." The Backyard had wine cellars designed as a background for entertainment. Hewn of solid rock, lined with dusty bottles, and equipped with a table spread with hors d'oeuvres, a piano, fireplace, and bar, the cellar was as hospitable a room as one could desire. Nowadays, a smart San Francisco restaurant can hardly afford to be without such a room.

The Gangplank resembled the deck of a ship, whose muraled walls duplicated the San Francisco skyline. Guests sat on kegs softened by cushions, and ate sandwiches, cold platters, and simple hot dishes from barrel tops. The nearest thing to it today is Bernstein's Fish Grotto, which sets its prow squarely on the sidewalk of Powell Street. I'm told that this lifelike dining ship is modeled—except for the rations—on the Nina of Columbus.

Nonconformists of real quality are few these days, and an honest Bohemian doesn't scare up much interest. Even pseudo-beatniks have largely left the scene, and the beard has taken on a kind of distinction akin to dignity. But innate in many solid San Francisco souls is a now-and-then desire to forsake their glamorous headquarters and to "come as they are" to a good, honest place with a bit of character.

There aren't too many spots that satisfy. Lupo's—discussed in detail in the section on Italian restaurants—is one of them that does. Frank Cantalupo, its owner, is one of the few genuine characters left around. Besides his remarkable personality, his cooking is really splendid. The Old Spaghetti Factory offers unlimited antiques and curiosities, arranged with a charming sense of humor, a musical review, food and beer. The Brighton Express serves dinners and gooey desserts—mud pie is probably the most notable—to parties of not more than six affiliated adults. They close with pleasant originality on Tuesdays and Wednesdays. Tommy's Joynt is good for hefty short orders served in a casual atmosphere. The stock of beer is enormous, but you can get everything else from Irish coffee to gin and tonic. At Juanita's Galley in Sausalito your order is cooked and served you according to the time you have punched on a kind of time clock; sometimes the wait is very long indeed, but nobody seems to mind. Juanita Musson, a bulky woman usually clad in a muu-muu, doesn't shy away from expressing her opinions, and is thereby often involved in rather well publicized altercations. The Galley, open twenty-four hours a day, has recently set up in a ferry boat berthed at the foot of Waldo Grade.

Most of the establishments that decorate with an elaborate motif are at least moderately deluxe. The most ingenious of these is Sally Stanford's Valhalla, also in Sausalito. Furnished to meet the highest standards of a bagnio parlor, it is artfully supplied with glorious Victorian settees, marble cupids, fringed lamp shades, flowered rugs, and a clutter of amusing bric-a-brac. There is a piano—and a piano player with an enormous repertoire—and a parrot, generally resting in a fine covered cage, but otherwise perched on her mistress' shoulder. She is not in the least reluctant to converse, but seems to be discreet. The hostesses are bouncy and—what a blessing of an innovation—dressed in their own clothes. If you told Sally that the entire production seemed to be too convincing, she would be most complimented: she was for years San Francisco's most celebrated madam, and supplied most of the furnishings herself. Her most recent (reformed) venture was a dashing fling at politics, when she ran—and swears to do it until she wins—for the Sausalito city council. Out of a field of eight trying for two seats, Sally came in third. A sharp and well-informed woman, she conducted her campaign with gusto, a swanky headquarters, a vintage Rolls Royce, and a mink stole. The issue most amusing to newspaper reporters, at least judging from the amount of copy that saw print, was Sally's proposal to convert Sausalito's brand new gazebo-shaped bus stop into a rest room for tourists.

There are four restaurant-bars that have retained something

of the old off-beat spirit. At least a good number of their patrons come primarily to eat or drink, rather than to stare at the natives. Their settings are honest, congenial, and interesting, and their food and drink is good, and what's more, inexpensive.

Mike's (or Dante's) Billiard Parlor ✳
521 BROADWAY

inexpensive

MIKE'S BILLIARD PARLOR IS JUST THAT, BUT IT ALSO SERVES EXcellent sandwiches, the best minestrone in the city, and a number of hearty hot dishes. Most people sit at the long bar, behind which on one end are stacks of long French breads, piles of jack and gorgonzola, salami, mortadella, coppa, and the other makings of a good torpedo sandwich; and on the other, an open kitchen, where your frittata, hamburger, or pasta will be cooked to order, and where sauces, stews, and minestrone simmer pungently along. There is a small adjoining room with tables, and a large area devoted to pool. The whole place is nicely run down—well used, you might say—and Mike's customers like it that way.

The man who made the place famous is Pasquale (Mike) Maiocco who labored hard there for twenty-eight years. He came to San Francisco at the age of seventeen from Damiano d'Asti near Torino and Genova, and went to work as a busboy at the very elegant Marchand's, where, as Mike sums it up, just about everything was served under silver covers. His career led him, as a waiter now, to Solari's, the dining salon of the St. Francis Hotel, the Fairmont, and as headwaiter, to Cabiria. All this time he dreamed of someday having an elegant business of his own. He started modestly in 1922 by buying with his savings his first place at 615 Broadway, devoted not to the satisfactions of the stomach, but to the game of pool. Five years later he moved to number 536 across the street. This forty- by ninety-foot hall contained a dozen pool tables, a soda fountain, and a cigar stand. Racketeering thrived in the neighborhood from about 1930 on, and in that era of hard times it was difficult to make an honest living. Billiards lost popularity, and Mike, faced with surviving this evolution, decided to sell food—bulging combination Italian sandwiches for fifteen cents. He nudged the pool tables a bit closer together, the hall took in a concessionaire barber shop, and a second lessee set up a lunch counter. Mike survived the evolution.

There was another move, in 1937, back to the other side of the street, leaving behind him Joe Ingrassia, who ended up owner and followed the neighborhood pattern of running a lunch counter that served excellent sandwiches and short orders. Joe's place is now called New Joe's, but Mike says that it was the original one, and that the various "Original Joe's" in the city were all started by people who once worked in the Broadway spot.

Mike had always wanted to remodel his pool hall and make it into a high class Italian restaurant, but his success with the sandwich was so phenomenal that he never broke away from the pattern he set for himself. During the war years Mike's was so crowded that a number of workers got into the habit of buying their sandwiches, taking them back to their trucks at the curb, climbing aboard, and enjoying them in the privacy of the cab.

When Mike retired a couple of years ago to his house on Beach Street, and his intricately planted and lovingly manicured garden in the yard behind, he sold out to a young society couple. They decided to raise wages, but in order to do this soundly, they also had to raise prices. The employees were shocked, especially Gino Ghio, an employee of long standing who kind of managed the place, John, an ex-wrestler, with Mike's for seventeen years, and Joe, who had washed those dishes for eighteen years. Nobody, least of all its employees, wanted Mike's to change, and a rise in prices would drive away a good number of the old clientele. In what must certainly be an unprecedented move in the annals of labor, the employees voted that their wages—and incidentally the prices—remain the same. They did.

Recently the place has changed hands again. The new owner is Enrico Banducci, the beret-wearing entrepreneur of the hungry i and Enrico's, the fancy coffee house just across the street. He is too good a showman, one hopes, to do anything rash. At this writing he has stepped up the advertising-public relations end of things, with a particular pitch to the socialite group—who have never been lacking among the patrons, but have never been primary either. We'll see. If, when you go there, it looks enticing from the street, all has been ruined!

Besides the huge delicatessen sandwiches, Mike's offers any number of other wonderfully arranged combinations—from butter and anchovies to a whole can of imported sardines complemented by large slices of onion. Mike's hamburger is excellent, sprinkled with just the proper amount of basil and parsley, and dripping with fried onions if you want them. There are daily hot specials: Monday—pot roast, Tuesday—beef stew, Wednesday—tripe, Thursday—corned beef and cabbage, Friday, baked fish, and Saturday—osso buco. On Sunday, try spaghetti with Italian sauce, or eggs, which Mike's does understanding things to, particularly eggs à la Mike: two eggs in a baking dish, surrounded by ham, peas and a splendid meat and tomato sauce, sprinkled with Parmesan cheese, and placed in the oven until the eggs set, the cheese melts, and the sauce sizzles.

Mike's is open every day, all year long from eleven in the morning until four the following a.m. At lunch time, you will find a good number of people from the nearby financial district; after two a.m., the minks mix with the pool hall types. Whenever you come, have a bowl of minestrone, which is made according to the following recipe. [Mike's gave me the recipe that they use, which produces around forty quarts. For those who plan to feed fewer than eighty or ninety guests, I have cut it down to four quarts, or ten to twelve generous helpings. Both sets of figures appear.]

MINESTRONE

2 lbs. (3 oz.) barley
3 lbs. (5 oz.) split peas
3 lbs. (5 oz.) dried lima beans
3 lbs. (5 oz.) dried red beans
2 heads (6 stalks) celery, chopped
2 bunches (6 leaves) chard, chopped
1 large head (¼ small head) curly Greek cabbage, shredded
3 or 4 (1) leeks, chopped
3 lbs. (5 oz.) salt pork chopped fine
4 or 5 (1) onions, chopped

garlic, to taste (1 clove)— optional
2 quarts tomato purée (1 cup purée, plus 2 cups solid pack tomatoes)
salt and pepper to taste (2 to 3 tbsp. salt, 1 tsp. pepper)
dry sweet basil to taste (2 tbsp. basil)
assortment of squash, eggplant, spinach, etc., cut into slices
1 lb. (3 oz.) uncooked macaroni (rice or other paste can substitute for, or supplement, the macaroni)
fresh grated Parmesan cheese

Rinse barley and peas and boil in 2 quarts of water for 1 hour. Rinse lima beans, boil in 1 quart of water for 1 hour; mash. Rinse red beans, boil in 6 cups water for 1 hour and 15 minutes; reserve. Add the chopped celery and chard, the shredded cabbage, the chopped leek and 1 quart of water, to the barley and split pea mixture. Cook over low flame. Sauté the diced salt pork with the chopped onion and garlic until lightly brown. Add the tomato purée and solid pack tomatoes. Cook a few minutes together, then add to the barley and split pea mixture. Add the mashed lima beans, salt and pepper, dry sweet basil. Cook for one-half hour. Add squash, eggplant, spinach, etc. Cook for one-half hour longer.

Cook macaroni ten minutes in 6 cups water. When soup is ready to serve, add cooked red beans and macaroni and heat through. Serve with a generous sprinkling of grated cheese.

The Buena Vista Cafe ✳

2765 HYDE STREET

inexpensive

AT THE CORNER OF HYDE AND BEACH STREETS, JUST WHERE THE cable car turns around, the Buena Vista Cafe dispenses good but simple food and an unusual range of drinks. It is a pleasantly ramshackle place, very crowded on week-end evenings, at Sunday brunches, and any night after the theatre. It is in favor with people from the neighborhood, businessmen from all over, socialites, and the sports car set—at least to judge by the variety and abundance of wire-wheeled, tonneau-covered two-seaters parked diagonally along its curbing.

William Niemann established the cafe in 1901, and stayed with it until his retirement in 1940. The present owners, John Koeppler and Vera and George Freeberg, have kept the place unpretentious; this is certainly, in a day of chrome and gilt, one of its great charms. Although it is primarily a bar, and has made its reputation as a place to drink, it is a pleasant place for lunch or snack, or a simple unlingered-over dinner.

Several years ago Stanton Delaplane, a *San Francisco Chronicle* travel writer and columnist, brought back from Shannon Airport in Ireland a drink that has made the Buena Vista famous, Joe Sheridan's Irish coffee. Nowadays you can order the Sheridan invention almost any place that keeps whipping cream on hand, but the Buena Vista is still the headquarters for drinkers with an addiction to seven-year-old pot-still Irish whiskey. They also mix up a smooth and authentic New Orleans Fizz—an excellent drink with which to begin a Sunday brunch. They are experts on that peppery combination, Tequila con Sangrita, the traditional nip at the cockfights in Guadalajara, and rapidly gaining aficionados in the Bay Area. They concoct and dispatch with authority negroni, Swedish punch, vermouth cassis, asbach uralt, amer picon punch, calvados "l'écusson," and the four varieties of Pimm's cup. They are proud to offer pisco punch, a drink from out of San Francisco's more boisterous past. And they have, what's more, one of the most distinguished and complete stocks of beer that it has been my pleasure to contemplate: from Germany, Norway, Austria, Denmark, Mexico, Malaya, Japan, Canada, France, Switzerland, England, Italy, Czechoslovakia, Holland, Australia, the Philippine Islands, Scotland, Ireland, and of course Milwaukee—in any shade from pale to extra dark.

Their wine card is impressive, listing mainly château bottlings from the best years of the last decade in France, and a limited but intelligent choice of German, Italian, and California wines. There is also on hand a small store of some of the really great vintages from abroad, but you have to ask about these. For people at the other end of a budget, there is house wine by the glass; or better, by the decanter—for less than the cost of one drink at the bar.

As for the Buena Vista's menu, Coney Island clam chowder, seafood cocktail, shrimp Louis—and fresh crab, in season—are standbys. You will find besides, an assortment of cold cuts, frankfurters, smoked oysters, imported herring tidbits, and brisling sardines, served with green salad or potato salad. If you are in the mood for cheese, there is a tray of imported favorites. If you feel like something more substantial, there are grilled ham or club steaks, and grilled steak sandwiches, pan fried chickens, French fried prawns or eastern scallops. Each day there are two or three special dishes, besides. On Mondays there are hamburger steaks, old-fashioned beef stew, and breaded veal cutlets; on Tuesdays, the menu lists potted Swiss steak, Italian pot roast with ravioli or tagliarini, and Irish stew; on Wednesday chicken sautéed with steamed rice, sauerbraten and potato pancakes, and braised sirloin tips with mushrooms; Thursday brings chicken pot pie, boiled beef with horseradish sauce, and Hungarian goulash with noodles; on Friday, besides pork sausage cakes with country gravy, there is a pot roast of beef, pounded steak, and a small and very inexpensive dinner steak added to the regular menu; on the week ends, there are always country sausages—or ham, bacon or link sausages, if you prefer—served up with a side of eggs, as well as pot roast, veal cutlet, and dinner steak. Every day there is soup for non-clam eaters, and an excellent velvety cheesecake.

Here are three recipes, given me by John Koeppler, for the best known drinks at the Buena Vista bar.

IRISH COFFEE

for each serving:

1 Irish coffee glass (short-stemmed, tulip shaped)	¾ cup hot black coffee
	1 jigger Irish whiskey
3 cubes domino sugar	lightly whipped heavy cream

Preheat the glasses by pouring in very hot water and letting them stand for a minute or two before emptying. Put three sugar cubes in each glass and fill immediately about three-quarters full of very hot coffee, stirring until the sugar is completely dissolved. Add Irish whiskey, and top with whipped cream, spilling it over a spoon to form an even head. Speed is important, because the drink must be served piping hot.

NEW ORLEANS FIZZ

for each portion:

1 tbsp. granulated sugar	1½ oz. heavy cream
1 tbsp. lemon juice	1 jigger gin
3 dashes orange-flower water	cracked ice
1 tbsp. egg white	2 oz. sparkling water

Combine all ingredients except sparkling water with an electric blender. Add sparkling water just before removing. Strain into chilled fizz glasses.

TEQUILA CON SANGRITA

Tequila, white or gold, according to preference.

sangrita:

12 oz. orange juice	1 oz. finely chopped onion
3 oz. lemon juice	1 tsp. salt
1 oz. Burgundy wine	1 tsp. tabasco sauce
1 oz. grenadine	

Combine all ingredients except tequila and chill well. Serve each person one glass of straight tequila, one glass (same size) of chilled sangrita. The Buena Vista uses long thin 2-oz. Mexican glasses, filling them with about 1¼ ounces each. To drink, alternate slow sips. Never mix, and—not that you could get much of that sangrita down in a hurry—take it easy. The sangrita in this recipe will make about fourteen servings.

❋ *Sam's Anchor Cafe*

27 MAIN STREET • TIBURON

moderate

SAM'S IS IN TIBURON BUT EVERYONE SEEMS TO THINK IT'S WORTH the twenty mile trip. In good weather customers arrive on foot, by car, and by boat, in any costume as long as it isn't fancy. They assemble by the dozens on Sam's fine rickety deck jammed with tables and chairs, and join other sunworshippers sipping ramos fizzes and munching giant hamburgers on sour dough rolls. From Sam's the view is always extraordinary. Beyond the bare feet, striped jerseys, and sun-tanned nouvelles blondes, is one of the great sights of the area: a stretch of bay, sometimes silver smooth, sometimes dark and turbulent, before a magnificent view of San Francisco.

Sam's is run these days by Hank Rubin and Jim Bigelow, who formed a company to manage just such places. It was, before their purchase in 1960, the property of its originator, a man of tremendous gusto and good will, Sam Vella. Now in his mid-seventies, he lives with his wife in an apartment only a few steps from the restaurant, and reminisces warmly about his many years on the water's edge in Tiburon.

He started out in 1920 with a two-burner coal-oil stove in a sixteen by eighteen foot tent, just where Sam's is now. He had arrived from his native Malta two years before, and worked as a fireman at the St. Francis Hotel and as a laundryman at the Palace. But on Sundays he always went for an outing to Tiburon. He decided to go into business there, and had to settle for the tent because the town had burned in a recent fire. The canvas cost him eighteen dollars in a local Army supply store. Besides its two-burner stove, it housed several tables set on saw horses, and three cots. Sam started his routine with an early swim in the bay, and then set to cooking up three meals a day for the three hundred workmen who ran the railroad barges to and from the city. Meanwhile, he also fed a small number of carpenters engaged in rebuilding activities, and took a good many swipes with the hammer himself, helping them build more permanent housing for his cooking operations.

During prohibition, when many a regular restaurant closed, Sam kept right on cooking, but ran his place like a boarding house, occasionally inviting the general public to partake of hot dogs or fresh clam chowder. In 1934, he opened as a genuine restaurant, and started off with fish dinners. Sam was a good cook, and his reputation spread. Before long, crowds were mounting to about twenty-five hundred people a week. Sam loves to recall the quantities of food and liquor consumed in those days: he ordered in fifty cases of gin and other spirits every two weeks—"why, we'd serve fifteen gallons of gin fizzes and one hundred cases of beer on Sundays alone!"—seven hundred loaves of French bread, and eighty dozen rolls a week! Between six and seven hundred people ate Sam's hamburgers every Sunday, and his wife—who made the salad dressing—spent eight hours fortnightly on each batch of fifteen gallons.

The most popular of all of Sam's dishes were his cioppino—still a favorite, and one of the recipes that we have here included—his steamed clams, and clam chowder. Sam—and Sam's—always cooks the cioppino to order; that is, the sauce, made well in advance, simmers on the stove, but the fish is added only when an order comes in. Sam used to dig his own clams, or buy them from the local clammers, about four miles away. They aren't available any more from such local diggings, but fresh clam chowder and steamed clams are still favorites on the menu. You can get a large serving of the clams—or fried prawns—as an hors d'oeuvre, one of the best accompaniments to a drink that I can imagine. In the old days, Sam used to soak his native clams for three days in various changes of water before steaming them with parsley, celery, and onions. He used half for orders of steamed clams, the rest for chowder. He put in a special bread oven, and made an impression on his customers by serving them only hot crusty French bread.

Up front Sam's has a fine dark bar dating from the old days; and at the end of the deck, a few steps down, sailors tie up an assortment of yachting craft. Sam recalls many an occasion when a big boat from Sacramento would anchor off shore and its cargo of government officials and businessmen would spend the whole week end dining at Sam's: cioppino on Saturday night, French toast, bacon, sausage and pork chops for Sunday breakfast, and a fine roast beef dinner before sailing back up the river.

Messrs. Rubin and Bigelow know the value of the property they have purchased. There has been little sprucing up, the menu remains very much the same, and habitués, though they miss the genial Sam, are relieved that the new management plans to carry on in the same casual fashion.

Sam's is open for breakfast and doesn't close again until 2 a.m. so that you can get a drink, meal or snack at your own pleasure. The menu lists salads and sandwiches—among them one of Sam's specialties, hamburger on French bread, and a rarer item, abalone on a French loaf; dinners and platters featuring excellent seafood and fish—sole stuffed with crab, sand dabs, pan fried rainbow trout among them; broiled meats and chicken; and a good cheese cake.

The most fun at Sam's is to come on a good day, lounge around on the open deck without having to rush, order whatever strikes your fancy, and enjoy it in a rare aura of relaxation—with view. Hank and Jim have given me the recipes for Sam's Special, and their delicious crab cioppino.

SAM'S SPECIAL

wine sauce: *4 to 6 servings*

3 tbsp. fresh creamery *unsalted* butter	1 cup milk, heated to lukewarm
3 tbsp. flour	1 tsp. freshly ground nutmeg
6 oz. fine dry sherry wine	1 generous pinch white pepper

fish: *per portion*

melted butter	1 tbsp. chopped shallots
1 large or 2 small filets of Pacific sole	1 tbsp. pimiento
	1 tsp. fresh lemon juice
3 oz. crabmeat	½ jigger sherry wine

Melt the butter in a heavy bottomed sauce pan. Add the flour, stirring constantly over low heat until all the butter is absorbed; add the sherry wine, a little at a time, stirring to avoid scorching. When smooth and free from lumps, add 1 cup of lukewarm milk, a little at a time, stirring continuously. When smooth and very thick, add freshly ground nutmeg, and a large pinch of white pepper. Simmer for three to five minutes to cook flour, stirring all the while. This makes enough sauce for four to six servings.

Brush bottom and sides of an eight-inch casserole boat generously with melted fresh butter. Line bottom of casserole with 1 large or 2 small filets of sole per portion. GENTLY, toss each 3 oz. of crabmeat with 2 or 3 tablespoons wine sauce, 1 tablespoon chopped shallots, and 1 tablespoon pimiento, being careful not to break up the claw meat. Spread the crabmeat over the filets of sole. Cover crabmeat with another layer of sole. Brush with melted butter. Sprinkle surface with 1 tsp. fresh lemon juice and ½ jigger of sherry wine. Bake in hot oven (400°) for 12 minutes. Remove from oven and spoon more wine sauce over the fish. Serve piping hot with plenty of warmed crusty French bread.

[I find that a light sprinkling of salt at the end is agreeable—at least to my taste.]

CRAB CIOPPINO

½ cup celery, diced fine

½ cup onions (use shallots in place of onions, if available), diced fine

½ cup bell peppers (sweet), diced fine

½ cup fine California olive oil

6 large fresh tomatoes, skinned and chopped

1 tsp. tomato paste

1 tsp. salt

½ tsp. hand rubbed dry oregano (remove all stems)

½ tsp. hand rubbed dry sweet basil

½ tsp. freshly ground black pepper

½ clove fresh garlic, crushed (optional—but don't leave it out)

1 pinch cayenne pepper (optional)

1 cup good quality California Barbera wine (if this wine is not available, use slightly more Pinot Noir or Cabernet Sauvignon)

1 cup water

1 large Dungeness crab

1 to 1½ doz. clams in their shells

1 doz. medium green shrimp in their shells

Sauté the diced celery, onions, and bell peppers in the olive oil until the vegetables are tender but not brown. Add the chopped tomatoes, tomato paste, salt, oregano, basil, pepper, garlic, cayenne, wine, and water. Simmer for at least two hours. If it becomes too thick, add water. Skim all oil from the surface. Correct seasoning.

Clean and remove the legs and claws from 1 large crab and divide the body section into quarters, leaving it in its shell. Scrub the clams with a stiff brush under cold running water to remove all sand. Wash thoroughly one dozen green shrimp under cold running water. Simmer the shellfish in the sauce for ten to fifteen minutes, or until the shrimp turn pink and clamshells open wide.

Serve family style in tureen with plenty of crusty French bread and a slightly chilled bottle of the same Barbera wine used in preparing the sauce. Serves two to six people, depending on their appetites and upon what else is served in the way of salads or dessert. The owners of Sam's prefer personally to have nothing else except a few strips of Monterey Jack cheese with strong black coffee. I won't argue.

The Glad Hand ✳

588 BRIDGEWAY · SAUSALITO

moderate

SNUG BETWEEN FANCIER SAUSALITO NEIGHBORS, THE BARN-RED Glad Hand nestles on a dock, bay windows facing out over the water to an unsurpassed view of San Francisco, often accented by a lean and gallant sloop lying at anchor off its pilings. On the same dock, but beyond the restaurant itself, and separated from it by a garden contained entirely in bidets, chamber pots, and other quaint pottery, squats a small cottage, once rented but now used as office space.

In this most unlikely setting, the Glad Hand pleases its customers with home-cooking at not too exorbitant prices, and a fine array of wines and beers. There is no hard liquor on the premises. A continuous show of paintings on the walls exhibits the not always successful efforts of various local artists, hung at no cost to them, and changed monthly.

The building, an old Victorian false front, was owned by one family until its more public days. The original owner rented launches, and brought the mail from San Francisco to Sausalito before ferry service took over in 1917.

After certain shady days during prohibition, and a later career as a cabaret called the Tin Angel, the premises became a restaurant in July of 1951, under the management of an ex ice-skating star. Albert K. Engel, one of the present owners, who joined and then bought out the originator, acts as both manager and chef. Bob Thompson, his partner, who also cooks, is married to Monica who used to live in the cottage out back. One of their assistants is artist Serge Trubach, who works part time as soup chef and dishwasher, and who ran in a recent municipal election as one of Sally Stanford's opponents for the Sausalito city council. They both lost, but Sally not so badly as Serge. In the summer months, the bar is often manned by vagrant intellectuals, the most notable of whom is the high school teacher and art collector Manug Terzian, who performs at the Glad Hand when he isn't off to Europe to add to his Picasso collection.

The place is cozy; at the bar you can order, besides a wide range of wines and beer, such good things as Rainwater Madeira, Mandorcrema, and champagne cocktails. There are a few tables in front, the kitchen down the middle, and nine or so tables in the rear, these with a view of Monica's flourishing geraniums and the San Francisco skyline. The atmosphere can best be described as rustic-Victorian, an amazing hodgepodge of old furniture, relics, and gew-gaws. The menus are charmers, each different from the other, and combining—with illustrations of the most quaint order—a sense of times-gone-by with the practical matter of the evening's fare. The clientele appears in all modes of attire, most often informal, feeling at home, cheerily amused, and ready for a good meal.

The cooking and menu are not complex, but have a homey touch and a reasonable price. First there is good homemade soup, served in individual pots with handles, and a wedge of iceberg lettuce covered with dressing. The entrées include a fine chicken sauté, lobster tails with drawn butter, steaks broiled crisply on the sides but juicy within, and inexpensive specials Monday through Thursdays. While they last they include such dishes as Italian veal, curried lamb, braised short ribs of beef, beef stroganoff, chicken and mushrooms, and oriental beef. On Fridays there is always a sea food casserole: paella; filet of sole Monica; or perhaps crab and shrimp in a winey sauce. Every week end there is a fine roast duck vin rosé with orange marmalade. Desserts are extra, but all made in the Glad Hand kitchens, and all delightfully gooey, rich, and calorific, the way a good dessert should be. There are a number of cakes, a fudgy chocolate standing out in my memory, trifle, not a usual item on Bay area menus, and—on the week ends—a smooth and creamy cheesecake. Here are two recipes, handed on to me by Albert.

GLAD HAND SALAD DRESSING

1 medium wedge blue cheese
½ cup hot water
1 heaping tsp. salt
1 heaping tsp. freshly ground
   black pepper

1 heaping tsp. garlic powder
   (or 2 cloves fresh garlic,
   squeezed)
¾ cup sherry wine
1 quart salad dressing or mayonnaise

Melt blue cheese in hot water; add dry ingredients plus sherry wine. Stir. Mix with salad dressing until blended thoroughly. Chill. Serve in generous helpings over large wedges of head lettuce. Stores well.

ROAST DUCKLING VIN ROSÉ WITH ORANGE MARMALADE

1 duckling, 4 to 4½ lbs.
salt and pepper

1 jar orange marmalade
½ cup rosé wine

Season the duckling with salt and pepper and lay on a large piece of foil in roasting pan. Coat generously with a good quality orange marmalade. Pour over it ½ cup of rosé wine. Wrap the foil around the duck completely, seal closed, and roast for 2½ hours in a moderate oven (350°). Uncover, baste with drippings and juices, bake ½ hour longer or until crisp and golden. Serves two to four.

7. CONTINENTAL STYLE

By far the largest number of good restaurants in San Francisco are continental in style. Most of them emphasize Italian or French cooking. They inherit their style of menu from San Francisco's days of greater gourmandise. Their typical huge dinner provides an assortment of hors d'oeuvres both local and imported, pastes or soup—and sometimes both—substantial entrées, a good dessert and coffee. They all feature excellent grilled meats, besides fancier recipes in lovely brown sauces. They have extensive à la carte service that costs considerably more than the dinners. Their decor, like their menus, covers quite a range: trattoria-style, old San Francisco, elegant, and modern architect designed. They include former "Fashion" restaurants, many "old-style" places, several places that are classified under "Italian," and such additional and worthy establishments as Del Vecchio's, Owl 'N Turtle, the Alta Mira Hotel in Sausalito, and Kirby Atterbury's La Caprice in Tiburon.

Adolph's ✳

641 VALLEJO STREET

moderate

ADOLPH'S IS A SMALL RESTAURANT BY DESIGN. ITS OWNER, ADOLPH Motta, limits the size to fifty-five diners so that he can greet his guests personally without neglecting his kitchen, bar, or dining room. He never wants anyone to be disappointed with food or service, and I can't imagine that anyone ever is. He knows almost every person who comes to dine with him, and delights them with continuously excellent food and personal service. Since there are not many tourists, but mainly San Franciscans among its clientele, the customers have developed a noticeable affection for both the restaurant and its personnel. If a waiter is out, the clients miss him with loyal concern. The waiters, in turn, call a great many customers by their first names. Adolph explained to me in his gentle fashion some of his feelings about restaurants: Their heartbeat is the kitchen. A cook, like a singer, is born—you can train either one, but if he doesn't have a feeling for it, he won't ever be more than ordinary. If a glass is dirty, you won't enjoy the best drink in it.

Adolph, who was a partner at the Paris Louvre for fifteen years, bought this spot on Vallejo Street a half dozen years ago. It had been going quietly for thirty years, but closed owing to a death in the owner's family. It was the kind of place that Adolph had been looking for. The bar takes up nearly half of the place, running its length to the kitchen; the dining room fills the other side. Adolph decorated the place gaily. There is a good deal of Pompeiian red splashed around, hanging ceramic plates from near Perugia, stores of bottles, duck presses, and chafing dishes.

Because the emphasis is on Italian-style foods, Adolph stocks several wines that go well with them: Bardolino, Valpolicella from the Verona region, Soave, and Verdicchio. The card also lists good French and California wines.

Dinner starts with an iced green salad mixed at the table with imported olive oil, and served on well-chilled plates. Along with it comes fresh cracked crab, assorted salami, and relishes. I could make a meal on this alone. But onion soup or consommé follows, and then an entrée cooked to order.

There are several specialties, all extremely good. Saltimbocca alla piemontese combines rolls of veal and prosciutto, smothered in mushrooms and white wine sauce. Veal scaloppine comes in a casserole layered with chicken livers and truffles, all bubbling through a sauce, Turin style. Adolph serves a fine filet, center slice, decked with slivers of white Alba truffles. There are three exceptionally fine chicken sautés. The first is a casserole of chicken and sweetbreads; the second a platter of chicken, fresh artichokes, and a delicious tangle of green tagliarini; the third, a classic spring chicken with herbs and fresh mushrooms. There are a number of other enticing dishes, including veal or chicken parmigiana, chicken cacciatore, sweetbreads or chicken livers sauté, boneless squab with wild rice, filet of rex sole en casserole, and a rack of lamb for two, roasted brown and crisp, but rare inside. There are steaks, chickens, squab, chops, and a fine lobster tail brochette grilled over charcoal. Whatever your order, it will be thoroughly hot, and dished up with a good deal of attention.

Another specialty is fresh cooked capellini, served in a casserole of enamelled ironware, ablaze. In fact, Adolph's is known as the house of capellini flambé. The flame, in this case on the outside, maintains the temperature and dazzles the audience, but is otherwise not essential to the recipe. Spaghetti and lasagne are available à la carte, but without a flame.

Besides ice cream and spumone, dessert includes banana fritters under freshly whipped cream, a frothy zabaglione, and Bel Paese cheese.

Adolph has explained to me how he cooks two of his specialties:

SCALOPPINE EN CASSEROLE

18 pieces of round of veal cut very thin (2 lbs.)	1 cup white wine
1 cup milk for dipping	salt and pepper
flour for dredging	1 lb. chicken livers
6 tbsp. butter	1 green onion, chopped fine
6 tbsp. oil	1 can white truffles

Pound the veal. Soak it in milk, then dip it in flour. Put half of the butter and half of the oil in a large skillet and sauté the veal until nicely browned. Remove it to a shallow casserole, deglaze the skillet with wine, and pour the gravy, salt, and pepper over the veal. Sauté the chicken livers—about three pieces per portion—with the chopped green onion in the remaining butter and oil until they are golden brown. Add the chicken livers to the veal, and braise together about ten minutes, over a very low flame, or in a moderate oven. A few minutes before serving, pour a little of the juice from the can of truffles over the meat, and garnish with slices of truffle distributed over the top. Serve very hot. Serves six.

⤙ · ADOLPH'S FILET

2 lbs. of heart of the tenderloin, defatted
¼ cup olive oil
4 handfuls fresh mushrooms

4 green onions
¼ cup red and white wine,
  half and half
1 can white truffles

Slice the filet into 8 pieces, each 1½ inches thick. [Each portion uses ½ lb. of meat, or two slices.] Fry them brown in very hot olive oil. If you like your meat rare, they will be ready when both sides are just brown; if you like your meat better done, extend cooking time to suit your taste. Put meat in heated shallow casserole (one large, or 4 individual). To the skillet, add one handful of mushrooms per portion, sliced vertically, and 1 chopped green onion per portion. Fry them fast. When the mushrooms are almost done, add the wine, and salt and pepper, scrape all the brown from the pan, and pour over the filets. Add a few drops of truffle juice to each serving, sprinkle generously with thin slices of white truffles, and serve very hot. Serves four.

❋ Panelli's

453 PINE STREET

moderate

I HAVE NEVER BEEN TO PANELLI'S WHEN THE GUESTS HAVEN'T seemed to be caught up in its characteristic feeling of warmth and animation. Although it opened only in 1944, it has that settled and comfortable look of a sexagenarian, and fits with ease into its building, which was constructed just after the 1906 fire. Part of its feeling derives from the original Edwardian ceiling, kept purposely intact. Besides the true spirit of hospitality, there is splendid cooking and enthusiastic service.

Four gentlemen share Panelli's success—Joseph Panelli, George Bacilo, Frederick Martelanz (the chef), and Louis Guffanti. But all of the personnel add to the conviviality. Frank, one of the bartenders, besides being a genial fellow, is likely to burst into a medley of old Italian songs as the evening goes on.

Since Panelli's is located in the heart of the financial district, its clientele, particularly at the noon hour, consists largely of brokers, bankers, insurance people, and attorneys, with a sprinkling of city officials, business girls, and those sagacious women shoppers who wouldn't think of passing up a solid San Francisco lunch for the old cliché of fruit and cottage cheese. The restaurant remains open all day, and there is an early evening jumble at cocktail time. One of the niceties at Panelli's is the attractive and tasty hors d'oeuvres that the house provides for its bar guests.

The bill of fare is extensive, and emphasizes Italian dishes. The house specialties include veal scaloppine alla Marsala, fettuccine al pesto, cannelloni with supreme sauce, rack of lamb, boneless squab with wild rice, a double sirloin with mustard sauce, tenderloin tips en brochette with wild rice—a San Francisco favorite for years—and a splendid chicken sauté with fresh mushrooms, carrots, peas, and potatoes parisienne en casserole.

The appetizers include salami, anchovies, shrimp, crab, oysters, prosciutto, imported sardines, and avocado cocktail. With a complete dinner you get an assortment of these, along with a mixed green salad bowl to start things off. Among the soups are a hearty minestrone, clear consommé, and zuppa maritata —wedding soup for two—a fine chicken broth cooked with pastina, then thickened to a creamy smoothness by the addition of egg yolks, butter, and grated Parmesan cheese.

There are delicious pastes here, and because many of them are cooked to order, they are served long before they have turned to unidentifiable mush. Besides spaghetti, cooked al dente, and done up with fresh mushrooms if you can afford them, there is homemade ravioli, capellini undisguised by anything less delicate than butter and cheese, tortellini bolognese, mostaccioli, lasagne, and tagliarini al pesto—that fine Genoese blend of garlic, fresh basil, oil, and cheese. There is, besides, an excellent risotto milanese, and you can order as an entrée chicken cooked with either risotto or capellini.

The rest of the menu is very extensive, running the whole gamut from steaks and chops to Welsh rarebit and Italian *frittata* (omelette). The desserts include assorted French pastries, cheeses, and ice creams, zabaglione, fried cream, banana fritters, crêpes suzette or French pancakes, and baked Alaska.

Panelli's has selected two of its favorite recipes for me:

➤ CHICKEN CACCIATORE

1 large onion	2 cups fresh or canned toma-
4 tbsp. olive oil	toes
1 roasting chicken, 3 to 3½ lbs.	1 cup coarsely chopped green peppers (1 whole pepper)
flour for dredging	¼ to ½ cup chicken stock or
salt and pepper	consommé

Chop the onion coarsely and brown it lightly in 2 tbsp. olive oil. Remove the onion pieces from the pan and reserve for later use. Cut the roasting chicken into serving pieces, and dredge them in flour seasoned with salt and pepper. Sauté the chicken until well browned on all sides in the oil in which the onion was browned, adding two more tablespoons olive oil. Add fresh or canned tomatoes, coarsely chopped green sweet peppers (remove seeds and ribs), and return the browned onion to the pan. Cover and simmer for fifteen minutes over a very low flame. Add a little chicken stock or consommé to the liquid in the pan, cover again, and simmer for about forty-five minutes, or until the chicken is tender. Serves four to six.

FROGS' LEGS PROVENÇALE

½ cup olive oil
2 sprigs dill, minced
1 tsp. chopped parsley
1 small clove garlic
½ tsp. granulated sugar

salt and pepper
12 small tomatoes
18 pairs small frogs' legs
4 cups chicken stock
1 sprig parsley, chopped

Heat olive oil to the smoking point with 2 sprigs of finely minced dill, one teaspoon of fine chopped parsley, a small clove of crushed garlic, and ½ teaspoon of granulated sugar. Add salt and pepper to taste. Peel and squeeze the seeds from the tomatoes [easier if you plunge them in boiling water for a minute], and add them to the mix. Cook over high flame, stirring constantly until the mixture is bubbling hot. Blanch the frogs' legs in boiling hot chicken stock. Drain well and add them to the oil and vegetables. Simmer gently for fifteen minutes. Arrange frogs' legs on a heated serving platter, cover with the sauce, and sprinkle with chopped parsley. Serves three.

The Red Knight ❋

624 SACRAMENTO STREET

expensive

THE RED KNIGHT, A COMPARATIVE INGENUE IN THE RESTAURANT field, has earned a reputation since its opening in 1959 for fine cooking, and especially for a dish characteristic of certain Swiss cities: fondue bourguignonne.

The twenty-five foot width of the Sacramento Street quarters was not too narrow for the gold assay office of Pony Express days that once occupied the site, but it challenged the Red Knight's designers. They came up with a scheme to string out the bar in front, put the open kitchen in the center, and the dining room in the remaining space all the way to the rear. Stairs lead up from the end of the bar to offices, storage rooms, and two private dining rooms, one of them (a current San Francisco necessity), a wine-decked, vine-trimmed "cellar." The decor, a marvelous complexity of rustic-medieval, mixes pecky cedar, crystal chandeliers (a dash of the Edwardian), "driftwood" stone walls, red and gold cut velvet wallpaper (there is Edward again), and an assortment of coats-of-arms, knights on horseback, heraldic emblems, shields, plaques, and one red knight in armor and long red undies.

There is less confusion in the cooking, executed by a Swiss chef, Ernest Lanker, who has spent more than thirty years at his calling, starting as a bus boy in an elegant Swiss hostelry. He spent the nine years preceding his move to the Red Knight as chef at Trader Vic's. In the years between he cooked for top restaurants in Europe and South America. Besides M. Lanker, the Red Knight personnel includes owners Roy Panelli and Max Stone, both long time restaurateurs. The place has an established air about it, largely owing to their presence, and the old-timers shake dice daily with confidence in their surroundings.

The Red Knight offers several appetizers often not listed elsewhere: Malasol caviar with blinis and sour cream, smoked sturgeon, a delightful lobster mousse, and one that you will have to ask the waiter for specially, hot crêpes filled with a delicate crab mixture, then covered over and baked, cannelloni style, in rich cream sauce. There are good soups here too, notable among them the vichyssoise.

There are a dozen entrées that are something quite special. Veal al papagallo contains Canadian bacon and Swiss cheese enclosed in a large steak cut from the eye of the veal, sautéed golden in butter, and finished with a sour cream sauce. Mignon of lamb Rity is a dish of lamb chops topped with beef marrow and marchand de vin sauce. Crab à la Red Knight is a great delicacy: fresh cracked crab poached in white vermouth, covered with chef's sauce, and served in abalone shells. Another good fish recipe is paupiette of sole cardinal: filet of sole stuffed with lobster mousse and covered with a subtle wine sauce. The Red Knight's lobster tail is poached in white wine, then dressed with oysters and sauce cardinal. Chef Lanker likes to stuff capon breasts with a mousse of chicken livers, or—as Chicken Three Colors, a variation on Chicken Cordon Bleu—with prosciutto and Swiss cheese, then glaze them with marchand de vin sauce, and serve with a foil of asparagus. Three beef specialties, tournedos Rossini, stuffed butterfly steak du chef, and the famous fondue bourguignonne, are the recipes which Roy Panelli selected for this book.

Among the desserts are banana fritters, crème caramel, pear belle Hélène, a light rum omelette, a lighter chocolate mousse, pastries baked on the premises, crêpes suzette, and assorted ice creams and cheeses. Strawberries à la Red Knight put a fine finish to a good meal: fresh strawberries, first bathed with cognac and Cointreau, are set aflame, then cascaded juicily over a mountain of ice cream.

TOURNEDOS ROSSINI

for each portion:

1 lb. filet (when fully trimmed it should come to about 12 oz.)
salt and pepper
1 strip of bacon
1 crouton or slice of toast the size of the filet

1 slice of pâté de foie gras (preferably from Strasbourg)
a few slices of truffle (black)
½ cup marchand de vin sauce (recipe below)

Season fully trimmed steaks with salt and pepper. Wrap a slice of bacon around the outer edge, and secure with a toothpick. Broil according to taste. Remove to a hot platter, placing it first on the crouton or toast. Top with a slice of pâté and a few slivers of truffle. Pour very hot marchand de vin sauce over all.

marchand de vin sauce:

6 or more beef and veal bones
2 tbsp. flour
1 carrot, 1 onion, in thick slices
1 stalk celery, cut in large pieces

oregano, parsley, bay leaf, salt and pepper
1 qt. water
1 tbsp. butter
1 tbsp. flour
1 cup Burgundy wine

Spread the bones in a roasting pan, sprinkle with 2 tbsp. flour, and cover with the onion and carrot slices. Bake in hot oven (400°) for at least ½ hour, or until the bones take on a good brown color. Remove them to a large kettle, add 1 stalk of celery in large pieces, oregano, parsley, bay leaf, salt and pepper, and 1 qt. of water. Remove fat from roasting pan, deglaze with a small amount of water, and add to the kettle. Boil the stock gently for three hours or more. During the cooking, skim off any scum that gathers. Strain.

Melt the butter in a skillet, add the flour, blending well, and cook until brown—but avoid burning it. Add 1 cup Burgundy wine, a little at a time. Cook until smooth. Strain and add to the stock. Heat well before using.

[This is a simplified version, an even easier method for home kitchens: discard the fat from the broiling pan, and deglaze the drippings with Burgundy wine.]

✂ STUFFED BUTTERFLY STEAK DU CHEF

16 oz. New York steak
salt and pepper
butter or olive oil
¼ cup or 2 oz. wild rice
6 medium size mushrooms, sliced vertically

2 shallots
1 tbsp. butter
light wine sauce, or sauce of your choice

Trim steak of all fat, slice it in half, but not quite through, and unfold it to resemble a book or butterfly. Season with salt and pepper to taste, and smear with butter or olive oil on the inside, but leave open. Broil one side quickly, then the other. Fill inside with wild rice prepared with mushrooms and shallots (see below), refold —as if closing a book—and secure with toothpicks. Serve very hot, accompanied by a light wine sauce or another of your choosing. Serves two.

WILD RICE: Wash the wild rice in cold water and drain thoroughly. Place in a skillet so that the rice can spread out and cook evenly. Cover ¼ cup rice with 2 cups cold salted water. Bring to a racing boil, then barely simmer about fifteen minutes. Bring to a boil again, turn down and simmer. Repeat this process until the rice is fluffy and all of the liquid is absorbed. Meanwhile, sauté the sliced mushrooms and finely minced shallots in 1 tbsp. butter until they are golden. Add to the cooked rice, and mix in.

WINE SAUCE: See marchand de vin sauce in following recipe. Or, use this simplified way of preparing the dish: Pan broil the steak in butter, instead of on a grill, remove steak, deglaze the pan with red wine, add a dash of Worcestershire sauce, a tiny amount of minced garlic or shallot, and reduce to desired consistency. Return steak to pan, heat through, and serve immediately, pouring the sauce over the steak.

FONDUE BOURGUIGNONNE

The Swiss make a special cooking pot for this fondue. It differs from the dish for cheese fondue, which will work, however, in this recipe, in that it is more upright and has higher sides. If you have neither of these a sauce pan about six inches in diameter and four and a half inches in height will serve the purpose nicely. You will need very long-handled forks, preferably with a wooden (or other cool) handle, one for each diner. And, since this dish must be cooked in the center of the table, you will need some kind of reliable flame, and a stand to hold the pot over it. You can get fondue bourguignonne equipment in specialty shops—and this dish is such fun to prepare that it is worth the considerable investment. Or you can adapt a chafing dish stand and burner, or use a simple sterno stove, available in drug and hardware stores.

filet, ½ lb. per person	assortment of sauces: mustard,
1 qt. clarified butter	soy sauce, catsup, chopped
	onion, sesame seed, curried
	mayonnaise, horseradish

Trim the filet completely, and cut it into cubes of about an inch. Place the meat on two serving platters, and put these on either side of the cooking equipment in the center of the table. Fill the pot not more than two-thirds full of clarified butter [or a mixture of vegetable oil and butter], heat to the bubbling point on the kitchen stove, and place over the table burner to keep it hot. Each diner spears a cube of beef and plunges it into the sizzling fat until it cooks to the degree of doneness he prefers. The sauces and condiments, each in a separate serving dish, should be spooned in dabs around the perimeter of each dinner plate. When the steak is done, the diner slips it off the cooking fork—never, NEVER put that hot fork in your mouth!—spears another piece, and cooks it while he eats the first, dipping it in one or another of the garnishes.

[There are several comments I have to make about this dish. First off, the amount of butter you use depends a great deal on how hot you can keep it at the table, and how many people are cooking in it at once. I find I get better results with about two inches of butter, and that if more than four people are cooking it is better to have two sets of pots going. The Swiss, at least in Lausanne where I first ate this dish, always keep two pots going anyway—one for the table, and the other bubbling on the stove, ready to replace the table pot as soon as it shows the least sign of cooling down. To clarify butter, heat it until it bubbles, skim the top, and after it cooks a bit, pour it into another container, discarding the residue of milk solids which settles to the bottom. As for the sauces, you can think up any number of other good complements to fine beef, the limits of your imagination being the only restriction.]

Ondine ✳

ONDINE IS ONE OF THE FINEST RESTAURANTS IN THE AREA, AND well worth the short trip to Sausalito, where it stands at the Bay's edge, commanding a sensational view. Its clientele is largely from San Francisco, and since its inception it has drawn a steady patronage of educated city diners.

When Fred Martinez and George Gutekunst opened in 1957, their restaurant was unique in several respects. For one thing, the total operation, including the building, was new and original. For another, by the time opening day came George and Fred had no money left, and discovered to their immediate dismay but later amusement that the cash registers contained not a sou with which to make change. They hurriedly floated a small loan in the neighborhood, put the necessary cash in the till, and have fortunately not had an empty register since. Ondine's success was instantaneous. The earnings went back into the business, and silent partners, architects, wine merchants, electricians and plumbers have long since been rewarded for their contributions to the undertaking.

Both Fred and George knew the restaurant business from long experience; between them they had thirty years as waiters in the very best places—both on land and at sea. Their ideas about their restaurant were sharp and definite: there would be no special play for the expense-account trade, and the menu would be primarily haute cuisine. They needed an outstanding chef, and found him in the person of Alfred Roblin, who was given immediate carte blanche in the kitchens. After two years of accolades, he became a full partner. Alfred has been chef at Romanoff's in San Francisco, and before that cooked in good hotels from Bermuda to Dublin to Marrakech. His associate at Ondine has always been Roger Chanteloube, who cooked with him in Bermuda and Marrakech.

The design and decor of Ondine are distinguished but quiet: architects Campbell and Wong preferred to exploit the wondrous view rather than compete with it. Their intelligent scheme, aided by the decorations of Roiccha and Sands, provides one of the area's handsomest dining settings.

Since its inception, the menu at Ondine has been undergoing a metamorphosis. Its direction is one of augmentation and refinement, with its focus narrowing—or expanding, if you prefer—toward the more classic cuisine that is the preference of its owners. The demands on the kitchen are great, depending on chefs and assistants of the highest skills and an expenditure of hours in time-consuming preparations. The management, however, retains several simple dishes on the menu to entice diners with timid palates, who benefit also by prices that are not as high as the haute cuisine justifies.

Chef Alfred is a loyal follower of Escoffier. He acknowledges no favorites among his clientele, however. When he was told some time back that two very prominent persons were among his guests, he announced that he would in the future be delighted to learn that he had been honored by celebrities, but only after they had left. Alfred believes in a good supply of veal, chicken, and white fish bones from which to extract classic stocks by reduction. Sauces made from these stocks are infinitely superior to more half-hearted preparations, and their appeal to the eye is enhanced by a subtle gloss and sheen. Alfred follows Escoffier's recommendations for garnishes; and he sends almost everything—except the dishes of greater simplicity—from the kitchen in silver service, first to be presented, then served. He feels that the greatest challenge to the chef is game, seafood, and fish cookery. He is delighted, when given adequate advance warning, to prepare partridge, grouse, wild goose, a saddle of venison, a fresh trout—in short, anything that an Ondine client has managed to bag, net, shoot, or snare. His greatest success, and anyone who has ever tasted one—or even laid eyes on one—will unstintingly agree, are his soufflés, whether they be orange, mocha, chocolate, Grand Marnier, or strawberry.

Ondine offers a regular dinner, with a dozen choices of entrées, and a full range of entrées à la carte, including some of the house specialties. You can order filet of sole véronique, piquant beneath a glaze of hollandaise and seedless white grapes; or a whole plump squab, boned, filled with wild rice, and sauced with port wine dotted with cherries. There are several fine dishes for two: rack of lamb, marinated before it begins to roast; capon mascotte, baked with tiny potatoes and artichoke hearts in a light veal gravy; pheasant, breast only, daubed with sour cream sauce over wild rice, or the classic bird en plumage; and a fine roast duckling bigarade, its own gravy sharpened by lemon and rounded by orange.

Entrecôte marchand de vin, chicken sauté polignac, grenadin of veal gentilhomme are classics; or there are splendid sweetbreads, chicken livers, tournedos, and steak au poivre or diane. There are a number of grilled meats and some enticing fish and seafood dishes: filet of sole ambassadeur, duglère, or rich with mushrooms bonne femme; there are frogs' legs provençale, broiled salmon in season, and lobster tail Newburg.

Some of the accompaniments are unusual: hollow potatoes soufflées or wilted spinach with crisp bacon. Among the soups is lobster bisque, and you can always enjoy a good double consommé here. The hors d'oeuvres are varied and excellent, and whether your whim is escargots, crab or oysters, herring in sour cream, blinis with caviar, prosciutto and melon, or celery Victor, you can find it well prepared.

If you should have forgotten to order your soufflé—I can think of no other reason to forego it—there are profiteroles filled with ice cream, and doused with chocolate sauce and whipped cream;

cherries jubilee; crêpes suzette; baked Alaska; a number of parfaits and coupes, including marrons glacée. And Ondine serves café filtre.

Here are three of Alfred's classic recipes, each depending for real success on a good stock or gravy.

➤ POULET SAUTÉ À LA DORIA

1 3-lb. chicken, disjointed	1 tbsp. veal gravy
olive oil and butter for frying	½ tsp. lemon juice
1 medium cucumber	2 tbsp. butter
salt and pepper	1 sprig of parsley, leaves only

Fry the chicken pieces in a mixture of oil and butter in a heavy skillet until they are well browned. Seed the cucumber, and cut into pieces the size and shape of garlic cloves. Add this to the chicken, season with salt and pepper, and cook a few minutes longer. Remove chicken and cucumber to a casserole, and finish cooking in a moderate oven (350°) for thirty minutes. While the chicken is stewing, pour off the fat from the skillet, add 1 tbsp. veal gravy and ½ tsp. lemon juice, and deglaze the pan. In another pan brown 2 tbsp. butter until it reaches the smoking point. Add a mince of the parsley leaves immediately, and stir this into the pan gravy. Just before serving, pour the pan gravy over the chicken and cucumbers, either in the casserole, or on a hot service platter. Serves six.

➤ FILETS DE SOLES POLIGNAC

3 mushrooms	1½ tbsp. butter
2 lbs. of filet of sole (or six filets)	2 tbsp. fish velouté (recipe below)
½ cup white wine	1 tbsp. julienned truffles (black)
4 tbsp. liquor from cooking mushrooms	1 oz. butter

Simmer the mushrooms in 1 cup of water until they are just tender. Remove and cool them, then mince into fine pieces. Reserve the cooking liquor. Poach the fish, folded double, about ten minutes in the white wine, 1½ tbsp. butter, and 4 tbsp. of the mushroom liquor. Butter an oval baking dish or shallow casserole, and arrange the drained filets in it. Reduce the cooking liquor until it is half its original amount. Add two tbsp. fish velouté, minced mushrooms, and julienned truffles; swirl in 1 ounce of butter until it melts and the sauce bubbles. Pour the sauce over the filets, and set in a hot oven (425°) for five minutes. Serves six.

velouté:

1 scant tbsp. butter	1 cup fish stock (recipe below)
1 heaping tbsp. flour	salt and pepper

Melt butter, blend in flour until smooth, add fish stock, heated, a little at a time, stirring constantly. Cook over low heat until thickened and smooth. Season to taste with salt and pepper.

fish stock:

1 onion, sliced	½ tsp. lemon juice
4 stalks of parsley, stems only	½ cup white wine
1 lb. white fish bones, heads, and scraps (Escoffier says that perfect stock derives only from the bones of sole or whiting; but in cases of dire emergency one part in four of turbot bones may be accepted)	½ cup water (or enough to cover)
	salt to taste

Put onions and parsley in a saucepan with bones, lemon juice, wine, and enough water to cover. Bring to a boil, skim the surface, then simmer uncovered for one half hour. Strain, and season to taste with salt. An acceptable—to me, but I don't know about Ondine—shortcut substitutes clam juice for fish bones. Proceed as above, using ¾ cup canned clam liquor instead of fish bones, and no salt. Yield: 1 cup of fish stock.

➤ ## TOURNEDOS MASCOTTE

6 raw artichoke bottoms,
quartered
1 tbsp. butter
1 lb. very small new potatoes
2 tbsp. butter
12 tournedos (round, thick
cuts of filet of beef)

2 or 3 black truffles, cut into 6
pieces, the size of olives
salt and pepper
2 tbsp. butter
¼ cup white wine
¼ cup brown stock or gravy

Fry the artichoke bottoms in 1 tbsp. butter until lightly browned. Cover, and cook over low heat about ten minutes, or until just tender. Peel the potatoes, and cut into olive shapes. Brown in 2 tbsp. butter, shaking the pan to prevent sticking. When evenly colored, cover and cook over low heat—with an occasional shake of the pan—for ten minutes, or until tender.

Season the tournedos with salt and pepper and fry quickly in butter. Place in a casserole and arrange the artichokes, potatoes, and truffles around them. Discard the fat from the tournedos pan, and deglaze with white wine. Add gravy or stock, and cook until it reduces by half. Strain and pour over the tournedos and garnishes. Put the casserole in the oven just long enough to heat through. Serves six.

✳ ## *Doros*

714 MONTGOMERY STREET

expensive

DOROS IS ONE OF THE FEW LUXURY RESTAURANTS THAT PROVIDES San Franciscans with both lunch and dinner, and caters besides to an adjoining private dining club. Doros' own dramatic interior has severe black leather chairs and banquettes juxtaposed to blood red carpeting, dark woods, antiqued mirrors, and gold washed brick. Lamps branch out of the ceiling, a hundred tiny lights twinkling in their own firmament. The bar is curtained off from the rest of the place by an old Italian device, a mobile beaded curtain, colored gold.

Only ten years ago Doros, then Piro's, was a small place with an open kitchen. Its success convinced the management to introduce silver service and serving carts, and finally to expand. They hired Mario Gaidano to plan a complete remodelling, and an extension into the building next door. At just about this time, owner Piro moved to Palm Springs, and the two remaining partners, Don Dianda and Roger Bertola (who has since retired because of ill health) renamed their showplace Doros—Do for Don and Ro for Roger.

Served by the same kitchen, and accessible from another street, are some of the most elegant eating facilities in the city, the Villa Taverna, belonging to a club of about two hundred members. It is named after the villa of the United States ambassador in Rome, and in luxury of detail it is somewhat reminiscent of the Hostaria dell'Orso restaurant in the same city. Housed in a former courtyard, and also designed by Gaidano, it is dedicated to "l'Idea del Buon Mangiare," expressed by a benevolent Italian marble Goddess of Good Food installed over the entry.

The façade of the villa, rugged grey stone with an irregular set to it, lends the building the granite solidity that suggests a nobleman's palazzo, and the enormous black iron and glass torchères which flank the entrance might, but for the fact that their flame is now fanned by electricity, cast light and shadow on the night wanderings of a long-ago people in a far-away place. The street, originally an alleylike passageway, has been planned by Thomas Church to become a thoroughfare as esteemed as the famous Maiden Lane in the center of the city. At this writing, the drawings show waves of mosaic tiles undulating gracefully down the street.

The Villa Taverna's interior has a remarkable quality that preserves, although it encloses it, the special charm of Italian

227

courtyard dining. Beyond this, it has managed to capture a clarity of light that one associates with the Umbrian sun, softened and playful as it filters through a translucent skylight against the whitewashed brick walls. A small railed terrazzo, with a striking black floor, is raised a few steps above the main courtyard. Across the way a balcony, festooned with a stunning red and Roman pink awning, provides added dining space, as well as the ceiling for an intimate and darkly pleasant bar. The only other decoration is a mural, Roman in feeling, and a rich array of polished wooden carts, glinting silver, and shimmering crystal. The tables, draped in long-skirted pink linen, bloom with gay arrangements of fresh flowers.

Doros is noted for its excellent complete dinners, with a choice from eighteen entrées. À la carte there is an even larger selection. There are the usual deluxe appetizers: crab legs on ice, prosciutto and figs, escargots, pâté de foie gras from Strasbourg, scampi, Beluga caviar by the ounce. Among the soups are green turtle laced with sherry, and a rich zuppa maritata. Doros fixes sole in a half dozen ways—with wine or cream sauces, mushrooms, spinach, or a swash of melted butter and a sprinkle of minced greenery. The pastes are numerous and varied; my own preference is for fettuccine tossed lavishly with no more than butter and cheese. The specialty of the house is cannelloni. There are also homemade ravioli and tortellini, a fine southern Italian plate of linguine with clams, spaghetti with Bolognese meat sauce, and risotto in the classic style of Milan.

Among the house specialties are golden breasts of chicken, bursting with herb butter à la Kiev, or with melting fontina cheese and slivers of ham in the manner of the Italian Valle d'Aosta. There are several delicate sautés, including chicken Jerusalem, dotted with mushrooms and hearts of artichokes, then bathed in cream and sherry wine. There are first rate meats and fowl from the grill, including several double cuts of prime beef. If you like zucchini—or better still, if you don't, but have an open mind about it—try one of the two ways that Doros serves them. The dessert list contains a happy number of rich and frothy combinations—zabaglione, soufflés, homemade cheese cake—and an assortment of delicious things in flames. They serve café espresso here and it is the best way to finish an Italian meal.

Don Dianda has kindly provided me with Doros' delicate recipe for veal piccata, another name for scaloppine.

VEAL PICCATA

2 lbs. veal, cut in very thin slices, 2 by 3 inches	½ cup white wine
	about 6 capers per portion
flour	3 or 4 small pieces of sweet butter
3 tbsp. butter	
1 tbsp. lemon juice	salt and pepper to taste

Pound the veal pieces flat with a mallet [or ask the butcher to prepare them]. Coat them with flour. Sauté the veal slices in 3 tbsp. melted butter until they are lightly browned on both sides. Add lemon juice, white wine, and capers. Reduce liquid slightly, and swirl in three or four small pieces of sweet butter to finish the sauce. Taste to correct seasoning with salt and pepper. Serve about four slices per portion. Serves 4 to 6.

Paoli's

MONTGOMERY AT CALIFORNIA

expensive

PAOLI'S A DOZEN YEARS AGO TOOK OVER THE SITE OF THE VENERABLE Collins and Wheeland Restaurant, a part of the Montgomery Street scene from the early 1860's until its demise before the Second World War. In the old days, when Sam Collins and Jim Wheeland ran things, their chief clientele came through the mud from the Mining Exchange across the street. No women entered the premises until the mid-Thirties. The all-male assemblage rollicked in the boisterous privacy of the bar, heartened by a free lunch of giant slabs of corned beef, turkey, ham, wedges of imported cheese—and on special occasions, chunks of crackling suckling pig to be hacked off by any hungry carver at will. Reports have it that A. P. Hotaling, whose name went down in history as the proprietor of a distillery left unscathed by the 1906 fire while all the churches burned, supplied Collins and Wheeland with an average of fifty-five barrels of liquor a week. The sight of all this cooperage lined up in front of the place was impressive even in those days of hyperbole. In one anemic but probably authentic version of the origin of Hangtown Fry, this one attributed to Duncan Nicol, the proprietor of the swanky Bank Exchange Saloon, a Collins and Wheeland cook by the name of Dennis simply thought the thing up one day. When the great fire razed San Francisco, Collins and Wheeland were not as blessed as Hotaling's Distillery. After the flames, a number of men from the old California Market, a property adjacent to Collins and Wheeland's California Street entrance, came into the business, and besides rebuilding and later redecorating were responsible for the eventual admission of ladies.

Joe Paoli, who bought the site and took over the tradition, but has otherwise no connection with the former restaurant, was born in Chicago of Italian parents who had emigrated from Camaiore, a small town near Florence. His father, a cement finisher, found work in San Francisco when Joe was two, completing decorative cornices and façades for elaborate residences typical of the Marina district. Jacopo Paoli housed his family in a flat on Osgood Place just across from the Gay Nineties, and by the time Joe reached grammar school he had secured a job as potato and onion peeler in that night club's kitchen. He grad-

uated to shucking oysters and serving cocktails at Alioto's restaurant on Fisherman's Wharf through his friendship with a
son of the family. His chosen career was engineering, and he
gave up his spare time restaurant work to attend engineering
college. During the war he worked first as a draftsman in the
shipyards, then went to sea as galley man on a Pacific transport.
By the war's end he had served on several liberty ships, become
chief steward, and acquired an enviable knowledge of food preparation. And most fortunately! After only a month's work for
a building contractor, he knew that construction engineering
was not for him. One evening, dining at Maye's Oyster House
on Polk Street, he quite impetuously offered the owner all of
his savings—some $9,000—for a share of the business. The
owner, with equal impetuosity, accepted, and for the next five
years Joe helped to run one of the city's fine old seafood restaurants. But Joe had learned about a lot more than fish in his
earlier experiences, and he was anxious to try a business on his
own. At this point he bought the old Collins and Wheeland
building.

Joe's partner in his new venture was his wife Rita, who contributed, besides energy and talent, a good number of the furnishings that were meant to complete the Paolis' new home.
The restaurant dining room, aided by Rita's not-yet-installed
living room wallpaper and several handsome antiques, took on
a homey warmth. Today Paoli's has expanded three times, its
menu is a lexicon of good foods, and its kitchens are guided by
chef de cuisine Patane and supervised by the celebrated French
chef Lucien Heyraud—for many of the great years executive
chef at the Palace.

At Paoli's there are two special dining rooms. One of these
is a room for private parties, which emulates the captain's quarters of an old English frigate. Here you can command in advance whatever feast you like. In the other, called the Lordship
Room, guests with reservations may choose from a special

gourmet menu that is a clear reflection of the genius of Messrs. Heyraud and Patane.

Paoli's appetizers are unusual: zampino, a small version of the delicious pork salami stuffed into the skin of a pig's foot by the good people of Modena, Italy; eggs à la russe; mushrooms in a fine marinade; smoked eastern sturgeon and Nova Scotia salmon; baked eggplant with Parmesan cheese; calves' tongues and pigs' feet; broiled scampi; pickled artichokes; and prosciutto from Parma. The soups include a petite marmite with paillettes de fromage (spangles of Parmesan cheese over the top turned brown and bubbly by the broiler) based on a stock that requires twenty pounds of beef, and available only in the Lordship Room. There are a dozen or more seafoods and fish, sautéed, broiled, poached, and fried, a fine stew of calamari and prawns, a curry of lobster, prawns (or chicken), and golden soft shell crabs from Chesapeake Bay. The selection of pastes is good: there are various spaghetti, gnocchi, fettuccine all'uovo in the style of Alfredo, tortellini, green tagliatelle, risotto milanese, cannelloni stuffed with veal and chicken, and linguine with clams. My favorite entrées from a long list are côte de veau, Cordon Bleu, garnished with gnocchi; the rack of spring lamb with parsley; and a heady mixture of chicken livers and mushrooms accompanied by risotto. There is delicious pheasant chicken baked in clay and served with soufflé potatoes and truffle sauce; on advance order there is salmon mousse decorated in the manner of the French master Carême. The vegetables are varied, and such succulent nourishments as baby carrots glazed with butter and chives, braised French endive, mushrooms sautéed in white wine, or giant white buttered asparagus from Belgium delicately touched with mace, or chilled with a vinaigrette topping, enliven the section that on many cartes du jour provides no more than a monotonous repetition of string beans and creamed spinach.

For dessert, besides soufflés, ices, and good things in flames, there is a fine, moldy gorgonzola, cream cheese with Bar-le-Duc, and a spectacular crema romana—creamy coffee-flavored pudding liberally laced with two liqueurs, crème de cacao and Tia Maria. Rita Paoli's grandmother used to feed this to her family in Italy, where Rita learned the recipe.

The restaurant is open—and jammed—for lunch. Its noontime menu is a brief résumé of the supper fare, with the addition of some light and appropriate dishes, salads and sandwiches, and a secretaries' lunch. This last, for a moderate fee, is guaranteed to forestall any hunger pangs for the rest of the afternoon, and includes good strong coffee—insurance against the inevitable throes of relaxation that might render somebody's right-hand girl heavy-lidded and bumbling for the rest of the afternoon.

Lucien Heyraud has given me the following six fine recipes:

PICKLED CELERY WITH ANCHOVIES

4 celery hearts	1 tsp. oregano
water to cover	a good dash of cayenne pepper
juice of ½ lemon	1 sprig thyme
1 pt. oil	1 bay leaf
juice of 6 lemons	salt and pepper
½ pt. wine vinegar	1 tin flat anchovy filets
1 clove of garlic, crushed	½ medium pimiento
1 tbsp. chopped parsley	

Trim, wash, and halve four select young celery hearts of equal size. Parboil for eight to ten minutes in water just to cover, to which has been added the juice of half a lemon. Prepare a mixture of the oil, remaining lemon juice, wine vinegar, garlic, parsley, and seasonings, and set it to boil. Add the parboiled celery and cook until tender. Remove celery to serving plate, and decorate each branch with filets of anchovies and strips of red pimiento. Serve very cold, as an hors d'oeuvre, accompanied by a few drops of the cooking liquor. Serves four.

CONTINENTAL STYLE

COLD CREAM VICHYSSOISE

4 medium leeks, white part only
1 oz. butter
3 medium potatoes, finely diced
1 pt. white chicken stock or consommé

1 pt. milk, boiled
½ oz. butter
salt and white pepper
1 pt. cream (whipping cream preferable)
1 tbsp. chopped chives

Mince the white part of the leeks into fine pieces. Stew the minced leeks gently for ten minutes with 1 oz. of butter. Add the finely diced potatoes. Moisten with the pint of white chicken stock or consommé, and set to cook gently for thirty minutes or more. When well cooked, add the boiled milk and ½ oz. butter. Stir in well. Now rub the whole through a fine sieve. Season to taste. Chill. When very cold and ready to serve, add 1 pt. of heavy cream and sprinkle one spoonful of chopped chives over the top. Makes about 2 quarts, or eight servings.

FILET OF SOLE AMANDINE

6 filets of sole
salt and pepper
milk
flour
¼ cup butter

2 tbsp. blanched, sliced almonds
juice of ½ lemon
1 sprig parsley, minced fine

Wash and dry the filets of sole, then season with salt and pepper. Dip them first in milk and then in flour. Heat the butter in a large skillet, and sauté the filets until they are golden brown on both sides. Remove them to a heated serving platter. In the remaining butter quickly fry the sliced almonds until they are golden brown. Pour the butter and almonds over the sole, add the lemon juice, and sprinkle over the parsley. Serves six.

CHICKEN SAUTÉ PERSILLADE

1 young 2½ lb. chicken, disjointed
salt and pepper
flour

3 tbsp. butter
½ cup dry white wine
1 small clove garlic, chopped
½ tbsp. chopped parsley

Season the chicken with salt and pepper, then dip in flour. [Shaking the pieces in a paper bag with a small amount of flour insures an even coating.] Sauté in butter in a large skillet. When nicely browned, remove to a hot platter. Add the white wine to the juices remaining in the pan. Add the chopped garlic and chopped parsley. Stir well to incorporate all of the brown particles. Taste for seasoning, then pour over the chicken. Serves four.

GREEN GODDESS SALAD

3 cups mayonnaise
8 to 10 filets of anchovies, chopped into small pieces
1 scallion, chopped fine
2 sprigs of parsley, chopped fine
2 tbsp. tarragon leaves, chopped fine

1 tbsp. chives, minced fine
½ cup tarragon vinegar
1 clove garlic
assorted salad greens: romaine, escarole, chicory, broken into pieces

Add the chopped anchovies, scallion, parsley, tarragon, chives, and vinegar to the mayonnaise, and mix well. Rub the salad bowl with a cut clove of garlic. Arrange washed and chilled salad greens in the bowl, add at least 1 tbsp. of dressing for each person, and toss together briskly.

STRAWBERRIES ROMANOFF

2 qts. strawberries
sugar to sweeten
1 pt. vanilla ice cream

1 cup whipping cream
juice of ½ lemon
¼ cup Cointreau

Wash and stem the berries, sweeten to taste, and put to chill. Whip slightly 1 pt. of vanilla ice cream. Whip heavy cream until very stiff and fold into the beaten ice cream. Add the lemon juice and Cointreau and stir in. Pour the cream mixture over the chilled berries, blend quickly and serve in iced bowls. Serves eight or more.

HENRY'S FASHION IS THE SOLE SURVIVING RESTAURANT OF A FOR-
mer half-dozen that used in their names a special designation
for individualistic cooking prepared in the style of—or in the
fashion of—a particular chef: Louis, Gus, Charles, or in this
case Henry. The term "fashion" borrowed meaning also from
the word "fashionable," and thus suggested to patrons that the
food would also be elegant, continental, and excellent. Henry's
Fashion retained more than its name well into the 1950's: diners
in the marble-floored, high-ceilinged room were seated at baro-
nial tables, or sealed in private booths, and summoned waiters
by ringing—and waiting—for them. Many customers came from
the ferries that docked at the foot of Market Street, a short, pleasant jaunt to Henry's on the Davis Street corner. The regulars
included one doctor who arrived daily for thirty years precisely
on the stroke of noon. The restaurant received a crippling blow
when ferry service was suspended, and limped along on the sentiment of a narrowed number of old-timers. It finally gave in
gracefully to the times, ripped out the walls and booths, and
replaced them with redwood and brick, mahogany and flagstone,
modern upholstery, and a number of fixtures designed to give
the place an air of cheerful modernity. Two things were retained:
that important word "fashion," and the warmth that had long
marked the place as one of forthright hospitality. When customers gather around the piano they raise their voices in a conviviality that is Henry's present fashion.

The original proprietor, Henry Cristiani, opened the place in
1919. One of the subsequent owners, George Rovetti, was known
for his garden of miniature pine trees grown with seeds sent him
from Italy. At Christmas time he gave crippled children at Shrin-
ers' Hospital a large number of them, tinselled and bejangled,

and their joy through his gift inspired Perry Patton to write a Christmas fantasy about Giorgio and his pine trees. George has passed away, but his son George, Jr. is one of the four men— all with a heritage of old restaurant families—who direct Henry's Fashion today. His partners are Benny Candela, Piero Tomei, and Tullio Picchi. Piero's operatic tenor voice often enlivens the cocktail hour.

The menu is sparked with such Italian savories as buttered linguine topped with pesto—a Genoese sauce of fresh sweet basil, Parmesan, oil, parsley, and sometimes walnuts, all macerated in an old-fashioned mortar with the pestle from which it takes its name. There is veal scaloppine or rollatine in several variations; a first-rate chicken cacciatore—or the same bird dressed with lasagne or risotto; saltimbocca, here prepared Bolognese style: a slice of veal layered over with one of prosciutto, sautéed in a winey brown sauce, and served handsomely decked with rice and vegetables. When melon or figs are in season, they are always on Henry's menu as the classic accompaniment to prosciutto. For dessert there are pancakes alla marmellata, zabaglione whipped with Marsala, and café espresso.

Henry's Fashion has a representative continental-style menu, with specialties such as glazed breast of capon cooked in white wine; or medallion of tenderloin, nicely browned in butter, perched—dripping brown juices—on a base of eggplant, and finished with mushrooms and gravy. Broiling is all done over charcoal, and a number of dishes come to the table for flaming in cognac before the final dabbling and swishing of the sauce. Henry's serves Chateaubriand Richelieu, a dish that would have sent Veblen into a double delirium: extra thick filet mignon is first packaged inside a round steak, then broiled over the coals, and served planked and wreathed with a gardenful of vegetables. But I would rather have, and I usually can't resist it, a plebeian broiled round nose sole along with an honest dish of homemade tartare sauce. Henry's does this to perfection.

Henry's complete dinner starts with assorted appetizers, goes on through courses of salad, soup or paste, entrée, and dessert. This is the only restaurant that I know of in the city where the excellent traditional fried cream and banana fritters are augmented by concoctions rarely tasted by those who read the menu from right hand column to left. At Henry's, crêpes suzette and cherries jubilee are part and parcel of the regular dinner.

Henry's is open for lunch—and it's a jolly place to eat—with a menu of good hot dishes (jumbo stuffed Louisiana shrimp, pot roast with tagliarini, lamb fries, calf's liver with onions or bacon), salads, soups, seafoods, a sandwich or two. And broiled round nose.

Chef George has given me these two fine recipes:

➤   CHICKEN CACCIATORE À LA EDY

¼ cup olive oil	1 tsp. rosemary
2 2-lb. chickens cut in pieces	¼ cup white wine
1 medium onion, sliced	1 cup tomatoes, mashed
1 large bell pepper, sliced	1 small can ripe olives
1 lb. fresh mushrooms, sliced	salt and pepper
1 clove garlic, chopped	

Heat olive oil in a large frying pan, add chicken, and brown on all sides. Remove chicken (keep warm), put in onions, bell pepper, and mushrooms. Cook for three minutes; add chopped garlic and rosemary, cook for ½ minute, then pour in wine. After 1 minute, add browned chicken, mashed tomatoes, and ripe olives. Add salt and pepper to taste. Simmer over low flame until tender—about twenty minutes. Serves four.

➤   GRENADINE OF BEEF À LA GIORGIO

3 lbs. filet mignon	¼ cup tomato sauce
flour	½ cup beef broth
1 tbsp. olive oil	½ tsp. rosemary
1 lb. fresh mushrooms, sliced	salt and pepper
1 clove garlic, chopped	1 sprig chopped parsley
3 oz. sherry	

Trim all fat from the filet, and slice it ½ inch thick. Flour it lightly [shake with a small amount of flour in a paper bag], and brown about one minute in very hot olive oil in a large skillet. Turn meat, add mushrooms, and cook about one minute more. Lower flame, add garlic, cook ½ minute, then add wine. When wine heats through, add tomato sauce, beef broth, rosemary, and salt and pepper to taste. Simmer for 6 minutes, sprinkle parsley over the top, and serve immediately. Serves four to six.

Lambros

315 BUSH STREET

moderate

LAMBROS, WHICH CHARLIE BARDELLI AND JOHN JEROME OPENED as recently as 1946, nevertheless has an authentic air of old San Francisco about it. The bar which runs the length of the room, is the original and famous Waldorf Bar, one of the most splendid along the early cocktail route, and later the chief adornment of the Palace Hotel's Comstock Room. Joseph Mares, the present proprietor, was formerly a partner in Grison's and the Paris Louvre. His menu lists a good cross-section of continental dishes, from wiener schnitzel to neapolitan spaghetti, and his planked steaks, sautés, and roasts are equally fine. The lunch crowd is mainly from the financial district, and the clientele is in general —Joe says about ninety-five percent—composed of local people.

Here are two recipes for typical Lambros dishes, kindly provided by Joe Mares.

➤ BEEF WITH SOUR CREAM SAUCE

1 2-lb. filet of beef
2 oz. fat bacon
2 oz. lard
1 onion chopped
7 oz. vegetables: 2 small carrots, 2 small stalks of celery, chopped
1 sprig parsley, minced
5 peppercorns

½ bay leaf
1 tsp. allspice
½ pt. sour cream
1 tsp. flour
a few drops of vinegar or lemon juice, or a little grated lemon peel
salt

Trim filet of fat and gristle. Thread strips of bacon through the meat. Melt the bacon fat in a baking tin and fry in it lightly the chopped onion and vegetables with the parsley, peppercorns, bay leaf, and allspice. Add the meat and cook in a moderate (375°) oven until brown (about 25 minutes), adding a little water if needed. When well browned, remove and slice the meat and keep hot. Mix the flour with the sour cream, add it to the sauce in the baking tin, and simmer on top of the stove for a few minutes. Pass the finished sauce through a sieve (along with the vegetables in it). It should be brownish and thick. Add salt to taste, a few drops of vinegar, lemon juice, or a small amount of grated lemon peel, according to your preference. Pour the sauce over the slices of filet, and serve with dumplings or noodles. Serves four or more.

➤ STUFFED CABBAGE LEAVES

1 large white cabbage
kettle of salted boiling water
1 lb. minced raw beef
8 oz. cooked rice
2 medium onions, grated, or finely minced

salt and pepper
½ to 1 cup tomato purée
¼ pt. water
3 tbsp. brown sugar
6 tbsp. sultanas (white raisins)
1 tsp. lemon juice

Pull the leaves of the cabbage except for the small ones at the heart. [To facilitate this, soak the cabbage head in the hot water just long enough to loosen the leaves.] Cut the hard core out of the largest leaves. Put the trimmed leaves in the salted boiling water for five minutes. Drain and dry them with a cloth. Mix the meat, rice, grated onions, salt and pepper, with a little of the tomato purée as binding. On each cabbage leaf spread flat, place 2 tbsp. of this stuffing mixture, roll up into a neat parcel and tuck the ends in. Line a pan with a few scalded cabbage leaves, and lay the parcels side by side on these. Pour over the remaining tomato purée, about ¼ pt. of water, the brown sugar, sultanas, and lemon juice. Cook over very low heat for at least two hours. If the liquid evaporates, add a little more water from time to time. Serve with sour cream on the side. Serves six.

The Domino Club ✳

25 TRINITY PLACE

moderate

ALTHOUGH MUCH OF THE DOMINO CLUB'S FAME IS OWING TO ITS collection of more than two hundred paintings—most of them of nudes—its owner Larry Geraldi, who comes from a Fisherman's Wharf restaurant family, is at least as proud of his kitchen and his cooking. All of his food is cooked to order by a kitchen staff entirely European-trained; all of the meats are hung and aged on the premises; all of the fish are brought in by Geraldi fishing boats. At noon the Montgomery Streeters who trek down the little Trinity Place alley for lunch find perennially amusing the Domino Club's most prominent painting: "Gloria," who lolls over one end of the bar, and who—after you've stared long enough—seems to move just a little. The artist comes in to check her lighting all the time (wrong lighting, no movement). Gloria unabashedly exposed herself to the eyes of 250,000 admission paying spectators during the 1939 San Francisco World's Fair, where she undulated no more, no less. Another noteworthy canvas is Benedetto Luti's "Betrothal of Aurora to Jupiter." Lest it be suspected that the Domino Club's remarkable collection derives solely from raffish interests, let us remember that the nude in the bar is a venerable San Francisco tradition which the Club merely perpetuates to generous excess.

Here is Larry's recipe for one of the many good dishes on his menu:

LOBSTER THERMIDOR

1 boiled lobster
1 tbsp. butter
2 shallots, chopped
6 mushrooms, sliced
1 tsp. English mustard
½ cup dry white wine
½ cup white cream sauce
salt and pepper
Parmesan cheese

Remove lobster without breaking the shell. Cut the lobster meat into ½ inch dice. Melt butter in sauté pan, add shallots and lobster meat, sauté until warm. Add fresh mushrooms, and sauté another minute or two. Add mustard and dry white wine. Reduce for five minutes. Add cream sauce slowly, blend well, and simmer for two or three minutes. Add salt and pepper to taste. Stuff the mixture back into the lobster shell, sprinkle with grated Parmesan cheese, and bake in a hot oven (400°) until the lobster obtains a rich golden brown color. Serves one.

✳ *Swiss Louis*

493 BROADWAY

moderate

THIS FINE SMALL RESTAURANT IN THE HEART OF NORTH BEACH has been going for a half dozen years, and owes its success largely to the personal attention of its two Swiss-Italian partners, John Marconcini and Louis Marguetti, who supervise bar, pantry, and kitchen, and know most of their guests. They have had a good deal of previous restaurant experience. Louis owned the Three Little Swiss for many years; John, who once worked there, cooked long before that for Tait's at the Beach, one of the famous old-timers. The menu is not large, but the food is good. John supervises as well as trains all the chefs himself. If you give advance notice, and if the schedule permits, he will fashion a delicate cheese fondue for your party. This with a good French bread for dunking, a crisp salad and a dry white wine makes a fine light supper. Twice a week there is polenta, generally with Swiss steak for Tuesday lunch, or with baked sea bass on Fridays. Other specialties are saltimbocca, and mustard culotte steak. Boiled beef is on the menu every day, in relief to the heavy spicings and sauces that one so often finds in continental cookery. There are always good fresh vegetables, and button mushrooms on the steaks. Louis' is noted for cappuccino—San Francisco style, that is—a velvet drink of steaming chocolate and brandy. John has given me three recipes for meat dishes, the first of which he prepares at tableside. You who have chafing dishes can do likewise.

SCALOPPINE

per portion:

¾ lb. choice cut of veal, cut into five thin pieces	chives, chopped fine
	4 or 5 sliced mushrooms
flour	½ glass sherry wine
oil and butter	chopped parsley

Pound the veal well, then dredge with flour [shake in a paper bag with small amount of flour]. Fry in oil and butter mixed, until nicely browned. Add finely chopped chives, sliced mushrooms, sherry wine, and chopped parsley. Simmer until cooked—about five minutes.

CONTINENTAL STYLE

CULOTTE STEAK

1 culotte steak, 1½ lbs.
¼ lb. butter
1 tbsp. mustard (prepared)
a few drops of Worcestershire
  sauce

1 tbsp. paprika
fresh ground black pepper
juice of 1 fresh lemon

Broil the steak over charcoal slightly under the degree of done-ness you prefer. Place in a fireproof serving platter over a low flame. [This is the time to use the chafing dish.] Add the butter, mustard, Worcestershire sauce, paprika, black pepper, and lemon juice. Turn and swish the steak until the butter and other ingredients blend, poking the meat with a fork so that it will absorb the flavors. Slice in wide slabs—three per portion—and serve on hot plates, pouring the juice over. Accompany with julienne cottage-fried potatoes. Serves two.

SALTIMBOCCA

per portion:

¾ lb. choice veal, cut into
  two slices
2 slices prosciutto
mixture of herbs, according to
  taste: oregano, rosemary,
  thyme, marjoram, sage
1 black truffle, chopped

garlic, amount according to
  taste, minced fine [op-
  tional]
1 2-oz. cube Monterey Jack
  cheese
flour
olive oil
½ glass white wine
½ cup mushroom gravy

Pound the veal with a mallet. On each slice put one slice of pros-ciutto. Smear with a mixture of herbs, chopped black truffle, and minced garlic. Put the cube of Monterey Jack cheese in the center, and roll up the veal slice. Dredge with flour, and fry in hot olive oil until browned—about four or five minutes. Add ½ glass white wine and ½ cup mushroom gravy, reduce heat, and simmer for about five minutes uncovered. Serve with wild rice and button mushrooms.

Rubini's ✳

10 OLEMA ROAD • FAIRFAX

moderate

RUBINI'S IS LOCATED IN FAIRFAX, A SHORT DRIVE FROM SAN FRAN-cisco. The pleasant, airy dining room overlooks a brook gurgling past alders and walnut trees. There is a piano bar—besides the standard one—a changing show of local artists' paintings, the warmth of a brick fireplace, and a general air of friendly well-being. Owners Dick Templeton, who serves as maître d'hôtel, and Gordon Jones, whose job is co-chef, met by chance in San Francisco a dozen years ago. Jim Duncanson, the other chef, once cooked for Samuel Goldwyn. The food is well prepared, and such small details as peeled tomatoes, well-iced relishes and good hot dinner plates are not neglected. The menu features rabbit à la Rubini, breast of capon Cordon Bleu, calf's sweet-breads with mushrooms, shallots, and Rhine wine, and gar-licky frogs' legs provençale. The co-chefs have supplied two reci-pes which are favorites with their patrons: lobster steak, and shish-kebab, the latter served in a darkened room on a flaming sword.

LOBSTER STEAK RUBINI ◄

per portion:

1 large lobster tail	1 tsp. chopped shallots
1 beaten egg	½ cup sliced mushrooms
¼ cup flour	½ cup white wine
¼ cup oil	¼ cup chicken stock
2 tbsp. butter	lemon wedge

Remove lobster from shell and cut down the center lengthwise, but not all the way through, so that the meat butterflies. Dip into egg, then flour. Sauté in hot oil until golden brown. Drain off oil, add butter, shallots, and mushrooms, and sauté until mushrooms are limp. Add wine and chicken stock, cover, and simmer over low flame for fifteen minutes. Remove lobster to a heated platter and reduce sauce to desired thickness. Pour over lobster and serve with garnish of lemon wedge.

SHISH KEBAB

1 4-lb. leg of lamb cut into two-inch cubes	¼ tsp. fresh ground pepper
	1½ tsp. oregano
one onion, chopped	2 cloves garlic, crushed
juice of two lemons	1 green pepper, cut in chunks
½ cup olive oil	8 mushroom caps
1 tsp. salt	2 onions, cut into quarters

and—if you are doing this à la Rubini's:

1 darkened room	1 fireproof vest
1 flaming sword	

Mix together the onion, lemon juice, olive oil, salt, black pepper, oregano, and crushed garlic. Add the lamb cubes, mix well, and marinate at least two hours. When ready to cook, alternate lamb, chunks of green pepper, mushroom caps, and onion quarters on skewers. Broil according to taste, preferably over charcoal. Turn to brown evenly, and baste, when needed, with butter. Serves four.

8. ITALIAN

When the corner of Davis and Pacific streets was still part of the Bay, an enterprising immigrant took over an abandoned sailing ship, anchored it there, and began cooking up batches of pasta and scaloppine. If this was not the city's first Italian eatery, at least it was its most unusual one. Signor Bazzuro had to give up his ship when the Bay was reclaimed, but he didn't give up his peasant-style restaurant. As soon as he could, he built new quarters close to the original spot. In 1906 he lost that establishment to the flames, but was among the first to rebuild, and his unpretentious new restaurant, managed by his family, thrived for years after he had passed from the scene.

The town has always been brimming with good Italian eating places. In the late 1930's, the Old Grotto was still dishing out its famous ravioli in the very same Washington Street spot where it started in 1862. Fior d'Italia, which opened in 1886, is still one of the city's best loved Italian restaurants. The Fly Trap, Bonini's, Coppa's, both Solari's, the Dante, Steve Sanguinetti's, Il Trovatore, the Gianduja, Buon Gusto, Campi's, Lombardi's—these are all old-time names, some of them still on the scene—of some local fame when the subject is Italian cookery.

San Francisco may be a Spanish name, but it is the name of an Italian saint. The city owes a great part of its charm and many of its mores to the color and size of the Italian population, which began arriving in force during the mining days. The early settlers —mostly fishermen—lived in perilously perched dwellings jutting from the side of Telegraph Hill. The fishing fleet is still Italian, and Fisherman's Wharf is a direct outgrowth of this enterprise. Every year the city joins in the annual blessing of the fleet.

The area called North Beach (because it was once exactly that) is now several blocks inland from the water, and the center of the Italian community. On upper Columbus Avenue, you will hear as much Italian as English. Factories and stores are full of hanging sausages and salami, racks of noodles stretching dry, bouquets of fresh basil and dandelion, baskets of dried codfish and mushrooms, and mountains of cheeses. In the early years of the century cellar windows looked on private wine presses all through the area. Down in the basement the grape harvest, piled into tubs, was crushed by human feet. Nowadays you will see instead shop windows lined with the straw-wrapped pudgy bottles of Chianti and Orvieto, or taller ones of Nebbiolo and Valpolicella. As you walk the streets, your nostrils will be pleasantly assaulted by the smell of coffee roasting black, or by a waft of Parmesan being freshly grated. The bakery windows fulfill childhood's wildest dreams: little cakes, big cakes, pilings and mountings of creams and colored icings, the most luscious confections that whimsy and tradition can supply.

There is for this large Italian community, a daily language paper, "L'Italia," as well as daily radio programs broadcast in the mother tongue. The whole city participates in the Columbus Day parade and celebration, and a commemorative statue of the Discoverer of America stands high on Telegraph Hill.

The North Beach neighborhood is brimming with Italian restaurants—and there are others dotted through the city. Buon Gusto, Jake's, and San Remo are typical of the legion of places that offer good meals for a very modest cost. On the other hand there are the expensive and deluxe Amelio's, an old-timer, and La Strada, a handsome newcomer. La Strada is designed like an avenue with alcoves along its way where bar patrons lounge all'italiana and watch the passersby—in this case diners on their way to the malfatti, cannelloni, piccate, costolette, and fagiani served in the dining room in the rear. Somewhere in between are Vanessi's, noted for nearly thirty years for its minestrone, now marketed commercially, and other Italian specialties; Ray's Bar, tucked away in one of the city's prime locations near the corner of Columbus and Broadway with accommodations for only a handful of diners who come for the thick broiled steaks, the excellent pastes, and salad with homemade vinegar dressing; and New Joe's, long a fixture on Broadway, and one of the most reliable short order restaurants in the city. The menu, lettered over the counter, serves as well for diners in the booths, and there are such excellent items as huge broiled hamburger steaks between pieces of French bread; roast prime ribs of beef piled high with an accompanying order of spaghetti; Joe's special: egg, spinach, ground beef, and a pick-me-up of seasoning; or an airy zabaglione whipped up right before your eyes. Nino's, in the financial district, is a fine upstairs place, noted for gnocchi, zuppa inglese, and the best frittata I have had in San Francisco, the eggs heavily accented with spinach, mushrooms, and prawns. At Pietro 311 on Washington Street, Italian specialties are served in an old San Francisco atmosphere replete with song—all of the busboys and waiters double on the vocal chords.

For more limited refreshment there are a number of Italian coffee houses and cafés. The Trieste Café offers, besides its excellent espresso and cappuccino (Italian-style), a caseful of tempting pastries, and a juke-box full of Italian melodies and operatic arias. The Tosca, noted especially for its San Francisco-style cappuccino, has a full range of bar specialties besides, and a machine stacked with old-time operatic records. One of my favorite places for espresso is not a coffee bar at all, but the Graffeo, a modest and shabby little shop run by Giovanni Repetto, a Genoese coffee merchant. He roasts to order your pound or more of beans—his own blend of eight varieties—with a sad eye, a shake of the head, and a short dissertation on the evils left lurking in the more lightly roasted American-style coffee. While the beans tumble and steam, he starts up a pleasantly grumbling espresso machine on the small counter, and after a decent interval, persuades it to yield up two demi-tasses of splendid black coffee, which he genteelly offers.

The restaurants that follow represent cooking from various regions of Italy. American taste, as well as an abundance that allows us to put more sauce than pasta on a plate, has somewhat changed the cuisine from what native Italian restaurants would offer. The cost of labor precludes the cooking of pasta firm—*al dente*—except at additional cost, and limits cannelloni to a pancake existence. This is not bad, but it is far inferior to the real thing, cannelloni made of sheets of the very lightest dough. Although in many cases San Francisco restaurants serve first soup and then paste, while any good Italian can tell you that they are one and the same course, or offer *pasta mista*—a platter of ravioli, tagliarini, *and* spaghetti—somewhat akin to serving steak, fish, and fowl all in the same dish, they manage in most instances to preserve the authentic flavors of old-world dishes, and sometimes improve upon them by the quality of the meat they are fortunate to have.

Oreste's ✳

118 JONES STREET

expensive

ORESTE'S IS A DELUXE RESTAURANT SET IN THE MIDST OF THE TOUGH and squalid downtown area known as the Tenderloin. Its owner, Joe Piccinini, counted on the city's love of good food to find the place out, and it did. Localites, opera stars, the city hall crowd, and numerous theatre people bask in the hospitable setting, surrounded by racks of wine, copper duck presses, Venetian chandeliers, Deruta pottery, a good quantity of dark red leather, and platefuls of pungent Tuscan cooking.

Joe was born in Lucca, and in 1946 fulfilled a lifelong ambition to come to the United States. He worked at several old-time restaurants in San Francisco: Vanessi's, Panelli's, and Amelio's, and there met another Tuscan immigrant, Oreste Orsi, who was making a local reputation as a chef. The two men first became friends, then business partners. Oreste's career started in Torino in 1927 as a dishwasher in the Ristorante Vittoria. He was promoted to cutting up vegetables, and by 1930 had started to cook. After some time in Milano, which he liked less well than Torino, he went to cook for the Italian Army, preparing the officers' mess for almost ten years. He was captured by the Germans and spent the next twenty-nine months a prisoner. He learned German from his captors, Russian and French from his fellow prisoners, and took to cooking for the other internees whenever there was anything to cook. There was, besides little to eat, little to do. So to pass the time he began whittling and working at the simple food that came for their mess. He finally constructed with the help of some of his fellows a delicately sculptured rose out of a potato, a batch of pasta from the starchy white bread, and a gorgeous pastry cake, iced with curlicues and flowers from peelings and scrapings. It was a thing of beauty, and they presented it to the German officers, who got the point, assigned them positions with a little more to do, and gave them a little more to eat. When Oreste was finally liberated from the Nazis by the Russians, he was forced to march through Poland—a good 725 kilometers—before he escaped to the American forces in West Germany with the assistance of the Polish underground. He and his closely-knit family came to California. He hopes to spend more time with them all, now that he has left Oreste's with plans to start a small place of his own.

The menu is large, and each portion individually prepared. There is a splendid assortment of pastes: spaghetti with ricotta or with vongole (tiny Italian clams), ravioli with meat sauce, tortellini, baked green lasagne, risotto, tagliatelle, and homemade cannelloni—these filled with chicken, veal, ricotta and Parmesan cheese, then baked in a covering of tomato and cream sauce. The excellent fettuccine is among the recipes that follow.

Sportsmen are invited to bring their own game, which will be prepared with traditional Tuscan expertness. Oreste's sauce for duck, for instance, is made from blood and bones, red wine, a little butter, laurel leaves, Worcestershire sauce, fresh ground pepper, dry mustard, and a suggestion of currant jelly. There are several other specialità della casa, all highly recommended: chicken alla toscana, a sauté of capon, artichokes, mushrooms, and olives; saltimbocca alla romana, a roll of thinly sliced veal enclosing prosciutto, melting fontina cheese, white truffles, and sage, simmered in a liberal dousing of white wine and Marsala. Rollatine are similar to saltimbocca but without the truffles. Scaloppine are kept classically simple, with just a dash of butter, a dash of lemon, and the gentle touch of a final scattering of parsley. One of Oreste's best fish dishes is filet of sole alla romana. Each portion consists of two filets rolled around a well-mixed filling of fresh crab meat, raw beaten egg, parsley, oregano, and a little tomato, then cooked until rosy, and served with a handsome accompaniment of polenta and spinach. Veal Oreste, and breast of capon Valdostana, are both specialties for which I give Oreste's recipes below.

Among the desserts, on a list that is complete with the usual fancy items, is an almost runny gorgonzola, zabaglione tipsy with Marsala and grenadine, and—given a day's notice—that elaboration on the English trifle, zuppa inglese, a spongy cake soaking up custard, liqueurs, sweetmeats, and whipped cream.

Here are three of Oreste's recipes:

BREAST OF CAPON, VALDOSTANA

1 whole breast of capon, boned	flour
3 oz. prosciutto	1 beaten egg
3 oz. fontina cheese	olive oil for deep frying

Cut breast in half at the front center. Cut each half lengthwise so that it opens like a book. Close half the prosciutto and fontina inside each half breast. Dip them in flour, then in beaten egg. Fry for fifteen to twenty minutes in enough olive oil to cover. Drain well and serve on heated platter with an accompaniment of fried zucchini and mushrooms dorée. Serves two.

⤞ FETTUCCINE ALL'ALFREDO (ALLA ROMANA)

1 lb. freshly made noodles
  (recipe below)
plenty of boiling, salted water

1 pt. half and half, ½ lb. butter, and 1 nutmeg (or, ½ pt. whipping cream, and ¼ lb. of butter)
4 or more handfuls of grated Parmesan cheese

Boil the noodles in briskly bubbling water for 3 or 4 minutes [if noodles are not homemade, the cooking time will be longer: boil until just tender]. Drain and dress immediately with one pint of half and half and ½ pound of butter. Grate a very little fresh nutmeg over the top, and simmer over very low flame until the sauce reduces to a creamy but not too thin consistency. Serve with a handful of grated Parmesan cheese on each portion.

or [I like this way better]

Melt ¼ pound of butter, add four or more handfuls of grated cheese, and ½ pint of heavy cream whipped slightly. Beat until light and well blended. Toss into cooked and drained noodles, and serve immediately. Serves four.

This is the way Oreste's makes noodles:

4 eggs
1 lb.—more or less—good flour, sifted (Oreste's suggests that you ask in a bakery for a hard, all-purpose flour to be used for pastes)

½ cup olive oil
salt

Break the eggs into a well in the flour. Mix in a little at a time with your fingers. When half the egg is mixed with the flour, add the olive oil and salt in the center. Continue mixing in the flour until it is all blended. If needed, add a few drops of water. Work the dough for at least fifteen minutes, but better for half an hour, until it is glossy smooth, light and elastic. When kneaded, roll out on a floured counter with a floured rolling pin until it is very thin like a sheet of paper. [If you are new at noodle making, divide the dough into two or three sections, work and roll out each one separately.] When it is thin and even, flour it lightly, and roll it up. With a sharp knife, cut it in ¼ inch widths. Pick up each cut roll by the center and shake—the noodles will unfurl like streamers of confetti. You can use them immediately, but it is preferable to dry them, spread on towels, for one half hour. Makes about one pound, or enough for four servings.

VEAL ORESTE

1½ lbs. filet of veal (rib eye or filet)
1 large piece of prosciutto
butter for frying

½ glass Marsala
½ glass sauterne
1 white truffle
½ oz. brandy, heated

Butterfly the filet by cutting sideways from one edge almost to the other so that it opens like a book. Put the prosciutto in the center and close the meat over it. Fry it gently in hot butter for about fifteen minutes, turning once to brown both sides. Pour Marsala and sauterne over it, and add the truffle in thin slices over the top. Simmer until sauce is reduced by half. Remove the veal to a heated serving dish, pour over it the sauce with all of the brown scrapings from the pan, and the heated brandy. Flame the brandy, and serve immediately. Oreste's suggests spinach or asparagus as a good accompaniment. Serves two.

NOTE: Beef can be made using the same recipe, but altering the cooking time for rare, medium, or well done, according to your taste.

✳ Fior d'Italia

621 UNION STREET

expensive

ANGELO DEL MONTE OPENED FIOR D'ITALIA ON MAY 1, 1886. IT has been ever since one of the city's finest Italian restaurants. Its clientele includes San Franciscans from every corner of the city, including a regular contingent of Italians who always celebrate their most important family occasions here. The list of celebrities who have become faithful patrons is impressive: Caruso and Tetrazzini, Mary Pickford and Douglas Fairbanks, Broderick Crawford, Rita Hayworth, Rex Harrison, Eva Gabor. The most loyal of all the Fior's guests was Louis Scaglione, who for more than fifty years happily ate all his lunches and dinners there. Once a year he made an exception and took Sunday dinner with his niece at her San Francisco home. He worked as a tailor at the fine gentlemen's haberdashery, Bullock and Jones, and put most of his funds into stocks. When the '29 crash came, he lost almost everything. He asked the owner, then Papa Marianetti, if he could charge his meals and pay at the end of the month. Papa obligingly kept a record, entering vague marks to satisfy his customer, but charging only a very modest sum when payment day came around. The last three years he wouldn't allow Scaglione to pay at all, reassuring him with an offhanded "Pagherà." ("You'll pay some day.") Marianetti, an immigrant from Maggiano, a town between Lucca and Pisa, came in as a partner in 1896. George and Frank Marianetti, his sons, Armando Lippi, brother of a later partner, and Leo Quattrin, the chef, run the business today.

George Marianetti loves to reminisce about the early days. It was his chore when he was very young to deliver the fresh, white aprons—hot, and all rolled up—to his father after school; his invariable reward was a dish of ice cream and a pastry. When he was in the first grade his teacher always dismissed him early so that he could fetch her an order of Fior's ravioli for her lunch. When he was twelve, George started to work after school. From the early 1900's through the First World War, when Fior devoted a second floor to revelry and entertainment, George was stationed at the bottom of the stairs to announce "Music and Dancing Upstairs." When he was fourteen his idol was a beautiful blonde who sang in the show, but whom he knew only by her picture posted at the outside entrance. Then his chance to see her finally came. His father ordered him upstairs one night —but alas, to the darkest recesses of the kitchen, there to wash a thousand dirty glasses with sandsoap and cloth. He got a dollar's pay and sore hands, but never saw that blonde singer. When he was sixteen he became a full-fledged busboy, and recalls with amusement and appreciation that his father followed close on his heels to speed him up.

Every day his father drove the Chrysler to market to buy produce for the restaurant. He would dump the load on the family table in the rear of the restaurant, and the boys and Papa would start in shelling peas and stringing beans. Pretty soon Basilio Lippi, another partner, would join the group, and conversation vied in animation with the nimble fingers at work on the beans. Barsotti the butcher would bring in a couple of legs of veal, and Papa Marianetti would sing out a "Come va?" and a "Vieni quà," and Barsotti, before he knew it, would be at work shelling peas. Salesmen who came in, Mr. Collins the cop on the beat, Father Mario, and everyone else who entered, would be invited to sit down and talk, and nine or ten people would be shelling peas and stringing beans before the hour was up.

The happiest time at the restaurant—and the happiest day that George ever saw—was November 11, 1918. The schools were closed because of the flu epidemic, and George was busily at work writing out the day's menu on the duplicating machine. About 11 a.m. the doors flew open. A bunch of workers from the biscuit factory nearby, flour flying in great clouds around them, burst in screaming "The war is over!" They were followed without pause by crowds of hilarious and joyful citizens, who celebrated the end of hostilities until six o'clock the following morning. They jammed into the dining room, and crowded straight out to the curb, eating and drinking in long-awaited release. Signor Puccinelli, whose father had owned Il Trovatore in the early years of the century, arrived with a group of fifty. The Marianettis opened the upstairs dining room and sent up a cook. Puccinelli, who knew the business, set it up and served. George, realizing after many hectic hours that he had had nothing to eat since breakfast, grabbed up a broiled steak, ran into one of the private booths designated for ladies, and gobbled it down. When the restaurant finally closed the next morning, after the most marvelous time in anyone's memory, it was completely out of everything: wine, bread, chicken, meat. Every crumb on the premises had been consumed.

During the depression years, Marianetti announced that the Fior d'Italia would never close. "If you think this is a depression," he would say, "you should see Italy!" He was at this point the sole owner, but he managed to see it through. With the same kind of determination he directed the restaurant's first move, from 492 to 504 Broadway. When the new quarters were remodelled, and it was time to start thinking about transferring to the new address, George asked his father how long he thought they would have to remain closed. "Closed?" was Papa's indignant reply, "Tomorrow we will serve in 504 Broadway." They fed their dinner guests as usual, including three friends whom George had brought for a farewell meal in the old place. As soon as the last customer left Papa began giving commands to the whole family, all of the personnel, and George's friends included. They moved everything: food, liquor, ice boxes, boardwalks, tables and chairs quickly refurbished with silver spray. By three a.m. they had finished. The next day at 11 a.m. Fior served lunch at 504 Broadway.

In 1954, in the restaurant's sixty-ninth year on Broadway, George decided to move it. His friends were aghast and counseled him against it. Beset by doubts and indecision, he went to look over the proposed new premises again. When he came out of the building and saw the park that faces it with a church across the lawns, he was sure he was right. The new restaurant, designed by Mario Gaidano with whitewashed used brick, strong Chinese reds, ink blacks, and gold trimmings, won a nationwide first prize for its architecture.

In this modern setting the Fior d'Italia serves largely Italian specialties, including almost all of the dishes that appeared on its first menu in 1886: risotto with clams (formerly ten cents); tortellini (then five cents); veal sauté (then five cents); squab casserole (forty cents); double porterhouse (sixty cents); and many others. Some are dishes that Papa Marianetti used to cook only for the family before George persuaded him to add them to the menu. George knows that some of them were first introduced to San Francisco at Fior d'Italia, and he thinks it likely that a few, even, were the first Italian dishes of their kind served in America. The menu has been supplemented over the years with such dishes as fettuccine, gnocchi, saltimbocca, cannelloni, tagliarini with pesto, lasagne with Italian sausages, chicken with polenta, a number of risottos, veal escalopes, chicken sautés, and charcoal broiled steaks and chops. During the spring season Fior serves capretto—suckling kid—a traditional Italian Easter dish, but a great delicacy anytime.

George has given me two fine recipes for traditional Italian dishes: risotto alla milanese, and osso buco.

RISOTTO ALLA MILANESE

½ cup minced onion
½ cup olive oil
1 cup sliced mushrooms (optional)
2 cups rice

2 quarts chicken broth
¼ tsp. powdered saffron
salt and pepper
1 lump of butter
1 cup grated Parmesan cheese

Brown the onion in the olive oil in a large skillet. When lightly brown, add mushrooms, and cook over a slow fire for about ten minutes. Add rice, and continue cooking for fifteen minutes, stirring constantly. Dissolve the saffron in ½ cup of the chicken broth. Add half the remaining broth, one cup at a time, stirring in well. Add the saffron, salt and pepper, and continue to cook, adding broth as needed, and stirring constantly. When rice reaches the chewy stage (*al dente*), remove it from the fire, stir in a large lump of butter, top with grated Parmesan cheese, and serve immediately. Serves four to eight, depending on the size of the portions.

OSSO BUCO

½ cup olive oil
4 veal shanks cut in thirds, with marrow in the center
1 cup flour
¼ cup chopped onion (¼ small onion)
¼ cup chopped celery (½ stalk)

¼ cup chopped carrot (½ small carrot)
¼ cup minced parsley (about 2 sprigs)
2 tbsp. tomato paste
1 cup water
salt and pepper

Heat the olive oil slowly in a large casserole or heavy pan (a Dutch oven is perfect). Dust the meat with flour [shake in a paper bag with a small amount of flour], and brown slowly in the olive oil. When well browned, remove meat from the pan, add vegetables, and sauté until glossy. Add tomato paste and water, salt, and pepper, and stir all together. Put veal back in the pan, cover, and simmer at least an hour, or until tender. Serve with risotto alla milanese, or plain rice. Serves four to six.

NOTE: This recipe is one that takes well to sitting in its own juices. It is a good dish to prepare early and reheat when you are ready to eat.

Veneto Restaurant ✳

MASON AT BAY

moderate

DECORATION IS A FINE THING WHEN TREATED WITH TASTE AND moderation; when abused it is flummery of the worst sort, and works evil on the digestion. At Veneto, I am happy to report, although the setting includes a real gondola afloat in a real canal—a prop that would ordinarily send me running—the management has succeeded in capturing and transmitting a genuine spirit of Italian gaiety, calculated to improve the spirits and foster the appetite.

The main dining room, Venetian style, is pleasantly dark and comfortable. Next to it is a central court, open to the sky, with a splashing fountain, flowers, and real sunshine—one of the pleasantest places in the city for lunch on a good day. Behind a renaissance balustrade the canal runs through the terrazzo into the adjoining bar room, just wide enough for passage of the gondola. On the wall behind it is a two-story-high mural of Piazzetta San Marco in Venice. The bar room is large and elegant, and abundantly walled in glass, allowing it an unbroken continuity with the flowery courtyard on one side, and its own shaded sidewalk cafe on the other. In the evening there is piano music, and a strolling gondolier-accordionist to cheer things along.

Another dining room, a favorite when you bring the children, houses an enormous collection of dolls. Veneto's owner, John P. Omizzolo, has gathered them from all over the world. The most popular room according to the staff, but one which frankly leaves me cold, is the Cave Room, a replica of an Italian grotto with an abundant crop of stalactites, a giant fireplace, a fine assortment of mellowed copper, red checkered tablecloths, and racks and rows of wine.

Mr. Omizzolo, from the Veneto province of Italy, started his restaurant in 1922 with one room. In today's enlarged and fancy quarters, he continues to provide such nice Italian touches as a large basket of fresh and dried fruits and nuts at the end of each meal. With drinks at the beginning there is a goblet full of cherry tomatoes and along with the meal a basket of hot sesame rolls dusted with cheese.

Veneto's menu has a good assortment of pastes: spaghetti with crab, or meat sauce, or fresh mushrooms; baked green lasagne made on the premises; risotto alla milanese; cannelloni; and tortellini layered like the lasagne with a sauce of meat and tomatoes. There is osso buco with risotto every Wednesday at lunch, and chicken alla cacciatore and baked sea bass, both with polenta, on Friday. The saltimbocca here is a medallion of veal sautéed in white wine and finely chopped mushrooms, covered with prosciutto and Monterey Jack cheese and a sprinkling of Parmesan, all served bountifully over a bed of wild rice. Another specialty, for which the recipe follows, is whole boneless squab chicken alla parmigiana served with wild rice. The menu ranges through veal scaloppine, a number of broiled steaks and chops, pheasant chicken in casserole, whole broiled lobster, rainbow trout, chicken livers sautéed, frogs' legs with butter sauce, and a juicy prime rib roast of beef. There is an excellent fried cream for dessert—Signor Omizzolo has been good enough to give me this recipe also—and a number of sundaes of more than passing interest: Rome Delight is sherbet covered with freshly squeezed lime juice, crème de menthe, whipped cream and a final scallop of lime rind and green cherry; the Galliano is ice cream with a float of Galliano, crushed pineapple, and a head of whipped cream. There are, for the timid, cheese and crackers, spumoni, and unadorned creams and ices.

Here are recipes for two of Veneto's specialties.

FRIED CREAM

1 qt. milk
1¼ cups semolina (Cream of
    Wheat is an excellent sub-
    stitute)
3 eggs
2 tsp. vanilla
salt to taste
3 tbsp. sugar
Saran wrap
flour

2 eggs beaten with a little milk
fine bread crumbs
mixture of vegetable oil or
    shortening and butter for
    deep frying
6 tsp. white sugar mixed with
    6 tsp. brown sugar
24 cloves
12 oz. rum or brandy

Bring the milk to a boil. Slowly add the semolina, stirring constantly, and continue to cook until very thick—about ten minutes. Stirring is essential to avoid lumps. When thick, and smooth, remove from fire. Add the three eggs, beaten, one at a time, and mix well until thoroughly blended. Add the vanilla, salt, and sugar and mix in well. Pour about 1 inch deep into rectangular or square baking dishes lined with Saran. This amount will just fill two pans 9 x 9 x 2 inches. Refrigerate several hours or overnight. When firmly chilled, turn out onto a flat cutting surface, and divide into twelve squares. Roll each square in flour, dip into beaten egg and milk, and roll in fine bread crumbs. Fry in a mixture of deep vegetable oil (or shortening) and butter until golden brown. Remove from fat, drain on absorbent paper, and place each square immediately into a very hot dessert bowl. (If you want it to flame, the hot bowl is the secret.) Sprinkle 2 tsp. of the brown and white sugar mixture over each square, and stick each one with two cloves. Pour one ounce of warmed brandy or rum over each portion. Flame. Serves twelve.

> CHICKEN ALLA PARMIGIANA

per portion:

1 squab chicken, boned	¼ cup Napolitana sauce
flour	(recipe below)
1 egg beaten with milk	4 thin finger-length strips of
bread crumbs	Jack cheese
1 tbsp. olive oil	1 tbsp. grated cheddar cheese
	1 tbsp. grated parmigiana

Dip the chicken in flour, then in egg beaten with milk, then in bread crumbs until it is evenly covered like a cutlet. Fry it in olive oil in a pan that can be put in the oven, ten minutes per side. Place the same frying pan in a 350° oven for about ten to fifteen minutes, or enough time to cook through. Remove from oven, pour ¼ cup of Napolitana sauce over the chicken, lay four strips of Jack cheese on top, cover with grated cheddar, then grated Parmesan, and put it under the broiler until it bubbles. Veneto serves this with wild rice.

NAPOLITANA SAUCE:

To one can of tomato sauce, add a sprinkling of oregano and basil, a little minced garlic, and a dash or two of Worcestershire sauce, and simmer for ten minutes.

* *Lupo's*

1042 KEARNY STREET

moderate

LUPO'S COOKING IS SOUTHERN STYLE—SOUTHERN ITALIAN, THAT is—and delicious. The small dining room is typical of a modest trattoria, more concerned with food than with surroundings. Although many San Franciscans know Lupo's for the excellent pizza, more come because they can get baked clams, calzone, squid, toasted peppers, and delicately cooked veal and chicken dishes, prepared with the love and attention of home cooking.

The owner, Frank Cantalupo, is one of the authentically great personalities of San Francisco. I love to talk with him, for he is a true individualist whose opinions are expressed in the choicest idioms of colloquial English, and delivered with a feeling and emphasis that suggest the theatrical talents of his parents. Both were connected with show business from 1905 until the mid-Twenties. Papa Eduardo came from Naples; Mama, who danced under her maiden name of Concetta de Nicolia, from Sorrento. Papa once played with Mary Pickford, sang with Caruso, and was a top-flight comic in New York and Naples. Concetta was a star dancer and specialized in the tarantella. Papa's restaurant experience stemmed from a café he opened in Sorrento in 1926, and a summer-garden restaurant in New York. His San Francisco pizzeria-trattoria has been going since 1936, originally a joint enterprise with Frank and brother Tony.

The crowds that come in include opera performers, the Italian colony, people from just about all branches of society, and a number of people from show business. Xavier Cugat loves Frank's squid, baked marinated oysters, clams on toasted French bread, and shrimp in tomato sauce; John Scott Trotter favors the spaghetti with clam sauce; José Greco is an avid fan of Frank's calzone imbottito—a kind of Italian-style filled turnover, his cold zucchini with vinaigrette dressing, calamari stewed in their own juices, and baked coo-coo clams; Jack Webb also goes for those clams, and once polished off four consecutive orders of them.

Frank is delighted to have you come with one of his specialties in mind, but he advises that you will eat best if you arrive with an open mind and an open stomach, ready to try whatever special dish he may have cooked up that night. This is sound advice, and you will eat well indeed if you ask the waiter what wonderful aromatic thing that is that Frank has simmering on the back of the stove. All of the baked foods have a special flavor, coming from an oakwood burning brick oven that Frank thinks is the only remaining one in the country that is still in daily use.

Frank serves no hard liquor, and in fact gets quite overcome by the thought of his good foods being judged by tastebuds dulled with too many preceding Scotches on-the-rocks. He heartily approves, and offers, Italian Marsala and vermouth to whet your appetite. He handles Italian table wines too—verdicchio, bardolino, valpolicella, grignolino, lacrima cristi, sparkling Asti spumante—but has a number of bottles of Louis Martini for those who prefer the California vintages.

Pizza at Lupo's comes in two sizes and an infinite variety, including any combination that isn't already on the menu. There is classic Neapolitan style with cheese and imported tomato sauce, and two deluxe pizzas that contain a veritable Italian delicatessen: mushrooms, capers, anchovies, olives, olive oil, ham, cheese, chicken, peppers, and tomato sauce—embellished with mushrooms on the one, Italian sausage, sweet basil, and garlic on the other. Lupo's offers a pizza with imported butterini cheese, and another with fresh clams, cheese, and tomato sauce. When Papa Cantalupo was alive, he sent two pizzas to President Eisenhower—not necessarily through political persuasion, Frank explained to me, but out of love and respect for the president of his adopted land.

Frank has a fine rapport with veal, chicken, and squid. He has an equally knowing way with melanzana alla parmigiana (eggplant baked with Parmesan cheese), Italian sausage, which he sautés with peppers, and a variety of vegetables, which he cooks and chills, then serves in salad form seasoned with oil, lemon or vinegar, and sometimes garlic. Lupo's offers two dozen dishes of spaghetti, sauced with everything from butter and cheese, or oil and garlic, to lobster, shrimp, squid, or crabmeat, and an unusual combination with garlicky sautéed broccoli.

There is, besides, home-made lasagne (recipe below), home-made stuffed manicotti (giant tubes of pasta), homemade ravioli, and fine macaroni dressed with Italian sausage, mushrooms, olive oil, garlic, and a fling of parsley. Lupo's will cook spaghetti *al dente* at a small additional charge.

For dessert there is a favorite sweet of southern Italy, home-made canoli; also imported Italian raisins, imported Italian cheese, tortoni, spumoni, zabaglione, and fresh fruit. Coffee, if you like the dark Italian style, comes in Neapolitan pots.

Frank has generously told me how to fix four of his dishes.

ZUCCHINI SALAD

4 zucchini
½ cup olive oil
1 clove garlic (optional)
½ cup oil and vinegar dressing (made with three parts
  oil to one part wine vinegar)

salt and pepper
½ tsp. oregano and sweet
  basil, mixed

Wash, trim, and slice zucchini. Fry in ½ cup olive oil with garlic (optional). Drain and chill in refrigerator. Dress with olive oil and wine vinegar dressing, sprinkled with salt, pepper, oregano and basil.

TOASTED PEPPER SALAD

4 bell peppers
½ cup oil and vinegar dressing
  (same as above)

salt, pepper
1 clove crushed garlic

Toast peppers whole over the flame of a gas stove (or better, over charcoal) until the skin is blackened and crinkly. (You can also bake them in a hot oven.) Cool and remove skin. Seed the pepper, and cut it into strips. Season with salt, pepper, and crushed garlic, and chill in the refrigerator. Dress with oil and vinegar dress-ing, or add this dressing before refrigerating. Serve on slices of French bread. Serves four.

ITALIAN

➤ ## LASAGNE

1 lb. lasagne noodles

2 cups tomato sauce seasoned with garlic, basil, oregano, or whatever Italian condiments you prefer

4 slices prosciutto, cut into small pieces

6 cooked mushrooms, sliced

½ cup cooked peas

2 hard boiled eggs, sliced

1 cup Parmesan cheese

8 oz. mozzarella, in slices

1 lb. ricotta

Boil noodles until tender but still firm, in a large kettle of salted, boiling water. Drain. Butter a large baking dish and put a little tomato sauce on the bottom. Add half of the noodles in a layer, then add a layer consisting of half of each of the other ingredients. Repeat, ending with a good sprinkling of Parmesan cheese. Bake in a 375° oven until bubbly—about twenty minutes. Serves eight.

➤ ## SAUSAGE AND PEPPERS

2 linguisa or Italian pork sausages

1 tbsp. olive oil

1 toasted pepper (see recipe above for toasted pepper salad)

1 glove garlic, minced

basil and oregano, according to taste

1 tsp. red wine vinegar

Sauté the sausage in oil. When browned on one side, turn and add strips of toasted pepper, minced garlic, a sprinkling of basil and oregano, and a teaspoon of red wine vinegar. Continue cooking slowly until well cooked—about twenty minutes. Serves two.

Sorrento ✳

314 COLUMBUS

moderate

JUST UP COLUMBUS AVENUE ABOVE BROADWAY IS A SMALL PIZ-
zeria whose owners, both from Sorrento, have fashioned it after
a place you might find on their part of the Amalfi peninsula.
Jerry and Camilla Criscuolo are good cooks and cordial hosts.
They have a loyal following of plain citizens, and an impressive
fan club of opera, stage, and screen stars. The most frequent
visitor from the southland is Danny Kaye; when he gets a yen
for spaghetti and clams, he hops in his plane and flies up. Jerry
or Camilla gives him an apron and a spot in the kitchen, and
he cooks up a batch of his own. He has been known to phone
up in the middle of the dinner hour with a plaintive, "Now, how
did you make that marinara sauce I had last week?" [Answer:
garlic, parsley, and tomato.]

The Criscuolos have been in California a dozen years, and
were before that in the East. In the Twenties, Jerry spent time
cooking in the merchant marine of India, but his skill with pizza
dates from even earlier days in Naples. When a participant on
the television show "You Asked For It" wanted to know how to
make pizza, Jerry and Camilla were chosen to demonstrate the
art. You have to know if the dough is right by the feel, Jerry
told me. Some people just mix up the ingredients and throw it
together. They can't tell that in the summer the flour is a little
weak, and the dough absorbs a little more. Jerry's sensitive
hands can detect the proper balance in an instant, as can those
of his assistants, and his two sons Jerry and Louis, who both toss
a pizza as easily as some children toss a football.

Camilla Criscuolo is inordinately fond of the opera. Her husband shares her passion, but they often attend separate per-
formances because someone has to mind the store. The signora

has been known to enjoy every instant of a given work, then leave the opera house, change her elegant furs for an apron, and disappear behind a steaming kettle of spaghetti in the Sorrento kitchen.

The pizzeria is lined with booths and a long row of linen-covered tables that stretch down the center between them. The kitchen in the rear is open to view so that you can watch the pizza tossing and the work at the giant brick oven. The ceiling is a canopy of grape leaves and twinkling lights, the wooden walls are decorated with paintings, handsome ceramic plates, and a full section of autographed pictures.

The menu at Sorrento offers a great variety of pizza. There is pizza Margellina covered with baby clams and tomato sauce; and pizza à la fisherman with tuna, baby clams, anchovies and sauce. The capriciosa has sausage, cheese, bell peppers, tomato sauce, anchovies, and mushrooms; but the epitome is pizza la suprema, which I confess I have never tried. The Criscuolos claim it has something of everything. Among their soups is stracciatella, a fine chicken broth into which beaten eggs and cheese are stirred and cooked to delicate shreds. The pastes include spaghetti, ravioli, linguine, homemade tagliarini, tortellini (also in broth), rigatoni either baked or cooked to order, fettuccine, lasagne, and cannelloni. The lasagne are baked with two layers of ricotta, hard boiled eggs, prosciutto, Italian sausage, Parmesan, and mozzarella; the cannelloni and manicotti are stuffed with a mixture of the ingredients that go into the lasagne, then baked with mozzarella, meat sauce, and grated cheese. A speciality of the house is eggplant baked with Parmesan cheese, and there is a good assortment of veal cutlets, scaloppine, and chicken dishes. For drinks there are beer, wine, and Neapolitan coffee.

Jerry has given me his recipes for clam sauce, both red and white, and for polpi, little octopi, which he prepares whenever they are available.

CLAM SAUCE (WHITE)

1 can imported Italian baby
  clams (vongole) or tiny
  Japanese clams
2 cloves garlic, minced

4 tbsp. olive oil
sprig or two of parsley, minced
½ lb. spaghetti or linguine

Drain the clams and place in skillet or saucepan, reserving the liquor from the can. Sprinkle the clams with the garlic, olive oil, parsley, and enough clam juice to make a sauce. Simmer until well blended—about ten minutes. Pour over spaghetti which has been cooked just tender (firm, not mushy) in a large kettle of rapidly boiling salted water, then drained, and tossed with a lump of butter. It is not traditional in Italy to serve cheese with this sauce. Serves two.

CLAM SAUCE (RED)

Same ingredients as above,
  plus 2 or 3 fresh tomatoes,
  mashed or coarsely puréed

Follow above instructions, adding only a little clam juice, and the puréed fresh tomatoes. Serves two.

POLPI

1 can polpi (little ones—usually canned, from Japan)
4 tbsp. olive oil
2 cloves garlic, minced

2 sprigs parsley, minced
3 fresh tomatoes, puréed
fresh ground black pepper

Drain the polpi and place in saucepan with tight fitting lid. Add the oil, garlic, parsley, puréed tomatoes, and a good sprinkling of freshly ground black pepper. Steam, covered, in their own juices (do not add any water) over low heat for ten minutes. Longer cooking toughens them. Serves one.

9. GERMAN

The Bay Area has a large German population dating from the earliest days of westward migration. As early as 1853 there were four German singing societies (Saengerbunde) in San Francisco. The city has always hosted a legion of other German organizations besides musical groups. There are clubs concerned with athletics, provincial kinships, and general camaraderie. Their headquarters is California Hall—originally Deutsches Haus—where nearly one hundred societies hold their meetings, and where the Rathskeller has provided them since 1912 with substantial food and drink. There is a German language paper that comes out weekly. The principal neighborhood congregation is in the Mission District, where there are German butcher shops filled with livers, rumps of beef, ducklings and geese, hare, pigs' feet, and veal cutlets; German delicatessens stocked with sauerkraut, head cheese, bratwurst, liverwurst, bauernwurst, bockwurst, and blutwurst; and German bakeries crammed with apfel strudel or streuselkuchen, schnecken, gugelhupf, and tortes of raspberries, hazelnuts, and almonds.

Zinkand's and the Louvre were the great German restaurants of the earliest days. By the 1900's, German family groups favored the Heidelberg Inn on Ellis Street, a faithful reconstruction of a typical German rathskeller. In its gemütlich atmosphere, they gathered round to drink their beer, stuff on sauerbraten, and chime in with the orchestra when they felt sufficiently expansive. There was also the Hof Brau on Market near Fourth, which attracted a large non-German clientele, and specialized in all forms of abalone dishes. Chef Herbert discovered the secret of cooking them tender, and they became quite the rage, along with another specialty, reindeer steak. During the first World War the name was diplomatically changed to the States Restaurant. The theme was carried out by assigning the names of states to the dining booths, and patrons competed to reserve their native states.

San Francisco German cooking is mainly north-central—robust and satisfying. There is little of the more delicate Bavarian-Austrian cuisine. Five restaurants provide the city with most of its German cooking: The Palm Garden Grill on Market, the Shadows, high on Telegraph Hill, the Captain's Galley in the Marina, and two large halls that merit further description: Schroeder's Cafe and the Rathskeller.

✳ Schroeder's Cafe

240 FRONT STREET

inexpensive

Schroeder's opened in 1893, serving merchant's lunch to men only until three o'clock every afternoon. It held to this pattern when it reopened after the fire, and only in 1935 did it permit women on the premises. But even then, only after half-past one, a rule that still applies. In 1935, too, it began to serve dinners, but it has never remained open on Saturday or Sunday. The present owner, T. M. Kniesche, Sr., bought the place from Schroeder's widow in 1922. He directs it along with his wife and son. The former took Max, Jr.'s place once when he went off to war and could never again be persuaded to stay at home. The clientele is world-wide, and every Christmas the Kniesches send out over nine thousand greeting cards.

The dining hall is huge but cheerful. Murals and crests and flags of different provinces enliven the wooden walls and posts. The kitchen is open to view and the antics of the busy chefs amuse the guests. The head chef is a cousin whom Mr. Kniesche, Sr., brought here from Germany when he was fifteen years old, and who has been working in the restaurant ever since. All the cooks and bartenders are German. There is one non-German-speaking waiter, an old-timer, but he's learning. There are no tablecloths to hide the highly polished oak tops. Mounted here and there are deer heads, antlers, and horns, samples of old Schroeder's prowess as a hunter. The rosewood and mahogany bar, well over a century old, came around the Horn. Some of the decorative old bottles with pewter handles and tops date from the days when beer came in bulk at the corner store, and junior went with such a bottle in hand to fetch it for the family dinner.

The murals, painted in 1933 by Herman Richter, are mainly humorous—a dice thrower with his other hand on the barmaid's derrière, a fisherman exaggerating his catch, much to the amusement of his audience, which includes a smiling fish mounted on the wall behind him. The pictures are filled with personal touches, portraying Henry Schroeder and his dog with Max Knieche, Jr., when he was eight or nine years old; the artist himself; and a number of old clients—some in the costume of monks—enjoying the food and beer.

The food at Schroeder's is excellent, and the prices remarkably modest. All of the bread—splendid dark pumpernickel and rye—and the desserts—huckleberry squares doused with whipped cream, and traditional apple-strudel—are baked especially for Schroeder's. The weekly bill of fare has been the same for years. All of the food is cooked fresh each day, except of course for the slaw, kraut, and sauerbraten. These marinate in crocks stored in Schroeder's spotless cellars, next to potatoes in reserve for the summer season, and enormous iceboxes of meats and barrels of light and dark beer.

Among the daily specials are such favorites as Monday's roulade of beef, schweizer bratwurst (pork and veal sausage) with red cabbage, wiener roast braten (steak and onions), liver dumplings with sauerkraut, kalbs haxen (veal shanks), and smoked tongue with spinach. Tuesday is sauerbraten and potato pancake day, along with frankfurters, corned beef and cabbage, and old-fashioned Irish stew. At midweek there is corned brisket of beef seasoned in the smokehouse, served with puréed split peas, roast duck or pork with applesauce, garlic sausage with lentils, and calf's head—turtle style or vinaigrette. On Thursday there are roasted prime ribs of beef, baked spare ribs with kraut, boiled beef with spinach or horseradish sauce, oxtails sautéed with vegetables, paprika chicken and noodles, and the classic Holstein schnitzel. The week ends with sauerbraten and potato pancakes, pig's knuckles and sauerkraut, fresh fish, and goulash with noodles. There is baked chicken every day.

Max, Jr., has given me several classic recipes from the menu:

GERMAN

➤ ROULADE OF BEEF

1 onion, 8 oz.
4 bottom round steaks, ½ lb.
    each, cut ¼ inch thick
salt and pepper
¼ tsp. rosemary
½ dill pickle
2 oz. salt pork
8 toothpicks
2 tbsp. shortening

½ cup flour
2 tbsp. paprika
1 clove garlic, finely chopped
¼ tsp. thyme
¼ tsp. marjoram
2 cups clear beef or chicken
    broth, warmed
1 cup tomato purée
1 cup red wine

Dice the onion finely. Salt and pepper the steaks on one side. Sprinkle with rosemary and one half the diced onion. Cut the dill pickle in four long slices and place on the steaks. Slice the salt pork into four slices and place on the steaks. Roll the steaks and fasten securely with two toothpicks.

Heat the shortening in a skillet and sauté the roulades over a high flame—about two or three minutes on each side—until they are golden brown. Remove them to a casserole. Add the other half of the onion to the skillet, and braise over low heat for five or six minutes. Add the flour, paprika, minced garlic, thyme, and marjoram, and blend in well. Add the warmed broth slowly, stirring constantly. When well blended, add the tomato purée, stir in, and bring the sauce to a boil. Cook until thickened and smooth, stirring while it cooks. Pour the sauce over the roulades in the casserole, and bake in a 350° oven for approximately one hour. Ten minutes before serving, add one cup of red wine. Serve with red cabbage and mashed potatoes. Serves four.

➤ RED CABBAGE

1 small head red cabbage, approximately 4 lbs.
2 cups chicken or beef broth
4 tbsp. butter
2 apples, peeled and diced
    (preferably green)

2 tbsp. wine vinegar
1 tbsp. sugar
½ stick cinnamon
2 cloves
salt and pepper
½ glass red wine

Trim cabbage, remove hard core, and shred into a large saucepan. Bring the broth to a boil and add to the cabbage along with the butter. Simmer for one hour. Add apples, vinegar, sugar, stick cinnamon, cloves, and salt and pepper to taste. Cook for twenty minutes more over low heat, mixing occasionally. Add red wine, and cook for ten minutes longer. Correct seasoning. Serves six.

LIVER DUMPLINGS

Schroeder's serves these excellent dumplings with two sauces, a brown sauce with bacon added, or—the one which I prefer— a light caper sauce. These dumplings, made half again as small as the recipe suggests, and kept warm in a chafing dish, with a stack of toothpicks easily available, make splendid cocktail fare; or with capers added before they cook, they make an excellent soup garnish.

1 cup bread crumbs	1 tsp. salt
1 cup milk	pepper
1 beaten egg	½ lb. chicken liver (or
1 tsp. grated onion	calf's liver)
¼ tsp. poultry seasoning	grated rind of ½ lemon
grated nutmeg	kettle of boiling, salted water

Combine bread crumbs and milk and cook until smooth. In a large bowl mix the egg, onion, poultry seasoning, a little grated nutmeg, salt, and pepper. Add the bread crumb mixture and stir in well. Remove any skin and membranes from the liver, and chop fine. Add to the mixture along with the grated lemon rind. When well mixed, form into small balls by rolling between the palms of the hands. Makes about sixteen to eighteen balls slightly smaller than golf-ball size. Bring a large kettle of salted water to a brisk boil. Poach the dumplings for ten minutes. Remove with a perforated spoon. Serves three or four. Serve with caper sauce.

CAPER SAUCE

2 tbsp. flour
1 tbsp. butter or other shortening
2 cups of stock in which
  dumplings were cooked (or
  soup stock)

¼ to ½ cup capers, drained
  (or any preferred amount)
salt and pepper to taste

Mix the flour and shortening to a paste over low heat. Heat the stock and add a little to the paste, until it is thoroughly dissolved. Add this to the remaining hot stock, stir in well, and continue cooking for ten minutes. Add capers just before serving. Correct seasoning. Schroeder's advises that if a tomato flavor is desired, a small amount of sauce or paste can be added. I prefer it without.

✳ *The Rathskeller*

600 TURK STREET AT POLK

inexpensive

THE RATHSKELLER, "HOME" FOR A LARGE SEGMENT OF SAN FRANcisco's German colony, follows its German prototype, even to the tile floor. Since its beginning in 1912 it has been located in Deutsches Hall, a huge building modelled after a German-style city hall.

The restaurant is an enormous room filled with heavy mahogany beams, an array of stag heads and steins, and a huge oldfashioned mahogany bar. It often vibrates with the music of visiting brass bands, accordionists, and lusty choristers. It is dark and worn, leisurely, and familiar; all of the personnel, save one Japanese busboy and a mynah bird that greets customers, are of German origin. There is a four-lane bowling alley continuous with the restaurant, one of the few alleys left with honest-to-goodness live pinsetters.

Besides the German societies, many other patrons march down the wide marble staircase for a modestly-priced meal of roast goose, sauerbraten with red cabbage, or wiener schnitzel. Because the Rathskeller is close by City Hall and Civic Center it attracts judges, juries, and music lovers on their way to the opera. On occasion groups of language students come to try out their German.

The owners are Fred Kuehn, Charlie Wagner, and the Heyden family. Agatha Marie Heyden's father was a pioneer who came from the Black Forest; she says some of his pioneering instincts have rubbed off on her. Her husband Arthur was born in Berlin, and courted his wife in the Rathskeller. Mrs. Heyden, whose love besides good German food is music, studied for nine years under Madame Schumann-Heink. She has a remarkable collection of folk costumes, one or another of which she dons when there is a festival at the Rathskeller. The chef, Robert Leguillon, has worked at Romanoff's, the French Club, Ernie's, and the New York St. Regis.

At the bar there are dark and light imported beers on tap, a number of chilled wines from the Moselle and the Rhine, and the usual stock of stronger beverages. The kitchen produces boiled pig's knuckles (hot with sauerkraut, cold with potato salad); schweizer bratwurst with red cabbage; potato pancakes with applesauce, or German-style rolled pancakes with strawberry or applesauce; beef goulash, rouladen, and sauerbraten; paprika chicken with Hungarian overtones; and every Tuesday evening hasenpfeffer with egg noodles. There are rollmops, marinated herring, and herring salad, as well as steamed smoked Alaska cod with melted butter. There is Westphalian ham or kalter aufschnitt (assorted cold cuts) with potato salad; Polish sausage, and spicy frankfurters with sauerkraut. The menu also

GERMAN

includes American-style steaks, chops, and chicken, and German-style potatoes—fried, boiled, in the form of pancakes, dumplings, or salad. There are cheeses for dessert, as well as Bavarian cream, strudel, and cheese cake.

Mrs. Heyden has given me several recipes, including the Rathskeller specialty, hasenpfeffer.

HASENPFEFFER

1 hare, preferably three months old
Burgundy wine vinegar
water
6 small onions, cut up
3 carrots, cut into medium size pieces
6 pieces celery, cut into medium size pieces

½ tsp. salt
6 peppercorns
1 bayleaf
flour
salt and pepper
3 tbsp. bacon drippings
1 to 2 tbsp. flour mixed with a little of the marinade
paprika

Disjoint the rabbit and place in a crock or casserole. Cover with wine vinegar, and water in equal parts [I find it is better to mix one part wine vinegar, one part Burgundy, two parts water]. Add the raw cut up vegetables, salt, peppercorns, and bayleaf. Refrigerate for four days. [Domestic rabbit marinates easily in two.] On the fifth day [or third] drain the rabbit, reserving the liquor and vegetables. Dredge the rabbit in flour, and season with salt and pepper. Melt the bacon drippings in a large skillet, and sauté the rabbit until it is well browned on all sides. Cover with the marinade and vegetables, and simmer with the lid on, over very low heat, for about two hours. Do not allow to boil. Add more marinade if needed during the cooking. Remove the rabbit and thicken the gravy by adding one or two tablespoons of flour mixed with a little marinade. When thickened, return rabbit to the sauce, heat through, and just before serving add a dash of paprika for color. Serve with egg noodles. Serves four.

SAUERBRATEN

1 large round steak, weighing about 3 lbs.	2 bay leaves
1 tbsp. salt	6 peppercorns
½ tsp. pepper	6 cloves
2 onions, chopped	1 tbsp. butter
1 carrot, chopped	2 tbsp. bacon drippings
1 celery stalk, chopped	4 tbsp. butter
½ pt. wine vinegar	4 tbsp. flour
2 pts. water	2 tbsp. sugar
	12 gingersnaps

Place the round steak in a large clay casserole with a cover, and sprinkle with salt and pepper. Add the chopped raw vegetables, bay leaves, peppercorns, cloves, vinegar and water. If the meat is not covered, add more vinegar and water in equal proportions. Marinate four days in the refrigerator. Drain the meat and reserve the liquor. Brown over high flame in a mixture of one tablespoon of butter and two tablespoons of bacon drippings. When well browned, cover with the reserved marinade, and simmer over low heat for about three hours. In a small skillet, melt four tablespoons of butter, add flour and stir to a smooth paste. Stir in the sugar and cook until dark brown, stirring to prevent scorching. Add to the meat sauce, cover, and simmer one half hour longer. Place meat on a heated platter. Crush the gingersnaps [roll with a heavy rolling pin between sheets of wax paper], add to the sauce, simmer a few minutes, and pour over the meat. Serves eight.

POTATO PANCAKES

6 peeled potatoes	pepper
½ onion	1 sprig parsley, minced
½ nutmeg	2 tbsp. flour
2 beaten eggs	fat for frying
1½ tsp. salt	

Soak potatoes in cold water until ready to use. Drain, one at a time, and grate into a large bowl. Press out liquid that accumulates, and pour off. Grate the onion and half a nutmeg into the potatoes. Add the beaten eggs, seasonings, and flour. Mix well. Fry one large spoonful for each pancake in hot fat in a large skillet or griddle.

GERMAN

When the edges brown and holes form in the center, the pancake is ready for turning. Serves eight.

⤚ KÖNIGSBERGER KLOPS (MEATBALLS) WITH CAPER SAUCE

1½ stale rolls	1 tsp. Worcestershire sauce
1½ lbs. veal	1 sprig parsley, minced
¼ lb. fatty pork	1 tsp. salt
2 tbsp. softened butter	½ tsp. pepper
½ tsp. grated lemon peel	¼ onion, grated
1 tbsp. lemon juice	1 tbsp. butter
3 beaten eggs	6 cups of stock or bouillon

Soak the rolls in cold water until soft. Squeeze out and put in a large mixing bowl. Grind the pork and veal several times until very fine (or have the butcher prepare it for you), and add to the bread, along with the softened butter. Mix together thoroughly. Add the grated lemon peel and juice, the beaten eggs, Worcestershire sauce, minced parsley, salt and pepper, and the grated onion, browned in one tablespoon of butter. Mix together and form into balls. Makes approximately two dozen meatballs slightly larger than the size of a ping-pong ball. Bring the stock or bouillon to a boil, and poach the meatballs, covered, for fifteen minutes over simmering heat. Drain meatballs in a perforated spoon, and remove to a warm platter. Serves six.

⤚ CAPER SAUCE

2 tbsp. butter	Worcestershire sauce
2 tbsp. flour	salt
1½ cups heated stock in which the meatballs cooked	3 tbsp. capers

Melt the butter, add flour, stir until smooth. Slowly add the heated stock, stirring continuously. Cook until thickened. Add several good dashes of Worcestershire sauce, salt, and capers, and cook a minute or two longer to blend the flavors. When ready to serve, pour over the meatballs.

10. JAPANESE

AFTER the 1906 fire, Japanese began to settle in force in the central blocks of a neighborhood which in the early days was the city's "Western Addition," a name that has clung to it along with "The Fillmore," which recognizes its principal street. Unscathed by quake or fire, it emerged as the city's leading business area in a boom that lasted only the half dozen years it took for

Market Street to recover fully. The fire spared the mansions built in the '70's and '80's, a conglomeration of turreted, pillared, and domed monstrosities, a large-scale clutter that has finally yielded to neglect, a cloak of grime, and the boarding house.

In the midst of the Victorian scrollwork, several blocks filled up with Japanese. Their neighborhood, "Little Osaka," started at Fillmore and occupied the streets east to about Octavia, north to Pine, and south to Geary. Amidst the hulks and relics of bonanza days, Japanese calligraphy announced bookstores, hardware, gold fish, produce, and tempura. The community supported two newspapers, a YMCA and YWCA, and housed the Golden Gate Institute, once the second largest school for the teaching of the Japanese language in the country. The old generation taught its children the traditional arts of painting and composing, flower arrangement and tea service, judo, karate, and the creation and cultivation of bonsai. They observed the March festival honoring girls with the traditional dolls, rice dumplings, kimono and obi; the May ceremony honoring boys with paper carp and wrestling; and the midsummer Halloween festival with masks, incense, chrysanthemums, and dancing in honor of the dead.

Then came the war. In a wave of vengeance whipped by hysteria the six thousand Japanese residents in San Francisco—many of them United States citizens—were deprived of their homes and businesses, and herded east to relocation camps in the name of "military necessity." General John De Witt at the head of the Western Defense Command gave the orders, but the national feeling was such that he was decorated rather than castigated by Congress. In saner moments the courts declared the entire episode illegal and ordered some attempt at compensation, but the relocation will remain an untidy blot on the pages of American democracy. The area the Japanese left behind filled to overflowing with war workers, Filipino and Negro families, many of whom stayed on when the hostilities ceased.

Returned from the concentration camps, the Japanese dispersed throughout the city, but many reestablished themselves in the old quarter. When within a few years the whole country ironically was emulating Japanese architecture, furnishings, objets d'art, and landscaping—drummed on by the dissertations of leading consumer magazines on how best to succeed in making the home *shibui*—the Japanese quarter began to feature imported artifacts in quantity sufficient to supply the vogue. This renaissance brightened the face of the slum, but only in small measure, and a general demolition and rebuilding is currently under way. The plans are magnificent. The core of the old Japanese quarter will give way to a three-block cultural and trade center, oriental in tradition and atmosphere, but modern in design, approach, and materials. The project will contain a sky-lighted shopping center, a continuum of narrow Japanese-style streets fronted with open shops; underground parking; an outdoor plaza; a trade exhibition hall; an inn with both Japanese- and American-style accommodation; a theatre in the traditional style of 17th century Japan; tea rooms; gardens; and a two million dollar theatre-restaurant. To be called the Kabuki Theatre Restaurant, the building will occupy nearly a full city block, and accommodate 750 main floor diners with a balcony for 250 patrons who are interested only in drama. The owner, Kunzio Matsuo, owns over a hundred theatres in Japan and is the director of the Grand Kabuki Theatre there. The productions will include modern Kabuki, as well as plays and revues of an international character.

The new center will please San Francisco's growing Japanese population—9,464 at last count—the increasing number of visiting Japanese nationals here on business, the rest of the local population whose intrigue with the orient is in full bloom these days, and an ever-increasing number of tourists, already won over by the charms of the Japanese Tea Garden in Golden Gate Park. This Garden, one of the highlights of the Exposition of 1894, is a wonderland of red-leafed maples, gnarled miniature pines, flowering fruit trees, meandering paths edged with thatched bamboo fencing, ponds afloat with lilies and accented with water iris, streams stocked with carp and forded by perfect bridges. It is marked by a two-story temple gate, a shinto shrine, and a tea house, on whose wisteria-shaded terrace kimono-gowned waitresses serve green tea and delicate cookies.

Although Japanese restaurants are no longer an oddity in the city, they were strange and foreign until long after the great fire. Clarence Edwords describes his visit during the first decade of this century to a place that he had heard about from a Japanese friend. To the astonishment of the little party of non-Japanese, their oriental colleague took them to a residence on O'Farrell Street which revealed only after their entry that it was set up to accommodate diners. They ate in a large front room amidst exquisitely arranged chrysanthemums on a table laid to perfection with lacquer ware, sparkling crystal, and silver (in deference to Occidental guests). The evening started with tea, served in delicate blue porcelain, honoring the host; then went on to the consumption of a good amount of saki, which continued throughout the meal. The first course was swallow's nest soup, shark's fin salad, and what the author at first took to be two cakes, angelfood and fruit cake, served with amusingly perverse oriental taste at the beginning of the meal. He discovered that the one "cake" was fish iced with minced lobster, while the other was the dark meat of chicken with a glaze of light meat. After more tea from no less beautiful yellow porcelain, the diners had a dish of mixed vegetables "immature . . . in a sort of sauté . . . flavored with a peculiar sauce." A huge California lobster came next, and the author was amazed to find that the "shredded coconut" with which it was covered was really the lobster meat. The shell, whole and empty, was for decoration. The kimono-clad waitresses next carried in a tub of water with a live trout circling in it, and after proper viewing by the assemblage, whisked it away to be returned in thin slices—raw—with a soy sauce for dunking. The author and his friends, no doubt encouraged by their Japanese companion, found that the "repulsive" stuff was as agreeable as oysters; they polished it off, declaring it "delicious." Tea in deep red pottery preceded a dessert so elusive that Edwords could only describe it as "unusual" in both taste and appearance. Finally there was fruit and candied ginger. The meal lasted over five hours, and since the quantities of food were more than the assembly could pack away, they were given carved teak boxes for the leftovers—not to placate Rover on arriving home, but because it would be very poor manners to suggest by leaving a morsel that the meal had not been perfection. Beyond this, all of the chrysanthemums were gathered up and pressed upon the departing diners, who left amid bows and good wishes, "with the feeling of having been transported to Fairyland of the Orient." [30]

In San Francisco today there are many Japanese restaurants and bars. We no longer boggle at fish cakes or bean sprouts, although some of us still retain a certain reserve in the face of raw fish. The mode and setting of Japanese dining is not such a mysterious experience, and alas, so many diners unschooled in Japanese etiquette have left this or that on a plate, that the carved teakwood box has disappeared from the dining room.

Of the modern establishments there are three or four different kinds. The one country-style Japanese restaurant is the charming Mingei-Ya, operated by Russ and Miyo Rudzinski, who lived some years in the Japanese countryside and brought back with them the folk pottery that they had admired and used. Besides filling their house with it, they have put it to use in the restaurant, and have stocked a shop with pottery, aprons, and other examples of Japanese craft. Mingei-Ya means folk art shop and restaurant. The restaurant itself is decidedly rural in its layout, decoration, and style of cooking. The food is very good,

[30] Edwords, *Bohemian San Francisco*, pp. 57-9.

though not inexpensive, and one dish, O-mizu-taki—a kind of Japanese beef stroganoff—most unusual. The waitress prepares a broth in a copper stove at your table, and into it you dip ribbons of prime rib beef, fresh mushrooms, bamboo shoots, tofu, and vegetables according to the season: green onions, fresh baby spinach, special (and highly edible) chrysanthemum leaves. The rich creamy sauce has a tang that suggests a dash of mustard, a grating of horseradish, and even sour cream. When you have finished dunking the solid parts of the meal in broth and sauce, you mix some soup with the remaining sauce and drink it from your bowl. At this stage the flavors are even better. Mr. Rudzinski likens them to a hearty borscht and sour cream. The pickled tidbits at Mingei-Ya are put up on the premises (not every restaurant bothers with this refinement) and the rice cakes and other hors d'oeuvres are similarly made fresh daily. Mr. Rudzinski toasts the green tea leaves every day. The Japanese peasants roast their utilitarian tea out of the necessity of improving it, and he reasons rightly that if such wonders can be performed with inferior leaves, the toasting of high quality tea should make a delicious brew.

The Japanese neighborhood has a number of inexpensive and unpretentious places that specialize in good tempura or sukiyaki, but they are in the path of the redevelopment. Closer to the center of town are more sukiyaki houses, and recently some short order Tokyo-style places that recapture the success of the old Tenkin Restaurant on Laguna, that used to serve nothing but tempura. Tokyo Sukiyaki, Bush Garden, and Nikko all specialize in sukiyaki, that fine table-cooked mixture of meat, bean curd, and vegetables. Nikko is designed as a garden restaurant, with three types of dining rooms: American-style (tables and chairs), Japanese-style (floor cushions), and Kotatsu style (on the floor, but legs fit in a space cut out under the table). At Tokyo Sukiyaki, located at Fisherman's Wharf, the chef is distinguished Naoichi Hayashi, who left the U.S. Embassy in Tokyo for this position. At San Pei on Broadway the menu consists largely of short-order dishes, broiled or fried on grills or in great vats behind the counter. (There are, besides counter seats, tables and Japanese-style private rooms with floor seating.) The specialties are yakitori: a variety of bite-sized, skewered items, marinated, then broiled; tempura: deep-fried batter-coated shrimp, fish, and vegetables; oden: cakes of fish, shrimp, fried soy-bean, and bean curd with taro root cooked in broth; and sashimi: rolls of thinly sliced raw fish of several varieties with a sharp dipping sauce. One of the advantages of this modern city-type restaurant is its hours—from late morning until almost dawn.

The two restaurants following are the most characteristic and the most celebrated of their respective types: the traditional sukiyaki house, and the modern Japanese city restaurant.

Yamato ✳

717 CALIFORNIA STREET

moderate

YAMATO IS THE OLDEST JAPANESE RESTAURANT IN THE WEST. IT was started early in the Thirties by J. T. Nakahara, primarily to provide an oriental hotel for Japanese travelers to this country. Not only were there Japanese-style sleeping accommodations, but all of the dining rooms—oriental or American—were separated according to the Japanese belief in dining in privacy.

In 1950 the Ishizaki brothers took over the restaurant. Ken is host, Kobo is manager, and Joe the superlative chef. Under their direction it has become one of San Francisco's most delightful places, combining the best of Japanese handicraft with the latest mechanical aids, a Western-style bar with Japanese-style tatami rooms, the whole aflutter with lovely kimono-clad waitresses.

JAPANESE

The restaurant has given up sleeping quarters altogether, but retains twenty-one private Japanese-style rooms with sliding panels, and two Western-style dining rooms. Altogether the place can seat three hundred guests, but so skillfully arranged are the public rooms that there is never a sense of dining with more than an intimate company.

The interiors were designed locally by Harada and Meu and prefabricated in Tokyo by the Shimizu Construction Company —so successfully, in fact, that the company now makes and exports prefabricated tea houses for American gardens. Once the plans were drawn with appropriate translations into the metric system, they were mailed to Tokyo. The Shimizu crews had to make more than seven thousand parts from over forty varieties of wood, much of it hand rubbed or veneered, and fifteen types of bamboo. They used hand-made rice paper for the walls, and hand-made fittings and hardware. The materials were reassembled here in authentic Japanese fashion, which relies on mortise joints and pegs instead of glue and nails. The most remarkable part of the new interior, a second floor garden pond amidst delightful Japanese landscaping, is approached by a traditional bridge (*nari bashi*) that has a built-in squeak (*shimusi*) to announce the presence of visitors with authentic oriental subtlety.

The food is cooked to order and arranged with an art that is to Japanese cuisine as important as the manner of preparing it. The specialty of the house is the imperial Sukiyaki dinner: clear broth (suimono), vegetable salad with tangy Japanese vinegar dressing (sunomono), shrimp tempura, skewered chicken teriyaki, sukiyaki, steamed rice, fruit or ices, fortune cookies, and a good amount of green tea. There are steak and salmon teriyaki, as well, and several simpler dinners. For the adamant Western palate there is steak. Yamato's kitchens can prepare a large variety of more specialized native delicacies, among them casseroles steaming with tender chicken or seafoods; steamed rice or noodles with tempura or broiled eel; fish cakes; seaweed; and scrambled eggs—oyako donburi—these mixed with chicken, vegetables and sauce, and poured over a heap of steaming rice. There is a special custard that can be prepared in a quarter of an hour for two or more, and a special banquet dinner that really starts back with the growing of bamboo stalks—in deliberately different shapes to present a pleasing appearance.

Such a ceremonial dinner was prepared in August of 1960 for one hundred Bay Area dignitaries who assembled to celebrate the one-hundredth birthday of Japanese-American comity. The hors d'oeuvres, arranged in those specially grown bamboo stalks, consisted of steamed eggs rolled in greens and seaweed; two-colored fish roll: a layer of pickled fish and another of omelette, rolled around celery and ginger in pinwheel fashion, then sliced; squid stuffed with smoked salmon; chicken yakitori: skewered bits of chicken dressed with teriyaki sauce and broiled; yakiebi: skewered bits of shrimp prepared like the yakitori; squid, pickled, then cut in gear designs; harusame age: fish in small chunks rolled in chopped yam noodles, then deep fried; and kazari yasai: pickled long white radishes carved to appear like cherry blossoms, cucumbers shaped into chrysanthemums, potatoes and cucumbers transformed into lotus blossoms, celery and carrots carved into narcissus, and green onions looking for all the world like iris. These hors d'oeuvres were garnished with more pickled white radishes, cucumbers, lemons, pickled lotus roots, tomatoes, ginger stems, curled celery, and red radishes cut in flower shapes; and assembled around a treasure ship centerpiece made of lobster shells—the head for the bow, the tail for the stern, and a mast and sail of vegetables—filled with raw lobster meat and served with a dipping sauce of soy.

Then came tray number one. This presented white bean paste soup garnished with diced fish cake; a splendid red and white salad made of marinated threads of long white radishes garnished with salmon and lobster; thin slices of raw filet of tuna served with a sauce of soy and grated horseradish; and icy egg custard diced in small cubes, served with a sauce made of powdered green tea. On the tray that followed there was duck dressed with teriyaki sauce, broiled, and served with tender bamboo shoots and a garnish of pine leaves; a small side dish of marinated pine mushrooms and jellyfish; white rice cooked with sesame seeds and green peas; and an assortment of bite-sized tsukemono—Japanese pickles: large white radishes in sake brine, fresh cucumber pickles, ginger pickles. For dessert there were fresh oranges, bananas, grapes, and apples.

In presenting me with three classic recipes, the Ishizakis also passed on several ideas about Japanese cooking. First of all, it is characterized by simplicity and variety. The practice is to blend, rather than combine flavors, and to develop the natural taste of each ingredient—often best accomplished by short cooking, or serving food raw (especially meats and seafoods) with a sauce and condiment. When the Japanese plan a meal, they attend to textures, harmonies of taste, and contrasts. Most cooking in Japan is done over charcoal in a brazier, so broiled dishes like yakitori are quite common.

Most typical of Japanese dishes is sashimi—raw seafood—and one of the favorite forms is lobster. Here is Joe Ishizaki's recipe:

LOBSTER SASHIMI

1 lobster tail	1 long white radish, shredded
garnish of assorted chopped green vegetables: green onions, chives, pepper, lettuce, parsley	(Japanese horseradish)

sauce:

2 tbsp. Kikkoman Shoyu (Japanese soy sauce)	a pinch of Aji-no-moto (monosodium glutamate)
	a dash of lemon juice

Cut off the soft undershell of the lobster tail, taking care not to damage it, and remove all meat. Cut out black vein and rinse meat in cold water. Cut into eight or ten small (bite-size) pieces. Chill in ice water about twelve minutes to make the texture firm; dry thoroughly with a cloth. After removing meat, boil the shell until it turns red. Cool. Line the shell with a garnish of green vegetables and some shredded radish. Place lobster meat on garnish. Mix soy, Aji-no-moto, and lemon juice, and serve in small, individual side bowls, with small mounds of the remaining grated fresh horseradish in separate condiment dishes. The diner mixes whatever proportion of horseradish he desires with his sauce and uses it for dipping. Each lobster serves one.

YAKITORI (BROILED CHICKEN)

1 1¾-lb. broiler or 2 small broilers, boned and cut into 1½-inch squares
the livers, cut into 1½-inch pieces (optional)

10 large scallions cut in 2 inch lengths
sansho or cayenne pepper

sauce:

¾ cup Kikkoman shoyu (Japanese soy sauce)
¼ cup sugar

¾ cup sake (Japanese rice wine)

Thread the chicken and scallion (and liver, if desired) alternately on wood or metal skewers about six inches long—about four pieces of chicken and three of scallion are sufficient for each skewer. Mix soy, sugar and sake. Baste skewered meat and scallions with this sauce and put to broil. An outdoor charcoal fire is best, though a wood fire, electric or gas broiler may be used. Keep skewers about four inches above hot coals, and remove three or four times for basting in sauce. Excessive broiling causes juices to escape and destroys some of the flavor. When nicely browned, but still juicy, serve on hot plates, and sprinkle with sansho or cayenne pepper. Serves six.

NOTE: Pork or veal can be used in place of chicken; pork should be cooked slightly longer.

➤ **BEEF SUKIYAKI**

To Americans Sukiyaki is the best known—and probably tastiest—of the Japanese dishes. Most restaurants follow the custom of preparing it at the table over a hibachi—although a chafing dish or electric hot plate will make an excellent substitute. When the sukiyaki is ready the Japanese diner, using chopsticks, transfers morsels of food directly from the sauce pan to his bowl, selecting the ingredients cooked according to his taste.

sauce for cooking:

½ cup Kikkoman shoyu
(Japanese soy sauce)

¼ cup sake (Japanese rice
wine; sherry or whiskey may
be substituted)
⅓ cup sugar

dipping sauces:

1 raw beaten egg per portion
(optional)

6 tsp. dry mustard
water

Arrange the following ingredients on a large serving platter and bring to the table:

4 oz. beef suet
2 lbs. tenderloin of beef,
sliced very thin into 2-inch
pieces
12 scallions cut in 2-inch
lengths
½ Chinese cabbage (sometimes called Napa cabbage
or spinach cabbage) cut in
2-inch lengths
½ lb. fresh spinach cut in
1-inch strips
2 cups cooked shirataki (or
one 8¾ oz. can)

12 large mushrooms in slices
(preferably fresh; canned
button mushrooms, canned
matsutake, or dried shiitake
may be substituted)
12 pieces tofu (soybean curd)
in 1-inch cubes (the 11 oz.
can contains 12 large pieces
which can be cut into 1-
inch cubes; handle carefully
to avoid breaking)
1 can bamboo shoots cut in
large bite sizes

(shirataki are translucent threads of gelatinous starch extracted from a yam root, and are cooked like vermicelli which they resemble.

The canned product is ready for use. Cold cooked egg noodles, preferably of a long, thin variety, may be substituted.)

sauce for cooking:

Mix soy, sake, and sugar, pour into a small pitcher, and set aside.

sauces for dipping:

Beat one raw egg for each diner (optional). The Japanese dip sukiyaki in raw egg just before eating it; the thin coating serves as an additional sauce, meanwhile cooling the sukiyaki just enough so that its full flavor can be appreciated.

Mix dry mustard with enough water to make a sauce to your taste. Spoon out in six small serving saucers, one for each diner. You can increase the amount of mustard if desired.

Sukiyaki:

Heat the pan. Use a heavy skillet, preferably of iron. Cut the suet into small pieces and melt half in the pan until the bottom is generously coated with fat. Take a slice of beef, dip in the cooking sauce to coat it, and place in the hot pan. As soon as one side turns color, turn and brown the other side lightly. This takes just an instant, since the thin beef can overcook quickly, and is most delicious when left as rare as possible. When cooked to desired state, dip in freshly prepared mustard, and eat. About one-third of the beef is consumed in this manner.

Melt the remaining suet and add enough cooking sauce to cover the bottom of the pan. Add the rest of the beef and cook lightly until it turns color. Place all the other ingredients on top of beef slices. Cook briefly. Bring the beef with chopsticks or tongs to the top of the vegetables. Do not stir. Continue to cook gently over a medium fire until vegetables are just tender. If sauce cooks down, add additional diluted sauce: three parts sauce to one part water. It is customary to accompany this dish with bowls of hot rice. The pan juices are delicious spooned over the rice. If you prefer, you can cook half of the sukiyaki at a time, replenishing the skillet from the platter after serving the first batch. Serves six.

NOTE: The platter can be arranged and stored in the refrigerator and the sauces can be made well in advance, making this a simple dish for a small dinner group. A Japanese-American friend tells me she often uses sukiyaki-no-tomo, a canned mixture of sliced bamboo shoots, sliced mushrooms, and shirataki (yam noodles) in place of the separate ingredients. For this recipe, two cans of the 8¾ oz. size will be sufficient.

✳ Cho Cho

1020 KEARNY STREET

moderate

CHO CHO, AS EVERYONE SINCE PUCCINI KNOWS, MEANS BUTTERFLY. Jim Sakata, whose energies and tastes created this excellent restaurant, chose the name as a symbol of beauty and pleasure. In his conception, just as the butterfly in its metamorphosis comes upon a world of loveliness, the guests of Cho Cho enter a realm of enjoyment and delight. His restaurant has become noted, since its recent beginning in 1960, for authentic Japanese cuisine of unusual variety. Its patrons have included the visiting Grand Kabuki troupe, professional Japanese wrestling teams, dignitaries visiting from Japan or resident in the local community, and a large number of other San Franciscans. They have delighted in its intimate Tokyo-style quarters, and even more in the prospect of discovery offered by its menu and gourmet cooking.

The American-style bar, a handsome slab of redwood burl retained from the days when the premises was known as Shanghai Lil's, specializes in first-rate martinis side by side with a sake and vermouth concoction known as Cho Cho San (recipe below). There is a good stock of Japanese rice wines, including

Shirayuki, one of the few sakes that are not served warm and can even withstand the addition of ice. Cho Cho has some of the best bar nibbles in town, in particular salted dried green peas that put to shame any variety of toasted nutmeats.

Over the counter and booths a row of small, handpainted banners flutter as a waitress whispers past. The banners are symbols appropriate to the month and season and are changed accordingly. At the counter itself, delicate tempura turn golden as they bubble before your eyes. Yakitori, spitted chunks of chicken breasts, prawns, or prime beef skewered with ginkgo nuts and vegetables, curl brownly and crisply over the embers of the grill. At the sushi bar—one of the first outside of Japan—chefs prepare an assortment of open-faced "sandwiches," patties, and rolls based on vinegar-flavored rice combined with eggs, raw fish, vegetables, and appropriate seasonings. At the tables—there are no floor cushions here—diners feast on simple country casseroles, or grill thinly sliced meats and vegetables on equipment adapted from the original samurai do-it-yourself technique of cooking over the campfire on metal armor and swords. One area of the kitchen is open, providing a continuous exhibition of Japanese cooking.

The chefs, all Tokyo-trained, come from generations of cooks and restaurant owners, and have prepared foods for the most outstanding restaurants in that city. The menu they offer at Cho Cho is enormous. It includes a southern Japanese adaptation of a famous Nagasaki chicken casserole, mizutaki. As with many of the original Nagasaki recipes, this one shows a Chinese influence, but Jim Sakata tells me that the southern (Hakata) variation is considered by many experienced eaters to be even better. There are several broiled foods glazed with teriyaki sauce: chicken, filet mignon, salmon and sea bass. There is splendid sashimi, raw fish—the variety depending on the season—so perfectly arranged that they are like a painting. The flavor is subtle and exquisite, underscored by a sharp dip of soy, freshly grated ginger root, and horseradish. And there are such delicately prepared dishes as whole trout skewered and broiled with coarse salt, charcoal broiled filet of lake eel, and broiled stuffed lobster served in its shell.

At lunch time there are several special dishes: nabe-yaki, noodles cooked up with oysters, abalone, and shrimp; katsudon, a slice of prime rib dipped in batter, deep fried, and baked in sauce en casserole; oyako domburi, baked chicken and eggs; and tendon, tempura and sauce cascaded over rice. There are a number of traditional side dishes—soups, salads, seafoods, pickles, custards—among them a coolly refreshing cucumber and shellfish salad; miso soup (based on fermented soy bean paste) with tiny mushrooms or vegetables; broiled herring roe; iced soy bean cakes with a special sauce; and lightly steamed fish cakes.

There are many-coursed dinners built around sashimi or teriyaki, but à la carte dishes can be ordered on a dinner basis also. The meal always starts with a soup—generally a shimmering clear broth touched with a garnish, and ranges through skewered yakitori, deep fried prawns, pickled vegetables, rice, and salad, to a gentle rounding off with snow peaches, loquats and lovely Nijiseiki pears. During the meal, yabe cha, a southern Japanese hand-rubbed green tea, is customarily consumed—along with an Ochoshi bottle of warm sake.

Jim Sakata has given me two recipes, one for mizutaki and the other for the excellent Cho Cho San cocktail, a Japanese "martini."

➤ MIZUTAKI (CHICKEN CASSEROLE)

5 lbs. unboned young chicken cut into bite-size pieces about 1½ to 2 inches (leave skin)

2 qts. water

1 small bunch spinach

½ lb. mushrooms

1 head Chinese cabbage (sometimes called Napa cabbage or spinach cabbage)

1 cup stock

1 tbsp. sake

1 tbsp. Japanese soy sauce

Bring two quarts of water to a boil. Add chicken and cook uncovered until the skin whitens and the meat is just tender. Boil one head of Chinese cabbage very quickly—just enough to soften the leaves. Boil one bunch of spinach. Drain and reserve liquid. Prepare vegetable rolls: lay out a leaf of cabbage, cover with a few leaves of spinach, and roll up neatly. The finished roll should be 2½ to 3 inches in length. Make at least two for each person. Clean mushrooms and cut in halves. Arrange chicken pieces, vegetable rolls, and mushrooms in sections in a casserole. They should be arranged with care for the pattern, making it as pleasing to the eye as possible. Cover with one cup of stock, a little of the reserved vegetable cooking liquid, 1 tbsp. sake, and 1 tbsp. Japanese soy sauce. Cover and cook in a moderate oven until just hot. The vegetable rolls will fall apart if cooking is prolonged.

dipping sauce:

juice of 2 lemons (about ½ cup)
½ cup Japanese soy sauce
monosodium glutamate

1 tbsp. mirin—sweetened rice wine (or ½ sake, ½ sugar)
1 tbsp. grated ginger
3 tbsp. minced scallions

Mix lemon juice and soy sauce with a pinch of monosodium glutamate and mirin (or sake sweetened with sugar). Divide into individual bowls. Serve the grated ginger and minced scallions in a separate dish. Each diner adds these according to taste to the dipping sauce, along with a few tablespoons of juice from the casserole. Serves six.

NOTE: It is customary to serve a large flat plate on the side to be used for bones. The secret of this recipe is the quality of the stock, which exchanges flavors with the other ingredients. The Japanese often make their stock from seaweed and shaved bonito to which they add monosodium glutamate, soy sauce, and sake. However, any good chicken stock will be appropriate.

JAPANESE

CHO CHO SAN

per portion:

⅔ oz. Martini dry vermouth
1½ oz. dry sake
orange bitters

a twist of orange peel
ginger shoot (comes in jars;
  if unavailable, use a small
  slice of fresh ginger)

Mix vermouth, sake, and orange bitters with a generous quantity of ice in a martini-type mixer. Do not allow to become too dilute. Rub the edge of a chilled martini glass with the twist of orange peel before pouring in drink. Decorate with ginger shoot (stirring rod fashion).

11. BRITISH

THE first settler of Yerba Buena village was Captain William A. Richardson, an Englishman. His countrymen have been prominent in the subsequent development of the city, from the invention of the cable car to the development of Golden Gate Park. It has been estimated that over 100,000 persons of British origin reside in the Bay Area. But their noticeable congregations are few. Their most colorful contingent is a group of pipers, who swirl willingly for many a non-British festivity; their favored hangout is a large smoky Scotch pub, The Edinburgh, where a

301

dart game is always in progress. One of the most recent outposts is the Old Chelsea at Larkin and Geary, an authentic fish 'n chip house with equipment imported from London, and fresh plaice and haddock shipped from the North Sea. There you can order up a paper full of properly fried tidbits—even doused with vinegar if you want to be all that authentic. (Myself, I think it makes the crispy stuff soggy.) If there is anything missing it is the traditional soupçon of printer's ink; our health regulations forbid the use of newsprint for packaging the finished product.

Besides a number of Indian curry places, that appeal to the British palate as well as to the memory of empire, there is one good British restaurant in the city.

✳ *The Coachman*

1057 POWELL STREET

moderate

THE COACHMAN IS A BUSTLING ENGLISH EATING HOUSE WITH REmarkably good food and moderate prices, the inspiration of two young Englishmen who met by chance one afternoon in San Francisco over tea at a vicarage. Peter Lomax had studied hotel management at college in Lucerne; his partner, Malcolm Stroud, had taken up the same courses in Blackpool, Lancashire. They had worked between them in England, the Bahamas, Canada, Alaska, on a number of English boats, and finally at Romanoff's, Le Trianon, and Fleur de Lys in San Francisco. But they never crossed paths until that afternoon at tea. They then became good friends—and roommates until Peter married—saved their money, and a few years ago launched The Coachman. Since then they have opened the Old Chelsea fish 'n chip house, and Peter has taken over the excellent continental restaurant, Monroe's.

Their Coachman restaurant reverberates with the congeniality of a good English inn. There are burly wooden benches and chairs, candles blazing on the tables, and a jolly hubbub in the air. An amusing conglomeration of hunting horns, tankards and mugs, old maps and lithographs, pictures of the hunt, a food guide to London restaurants, and another to her theatres, is mounted against dashing hunter's red walls. The bar is well forward with the open kitchen just beyond, as cheerful as a blazing hearth.

The menu is limited to a few excellent dishes, all of which are preceded by steaming cups of Scotch broth, and tossed salad. There are ales and stout and several good wines to go with dinner—perhaps a generous steak and kidney pie under a buttery crust (one of the recipes which Malcolm has kindly given me). The traditional mixed grill consists of a broiled loin lamb chop, a plump lamb kidney, brown pork sausage, onion, mushrooms, and a medallion of beef wrapped in bacon and laved with a good béarnaise sauce. There is also a fine filet brochette, curried chicken, and royal trout. Dinner comes with coffee; dessert is extra. If you are inclined toward something rich, there is ambrosial cheesecake. But the better choice after such hearty fare is fresh fruit doused with Mandorcrema, an almond-flavored Marsala.

Malcolm has given me his recipe for Scotch broth, and it is well worth the time it takes.

SCOTCH BROTH

stock:

4 lamb shanks	one sprig parsley, chopped
1 gal. water	1 onion, diced
salt and pepper	1 carrot, diced
1 bay leaf	3 or 4 stalks of celery, diced
a good dash of monosodium glutamate	

soup:

finished stock (above)
1 large onion, diced fine
two carrots, diced fine

four stalks of celery without
  leaves, diced fine
1 potato, diced
½ cup barley

STOCK: Put all ingredients for stock into a large kettle. Bring to a boil, then reduce heat and barely simmer for twelve hours. Skim the surface from time to time. When cooking is completed, remove the shanks, and strain the stock. Take the meat off the shanks and dice up very small. Reserve.

SOUP: Add the diced onion, carrots and celery to the strained stock. Simmer for five hours, skimming when necessary. Add the cubed potato, and barley which has been rinsed first in cold water. Cook for at least one hour longer. About one-half hour before serving, add the diced lamb and correct the seasoning. Serves eight.

STEAK AND KIDNEY PIE

½ lb. beef kidney
1 lb. top round steak
⅛ lb. butter
1 finely shredded onion
1 tbsp. tomato paste

1 tbsp. flour, or more as
  needed
salt and pepper
1 tsp. monosodium glutamate
2 cups or more of stock

pastry:

1½ cups flour
1 pinch salt

1 cup butter
1 oz. ice water

Remove suet from kidney, place kidney in a pot, cover with cold water, and bring to a boil. Remove from water immediately, drain, and cool. Dice steak and kidney into cubes one inch or larger. Melt the butter in a skillet, add onion, and cook until soft. Add the diced steak and kidney and cook until well browned. Add tomato paste mixed with the flour, salt, pepper, and monosodium glutamate. Simmer until sauce is slightly thickened but still runny. If too liquid, add a little more flour. Transfer to a round baking pan or casserole. Add stock until it covers the top of the meat. Bake at 300° for about two hours or until tender. Add more stock as needed—mixture should remain juicy. About one half hour before meat is baked, prepare the crust. Raise the oven temperature to 450° before baking it.

PASTRY: Sift dry ingredients. Cut in butter. Add ice water a few drops at a time, mixing in lightly. The secret of this pastry is in the mixing: never press the dough together—it should always remain crumbly like bread crumbs. Collect the dough gently and mound it on a board lined with heavily floured wax paper. Roll out tenderly with a well floured rolling pin to the shape of a pie top. About twenty minutes before the meat is done, add the pastry top (carefully invert the wax paper over the casserole), and continue baking at 450° until golden. Serves four.

NOTE: In England boiled potatoes are the traditional accompaniment to this dish. The pastry, with the addition of one egg yolk and 1 tsp. sugar, makes a marvelous dessert flan. Press dough by hand in a flan mold, and bake empty or filled, according to type. Use with any desired cream or fruit filling. One suggestion: peel, core, and thinly slice four large green apples (if you ever come across Astrakhan apples, these are by far the best for tarts and pies). Arrange in overlapping circles on the unbaked flan dough. Sprinkle generously with grated nutmeg, a dash of cinnamon, granulated sugar, and salt. Squeeze a little fresh lemon over the apples. Spread with a good tart jam—apricot or plum is just right—dot with butter, and bake in a 250° to 275° oven until the apples are tender and a glaze has formed over them (at least an hour and a half, but probably more).

12. INDIAN

THE sikh turban and gossamer sari are not strange sights on San Francisco streets, but the resident population of Indians and Pakistani, largely students, is too small to support an Indian colony. The four restaurants that provide Indian cooking exist rather because so many San Franciscans like the taste of curry, unleavened bread, and good chutney. They are Little India, in the Tenderloin; the Curry Bowl, out on the Russian end of Geary Boulevard, unique in that it is open only on Friday and Saturday; India House, with cooking characteristic of Madras in central India; and Taj of India, with specialties from the northern Punjab, which Dharam Jit Singh calls "the Cordon Bleu region of Indian cooking." [31]

[31] Dharam Jit Singh, *Classic Cooking from India*, Boston, Houghton Mifflin Company, 1956, p. 5.

India House   ✳

IN A DARKLY EXOTIC ATMOSPHERE, DAVID RICHARDS BROWN, AN Englishman who bears a sinister resemblance to Noël Coward, and his handsome blonde San Francisco wife, Patricia, who could easily qualify for the feminine lead in a Coward play, preside over India House. When Mr. Brown first came from England in 1934, he was a trainee for the Shell Oil Company. This affiliation kept him traveling all around in subsequent years until he finally decided to give up the desk for the restaurant business. In spite of the fact that his restaurant experience had been solely as a customer, and his acquaintance with Indian cuisine derived only from his pleasurable visits to a couple of London curry houses, in 1948 he launched a ten-table, one-waiter establishment devoted to the service of splendid Indian curries. The cooking was—and still is—done by two women trained by Mr. Brown himself. By the end of the first highly successful year the Browns moved from Clay Street around the corner to their present and larger quarters on Washington. They did the decorating themselves, with such success that one expects at any moment a brigade of Bengal lancers to come charging through. Outside, in dashing protest to the overabundance of neon and garish electrical lighting so characteristic of this age, Indian carriage lamps burning kerosene blaze the way. The bar is a cross between English pub and English club, with a shelf of initialled pewter tankards belonging to habitués—among them true-born Englishmen, Qantas chaps from Australia, and dignitaries from India. As you sip a gimlet or a Pimm's Cup number 1, 2, 3, or 4 (of which the Browns sell more, according to the distributor, than anyone else in the country), or dally over a fine old sherry, a waiter serves crackers with appetizers; tiny sizzling curried meatballs from a chafing dish; and devilled crab delicately laced with curry, sherry, and a flourish of Parmesan cheese, bubbling on half clam shells and served with tiny forks to scoop them out.

Perhaps the most unusual characteristic of the restaurant is its personnel: waiters who are all gentlemen and scholars from Pakistan and India, working toward degrees at colleges in the Bay Area. Sikhs and Pakistani, Hindus and Moslems labor side by side in an atmosphere—unheard of in India—of cordial amicability. The waiters wear their native coats and turbans. The Moslems sometimes prefer simpler Astrakhan caps and the Hindus plainer white linen ones. The sikhs' skilfully wound colored turbans are the most intriguing of all.

At India House the menu emphasizes curry. Chicken, beef, lamb, shrimp, crab, lobster, meatballs, eggs, and vegetables all take well to blends of exotic spices. Authentic curry is, of course, not just one seasoning, but a carefully considered mixture designed to complement the particular food being cooked. An Indian cook would no more think of dousing each dish with the same prepared curry powder than a Frenchman would of laving all he prepared in brandy, or an American of rendering chicken, steak, and salmon equally anonymous by cooking them in an impartial coating of ketchup. Even when you taste Bakre Ka Salan and Khorma, both excellent lamb curries, you find that they are quite differently flavored; in India the first might satisfy ordinary good taste, but the second—rolled subtly in turmeric and braised gently in spices—would be fit for the palace of a maharajah.

Of extreme importance in the eating of curry are the sambals or condiments, side dishes that contrast sweet, sour, and salt flavors with the heat of the sauce. India House serves grated coconut, Major Grey's mango chutney, sweet pickle relish, mustard pickles, ground peanuts, raisins, quarters of fresh limes (particularly good with the seafood), and fresh onions, which the diner can combine in whatever proportion his taste dictates.

There are a few dishes for diners who are willing to forego curry, as well as hotter sauces for the incurably adventuresome. The timid can fare very well indeed on English mixed grill, steak and kidney pie, or Bermuda chicken baked in a cream sauce that is well fortified with dry sack sherry. Whether you choose to avoid or embrace the curry, you should try chapattis, bread of whole wheat unleavened dough—a staple of Punjabi cooking— baked puffy to your order. It is served hot to be eaten dripping with melted butter. The Browns' recipe is below.

The India House menu includes yoghurt, various chutneys and pickles, poppadoms (another bread, these very thin rounds, spicy and brittle, served just brown from under the broiler), Bombay duck (which is really a fish), curried beans and egg- plant, and such desserts as imported sliced mangoes, plain or with ice cream. The standard dinner starts with salad, and in- cludes rice and sambals with your entrée, a bowl of fresh fruit and Liederkranz cheese with crackers afterwards. The Amir Ka Khana is the royal dinner, and includes, besides the curry of your choice, a taste of just about everything else on the menu.

There is a good wine list, but my own preference with a meal of curry is for a cool draught of beer or a balm of Pimm's cup made with gin.

Here are three excellent recipes from the Browns:

CHAPATTIS (UNLEAVENED INDIAN BREAD)

2½ cups whole wheat flour, sifted

approximately 1 scant cup of water

¾ tsp. salt

Prepare a dough of the whole wheat flour by adding the water little by little, mixing out any lumps. Knead on a well-floured board until smooth. Shape the dough into rounds about the size of golf balls. Roll out each one flat, and very thin, so that it looks like a Mexican tortilla. Place on a warm griddle for about fifteen seconds on each side, then hold with tongs over the flame of an open gas burner (the flame should not quite touch the chapatti). After a few moments the chapatti will puff up. Turn it over for a few seconds, and serve immediately, coated with butter. Makes about 1½ dozen. [This is one that my children love not only to eat, but to make.]

CHICKEN CURRY

1 cup onion, chopped fine
2 cloves garlic, minced
4 tbsp. butter
1 tbsp. curry powder
¼ tsp. cayenne pepper
salt to taste (about ½ tsp.)
curry powder for dressing
   chicken

1 2½ lb. fryer, disjointed
2 tsp. ground coriander
a dash of ground cinnamon
a dash of ground cloves
1 cup chicken stock
1 tbsp. tomato purée
juice of ½ lemon

Fry the finely chopped onion and garlic in the butter. When lightly browned, add curry, cayenne, and salt. Mix in well and cook for a few minutes longer. Dust the chicken lightly with curry powder, rub it in, and add to the onion mixture on the stove. Sprinkle with coriander, cinnamon, and cloves, and cover with chicken stock and tomato purée. Simmer with the lid on for about forty minutes or until the chicken is tender. Before serving, pour over it the juice of half a lemon. Serves two. Accompany with rice and a tray of assorted condiments.

BEEF VINDALOO

3 tbsp. vinegar, or more as
   needed
1 medium onion, minced fine
2 cloves garlic, minced fine
2 tbsp. coriander
1 tbsp. ground turmerie
1 tsp. ground cumin seed
1 tsp. ground ginger

1 tsp. ground red chilies
½ tsp. ground mustard seed
¼ tsp. ground fenugreek
1 lb. beef cut into ¾-inch
   cubes
¼ cup oil
½ pt. water
salt to taste

Make a thickish paste of the vinegar, onion, garlic, and spices. Mix with the meat cubes and allow to marinate for at least four hours. Then add ¼ cup of oil and ½ pint of water. Simmer covered until tender. Add salt to taste. Serves two. Serve with rice and a tray of condiments.

[NOTE: Fenugreek, once bottled by the Spice Islands Company, has become elusive in these days of slackened trade with certain areas of the East. It abounds as the odoriferous *trigonella foenum-graecum* in the fields of California, where it is used as one of the principal agricultural ground covers. Nobody markets it as a spice, except for one Oakland herbalist, and his product is designed for therapy rather than cookery. In short, leave it out.]

Taj of India ✳

825 PACIFIC

moderate

TAJ OF INDIA IS ONE OF THE FEW RESTAURANTS IN THE NORTHERN Hemisphere that specializes in Punjab cooking. The Punjab—lush northern plains at the foot of the Himalayas—is a great wheat-growing district, and whole wheat breads, mostly unleavened, are a staple of the diet, along with dairy products such as yoghurt and ghee, a kind of clarified butter. The shellfish on the Taj menu is an exception to the regional cuisine.

The restaurant is directed by Harnam Singh, descendant of Sikhs, a Punjab sect. Harnam has never himself been to India, but has a strong feeling for the place of his family's origin. He has been cooking since he was nine, and received a final apprenticeship as restaurateur by working for the Browns at India House. The actual cooking at Taj is done by an Indian woman from the Punjab, under the direction of Harnam and his wife Alice, who is also an expert at the stove.

The decor of Taj is handsomely Indian, from the brass doorplates down the carpeted stairs to the bar set with low cushioned couches, antique candle lamps, and round brass tables. The walls are persimmon red. There are intricate screens from the Kashmir carved from shisham wood, pillows covered in striped Madras cloth, dining chairs from Suwa, and statues of various Indian Gods: Nakras, the God of Dance, who dances in his son's body; and Ganasha, the God of Wealth, Prosperity, and Wisdom, who the Hindus believe is good luck to have around in shops and business places. There is Indian background music, and besides the waiters, an occasional sari-clad waitress.

The menu lists à la carte items, and two kinds of dinners—the simpler one consists of soup, rice, bread, entrée, condiments, curried vegetables, pulse (beans, lentils, and such), beverage and dessert. The Moghul banquet adds such traditional items as Bombay Duck (bumaloe fish from the Arabian Sea, fried crisp— a fine thing to sprinkle over a dish of curry), thin-layered buttered bread, and fried garbanzo droplets in buttermilk and sour cream. There are several curries: lamb, chicken, pork, prawns, vegetables, and tiny shrimp Doh-Peeazah style, cooked first with ground onions, then with sliced onions. For non-curry eaters there are several other authentic Indian dishes. (Harnam points out that, contrary to popular understanding, curry is not the be-all of Indian cooking.) Among these are baby leg of spring lamb, spiced chicken, ground beef rissoles, and marinated giant Cochin shrimp served in their shells doused with sesame sauce. For mothers-in-law who don't eat Indian food, curry or no curry, there is chicken baked en casserole with wine and herbs, or broiled steak.

The standard condiments at Taj—all of them specially prepared—are coriander chutney (Chinese parsley with fruits added to give it base), garbanzos, onions, yoghurt, shredded macaroon coconut, and raisins; but one can order additionally such relishes as sweet and sour tamarind sauce, and imported lime or mango pickles preserved in very hot mustard oil from the Punjab—the best oil, they say, in all of India.

Alice Singh has generously provided me with a number of recipes for relishes, curries, and an oven-baked bread.

MURGA KA KORMA (CHICKEN CURRY)   ◄

This curry is a specialty at Taj of India.

2 2½ lb. fryers, disjointed	2 tsp. turmeric
2 cups yoghurt	4 tsp. ground coriander
3 tsp. salt	¼ tsp. ground cloves
2 tbsp. butter	¼ tsp. cinnamon
2 cloves garlic, minced	¼ tsp. freshly ground black
1 tsp. minced green ginger	pepper
or ½ tsp. powdered ginger	⅛ tsp. ground cardamom
1 green pepper (sweet),	1 tbsp. grated coconut
thinly sliced	2 tomatoes, halved and sliced
1 onion, halved and thinly	
sliced	

Combine the chicken and yoghurt in a Dutch oven or heavy saucepan; let it marinate overnight. Add 2 tsp. salt, cover and cook over low heat for fifty minutes or until tender. Uncover and cook until almost dry (raise heat to high). Melt the butter in a skillet and sauté the garlic, ginger, green pepper, and onion three minutes, stirring almost constantly. Add the turmeric, coriander, the remaining tsp. of salt, cloves, cinnamon, pepper, cardamom and coconut. Cook over low heat ten minutes or until pepper and onions are tender; add a drop or two of moisture if needed. Stir frequently. Add tomatoes, cook three minutes. Stir mixture into the chicken; cook fifteen minutes, uncovered. Garnish with additional coconut if desired. Serves six to eight.

GHEE   ◄

Ghee has a much higher smoking temperature than unclarified butter and can be used for deep frying.

METHOD: Place butter in saucepan with high sides. Cook over low fire for thirty to sixty minutes, or until solid particles are formed. Be careful not to let it brown. Strain through cheese cloth. Finished ghee should be yellow.

CHICKEN CURRY (DELICATE)

¾ cup onions thinly sliced,
then cut into small pieces
3½ tbsp. butter
¾ tbsp. turmeric
¾ tbsp. coriander
1 tsp. cumin
¼ tsp. cayenne
¼ tsp. black pepper
½ tsp. ginger (or preferably
a small piece of fresh ginger
root, minced)

3 lb. fryer, disjointed
½ cup cold water
1 tsp. salt (to taste)
½ cup diced tomatoes
4 tbsp. yoghurt
2 tbsp. sesame seeds
sesame or vegetable oil
1 sprig of fresh coriander
(Chinese parsley), if available

In a Dutch oven sauté the onions in butter until golden. Add spices, and sizzle for a few minutes, stirring constantly. Place disjointed chicken in the pot, stir lightly until all pieces are well coated. Fry a few minutes, add water, cover pan tightly, and cook until tender—½ to ¾ hour. Add salt to taste, diced tomatoes, and yoghurt. Mix lightly, cook about five minutes more. Remove from fire. Arrange on heated serving dish, and sprinkle with sesame seeds which have been toasted dry or with a little sesame seed oil or other vegetable oil in a shallow pan in the oven. If fresh coriander is available, break a few leaves into small pieces and sprinkle over the top. Serves four.

NOTE: For dryer chicken, use less water; for more sauce, add a half cup more water in small amounts at intervals during the cooking. Serve with Tunduri Roti (recipe above).

CUCUMBER RAITA

1 pt. yoghurt
1 small red onion, grated
½ medium cucumber, grated
¾ tsp. salt

½ tsp. cayenne (optional, but
good)
¼ tsp. cinnamon
a dash of ground cloves
½ tsp. caraway seeds

Beat yoghurt. Add other ingredients, and mix well. Refrigerate. Always serve cold. Stores well in refrigerator.

PODINA CHUTNEY (MINT CHUTNEY)   ⤙

This fresh mint chutney, as well as the yoghurt and cucumber raita, are of general use in Indian homes.

1 cup mint leaves (fresh coriander leaves may be substituted)	2 fresh hot chilies
	1 tsp. salt
	1 tsp. sugar
6 green onions, bulb only, or shallots	2 tbsp. lemon juice

Be sure mint leaves are free from stems. Put in a blender. Cut onions and chilies into small pieces. Add to blender with spices and lemon juice. Turn on and off until it just becomes a paste. Too long in the blender makes the chutney too watery. Alternate method: Mince mint, onions, and chilies. Put into a mortar with the spices. Grind with a pestle, adding lemon juice gradually. Serve chilled. Will store for several days in the refrigerator; may be frozen.

TUNDURI ROTI (OVEN BAKED BREAD)   ⤙

2 cups whole wheat flour	1 cup warm water
2 cups white flour	¼ cup yoghurt
1 pkg. dry yeast dissolved in ¼ cup warm water	1½ tsp. salt
	3 tbsp. melted butter

Sift flours together into mixing bowl. Dissolve yeast, stir into 1 cup lukewarm water in another bowl, add yoghurt and salt, and mix well. Mix the liquid into the flour, then knead in the melted butter. The dough should be rather stiff. Let rise in a warm place until a dent remains in surface when touched with finger. (Or put into a tightly covered container and leave for a few hours until baking time. Allow enough room in the container for expansion, then punch down before using.) Take enough dough to make a ball slightly smaller than a tennis ball, and flatten into a round between the palms of hands dampened with a little cold water. A brief kneading before may make this easier. Place on slightly oiled baking sheet. Bake 8 to 10 minutes in a hot oven (400° to 425°) or until slightly browned. Turn and bake about one minute on the other side. Remove to a bread basket or serving plate and spread with softened butter. Serve immediately while still hot.

315

>   EGGPLANT BOATS WITH BEEF

2 large eggplants
3 oz. ghee (recipe p.313)
  or butter
1 onion, minced
1 lb. lean ground beef
2 tbsp. minced fresh coriander
  (Chinese parsley)
1 small hot green chili,
  minced

salt
¼ tsp. cayenne
1½ tsp. garam masala spice
  mixture (see below)
2 tomatoes cut into 8 wedges
  each
2 8-oz. cans tomato sauce

garam masala spice mixture:

¼ tsp. black pepper
1 tsp. ground coriander
¼ tsp. caraway seeds,
  ground

⅛ tsp. ground cardamom
¼ tsp. ground cloves
¼ tsp. cinnamon

Quarter the eggplants lengthwise. Make a slit lengthwise through the center of each piece, being careful not to cut through the skin. Sauté in 4 tbsp. ghee until browned and softened, but not mushy; set aside. Filling: Sauté minced onion in 4 tbsp. ghee. Remove from fire, add ground beef, minced fresh coriander, chili, salt, cayenne, and special spice mixture. Mix well, and cook just two or three minutes. Fill the slits in the sautéed eggplant, leaving a little space at the top. Place two tomato wedges in top of each slit. Pour over them the tomato sauce and any leftover meat filling, and bake in medium oven until tender—about twenty to thirty minutes. The size of the eggplant will alter cooking time and amount of filling used. Serves eight.

NOTE: Garam masala is a mixture that the Indian housewife always keeps on hand, preparing it in large batches and storing for future use.

13. ARMENIAN

ALTHOUGH the colony of Armenians in the Bay Area is comparatively small, they have made an unmistakable impression on the community. They are mostly in business, particularly the selling and cleaning of rugs. To them goes the credit for one of the city's most charming trademarks, the sidewalk flower stands, which splash the downtown streets with bouquets of chrysanthemums, oak boughs, and calendula, spring daffodils, iris, and jaunty bells of Ireland. Two local Armenians have reached national eminence: William Saroyan, the Pulitzer prize-winning author, and (more pertinent here) George Mardikian, the owner of the famous restaurant Omar Khayyam's.

There are two other Armenian restaurants in the city, Bali's, notable for its excellently marinated lamb dishes, and the modest Cairo, which with Omar Khayyam's is discussed below.

✳ The Cairo

77 FOURTH STREET

inexpensive

THE CAIRO RESTAURANT IS DECIDEDLY ON THE WRONG SIDE OF THE tracks. There is a long pull up a sizeable flight of stairs to reach the dark and pleasantly worn dining room. There is no bar, nor even wine and beer. Yet the cooking is so good and the atmosphere so hospitable that there is seldom an empty table. The place was opened by the Garabedian family in 1919 in the same Fourth Street location, and has been run since 1946 by their daughter-in-law Novie. Mrs. Garabedian provides her customers with a large selection of home-cooked Armenian-Turkish foods. Armenian-Turkish cooking, she says, is the best in the world.

One of the principal foods of the Near East is pilaf, and Mrs. Garabedian makes two kinds every day, one of rice, one of cracked wheat. There is no end to the variety that can be produced by the addition of nuts, raisins, meat, or chicken. In two hours, Novie's friends tell me, she can turn out twenty different kinds of pilaf, and they swear to having tasted at least forty varieties all told. All you need is imagination, she claims. One of the best of these dishes is Istanbul pilaf: rice, fried noodles, finely cut string beans, tomato paste—and imagination. A favorite Armenian vegetable is eggplant, and Mrs. Garabedian says that in order to duplicate the native recipes as closely as possible one should use the smallest eggplants available. She herself tried to grow them from seeds brought over from Turkey, since even the small ones here are only a pale approximation of the real thing. She once managed to produce an acceptable crop in the soil of San Jose. At first they were very sweet, but later they grew acclimated and bitter. At Cairo there are two dishes made with eggplant that are highly recommended: imam bayeldi —eggplant sautéed with onions and tomatoes in olive oil; and patlijan moussaka—baked eggplant layered with spiced ground meat and tomatoes. Imam bayeldi means "the priest fainted" and got its name—according to legend—when an Armenian imam ate so much of the delectable stuff that he slipped into contented sleep. When friends arrived and saw him stretched out on the floor by the table, his wife explained that her husband had fainted.

Specialties of the house include another vegetable dish, dolma: baked zucchini, bell peppers, tomatoes, grape leaves and cabbage leaves, all filled with a mixture of beef, lamb, rice, and cracked wheat. Mrs. Garabedian's recipe follows. Two lamb dishes are especially noteworthy: orman kebab, a buttery sauté of lamb chunks and onions, and shish kebab, a dish of charcoal-broiled, skewered lamb flavored first in a winey marinade. I am exceptionally fond of lula kebab—highly seasoned lamb meatballs that are grilled over the coals; and kouzou kzartma—lamb shanks baked tender in a brown tomato sauce.

If your dinner does not come with sarma—grape and cabbage leaves rolled around delicately spiced meat fillings—these should not be overlooked. They are good either as a hot side dish or as a cold appetizer. Madzoon (yoghurt) is made on the premises, and adds incomparable flavor to pilaf, or anything else you choose to dab it on, for that matter. It is refreshing alone, and makes a delicious dessert when sweetened, or served with fruit. Mrs. Garabedian's paklava—uncountable layers of crisp tissue-thin pastry exuding honey rich with crushed walnuts—is so good that the Cairo sometimes runs short. If you want to try this royal pastry of Armenia, ask the waiter to put it aside at the beginning of the meal. There are other desserts, including authentic cookies, and candies like halva and lokoum. You may order a thick Turkish coffee, and read your fortune in the drops of dark syrup that run into the saucer when the emptied cup is traditionally turned over.

Here are two recipes kindly provided by Mrs. Garabedian.

EGGPLANT

4 small onions
1 large or 2 small green peppers
2 eggplants
1 No. 2 can solid pack tomatoes
½ cup (1 demitasse) olive oil
1 cup water
salt and pepper

Cut up the onion, green pepper and eggplant into squares. Arrange in a large skillet in alternating layers: eggplant, onion, then green pepper, until all vegetables are used. Pour solid pack tomato over them (use a brand that is not too watery). Add olive oil, half of the water, and salt and pepper. Cook over a very hot fire for twenty minutes, adding more water as needed. Serves four to eight.

VICTORY GARDEN DOLMA

1 lb. ground beef
½ lb. ground lamb
1 chopped onion
½ demitasse of uncooked bulghur (Ala, or cracked wheat)
½ demitasse of uncooked rice
1 can tomato paste
salt and pepper
1 cup cold water
4 zucchini
4 tomatoes
2 bell peppers
cabbage leaves
grape leaves
1 qt. water

Mix together in a large bowl the meat, chopped onion, wheat, rice, ½ of the tomato paste, and salt and pepper. Add one cup of cold water and mix well. Scoop out the zucchini and the tomatoes, and add the pulp of each to the meat mixture, stirring in. Fill the zucchini and tomatoes with the meat mixture. Cut each bell pepper in half, remove seeds and veins, and stuff with the meat mixture. Scald the cabbage leaves until they are soft enough to roll without splitting. Drain and pat dry. Lay them flat, put a spoonful or two of the meat mixture in the center of each, and roll up. Lay out the grape leaves and stuff in the same manner. Continue until all the meat is used up. Arrange side by side in a large low baking pan, casserole, or enamel roaster. Dilute the remaining tomato paste with one quart of water, and pour over the filled vegetables and leaves. Bake covered for one hour at 350°. Serves four or more.

Omar Khayyam's ✳
196 O'FARRELL STREET

moderate

OMAR KHAYYAM'S IS PERHAPS MORE FAMILIAR TO TOURISTS THAN to natives, yet its sound cooking and moderate prices exempt it from the suspicion that its fame is based primarily on public relations. George Mardikian, the owner of Omar Khayyam's, is one of this country's most famous restaurateurs. His is a Success Story, and he a great champion of Americanism. He came to this country, he tells us, in 1922, a refugee from Armenia where he had experienced the rigors of famine and war, had seen the Turks massacre his father, and had himself been incarcerated by the enemy. Rescued by Americans of the Near East Relief, he came to America to join a brother who had preceded him. As he recalls it, he had no money except what his brother sent him for his journey, and knew nothing of the language. On the train from New York to San Francisco he could make out only one hopefully familiar item on the menu, potato

salad—*patates salata* in Armenian—and had nothing else to eat
on the entire seven-day journey. It wasn't very good, and it
prompted him in later years to work out a potato salad recipe
that was. He serves it on all of the most festive occasions right
next to the caviar, finished like a cake, the appropriate greeting
spelled out in colored mayonnaise.

According to custom in Armenia, George and his brother
learned a trade early, something that they could always fall back
on, a *voski abaranchan* or "golden bracelet." George's was cooking. So when he came to San Francisco he sought work and found
it in a restaurant—but not as a cook; rather as a $12 a week dish-
washer in a spot called Coffee Dan's. Fourteen years later he
bought the very same place and later opened his own restaurant
there. In the years in between, he worked in various San Francisco restaurants and toured the world working as a ship's steward. In 1930 he opened his first Omar Khayyam's in Fresno, a
city that houses one of the three largest settlements of Armenians
in this country, and is as well the seat of a bishopric of the Armenian Gregorian Church. Within five years, he opened a second Omar's in Fresno, and had become known throughout the
area for Armenian shish kebab and paklava, as well as juicy American raisin pies—a regional dessert using raisins that are a primary product of the Fresno area. He presently owns only the
San Francisco Omar Khayyam's, but he has acquired along the
way several ranches and a radio station, has conducted a weekly
radio program for women, and has authored two books—one
the facts of Armenian cooking, the other the story of his life.

During World War II, Mr. Mardikian began a twelve-year
career as a special food consultant to the Army. Called first to
Camp Roberts to see what could be done to improve the food,
he suggested a series of innovations that were eventually adopted
in American bases around the world. Most important of all, he
attempted to remove the stigma attached to an assignment in
the kitchen by recruiting men who liked to prepare food instead

of those who were being punished by doing it, and dressing them respectfully in the tall chef's hats and white uniforms appropriate to their service. Dining halls were made more homelike and cheerful, and cooking seminars provided a range of recipes more attractive to the eye, and decidedly more appealing to the appetite. He helped to revise the Army's basic cooking manual, and toured the kitchens of bases in this country, France, Germany, Austria, Italy, and eventually Korea. At home, no soldier wearing a purple heart was ever allowed to pay for a meal at Mardikian's restaurant, and on Christmas and Thanksgiving the restaurant's festivities were entirely reserved for members of the armed services. For his work as a food consultant, George received a half dozen commendations from the War Department, and citations from Presidents Hoover, Truman and Eisenhower. He says that he was only repaying his adopted country for the opportunities it offered him.

Although he has become a United States citizen, he has not forgotten Armenia. He organized the American National Committee to Aid Homeless Armenians—a group concerned with a program for three-thousand displaced persons camped in Stuttgart, Germany. He and his wife annually revive an old Armenian custom. Every Christmas Eve, they invite their employees with their families to a gala party, and the Mardikians do all the serving.

The restaurant, down a wide flight of stairs from the street, is darkly panelled, comfortably appointed, and full of Persian carpeting. Its walls are a show case for eleven illuminated paintings depicting scenes from the "Rubaiyat of Omar Khayyam." The menu contains Armenian specialties, as well as salads, sandwiches, steaks, eggs, and such other American dishes as breaded veal cutlets and baked Virginia ham. The regular dinner starts with soup—generally a barley soup made with good lamb stock —and includes an unusual raw spinach salad, entrée, dessert— fruit, ice cream, Armenian cheese, or paklava—and beverage.

ARMENIAN

The shish kebab is always good, and a deluxe version is threaded with peppers, onions, and tomatoes. Lamb shanks and chicken Tchakhokhbelli are both cooked in tomato sauce, but the chicken hints of additional sherry. There are always two kinds of pilaf, rice or cracked wheat, both deliciously steamed and buttery. There are cold yalanji dolma, grape leaves with rice and onion filling, that makes a fine appetizer à la carte. For Omar's baked cheese-stuffed pastries I would be willing to forego some of my broiled lamb. Omar's regularly serves lavash; large cracker-like, but leavened, breads that resemble *matzoh*. They are traditional bread of Armenia, and the custom is to break one with your host, but I have never had the good fortune to find him in the restaurant.

Following are three Omar Khayyam recipes, including the famous potato salad.

POTATO SALAD

3 potatoes (average size)	2 hard boiled eggs
1 small onion	⅔ cup mayonnaise
1 tsp. salt	2 sprigs of parsley, chopped
¼ cup vinegar	salt and pepper (preferably
1 pimiento	white pepper)

Without peeling them, put the potatoes to boil. While they are cooking, slice the onion into a bowl and sprinkle 1 tsp. salt over it. Press out all of the onion juice, then rinse away the salt by washing the onion in a sieve under cold water. Chop it into coarse pieces, and reserve. When the potatoes are tender, let them cool, then peel and cut into medium dice. Mix well with the vinegar in a large bowl, and let stand for several minutes. Cut the pimiento into strips or dice and chop the eggs into large pieces. Add the onions, pimiento, eggs, mayonnaise, chopped parsley, and salt and pepper to taste, to the cubed potatoes and vinegar. Mix well. Refrigerate several hours before serving. Serves four.

RICE PILAF ⤝

¼ lb. butter

2 cups rice (long grain variety)

4 cups stock or broth

salt and pepper to taste

Melt the butter in an oven-proof casserole that can also be used on the top of the stove. Add the rice and stir until all the grains are well coated with melted butter, and the mixture is bubbling hot. In another pot bring the four cups of stock or broth to the boiling point, and add to the rice. Add salt and pepper. Cover tightly and bake for thirty minutes at 400°. Stir well once, and continue cooking—covered—for another quarter of an hour. Serves six to eight.

RAW SPINACH SALAD ⤝

Omar Khayyam's gave me the ingredients but not the exact proportions for this excellent salad, since one may vary it to his taste. The quantities suggested will give a reasonably good result.

1 bunch fresh young spinach

⅔ cup oil and ⅓ cup vinegar, mixed

½ pt. yoghurt

3 to 4 tbsp. ketchup

dash of dry mustard

dash of Worcestershire sauce

dash of paprika

a little fresh lemon juice or vinegar

salt to taste

2 or 3 slices of pickled beets, per portion

1 or 2 tomato wedges, per portion

1 hard boiled egg, grated

Trim the spinach, so that only fresh, firm leaves without stems remain. Wash well, drain thoroughly, and toss just for an instant in a large bowl with the oil and vinegar mixture. Put in a large sieve to drain off the dressing. Chill the drained leaves.

Mix the yoghurt, ketchup, mustard, Worcestershire, paprika, lemon juice, and salt to taste. Refrigerate until ready to use. Arrange the spinach leaves in individual bowls with a garnish of beets and tomato wedges. Pour three or four spoonsful of dressing over each salad, and sprinkle with grated egg.

NOTE: Since this salad tastes best when well chilled, it is preferable to make and chill the dressing in advance.

14. FISHERMAN'S WHARF
and Other Piscatorial Locations

Fisherman's Wharf lies over at North Beach, at the end of Meiggs's Wharf, where the Customs Officers have their station, and to reach it one takes either the Powell and North Beach cars, or the Kearny and North Beach cars, and at the end of either walks two blocks. When you get that far anybody you see can tell you where to go.

So wrote Clarence Edwords in 1914.[32] It seems incredible that

[32] Edwords, *Bohemian San Francisco*, p. 76.

326

anyone ever needed directions to Fisherman's Wharf, for nowadays the place is a major tourist attraction, dolled up with blazing signs, hawkers, curio and gift shops, museums, restaurants, sidewalk refrigerators, and enormous crab pots. You can find it merely by following the unmistakable smell of cooking crabs.

At first the fishermen operated from a pier at the end of Union Street in the shadow of Telegraph Hill. In 1900 they moved to Meiggs' Wharf, a substantial structure that reached two thousand feet into the bay. It was built in 1853 as a moorage for the lumber schooners of its builder, Henry Meiggs—or Honest Harry. He owned a sawmill at Mason and Powell Streets, one of too many investments that found him heavily in debt during the financial decline of 1854. As a city alderman he yielded to the temptation to save himself by forging city warrants as security for his losses, and finally fled to South America leaving $800,000 of debts behind him. Although he became a figure of international prominence owing to the successes of his railroad construction, notably in Peru, and amassed staggering fortunes —and it is said, paid off his old debts with interest—his desire to return to San Francisco remained unfulfilled. In 1874 he came as close as a bill passed by the legislature allowing him re-entry. But it was vetoed by the governor.

An abandoned ship was the first restaurant of prominence on the waterfront. Its Genoese proprietor, Giuseppe Bazzuro, is in some histories credited with having introduced cioppino to the city, a dish that turned out to be Fisherman's Wharf's most famous. He served up a fish stew called "ciopin," acclaimed as a favorite recipe along the coast of Liguria. According to an article in the February, 1961, *Gourmet* magazine, there is some possibility that Bazzuro did introduce San Francisco to his native dish. They point out that in Geneose dialect the word "cioppin" means a stew of various fish; and further, that the "Chiappa" was Genoa's great fish market.[33] The rest of Italy calls its fish stews by other names.

[33] "Cioppino," *Gourmet Magazine*, XXI (Feb., 1961), p. 47.

An even more unusual place, just at the beginning of Meiggs' Wharf, was Abe Warner's Cobweb Palace, cluttered with curios, a thriving and varying menagerie, and a gentle curtain of spider webs made heavy by years of accumulated dust. From 1856 to 1897 Abe dispensed excellent crab dishes and clams, and offered as well a stock of bar goods of impeccable quality. After the fishing fleet moved to the Wharf, the area was draped with drying nets and all the paraphernalia for keeping the equipment in good order. But at first only the fishermen ate there. In Edwords' day, the returning men of the fishing fleet breakfasted on deck, grilling some of their catch over charcoal fires, and accompanying it with heavy black bread and steaming coffee. They sold a good part of their catch to a daily assemblage of poor folk and contingents of the foreign population, who exchanged a few coins for a bounty of fresh seafood. The rest went to market on the Wharf, where it sold at low prices to the proprietors of boarding houses and family-style places, and to anyone else of the general population who knew a bargain and appreciated fresh fish. One of the fishermen, Tomaso Castagnola, began to offer seafood cocktails at his stand a few years before the first world war. A little later someone started cooking up batchs of clam chowder to be consumed on the spot, and before long most of the market stalls were selling seafood on short order. The crabs were picked out live, and boiled in great cauldrons. By the Twenties, the Wharf had taken on the character of a "drive-in," and motorists ate their crab Louis (an invention which is generally attributed to Tomaso Castagnola) from trays in their cars. Meanwhile Castagnola's and Alioto's had put in tables. By the Thirties there were a number of good restaurants, and the next decade brought even more, along with the enormous popularity with which the Wharf is coping, not too gracefully, today. Now the fishing fleet seems secondary in consideration to the clutter of gift shops, souvenir stands, and crammed parking lots. The rebuilding several years back, intended to modernize and improve the Wharf's appearance, served instead to cheapen it, replacing much that was honest and authentic with sterile equipment and tawdry gimcracks. The San Francisco Port Authority, awakened by the complaints of fishermen, restaurateurs, and the general San Francisco public, has begun planning a project to refurbish the whole area. Pier facilities would be increased and improved, and the dismal aura of Coney Island mediocrity would be swept aside in favor of modern concourses, sidewalk cafés, attractive shops, rebuilt restaurants, and perhaps even theatres and offices. It is too late to recall the men sitting in the sun mending their nets with large wooden shuttles; the lateen sails haven't been around for decades; the tasseled Sicilian fisherman's caps are worn by the waiters these days; the crab pots no longer bubble from the heat of the open fires beneath them—they use gas for their fuel; and party fishing boats don't rent out for $3.00 a day, cioppino included. Perhaps the next best thing *is* to build a totally new area, designed to face the modern facts of fishing. We'll have to wait and see.

Fish restaurants have never been confined to the Wharf. The French and Italian places have always offered quantities of fish and seafood. Before the fire, there was Darbee and Immel's and a whole battery of other places in the California Market. There was Gobey's, whose specialty was crab stew, and Delmonico's on O'Farrell, where lobster was cooked to perfection. A few years later, the Vesuvius, an inexpensive Italian restaurant, insured service of only the freshest possible fish by sending a messenger to the markets on Clay Street where he purchased each fish on order and brought it to the kitchen often still alive. The Buon Gusto was famous for its cioppino, which must have been considerably thicker than some served nowadays, since they customarily served it with polenta. The popular Gordon's Sea Food Grotto was at the corner of Sacramento and Market in 1877; the owner's son opened a second in 1920 in the Ferry Building. The Polk and Sutter Oyster House dedicated a pan roast to Governor James Rolph, Jr., who was among the most loyal of its clientele. He loved those clams, California oysters, lobster, shrimp and crab stewed together briefly in clam juice with a dash of Worcestershire, a dab of butter, and a good sprinkle of salt, pepper, and parsley.

Tadich's Grill has been famous for seafood for over a century, and it is still the old standby of many San Franciscans. Sam's on Bush Street (described, with Tadich's, elsewhere in this volume) was importing live deep sea turtles as late as the Thirties, and was known for green turtle soup and breaded turtle steaks. Turtle soup is still on the menu, but it is outranked in popularity these days by devilled crab. Buich's, whose owner Mitch did Tadich's cooking for forty years, is the newest seafood place in town, and promises to become one of the best. Maye's Oyster House, which dates back to the California Market, will be discussed at greater length below, along with three restaurants that are typical of the dozen or more at Fisherman's Wharf.

✳ *Fisherman's Grotto (No. 9)*
ON FISHERMAN'S WHARF

inexpensive

FISHERMAN'S GROTTO OPENED IN THE THIRTIES, UNDER THE DIRECtion of Mike Geraldi and Art Belcher. Mike had been a fisherman for twenty-six years, and his family numbered generations of Italian fishing folk. Art, on the other hand, was a San Franciscan, a stock broker and banker whose consuming interest was food. The two men became partners, built the first two-story restaurant on the Wharf, and began serving an extensive repertory of fish and seafood dishes. Four sons of Mike Geraldi now direct the establishment: Larry (who also owns the Domino Club), Nino, Mike, and Al. The decor is partly Venetian, with enough striped poles to moor that entire Italian city's fleet of gondolas. The view from the windows over the fishing boats bobbing at the docks is the most splendid assistance that any decor could have. The menu is extensive; there are over 150 items, from the simplest salads and grilled fish to epicurean turbot stuffed with crab meat, or lobster baked in its shell Princess style. Here are two recipes from Fisherman's Grotto.

SPAGHETTI WITH CRAB SAUCE

1 tsp. chopped celery
1 tsp. chopped parsley
1 tsp. chopped garlic
1 chopped onion
¼ cup olive oil
1 cup solid pack tomatoes
1 cup tomato sauce
1½ cups water

¼ tsp. paprika
salt (approximately 2 tsp.)
½ tsp. black pepper (less if you don't like your food "hot")
1 lb. fresh crab meat
¼ cup sherry wine
1 lb. spaghetti
grated Parmesan cheese

Sauté the chopped celery, parsley, garlic, and onion in the olive oil until delicately browned. Use a skillet that will be large enough to hold the spaghetti. Add the tomatoes, tomato sauce, water, paprika, salt and pepper, and simmer for an hour uncovered. Pick over the crab meat for bits of shell, wash and drain thoroughly. Add the crab and sherry wine to the tomato mixture, and simmer until it bubbles. Cook the spaghetti in a large kettle of boiling, salted water. When it is just tender, drain (do not rinse), and add to the tomato and crab sauce. Serve covered with grated Parmesan cheese on a well-heated platter. Serves four to six.

CHEF'S SEAFOOD SALAD DRESSING

2 cups mayonnaise
1½ cups chili sauce
1 tsp. lemon juice
1 tsp. horseradish

¼ cup sour pickles, chopped or ground fine
¼ cup celery, chopped or ground fine
½ tsp. Worcestershire sauce.

Mix all ingredients in a large bowl. When well blended, store in a cool place in a covered jar. Do not refrigerate. Can be used with any seafood salad.

✳ Tarantino's

ON FISHERMAN'S WHARF

moderate

TARANTINO'S IS OWNED BY EUGENE MC ATEER, A PROMINENT LOCAL politician, who chose the name of the old local fishing family rather than his own, because it seemed more in the spirit of the Wharf. The restaurant has been in operation since 1946, housed in the renovated quarters of the Crab Fisherman's Protective Association. The Association is an enterprise whose members own their own boats and equipment but act in unison to protect their fishing rights, much in the manner of a lobby. Their meetings used to take place in the area of Tarantino's present dining room. Thirty years ago the cocktail lounge was a classroom for immigrants training for their citizenship examinations. I'm not sure where the card games were played. Today the restaurant is handsome and comfortably appointed, with a long view over the Wharf, across the fishing boats, many painted blue and white in honor of Santa Maria del Lume, the patron saint of the fishermen. Beyond them you can see the red of the Golden Gate Bridge and the hills of Marin.

The menu includes filet of sole en papillote: sole covered with cream sauce, wine, shallots, green onions and mushrooms in dice, then baked in buttered parchment; shell fish creole style or curried; Hangtown fry; delicately browned abalone steaks; oyster stew; and cioppino—here made with cracked crab, prawns, clams, and eastern oysters—either in the shell, or "lazy man's" style. In either case you get a large apron-bib against splatter, and chunks of garlic bread to mop up the spicy tomato sauce. Here are recipes for two of Tarantino's specialties.

332

OYSTERS TARANTINO'S STYLE

¼ cup thick cream sauce
2 tbsp. cooked spinach,
  chopped fine
1 green onion, chopped fine
1 tsp. grated Parmesan
  cheese
2 tbsp. dry white wine

salt and pepper
1 or 2 egg yolks
rock salt
6 fresh oysters on the half
  shell
grated Parmesan cheese
melted butter
1 lemon quartered

Heat the cream sauce in a small pan. Add the chopped spinach, green onion, grated cheese, dry white wine, and salt and pepper to taste. Bring to a rolling boil, stirring constantly. While the sauce is boiling, beat in one egg yolk until the sauce stands when heaped on a spoon. It may take two yolks to thicken the sauce sufficiently. In a pie tin put six mounds of rock salt. On each pile of salt, settle in one oyster shell, deep side down, until it is steady and will not tip. Place the oysters in the shells, and heap with the sauce. Finish with a sprinkling of grated cheese. Brush with melted butter. Bake in a hot oven—450°—until golden brown. Serve immediately with quartered lemon. Makes one portion, or two if served as a first course.

HALIBUT FLORENTINE

2 halibut steaks or filets, 6
  to 8 oz. each
water
1 oz. dry white wine
juice of 1 lemon
¼ cup thick cream sauce

2 oz. cooked spinach,
  chopped
1 green onion, chopped
salt and pepper
1 egg yolk, beaten
grated Parmesan cheese

FLORENTINE SAUCE: Place halibut in a shallow casserole or saucepan. Cover with water. Add dry white wine and lemon juice. Cover and reduce to two-thirds over high heat. (Takes about five minutes.) In another saucepan, heat the cream sauce, and stirring constantly, add the cooking liquor from the halibut. When well blended, add the chopped spinach and onion (they should be chopped very fine), and salt and pepper to taste. Bring to a boil. Remove at once from the fire and stir in the beaten egg yolk.

HALIBUT: Place poached halibut in a buttered baking dish, or in individual buttered casseroles. Pour the Florentine sauce over the halibut, and dust generously with grated Parmesan cheese. Bake at 400° until the top is golden. Serve in the baking dish. Serves two.

✳ *Castagnola's*

ON FISHERMAN'S WHARF

inexpensive

MANY OF CASTAGNOLA'S RECIPES GO BACK THREE GENERATIONS TO the owner's great grandmother. Besides venerable recipes, the management believes in using high quality ingredients—Andy Castagnola told me, "After all, if you start with something bad, the result can't be very good"—and in letting the customer know when something is frozen, and when it is fresh. Beyond this, says Andy, they concentrate on providing good bread, good coffee, and good service. Besides Andy, the other owners include Tom Castagnola, a commercial fisherman who came to the Wharf in 1900, and is credited with having sold the first prepared food at his Wharf stand; Joe Borruso, who has been on the Wharf well over thirty years; and Anthony (Joe) Ferrari, who after fishing commercially for twenty-two years for the Paladini Company—the largest in the area—managed their plants for another seven. Andy used to have a restaurant way out on the end of the Wharf near a bridge that joined it to the lookout point. When the bridge was removed, the crowds stopped walking out to the end of the pier, and Andy had to give up his restaurant there. He called on three of his relatives —Messrs. Tom, Joe, and Anthony—and the new Castagnola was born.

The menu is very large, and includes dozens of fish, shellfish, salads, and chowders—and even crab, shrimp, oyster, and abalone sandwiches. The management recommends several special dishes, among them fresh-baked clams, one of those recipes that date back to great-grandmother: fresh clams diced, mixed with spices and sauces, stuffed baked in the shell and toasted in a hot oven. There is also stuffed calamari—or deep fried, if you prefer your squid that way—served with fried potatoes and fresh tomatoes. There are prawns sautéed Spanish style, and served with rice; or cooked in the manner of the Chinese with mushrooms and delicate herbs. Lobster tails, scallops, and baby shrimp come in sherry and mushroom sauce. Salmon, halibut, and sea bass are baked in a fisherman's creole sauce, poached and served with egg sauce, or broiled simply with a coating of melted butter and a sprinkle of parsley. Castagnola's has a fresh water tank stocked with live mountain rainbow trout, to cook to order.

Here are three recipes for favorite Castagnola dishes.

SHRIMP OR CRAB CREOLE

1 onion, diced	pinch of sweet basil, laurel
1 clove garlic, diced	(bay), rosemary leaves
3 stalks celery, diced	dash of cayenne, paprika, and
3 tbsp. olive oil	Worcestershire sauce
2 tbsp. flour	salt and pepper to taste
2 cans solid pack tomatoes,	1 lb. shrimp (cooked, or
No. 2 size	shelled green)
1 can tomato purée, No. 2	or
size (or 2½ cups)	1 lb. cooked crab meat

Sauté the diced onion, garlic and celery in the olive oil until they are lightly browned. Blend in the flour, and cook until smooth. Add the tomatoes, purée, herbs, salt and pepper, and simmer for four hours. When ready to serve, add the shrimp or crab [why not both?] and cook for ten minutes. Serves four.

CRAB NEWBURG

4 tbsp. butter
6 tbsp. flour
3 cups warm milk
1 tsp. salt
dash of Worcestershire
    sauce

1 tbsp. sherry wine
1 tsp. fresh lemon juice
4 cups of crab meat (lobster
    may also be used)

Melt butter, slowly stir in flour, and cook until smooth. Add warmed milk slowly, stirring constantly, and cook until thickened and creamy. Add salt, Worcestershire, sherry, and lemon juice, and mix well. Add crab (or lobster) meat, stir in, and cook until heated through. Serve immediately. Serves four.

ZABAIONE

per portion:

1 egg yolk
1 tbsp. sugar

½ eggshell sherry

In the top part of a double boiler, whip egg yolks, sugar and sherry over just simmering water (too hot, and the zabaione will curdle). Whip until very thick (this takes quite a while). Pile immediately into stemmed glasses—Castagnola recommends champagne glasses—and serve at once.

NOTE: Castagnola uses 3 parts sugar to 1 part vanilla extract, but I prefer the pristine form given above; they also garnish with half a cherry and a dash of nutmeg, gilding the lily to my way of cooking.

Maye's Oyster House ✷

MAYE'S OPENED IN 1867 IN THE CALIFORNIA MARKET, ALTHOUGH there have been several restaurants with the same name, this is the only one that derives from the original. When the two partners decided to divide the business, one opened a second Maye's on Polk Street; another move to a place a few doors away established Maye's in its present location. A succession of Yugoslavians with an admirable knowledge of fish cookery has always been in charge. In this tradition, Albert Joseph, Phil Modrich, and Marion Beroch direct the establishment today. The quarters are pleasant and comfortable, and the prices very moderate. The large array of fish and seafood dishes includes a number of oyster roasts; crab, devilled, or sauced with tomatoes, peppers, and onions, creole style; boneless fried sand dabs; rex sole stuffed with creamed crab; and buttery broiled petrale. There is a good assortment of other dishes: baked ravioli, broiled sweetbreads, lamb curry, boiled beef tongue, and one of the house specialties —veal scaloppine. Another specialty, one which can be ordered to take out, is the old San Francisco favorite, oyster loaf. Here is Maye's recipe for it, along with another from their menu, the old-timer Hangtown fry.

HANGTOWN FRY ◄

½ lb. bacon
2 tbsp. butter
1 doz. medium small oysters
flour
1 beaten egg for dipping

1 cup bread crumbs
6 beaten eggs
salt and fresh ground
    pepper

Fry the bacon in a large skillet. When well browned, remove to absorbent paper. Pour off the bacon fat, and add 2 tbsp. butter to the pan. Dip each oyster in flour, egg, and breadcrumbs. Fry lightly in the butter. When golden and crisp, add the six beaten eggs with a sprinkling of salt and a good grinding of fresh pepper over the top. Cook over medium heat until set on the bottom. Turn over, omelette fashion, to brown the other side. Add bacon over the top and continue cooking until firm. Serves three or four.

NOTE: Some cooks sprinkle in chopped green onion, or a fine dice of green pepper when they add the eggs.

OYSTER LOAF

1 loaf of French bread (size depending on number of portions)
1 clove garlic (optional)
beaten egg
salt and pepper
good dash of tabasco
good dash of Worcestershire sauce

½ doz. oysters per portion (minimum)
flour
bread crumbs
butter
French fried potatoes (optional)

Cut off the top of the bread so that it forms a lid. Hollow out the bottom, and remove any excess bread from the top crust. If desired, rub the inside of the loaf with a cut clove of garlic, and brush with butter. Then toast until crisp in the oven. Add salt, pepper, tabasco and Worcestershire sauce to the beaten egg. Dip the oysters in flour, egg, and breadcrumbs, and fry crisp and brown in butter. Fill the loaf with the hot, fried oysters, and top with French fried potatoes if desired (Maye's serves their oyster loaf this way). Put on the lid, and keep warm in the oven until ready to serve. One standard loaf of French bread holds about two dozen oysters (without potatoes) and will feed from two to four.

15. STEAK AND
CHICKEN HOUSES

Since beef is one of our best meats, the broiled steak has become special to the American menu, and one of our favorite foods. Although the art of broiling belongs to many cuisines, the tradition of the barbecue dates back in the West to the days of the hospitable Spanish and their entertainments. There are few

San Francisco restaurants that do not include broiled steak among their other listings, but several establishments specialize in this form of cookery. In San Francisco some of the steak houses have created sister establishments especially devoted to the glorification of chicken. Thus the present category.

* *Alfred's*

886 BROADWAY

expensive

ALFRED'S IS MUCH MORE THAN A STEAK HOUSE, BUT PRIME BEEF is its specialty. It is a deluxe restaurant with Italian cooking, and traditional San Francisco dinners that go from cracked crab, pickled pig's feet, and homemade ravioli, all the way to fried cream flambé—with all the trimmings. There is also fine squab, boned and stuffed with wild rice and baked plump en casserole, that is almost as popular as steak. The menu includes frogs' legs, sweetbreads, and a host of other dishes, but steak is the real treat. Every week the restaurant receives its entire supply of corn-fed beef directly by van from Chicago, where Alfred maintains a man in the Union Stock Yard to do all his purchasing. Once in Alfred's domain, the beef hangs in four enormous walk-in refrigerators to acquire the proper age. After about twenty days the flavor is superb, and the meat has acquired the right buttery tenderness.

Alfred Bacchini, whose excellent establishment this is, was born in Cattolica, Italy, which he left at seventeen to come to San Francisco in 1920. His father Giuseppe was a prominent chef, and later taught Alfred a great deal about that end of the restaurant business. Alfred started his own career as a busboy in the old Antella Hotel on Columbus. After two months of apprenticeship, he became a waiter, then a maître d'hôtel, and finally manager of a number of restaurants in the city. His real ambition was to sing professionally, and all the while that he was working in restaurants, he was practising for the opera. Alfred's career was finally determined while he was employed as the manager of an O'Farrell Street grill named after the great Italian tenor Beniamino Gigli. Gigli was a frequent patron and Alfred discussed his ambitions with him. Gigli agreed to audition him, and Alfred has been a restaurateur ever since.

He opened his own place in 1929, a fine old-style establishment, whose menu was little different than it is today. For years it was known as the 886, its number on Broadway. In 1958 the tone was changed by major redecoration. Old San Francisco yielded to golden Italian scrollwork, wall lamps from France, and chandeliers—exact copies of those in the Vienna Opera House—ashimmer with over a thousand faceted Czechoslovakian crystals. Behind the bar the wall is covered with growing orchids, a personal collection that includes some rare species.

Here is a recipe for Alfred's excellent squab.

BONELESS STUFFED SQUAB

½ cup wild rice
2 tbsp. butter
2 chopped green onions
2 boneless squabs
thyme
salt and pepper
1 tsp. olive oil
1 tsp. butter
1 oz. sherry wine
4 thin slices of prosciutto
2 tbsp. olive oil

¼ onion, diced
1 stalk celery, diced
10 button mushrooms (preferably fresh)
10 potatoes Parisian (directions below)
10 carrots Parisian (directions below)
2 tbsp. solid pack tomato
salt and pepper
2 tbsp. cooked green peas

Boil wild rice for ½ hour, then sauté in 2 tbsp. butter with two chopped green onions. Season the squabs inside and out with

341

thyme, salt, and pepper. Stuff with the wild rice mixture. Place in a well buttered casserole, add 1 tsp. of olive oil and 1 tsp. of butter over the top, and roast uncovered in a 500° oven for twenty-five minutes, or until golden brown. Splash one ounce of sherry wine over the squabs.

Meanwhile dice the prosciutto and sauté 1 minute in 2 tbsp. olive oil. Add the diced onion and celery, button mushrooms, potatoes and carrots Parisian, solid pack tomato, and salt and pepper. Sauté for ten minutes. Surround the squabs with the sautéed vegetables and prosciutto, cover, and cook for thirty minutes in a 400° oven. Sprinkle with two tbsp. cooked green peas and serve in the casserole. Serves two.

➤ POTATOES AND CARROTS PARISIAN

Peel enough firm potatoes to scoop out ten balls with a potato scoop. If you do not have a scoop, cut the potatoes in chunks, and round to the size of large marbles with a sharp paring knife. Sauté gently in butter until tender and golden. For carrots Parisian, use baby carrots, or shape young carrots to correspond to the size of the potatoes. Sauté in butter until just tender.

✳ *The Barbary*

490 PACIFIC

moderate

THE BARBARY RESTAURANT IS LOCATED SMACK IN THE FORMER center of San Francisco's liveliest scenes of carousal, an area which immediately with the Gold Rush was dedicated to sin. The very name conjures up visions of iniquities so debauched and flagrant as to run strong competition to history's most infamous orgiastic enterprises. Women were imported to provide for the needs of an influx of miners in a womanless community, and established in bordellos at the beachhead—the old Broadway and Pacific waterfront, long since filled in, but then within striking distance of arriving ships. The harlots were shortly joined by assorted ne'er-do-wells and criminals from Australia, whose escapades and forages into the more upright sections of town were primary among the instigations that established the vigilantes. In their honor, or dishonor, the section was called Sydney Town, a name that was replaced in the Sixties with the more descriptive term Barbary Coast. Within a few blocks, such viciousness prospered as to make the quarter totally unsafe to all but its own inhabitants. Drugging, slugging, and murder were commonplace. In the bars, those innocents who managed to withstand the rotgut they were served succumbed to the Mickey Finn; or if they got as far as the door still conscious, to a smart clobber on the pate with the inevitable bung starter. Trap doors opened at the bar's edge, and the unsuspecting reveler who at one minute had one foot on the floor and the other on the bar rail found himself an instant later sailing through the black air beneath it. At the least, seekers after ecstasies and overindulgence found themselves robbed of all they carried with them; he who fared less lucky found himself sailing to some hellspot as an unwitting member of a ship's crew. Those on whom the gods really frowned never came back out of the Coast at all. "Shanghai" was not the only word the language took on from the thriving days of the Barbary. The gang of juvenile delinquents of the day—so depraved and corrupt as to make modern offenders look like members of a boys' choir—were dubbed "Hoodlums," a noun whose meaning has paled since their sadistic operations. The scene for most of this outrageous criminality was any one of a plethora of dance halls, whiskey-houses, and melodeons, where lewd entertainments to the tune of the reed organ sucked the victims into the trap. Bacchus and Venus were worshipped in the Hippodrome, the Thalia, the Moulin Rouge, and—the most famous of them all—the Bella Union.

The Fire wiped out the scene, but only temporarily. In the

new era, the section became a favorite place for the rest of the town to slum in: parties of respectable citizens arrived in droves hoping for titillation from the girlie-shows and from the miscellany of dubious characters that abounded. They forked over their money willingly for the privilege of ogling, and the clout on the head and the knock-out drop became less necessary and consequently less common. The area was still a disgrace of major proportions, and was closed down after a citizens' and editorial campaign by the end of the First World War. There have since been revivals of the risqué shows, and of clip joints modernized to extract exorbitant fees from voluntary victims—but both have been on the pale side for such notorious territory. For a few years now the area has actually become chic, and reminiscent of its former activities only in a few strip places (one of which holds a weekly amateur night) on its fringes. Old "Devil's Acre" is now fastidiously groomed, housing a crop of interior decorator's studios, and the showrooms of many of the notables of the world of furniture and household design. It is, in its new way, a handsome neighborhood, and were it not for the awning over the restaurant spelling out the potent old label, the Barbary Coast would not be conjured up even in memory.

In a few years, the Barbary restaurant has become known for its good steak, its simplicity, and its hospitality. Its owners, Claude Franceschi and Jim Roukes, have both been employed at the bars and in the service of various San Francisco restaurants—Alfred's, the Shadows, and Veneto among them. They designed the convivial setting themselves, and dispense therein excellent bar goods, steaks, sweetbreads, chicken sec, and pollo a mattone. Pasta, not even listed on the menu, is first-rate: usually linguine, cooked expertly firm if you just say the word, tossed in melted butter, then smothered in grated Parmesan cheese. Salad comes with every order, tangy and crisp, potatoes, a vegetable in season, and strong dark coffee. The last time I was there eight or so hearts of very green artichokes braised just tender and full of flavor crowded the oval dinner plate. The double New York steak is the thing to have here. It is several inches thick and twice as wide, and you may end up taking some home to Rover. Once the waiter has paraded the impressive thing whole, brown, and glistening before you, it is sliced in juicy slabs comparable to many a Chateaubriand in more elegant surroundings —and half the price. The other items are well cooked and more than ample in proportion to the average restaurant serving. The most unusual dish among them is pollo a mattone, reminiscent of chicken alla diavola, but with the northern touches of Claude's home town, Lucca. It is a fried chicken weighted down in cooking with a brick (the Lucchese use a whole brick press, as I understand it, in which the bird cooks) so that it becomes unexcelled in the crispness of its skin and the contrasting succulence of its meat. There is one other special dish that is never on the menu, and unique in that it never costs the guests who eat it anything at all. Claude is a great hunter, and when the duck season is on he cooks up his catch for appreciative customers.

Here are Claude's recipes for two fine dishes.

SWEETBREADS

1 lb. sweetbreads
white wine or bouillon for
    parboiling
3 tbsp. olive oil
small clove garlic, minced

1 tsp. powdered sage
½ lb. mushrooms, sliced
salt and pepper
1¼ cups sauterne or other
    white wine

Parboil the sweetbreads in wine or bouillon. Trim them, remove membranes, and slice or cut into several pieces. Heat olive oil in a skillet. Add the sweetbreads, minced garlic, and sage, and sauté until brown. Add sliced mushrooms, cook a few minutes until they start to brown. Add salt and pepper and white wine. Cook briskly for about fifteen minutes, or until the sauce is reduced by about half. Serve immediately. Serves three or four.

Note: At the Barbary, they cook sirloin tips the same way.

➤ ## POLLO A MATTONE

2 small chickens, approximately 1¼ lbs. each, cut
in halves
½ cup olive oil

1 tsp. powdered sage
1 clove garlic, minced
salt and pepper
2 large bricks

Clean the chickens. Put the olive oil in a large, heavy skillet.
Add the chicken halves and sprinkle with sage, garlic, salt and
pepper. Place the bricks on top so that the chickens are weighted
down evenly and completely. Fry over a fairly high fire for about
ten or fifteen minutes. Remove bricks, turn chickens, replace
bricks, and continue to cook—no longer than ten minutes more.
The chicken must be golden brown on the outside but remain
moist inside. Serves four.

NOTE: If you don't have any bricks handy, it is perfectly acceptable to cover the chickens with a lid enough smaller than the skillet
in which they are cooking so that it rests directly on them. Weight
it down with a large kettle filled with hot water, or heavy rocks and
stones of any structure aesthetic enough to be at home in the
kitchen. An iron is weighty, but it tends to get splattered. If you
have difficulty finding chickens this small, you can use larger fry-
ers, but increase the cooking time accordingly.

✳ ## *Grison's*

VAN NESS AND PACIFIC

STEAK: *expensive*   CHICKEN: *moderate*

THERE ARE TWO GRISON'S SIDE BY SIDE ON VAN NESS AVENUE, ONE
devoted to steaks, the other to chicken. The steak house offers
prime corn fed beef from Kansas City, live Maine lobster, cherry-
stone clams, and other such delicacies from a seafood bar, additional entrées such as chicken livers and thick broiled chops,
and fine coffee made fresh at each table. There are home-made
biscuits served with honey, and every order is garnished with

rings of French fried onions and giant baked potatoes. The restaurant is large but efficient, and has been specializing in quality steaks ever since it opened over twenty-five years ago.

The chicken house specializes in Southern fried chicken, chicken pot pie, rainbow trout, short ribs of beef, and prime ribs served from a wheeled cart, English fashion. Dinners come with all the appropriate fixings.

On Christmas both establishments roast whole turkeys for groups of six or more (arrangements must be made in advance). And, to insure these diners the fun of holiday leftovers, a box is provided to cart them home in.

Both of these reliable restaurants are owned and managed by Robert Grison, a Swiss gentleman whose classic chef's training was acquired abroad. Here are three recipes which he kindly gave me.

BROOK TROUT, SAUTÉ MEUNIÈRE

1 trout per portion	fresh lemon
flour	chopped parsley
clarified butter (directions below)	2 tbsp. butter

Clean the trout, cut off fins and tail, but leave the head on. Dip lightly in flour, and fry in clarified butter until browned. Place on platter, squeeze fresh lemon over the fish, and sprinkle with finely chopped parsley. Add two tablespoons of butter to the pan in which the trout was cooked. When the butter takes on a brown color, pour it over the fish and serve immediately.

CLARIFIED BUTTER: heat butter very slowly for about thirty minutes until solid particles settle out. Strain through very fine sieve or cloth.

➤ ## CAESAR SALAD

2 small heads Romaine lettuce, thoroughly chilled
¼ clove garlic
salt and pepper
⅛ tsp. dry mustard
½ tsp. Worcestershire
sauce
1 tbsp. lemon juice

1 tbsp. olive oil
3 anchovy filets
1 coddled egg (recipe below)
¾ cup croutons (recipe
below)
1 tbsp. grated Parmesan
cheese

Wash romaine thoroughly, remove all outside leaves, and cut the remainder crosswise in pieces about one-half inch wide. Refrigerate until ready to use. Then place in a wooden salad bowl that has first been rubbed with garlic. In a small mixing bowl put salt, fresh ground pepper, dry mustard, Worcestershire sauce, and lemon juice. Mix thoroughly. Add olive oil and cut-up anchovies. Break the egg over the greens, pour on the salad dressing, and toss together lightly. Add croutons and half the cheese, and toss again lightly. Place on chilled salad plates. Sprinkle remainder of cheese on top. Serves three.

CODDLED EGG: Cook whole egg in hot but not boiling water for two minutes.

CROUTONS: Cut stale French bread in small squares. Soak them in olive oil, then put in the oven until they toast brown. Garlic lovers can rub them first with a cut clove of garlic.

➤ ## BAKED ALASKA

sponge cake
1 solidly frozen half-gallon ice
cream, brick or round form

4 egg whites
6 tbsp. granulated sugar

Cover a bread board or oven plank with heavy white paper. Place a thin layer of sponge cake on it, then lay the ice cream on top. The cake should extend all around about half an inch beyond the ice cream. Cover *completely* with a thick coating of meringue made from four egg whites beaten stiff with six tablespoons of sugar.

Brown quickly in a very hot oven. Slip from the paper onto a chilled platter. Serve immediately.

[I think the addition of a handful or two of slivered almonds, tossed all over the meringue before it goes in the oven, makes the dish twice as good.]

The Leopard ✳

140 FRONT STREET

expensive

THE SOMALI LEOPARD MOUNTED OVER THE BAR AT THE LEOPARD has a history. Its name is Singha after a native bearer it once did in on an African safari conducted by a young California hunter. Killed in turn, the stuffed leopard was presented to Mr. Bob Antraccoli, who made it the central motif of his restaurant's decor. It is now augmented by spears, shields, African masks, leopard print menus, and another leopard skin in the bar (I didn't get the story of that one).

The Leopard specializes in New York and filet mignon steaks, each cut to at least a pound. There are, besides, double cut lamb and pork chops, grilled salmon and rex sole, and a glorified hamburger of ground filet. Everything is à la carte, so you can make your meal as simple or as ample as your appetite dictates. There is onion or chicken soup, salad, potatoes, vegetables, including pan or French fried onions, and such deserts as cheese cake, or Liederkranz and crackers.

At noon the Leopard serves buffet luncheons. It is a favorite place with the sports world, and the San Francisco Giants baseball club holds its weekly meetings here.

Here are two recipes from the Leopard, one of them for their special baked potato.

> GLAZED NEW YORK STEAK

2 lb. New York steak, cut
thick

4 oz. sour cream
2 oz. Roquefort cheese

Broil the steak on each side for nine minutes. Spread the top with sour cream, then sprinkle with crumbled Roquefort cheese. Replace under the broiler until the cheese melts—about three minutes. Serves two.

NOTE: The Leopard suggests serving this with a chilled tossed salad and a bottle of good cabernet.

> POTATO PRINCESS

per portion:

1 good baking potato
2 tbsp. grated cheddar
cheese

2 tbsp. cream
2 tbsp. butter, softened

Bake the potato. Cut off the top, and scoop out the inside, taking care not to break the skin. Mix the potato with grated cheddar cheese, cream, and softened butter. Replace the potato mixture in the skin, and bake in a very hot oven for four minutes.

✳ *Le Boeuf and Le Poulet*

545 and 535 WASHINGTON STREET

expensive AND moderate

LE BOEUF SPECIALIZES IN STEAKS, AND ITS NEXT DOOR NEIGHBOR (and close relation) in dishes of chicken and fowl with an international flavor. In the steak house you select the size and cut of your steak, and pay by the weight. While it is cooking, there is salad with a choice of dressings, a relish tray, and good French bread. The sizzling steak comes with French fried onions and a baked potato. A tray of mints, nuts, and chocolates arrives with coffee, and there is à la carte cheese cake, Turkish pastry, and ice cream if you are still hungry.

Le Poulet has more to offer than chicken and fowl. The menu includes veal Cordon Bleu, lamb shish kebab, noisettes of beef, and roast prime ribs.

Both establishments are pleasantly modern in decor, rather darkly lighted, yet cheerfully arranged with fresh flowers. The three gentlemen who direct them are Ian Macdonald, manager; Henry Warren, maître d'hôtel; and Tony Vidak, chef. Here is their recipe for one of Le Poulet's specialties.

CHICKEN HAWAIIAN

1 fresh medium sized pineapple
2 to 2½ lb. fresh young
chicken
⅓ cup all-purpose flour
¼ lb. butter
1 tsp. salt
½ tsp. pepper

½ cup shredded coconut
pinch of dry mustard
1 spare tbsp. fresh grated
ginger (this is hot; you
may prefer less)
1 oz. soy sauce
1 cup chicken broth
½ cup rice

Cut pineapple in half, and dig out the fruit from the shell. Reserve both. Cut chicken into four parts. Coat the chicken with flour seasoned with salt and pepper. Fry the chicken in butter, taking care not to overcook. Drain off the butter, and put the chicken in a greased oven-proof casserole. Grate the pineapple pulp over the chicken, sprinkle the coconut and dry mustard over the top, add the fresh ginger, soy sauce, and additional salt to taste. Pour the chicken broth over all, and bake in a 350° oven until chicken is tender—about twenty to twenty-five minutes.

While the chicken is baking, prepare the rice: boil it in one cup of salted water until tender. When chicken is done, line the pineapple halves with a bed of steamed rice, and arrange the chicken and sauce on top. Serve immediately. Serves two.

351

✳ *Lew Lehr's*

3345 STEINER STREET

expensive

THIS STEAKERY IS HOUSED IN THE OLD MARINA DISTRICT POST OF-fice, but the only governmental vestiges are a few peep holes from upstairs offices that now look over the main dining room. Tak Enamoto redesigned the building and the interiors and decorated them with pleasant grass cloth, wood, shojii-type panels, and warm cocoa brown tablecloths.

Lew Lehr started his career as a barker in burlesque during the '33 Chicago fair. When he met up with the other Lew Lehr, who had priority on the name as far as show business was concerned, he took on a succession of new names. After a half dozen years, he decided to open a bar in Chicago, expanded it to include a restaurant, and finally moved on to the Gibson Steak House in Miami. He came west to visit his brothers Phil and Murray, and liked it so well that he never went back. At one time they were all together in the Olympic Hotel steakery, but that is now the sole domain of Phil, while Murray owns the Canterbury Hotel in San Francisco, and the Claremont in Berkeley.

The beef that is served at Lew Lehr's is sometimes show beef —he bids at all the livestock shows, and has several champions' ribbons to prove it. All the meat is aged at least twenty-one days when it is delivered, and hangs several more in Lehr's large refrigerators. When you enter Lehr's you take your choice of filet, New York, or eye of the round, displayed in a large refrigerated case, and tell the counter man exactly how much to cut off, and how you want it cooked. Then it is broiled on a special dripless grill, over white hot lava rocks. The broiler is slanted so that temperatures of from 500° to 800° can be maintained simultaneously, allowing rare and well done orders for the same group to be finished at the same time. As the steaks broil, the chef bastes them with butter and a little monosodium glutamate. You can have garlic butter, if you prefer it. No salt or pepper is used. The finished steak is served on planked metal platters that keep the meat hot through the entire meal. Since they sizzle hard enough to splatter, a bib covers each diner before his steak arrives. The weight of the steak determines the price of the dinner, which includes a crisp salad served from a rolling cart with a choice of dressings; a stuffed baked potato, with butter, sour cream, chives, or bacon to top it; French fried onion rings; relishes; French bread; and coffee. For those who don't like steak, there are African lobster tails.

Here is Lew Lehr's recipe for an especially good baked potato.

BAKED STUFFED POTATO ◀

per portion:

1 large baking potato	2 tbsp. milk
monosodium glutamate	4 tbsp. grated Parmesan
salt and pepper	cheese
4 tbsp. cream	

Bake the potato for one and a half hours in a slow oven—about 300°. Cut off the top, and scoop out the potato. Mash it in a bowl with a sprinkle of monosodium glutamate, salt and pepper, cream, milk, and grated cheese. Fill the shell with this mixture, and refrigerate for fifteen hours. Let stand at room temperature about three hours before reheating. Place in a moderately hot oven until the potato is thoroughly heated through.

III

Directory of Restaurants

ADOLPH'S (*Continental Style*)
641 Vallejo Street
EX. 2-6333
4:30–10:30 p.m., daily
Closed Monday
moderate

ALFRED'S
(*Steak and Continental*)
886 Broadway
SU. 1-7058
4 p.m.–12:30 a.m., daily
3 p.m.–12:30 a.m., Sunday and
holidays
expensive

ALOUETTE (*French*)
1121 Polk Street
GR. 4-1764
5:30–10:30 p.m., daily
Closed Monday
moderate

BARBARY (*Steak*)
490 Pacific
SU. 1-8420
11:30 a.m.–11 p.m., daily
Closed Sunday
moderate

BARDELLI'S
(*Old-Style San Francisco*)
243 O'Farrell Street
YU. 2-0243
11:30 a.m.–11 p.m., Monday–
Friday
4–11 p.m., Saturday
Closed Sunday
moderate

BLUE FOX (*Elegant*)
659 Merchant Street
YU. 1-1177
6 p.m.–midnight, daily
Closed Sunday
expensive

DIRECTORY OF RESTAURANTS

BUENA VISTA CAFE
(Off-Beat)
2765 Hyde Street
GR. 4-5044
10 a.m.–2 a.m., daily
inexpensive

CAIRO (Armenian)
77 Fourth Street
SU. 1-6819
5–9 p.m., daily
5–10 p.m., Saturday
Closed Sunday
inexpensive

CASTAGNOLA'S
(Fish and Seafood)
Fisherman's Wharf
PR. 6-5015
11 a.m.–11:30 p.m.
inexpensive

CHEZ LÉON (French)
124 Ellis Street
YU. 2-1093
5:30–10:30 p.m., daily
Closed Sunday and Monday
moderate

CHEZ MARGUERITE
(French)
2330 Taylor Street
PR. 5-9785
6–10 p.m., Wednesday–Saturday
5:30–9:30 p.m., Sunday

Closed Monday and Tuesday
moderate

CHO CHO (Japanese)
1020 Kearny Street
EX. 7-3066
6 p.m.–2 a.m., daily
Closed Sunday
moderate

COACHMAN (British)
1057 Powell Street
EX. 2-9903
5:30–10:30 p.m., daily
moderate

DES ALPES RESTAURANT
(Family Style)
732 Broadway
GA. 1-9909
5:30–9:00 p.m., daily
Closed Monday
inexpensive

DOMINO CLUB
(Continental Style)
25 Trinity Place
EX. 2-5579
11–2 a.m., Monday–Saturday
Dinner, daily and Sunday
moderate

DOROS (Continental Style)
714 Montgomery Street
EX. 7-6822
Lunch and dinner, daily
expensive

EL PRADO (*Elegant—lunch*)
Plaza Hotel
Union Square (Post near Stockton)
SU. 1-7200
Noon–9 p.m., daily
Closed Sunday and holidays
expensive

ERNIE'S (*Elegant*)
847 Montgomery Street
EX. 7-5969
5:30–11 p.m., daily
expensive

FIOR D'ITALIA (*Italian*)
621 Union Street
YU. 6-1886
11:30 a.m.–midnight, daily
4 p.m.–midnight, Saturday and Sunday
2–11 p.m., holidays
expensive

FISHERMAN'S GROTTO #9
(*Fish and Seafood*)
Fisherman's Wharf
OR. 3-7025
9:30–2 a.m., daily
inexpensive

FLEUR DE LYS (*French*)
777 Sutter Street
OR. 3-7779
5:30–11:30 p.m., daily
Closed Sunday and Monday
expensive

FLY TRAP
(*Old-Style San Francisco*)
73 Sutter Street
DO. 2-9781
11 a.m.–9 p.m., daily
3–9 p.m., Sunday
Closed Saturday
moderate

GARDEN COURT
(*Elegant—lunch*)
The Palace Hotel
New Montgomery at Market
EX. 2-8600
Breakfast: 6:15–11:00 a.m., daily
Lunch: 11:30 a.m.–2 p.m., daily
Dinner (with theatre): 6 p.m., curtain at 8:30 p.m., Monday–Saturday;
5:30 p.m., curtain at 8 p.m., Sunday
expensive

GLAD HAND (*Off-Beat*)
588 Bridgeway, Sausalito
ED. 2-9775
5:30–10:30 p.m., daily
4–10:30 p.m., Sunday
moderate

GRISON'S (*Steak and Chicken*)
Van Ness and Pacific
Steak House: OR. 3-1888
5–11 p.m., daily

359

GRISON'S (continued)
3–11 p.m., Sunday
Closed Tuesday
expensive
Chicken House: TU. 5-2050
4–10 p.m., daily
2–10 p.m., Sunday
Closed Monday
moderate

**HENRY'S FASHION RES-
TAURANT**
(*Continental Style*)
22 Davis Street
SU. 1-8485
11 a.m.–11 p.m., daily
Closed Sunday
moderate

HOTEL DE FRANCE
(*Family Style*)
780 Broadway
GA. 1-6410
5–10 p.m., daily
inexpensive

IMPERIAL PALACE
(*Chinese*)
919 Grant Avenue
YU. 2-4440
11:30 a.m.–midnight, Sunday–
Thursday
11:30–2:30 a.m., Friday and
Saturday
expensive

INDIA HOUSE (*Indian*)
629 Washington Street
EX. 2-0744
5:30–10:30 p.m., daily
Closed Sunday
expensive

JACK'S (*French*)
615 Sacramento Street
GA. 1-9854
11:30 a.m.–9:30 p.m., daily
4–9:30 p.m., Sunday
expensive

KAN'S (*Chinese*)
708 Grant Avenue
YU. 2-2388
Noon–11 p.m., Monday–Fri-
day
4:30–11:30 p.m., Saturday
5–11 p.m., Sunday
expensive

KOE'S AUBERGE (*French*)
1205 Stockton Street
EX. 2-1608
6–10:30 p.m., daily
Closed Sunday
moderate

LA BOURGOGNE (*French*)
320 Mason Street
DO. 2-7352
5 p.m.–midnight, daily
Closed Sunday
expensive

LAMBROS (*Continental Style*)
315 Bush Street
YU. 6-6165
11 a.m.–10:30 p.m., daily
moderate

LA PETITE AUBERGE
(*French*)
704–4th Street, San Rafael
456-5808
5:30 p.m.–midnight, Tuesday–
Saturday
4–10:30 p.m., Sunday
Closed Monday
expensive

LE BOEUF (*Steak*)
545 Washington Street
GA. 1-2914
11:30 a.m.–11 p.m., daily
expensive

LEW LEHR'S (*Steak*)
3345 Steiner Street
WE. 1-0575
5–11 p.m., daily
4–10:30 p.m., Sunday
expensive

LEOPARD CAFE (*Steak*)
140 Front Street
EX. 2-3348
11:30 a.m.–2:30 p.m., daily
5–11 p.m., daily
expensive

LE POULET (*Chicken*)
535 Washington Street
YU. 1-0417
11:30 a.m.–11 p.m., daily
moderate

LUPO'S (*Italian*)
1042 Kearny Street
SU. 1-9938
from 5 p.m. daily
Closed Tuesday
moderate

MAYE'S OYSTER HOUSE
(*Fish and Seafood*)
1233 Polk Street
GR. 4-7674
11 a.m.–11:30 p.m., daily
Closed Holidays
inexpensive

MIKE'S (or DANTE'S)
BILLIARD PARLOR
(*Off-Beat*)
521 Broadway
YU. 2-8872
11–4 a.m., daily
inexpensive

NAM YUEN (*Chinese*)
740 Washington Street
SU. 1-5636
11:30–2:45 a.m., daily
Closed Monday
inexpensive

361

OMAR KHAYYAM'S
(*Armenian*)
196 O'Farrell Street
SU. 1-1010
4 p.m.–midnight, daily
2 p.m.–midnight, Sunday and
most holidays
Noon–midnight, special holidays
moderate

ONDINE (*Continental Style*)
558 Bridgeway, Sausalito
ED. 2-7091, or YU. 2-1740 in
San Francisco
5:30 p.m. on, daily
5 p.m. on, Sunday
expensive

ORESTE'S (*Italian*)
118 Jones Street
GR. 4-5811
11:30 a.m.–midnight, daily
4 p.m.–midnight, Saturday,
Sunday, holidays
expensive

PANELLI'S (*Continental Style*)
453 Pine Street
DO. 2-7198
11:30 a.m.–midnight, daily
moderate

PAOLI'S (*Continental Style*)
Montgomery at California
SU. 1-7115
11–1 a.m., daily
4 p.m.–2 a.m., Saturday, Sunday, and Holidays
expensive

PLACE PIGALLE (*French*)
3721 Buchanan Street
WE. 1-5644
6 p.m.–midnight daily
5 p.m.–midnight, Sunday
Closed Monday
moderate

RATHSKELLER (*German*)
600 Turk Street
PR. 5-3188
11 a.m.–10 p.m., bar until 2
a.m., Monday–Friday
4–10 p.m., bar until 2
a.m., Saturday and Sunday
inexpensive

RED KNIGHT
(*Continental Style*)
624 Sacramento Street
EX. 7-4257
Lunch, 11:30 a.m.–3 p.m.,
Monday–Friday
Dinner, 5:30–11 p.m.
Monday–Saturday
Closed Sunday
expensive

REDWOOD ROOM
(*Elegant—*lunch)
Clift Hotel
Geary Street at Taylor
PR. 5-4700
11 a.m.–11 p.m., daily
expensive

RITZ OLD POODLE DOG
(*French*)
65 Post Street
SU. 1-1919
11:30 a.m.–10:30 p.m., daily
4–10:30 p.m., Sunday
expensive

RUBINI'S (*Continental Style*)
10 Olema Road, Fairfax
GL. 6-3870
5–10 p.m.
Closed Monday and Tuesday
moderate

SAI YON (*Chinese*)
641 Jackson Street
YU. 2-3814
11–6:30 a.m., daily
inexpensive

SAM'S GRILL
(*Old-Style San Francisco*)
374 Bush Street
GA. 1-0594
11 a.m.–8:30 p.m., daily
Closed Saturday and Sunday
moderate

SAM'S ANCHOR CAFE
(*Off-Beat*)
27 Main Street, Tiburon
GE. 5-4527
breakfast, lunch, dinner:
10–2 a.m., daily
moderate

SAM WO (*Chinese*)
813 Washington Street
YU. 2-0596
11 a.m.–1:30 p.m.; 7 p.m.–9
a.m., daily
Closed Sunday
very inexpensive

SCHROEDER'S CAFE
(*German*)
240 Front Street
GA. 1-4778
11 a.m.–9:30 p.m., daily (no
women until after 1:30 p.m.)
Closed Saturday and Sunday
inexpensive

SORRENTO (*Italian*)
314 Columbus
SU. 1-5037
4 p.m.–2 a.m., daily
moderate

363

SUN HUNG HEUNG
(Chinese)
744 Washington Street
YU. 2-2319
11:30–3 a.m., daily
Closed Tuesday
inexpensive

SWISS LOUIS (Continental)
493 Broadway
GA. 1-2913
Noon–11 p.m., bar until 2 a.m.,
Monday–Friday
4–11 p.m., bar until 2 a.m.,
Saturday and Sunday
moderate

TADICH GRILL
(Old-Style San Francisco)
545 Clay Street
SU. 1-9754
11 a.m.–10:30 p.m., daily
Closed Sunday
moderate

TAJ OF INDIA (Indian)
825 Pacific
EX. 2-0089
6–10:30 p.m., Monday–Thursday
6–11 p.m., Friday and Saturday
5–10 p.m., Sunday
moderate

TAO TAO (Chinese)
675 Jackson Street
YU. 2-6125

4:30 p.m.–2 a.m., daily
Closed Thursday
moderate

TARANTINO'S
(Fish and Seafood)
Fisherman's Wharf
PR. 5-5600
11 a.m.–midnight
moderate

TRADER VIC'S (Elegant)
20 Cosmo Place
PR. 6-2232
Lunch: 11:30 a.m.–2:30 p.m.,
daily
Dinner: 5:00 p.m.–12:30 a.m.,
daily
expensive

VENETO (Italian)
Mason at Bay
YU. 6-4553
11–1 a.m., daily
4 p.m.–1 a.m., Saturday
2 p.m.–midnight, Sunday
moderate

YAMATO (Japanese)
717 California Street
EX. 7-3456
11:45 a.m.–2 p.m.; 5–10 p.m.,
Tuesday–Saturday
3–10 p.m., Sunday
Closed Monday
moderate

Index of Recipes

INDEX

INDEX

rent customers include Coldplay, Jake Gyllenhaal, and Sky, the UK-based television and communications firm. Myclimate counts Coca-Cola, Ben & Jerry's, Virgin Atlantic, and Unilever among its clients. Gatherings including the 2006 G8 summit and the 2008 Democratic National Convention as well as high-profile annual events such as the Oscars also procure voluntary offsets. Joining along are surging numbers of everyday fliers and drivers headed to business meetings and vacations. Growth in voluntary offsets has spiked in recent years, and the market is expected to be worth $4 billion by 2010.

But as the industry matures and expands, some crucial aspects of retail offsets marketed to the public remain obscure. Differing from credits generated via cap-and-trade policies mandated under the Kyoto framework—issued primarily to large companies, not individuals, and monitored by a United Nations agency—retail offsets are entirely voluntary. They're also entirely unregulated. Offset brokers are not compelled to meet any standards, have no required inspections, project approvals, or reviews, and no obligatory follow-up assessments to ensure the efficacy of the carbon remediation. Although organizations exist that offer certification for projects that meet a set of guidelines, such as the Gold Standard, these efforts are in no way mandatory. And, as I found out, the certifiers don't always maintain the highest standards themselves.

Even the more visible aspects of offsetting such as pricing are dubious. In this market the product for sale is the "credit," which is equal to a ton of CO_2. Emissions caused by activities that require burning fossil fuels, such as running errands in the car or taking a flight to visit family, can be measured, but these metrics vary widely. Each offset firm comes up with its own formula to calibrate its website's "carbon calculator." The calculator prompts the conscientious eco-shopper to confess the miles he or she plans to travel, and whether it's air or road; those seeking full absolution will also find inputs for daily energy use. After entering the information, out comes a pollution quotient and a correlating dollar amount. In part because the market is still new, no standard prices exist so the numbers are all over the map. Consider the varying fees to neutralize the CO_2 emissions from a round-trip New York City–Mumbai flight. The CarbonNeutral Company offers three options that range in price between $36 and $87. To do the same job, Myclimate charges considerably more: for their credits a consumer would pay $250 to contribute to an offset project in a developing country such as India, or $760 toward a project in Switzerland. Beyond cost, there's no official industry registry so it's impossible to know how many credits exist for any given project, and how many have been sold and to whom. Consequently, it's impossible to know if companies are vending the same credits multiple times. The industry is riddled with inconsistencies and an overall lack of transparency, leaving tremendous room for fraud that cheats consumers and the atmosphere.

Further, to get the job done, greenhouse gas neutralization doesn't happen immediately but only over the life of the project. That means trees planted to sop up carbon from today's long-haul flight or cross-country tour will only absorb the CO_2 over the life of the tree, which could be one hundred years or more, depending on the species. Since CO_2 absorption is lower in saplings than in mature specimens, it takes time for a newly planted tree to reach meaningful sequestration levels. The remedy might seem obvious: plant trees with shorter life spans that reach maturity sooner. However, these trees also die sooner, and upon expiring— as is true with all trees—begin releasing the entire carbon load they've soaked up. In other words, even when trees have full, healthy lives (unlike Coldplay's mango forest), they invariably dump the CO_2 they've absorbed right back into the atmosphere. Trees with shorter life spans of, say, thirty years as is the case with willows, or fifty years, as with birch (TCNC uses both varieties in reforestation projects), if planted today will begin releasing their stored CO_2 between the years of 2040 and 2060. At that time, it's likely the world will still be struggling to bring down carbon levels; how will we handle those deferred emissions then? Alternately, when trees take in CO_2 over a much longer time, say a century, greenhouse gas levels continue to rise in the immediate future, precisely when they need to come down.

Sadly, marketing the prospect of neutralizing a consumer's greenhouse gases conveys to people that their contribution to global warming can successfully, and quickly, be annulled. Statements of relief about this from the British pop musician KT Tunstall indicate how misleading this system can be. To cleanse the greenhouse gases from her release *Eye to the Telescope*, the musician paid TCNC to plant fifteen hundred trees in Scotland. "I can now say that producing this album hasn't harmed the environment at all," Tunstall told a reporter in 2005. "It's going to be carbon neutral for me from herein. Each time I use the tour bus, each time I play a gig, more trees will be planted." The musician explained how shocked she was when TCNC told her she emitted almost seventy times more carbon than the average Brit. "I said immediately whatever proportion of my earnings it takes to put back into the environment what I've taken out, that's fine. I just wanted to put back in what I've taken out."

Stuffing the global-warming genie back into the bottle is the tough task offset companies promise to fulfill. But what's actually going down in the places where these guilt- and carbon-scrubbing projects materialize? In addition to tree planting, offset money also funds renewable energy projects such as wind, solar, and biomass meant to provide power that would otherwise come from fossil fuels. India is host to more than a quarter of carbon-offset ventures globally, in part because it costs considerably less to build these projects in developing countries. In the fall of 2008, I visit the southern state of Karnataka, which has its fair share of CO_2 neutralization projects; here some light might be shed on what transpires after a consumer sitting at his or her computer in New York City or London clicks the OFFSET MY CARBON NOW button and pays up with the credit card.

GUDIBANDA AND BANGALORE

It's nighttime and I'm at a cooperative dairy in a remote village that's part of Gudibanda. I'm here to find out what happens to the vestiges of a failed offset project, in this case the Coldplay mango forest. In the room with me are about nine men; most of them are standing because there are only a few chairs. I am sitting, and they are all staring at me. The room is dank and the air musky with the smell of milk just out of the body of a cow. The green paint on the concrete walls is faded and chipped and, in some places, splattered with mud. The president of the dairy has positioned himself behind a beat-up metal desk. His hair is coiffed and oiled, and he wears slacks and shined shoes. It's the uniform of a man on the take; he clearly doesn't earn his living as a farmer. All the other men do, and they're scruffy, their lungis are soiled and they have cheap plastic sandals on their feet. Resting on the desk, the president's fists are studded with a dazzle of gold rings.

More men gather in front of the building outside the room's only window, which has bars over it. The drone of the cooling vats where farmers deposit their day's milk muffles any sound from outside and, I realize, any sound that might come from this room. "I don't know what you're talking about," the dairy president says to me, smiling through his combed mustache. His expression comes across as menacing, and as I ask more questions, the tension mounts. Back in 2002 the dairy president was a member of the local governing body known as the panchayat. I am told by current panchayat members that he would at least have heard of the mango project. In a specious manner, the president tells me of some development projects that have come along in the last few years, but he can't remember the names of the NGOs involved. He consults with the farmers; everyone says he knows nothing about the Coldplay mango forest.

Most of the farmers here raise livestock or grow peanuts, millet, or lentils; others have mango plantations. One mango farmer sits down next to my translator and confesses that he remembers the project. The president interrupts, blustering that the man doesn't know what he's talking about, then stares him down. The terse, nonverbal exchange is over within seconds. The farmer doesn't say another word. Some of the nut growers have brought handfuls of dried peanut plants into the room and set them on the desk. The president sifts through the leaves for the shells, cracks them open, and eats the nuts raw. They are shriveled like raisins. The men talk about the ongoing drought and how this year's harvest is stunted. As he eats, the president lets the shells fall across the desk and onto the floor. Someone else will clean them up.

A couple of farmers offer to roast some nuts. A few minutes later, in the dirt patch in front of the dairy, they use matches to light the bundles on fire. The flames are short and fast, streaks in the darkness. One of the men stands over the burning, staring as if in a trance. Soon he lifts his leg and stamps the fire out. The scorched peanuts taste like soot and smoke and make me nauseous. When my translator and I get up to leave, the president asks us to stay a little longer. My translator suggests we don't. The group of men escorts us to our car.

As we drive away, our headlights shoot their beams on darkened houses made of granite. In this part of Karnataka the rock is more abundant than wood, so peasants drag thick slabs from the hillsides back to the village to build their shacks. The village is quiet and no one is around. I spot a tiny shop; from inside, the green-white glow of a fluorescent tube washes onto the dirt road. We pull over to talk to the couple crammed behind the counter. I buy some fried lentil biscuits, and as I'm paying, my translator asks if they know anything about the mango forest. The woman keeps her mouth shut as the man steps forward. He begins to answer, but then his eyes wander. I turn around and the man with the rings is behind me. The shopkeeper immediately tells him we were asking about the mango trees. "You believe *me*," the president of the dairy commands in a low voice. The farmer who told us he knew of the project is also here and invites me to come with them; he wants to show me his farm. It's pitch-black outside, I say no. The man with the rings insists. My translator and I jump into our car and get the hell out of there.

Anandi Sharan's name is listed on the website of a renewable energy company called Decentralized Energy Systems India Private Limited, or DESI. The firm is based in Bangalore and is chaired by Anandi's father, Dr. K. S. Sharan. The green-energy outfit is focused on a project to bring renewable biomass electricity to one hundred villages and is currently receiving money from Myclimate, a trusted Swiss voluntary offsetter. DESI purchases biomass gasifier generators for its project from a company called NetPro, which it shares an office with and which is owned by Dr. Sharan's brother. And rather astoundingly, the certifier of the hundred-village venture is Anandi Sharan herself. After the mango tree fiasco, she didn't back away from offsets but has instead expanded her reach. Her company is called CER India Private Ltd.; among its services are verification of the feasibility and efficacy of both voluntary and UN-regulated CDM projects. Apparently, the Sharans offer one-stop CO_2 offset shopping.

Every time I call to make an appointment to interview someone at DESI's Bangalore office, the woman on the other end of the line tells me no one's there and to try again in a few days. Finally, one afternoon I just show up. The office seems deserted; the lights are off and only a few people quietly mill about. The company's development engineer, Kaveri Uthaiah, agrees to an interview. She is tall and thin, only a few years out of college, and has a bad cold. Having graduated with a degree in environmental science, Uthaiah now works on DESI's hundred-village project, being carried out far from here in the northeastern state of Bihar. It is India's poorest, least developed, and most lawless region. In the last two years, DESI has installed four NetPro biogas electricity-generation units in three adjacent villages in Bihar.

Uthaiah explains that her job is to oversee the women's self-help groups DESI initiated to encourage business activity in the villages with the aim of strengthening demand for electricity. ("If we didn't, we wouldn't be able to generate the power and offset the carbon," she tells me.) Stemming from this work, dozens of businesses have been established, she proudly states, which means the project serves both the environmental and social good. When I ask for some examples, Uthaiah stammers, then says she knows of a rice mill and a workshop. What kind of workshop? "I'll have to get back to you with that information."

What Uthaiah does have is a video about NetPro's biogas technology. She hits PLAY on a laptop and a bold classical score, clearly influenced by *Star Wars,* issues forth from the tinny speakers. As the video rolls, it becomes clear that its aim is to obscure rather than illuminate. The movie doesn't show any images of real equipment, but instead begrudgingly leads the eye through a 3-D animated version of a biogas power plant. All of the equipment is rendered only as a series of cylinders, boxes, and rectangles, with no views of what would be happening inside the machine, no explanation of what the fuel source is, and not a word about how much energy can be produced. What I'm watching more closely resembles an experimental art film than an industrial video.

I ask if I can see pictures of the power plants and the new businesses in Bihar. Uthaiah says she doesn't have any. "They're all on Dr. Sharan's laptop, which he has with him"—and he's not here. Anandi Sharan's cousin Aklavya, who's an engineer at NetPro, comes into the room and says he has photos in his office. I wonder why DESI works in the remote and dangerous region of Bihar. Aklavya tells me Bihar is where the Sharan family comes from. "Our grandfather was a lawyer and earned the people's respect, so everyone will do what we say now," he states. Aklavya also boasts, as did Uthaiah, that in 2006 DESI won a $200,000 award from the World Bank for its initial work in Bihar.

At his computer Aklavya clicks through a PowerPoint presentation, scrolling to a photograph of a real biogas power generator. "This is what it looks like," he says. "But this isn't a machine that's in Bihar, this one is in Tamil Nadu," a state in the country's far south. I press for something that depicts the work they're doing in Bihar. He offers two other pictures. In the first a row of five or six women dressed in brightly colored saris pose for the camera with the countryside in the background. The other shows about twenty women seated in a room for what looks like a meeting; evidently this is one of the women's self-help groups. Aklavya says he has no other photos.

I ask Uthaiah and Aklavya—representatives of this award-winning renewable energy company that's helping lift the most vulnerable out of poverty—for a brochure detailing its activities, but DESI has no such literature. Before I leave, Uthaiah says that in the coming year DESI will expand its hundred-village project to twenty more locations—an ambitious plan from a company that has just five employees. I subsequently find a news article in which Dr. Sharan says this expansion will be accomplished in eighteen months. The article also says that, according to Dr. Sharan, DESI gets 50 percent of its investments from selling carbon credits, so the faster it gets projects on the books, the fuller its pockets will be.

The Sharans make the biogas units, they get the carbon offset money and run the social programs, they do their own offset verification, and they are politically influential in the region where the projects are implemented, which is a dangerous place for outsiders to visit uninvited. It's a self-contained system, one that's effectively closed to people such as me who might check on the validity of their offset enterprise.

Perhaps the project in Bihar is happening; perhaps micro-entrepreneurs are getting green power and gaining opportunities they wouldn't otherwise have. Maybe the biogas plants work and truly are renewable, maybe they are keeping CO_2 from spilling into the sky. Ultimately it's impossible to know what's really going on with voluntary offset ventures. Official CDM projects require more documentation, audits, and verifications, yet even this information is limited in its ability to truly capture what's happening in situ. For any given CO_2 offset endeavor, the official "project development documents," letters from host countries, and stakeholder comments offer convincing assurances that this endeavor will eliminate carbon dioxide and most certainly improve the livelihoods of the rural poor. But that isn't always the case.

MALAVALLI

The power is out again in the hamlet of Heggur, in Karnataka State. Manini, as I will call her, moves from her kitchen into the small brick-and-mud dwelling's only other room and flicks the switch once to make sure. No current. The mother of two teenage children feels with her hands for the kerosene lamp that's fashioned from a used glass flask and a short line of twine. It's stored on the room's only shelf, near the narrow wood bench that also serves as the family's bed. The match pops when it lights and gulps brighter when it touches the fuel-soaked wick. Her brother, who has been talking with some friends after a day laboring in the fields—it's sugarcane-harvesting season and they have work for the time being—reaches for a second lamp in the dim glow. Manini resumes her work in the kitchen; the small ceramic stove that rises about two feet off the floor radiates heat, but not much light. She knows where everything is, though; she feels for the silver water jug and pours the liquid into the pot that's heating on the stove as a faint trail of smoke begins filling the enclosed room.

The electricity comes back on in about half an hour. In this impoverished rural farming region of Karnataka, blackouts are normal and it can take six, seven, or more hours before voltage again courses through the village lines. Most power from the central grid is absorbed by the teeming city of Bangalore, home to almost 6 million. According to the people I talk to in the village of Heggur, the Indian government first installed transmission cables through this part of Karnataka in the 1970s, but the supply has always been unpredictable. With the rise of India as a global economic force, and Bangalore as the Asian hub of the information technology sector, millions of new city dwellers and power-intensive businesses now draw on a supply that cannot keep pace.

A new kind of energy company, Malavalli Power Plant Private Ltd., or MPPL, walked into this situation in 2001. The company had a unique plan for Heggur and its neighboring villages in an area called Malavalli, from which the firm derived its name. MPPL would build a forty-five-hundred-kilowatt biomass power plant, which could burn organic residues such as sugarcane leaves and rice straw left in fields after harvest, mill wastes, including sawdust, dead palm fronds, and branches trimmed from trees felled for paper pulp or construction. Unlike coal, oil, and natural gas, which release concentrations of carbon stored up over millennia, when organic matter is burned, it emits no more CO_2 than the plant took in while it was alive. The facility would channel its renewable electricity to the surrounding energy-deficient villages and provide work and training that would promote higher living standards, upward mobility, and stable incomes.

Government bodies such as Karnataka Renewable Energy Development Ltd. liked the plan for its environmental pathbreaking; according to MPPL, no such project had been developed anywhere in the country. The only problem was that MPPL needed more than just government support such as tax breaks and subsidies to cover the high cost of biomass incineration technology. But MPPL knew they could turn to another source: the emerging retail carbon-offset sector. So when the alt-energy company was approached by Myclimate, they took the deal.

"We are planning on building two more in Karnataka, and over fifty small-scale plants in Punjab," P. Sekhar, the director of MPPL, tells me as we talk in the company's bustling office in Bangalore. "Malavalli is an experimental plant. That's where we worked out the system: establishing the fuel-supply-chain model, processing the fuel, and how to design and build the equipment to adequately take and use this fuel." In addition to Myclimate, MPPL has received money for its Malavalli plant from several other offset entities based in the United States, Canada, and France, including Sustainable Travel International, PURE, and Climat Mundi. Companies like these typically contribute to several projects; the amount paid by a consumer is pooled with everyone else's money, then distributed to the various projects. Myclimate invests both in Switzerland and internationally in endeavors aimed mostly at fostering renewable energy. With a translator I make the 120-kilometer journey from Bangalore to Malavalli to find out more.

Tiny villages and shantytowns dot the lush farmland that surrenders to the swell of granite hills in the water-rich district of Mandya, where Malavalli and MPPL are located. Rutted, narrow roads cut through a patchwork of small plots chockablock with sugarcane, rice, millet, peanuts, and coconut palms. The villages are typically situated up winding dirt paths nestled within the fields. This part of the district also has many shantytowns where the landless live clustered along the main road and near the canals that run throughout the area. Their makeshift shelters are fashioned from dead palm fronds, blue tarps, and sheets of black plastic. Children play between the tentlike structures as women tend smoldering outdoor cooking fires and wash clothes in the narrow canals that run with muddy irrigation water.

Those who live in the villages are decidedly less destitute, having inherited houses and land from their families, who've been here for generations. But times are hard for some who, to give their offspring a place to farm, have divided their parcels so much that little is left for anyone to earn a living from. "It used to be much easier here, it was inexpensive to live and plenty of space," explains the wizened matriarch of a family in another village in Malavalli called Chikke Gowda Halli. "When we were raising our children, we had no worries about how we would survive." Her large family is now struggling, most of them having sold off their land to raise money with the hopes of finding work in one of the rice- or sawmills, or possibly the biomass plant.

One of the matriarch's sons tried to secure a job at MPPL for his own grown son. "But the people there had a lot of favoritism and asked me for a bribe," he recalls, still angry. "They only hired people they knew or people who paid them off." He claims the going price at the time was thirty thousand rupees, US$620, a sum he could not raise. Although the weather-beaten, middle-aged man hoped to see his son with a white-collar job, they both must now search for temporary labor in other farmers' fields, where they can expect to earn about US$1.50 per day.

Back in nearby Heggur, I find some men who are among those fortunate enough to have got jobs at the MPPL biomass station. A man I will refer to as Sakash says he started working there just under a year ago, while a fellow villager I'll call Amalendu got his job a few months after that (neither were asked to pay bribes; in fact the subject never comes up in our conversations). They both work among the hundred or so men who pull the leaves, branches, and husks from the outdoor storage yard into the building to feed the furnaces.

In his thirties, Sakash is lean and has a thick mustache. He wears clean shorts with a collared shirt accented with a terry-cloth towel thrown over his right shoulder and around his neck, a standard local look. When he started at MPPL, Sakash didn't realize the plant had worker safety issues. Neither did Amalendu, who's also in his thirties and sports a mustache and towel. The men say they are given no protective gear at the plant, and that the company has failed to install safety devices on its fuel-processing equipment. When I inquire MPPL tells me the facility provides hard hats and goggles, which are required for workers in the boiler-feeding area. However, the photos of the facility posted on Myclimate's website, which the offsetter and MPPL perhaps haven't reviewed, show men working in the boiler room, and none of them wear hats or eye shields.

Amalendu works the night shift hauling sugarcane leaves, palm fronds, and other fuel from the yard outside the power station into the boiler room. He explains that the leaves and branches stored outside form nests for the many snakes common in the region, which include cobras. The workers use their hands to load and move the material, but are given no gloves, and the facility doesn't adequately light the yard for the night-shift workers to help them avoid snakes. Consequently, workers must endure frequent poisonous bites. Amalendu was recently struck in the forearm; after a week's recuperation—without pay—he was back to good health. But that's not always the case. Sakash confirms that the workers are in constant fear of snakebites and tells me of a coworker who died from a bite he got on the job.

The equipment the plant uses also presents hazards. Before wood goes into the fire it must be sent through a shredder. The mouth of the machine is so large, Sakash tells me, "an entire human body could fit through it." But, he says, it has no safety guards, a charge neither MPPL nor Myclimate disputes in our communications. Sakash speaks of another laborer who lost his hand when he reached in to clear a jammed piece of wood. When I ask Amalendu about precautionary measures at the plant, he tells me there basically are none. "What goes on in the factory is a hush-hush thing," he says. "When Westerners come, you don't let them into the factory." Indeed MPPL denied my request to see the power station.

The MPPL website, like Myclimate's, paints a very different picture of its biomass project from what I found. MPPL's take highlights the benefits that are accruing to villagers such as those in Heggur with a flowchart tracing the social and environmental good works of distributing its carbon neutral power locally and creating jobs.

According to MPPL's website, the green energy leaves its facility, enters a "switch yard," and flows out for "rural electricity distribution." Since the peasants and laborers in the surrounding area lack an adequate supply, increased access to electricity would undoubtedly improve quality of life. A case study currently available from one of MPPL's certifiers, the Gold Standard, states that the facility "provides reliable energy for 18 hours per day, and with improved voltage." However, that's not an accurate depiction of what daily life in Malavalli entails. The energy produced at the biomass plant isn't sent by special lines to the nearby villages, but instead goes into the central grid. Everyone I ask in several of the surrounding villages says they get a maximum of twelve hours of power, six in the morning and six in the evening, riddled with unpredictable blackouts.

In terms of jobs, MPPL says the biomass facility's presence has created more than 400 jobs in the community. Myclimate says the project generates $1 million annually for local farmers who sell their crop wastes and that it has led to 650 new jobs. According to MPPL those include positions for metering and issuing bills, as well as bill collection and "complaints recording," the latter two performed by women's self-help groups, as the company's website states. Yet there are no metering, billing, or customer service jobs. Household power bills are ascertained, issued by, and paid directly to the state government, the same system that was in place before MPPL's power plant arrived. In mid-2009, when I ask about the discrepancy between what I found and what MPPL claims, the company says the jobs were part of a pilot project that was active from June 2004 until April 2005. MPPL's chairman, K. Krishan, tells me the firm has been "remiss" in keeping its website current on this point.

The flowchart on MPPL's website also illustrates that the company is composting its only by-product, ash, into a usable "organic fertilizer," which creates more jobs. MPPL's Krishan says the company employs twenty workers to process waste ash with cane trash and cow dung into fertilizer. In addition, the company's website states, outside jobs are generated because women's self-help groups sell the compost to area farmers. In mid-2009 MPPL sends me photos it says were recently taken at the composting operation, and maps of where the facility is located. It's in the village of Heggur. Everyone I talked to over the two days I'd spent in Heggur—a tiny village—including farmers and MPPL workers, however, said no compost facility exists (not to mention any fertilizer-selling women's self-help groups, which, in our exchange, Krishan admits were also part of the long-defunct pilot project). Further, when I was in Heggur, no ash-processing operation was visible in the countryside around the village. Perhaps MPPL is composting, but I saw no trace of it.

As for the jobs that have materialized, I meet no one in the villages around MPPL who has been given a chance to work in the power plant's offices, where fifty people are employed. Everyone I talk to says these better-paid positions are reserved for outsiders who've already earned higher degrees. The only direct jobs the villagers seem to have access to is loading the fuel into the boiler, which number about one hundred. Other new jobs that have come about are with hauling contractors who collect crop wastes to deliver to the plant. According to MPPL these jobs total almost four hundred, which, based on interviews I did with two contractors, seems slightly high but nevertheless realistic.

Environmentally, the one undisputable success of the project is that it generates energy without burning fossil fuels. This has created a booming local market for combustibles, however. Consequently, people such as Manini, who earns $1 a day when she can find work, must often buy wood whereas before she could gather crop wastes and dead branches as needed. The effects on the poorest are substantial because they make fires multiple times a day for cooking and to heat water for washing. And with more people buying firewood, vendors are felling increasing numbers of trees to meet demand. What's more, Sakash tells me he cuts trees on his land to sell directly to the power station to earn extra money. He knows others who do the same. While MPPL's chairman says the company does "not at all contribute to residents cutting down trees," Amalendu as well as Manini's brothers say they've seen an uptick in tree clearing since MPPL opened.

Sakash assures me that he plants saplings to replace whatever he's cut down, and perhaps the others do, too. But either way, what's happening inevitably puts pressure on the land, and on water systems, which suffer when trees are felled. When organic materials are used for fuel, they will compete for soil with either food crops or natural ecosystems. Using what are truly wastes to generate electricity is a viable solution, but it has limits that are easily disregarded.

MPPL's biomass plant carries a seal of approval from the Gold Standard, the most highly respected third-party certifier in the over-the-counter offset market. The Gold Standard is a nonprofit entity started in 2003 by a small group of nongovernmental organizations, including the World Wildlife Fund, or WWF. According to WWF's website the Gold Standard (GS) was formed to "ensure top quality projects." To do so GS dispatches inspectors to verify a project's social and environmental claims. When I contacted GS, the representative said what I had found at MPPL was "alarming" and that "this project in particular has been subject to extensive reviews, research, and monitoring both by the carbon community and independent groups." (She also tells me that GS has yet to issue its license to MPPL from 2008, even though both Myclimate and MPPL continue to use the GS logo.) That professionally trained inspectors miss what an outsider could learn in days begs the question of whether it's realistic to think any certification body can and will keep up with what's actually going on. Maybe some inspectors are lazy, or on the take, but what seems most likely is that such a job—of making sure carbon is reduced while the surrounding ecosystem is protected and social well-being is improved— simply can't be done.

NAGARLE

Harish Hande doesn't like carbon offsets. "It's a load of rubbish," he tells me when we meet at the Bangalore headquarters of his firm, Solar Electric Light Company, or SELCO. "Windmill companies, carbon offset verification companies, they're all pitching projects as investments to make the most money in the quickest period of time. It's not about renewable energy, it's about making money, that's it, that's all." He's pissed off. "Good things could be happening with this money, it's not that I'm opposed to companies paying to help subsidize renewable energy, it's just that it's not being used that way. It's criminal."

Despite his scathing criticism, Hande accepts money from The CarbonNeutral Company. He uses the funds to help propel SELCO, a for-profit maker of solar panels and lighting systems for "underserved households," mostly the rural poor. Hande sees himself not so much as an environmentalist as a social entrepreneur. While SELCO is primarily a manufacturer of micro-solar systems, its business model includes assisting many of its customers in securing loans from rural banks to purchase the firm's products. By doing so, SELCO hopes to take away a barrier that keeps those with few resources from tapping into off-grid energy: the initial outlay for the hardware. A typical SELCO package includes a twenty-watt panel hooked up to two light fixtures, and a battery that stores enough power for three to four hours of juice. It costs about $260. Although the price is high for someone who earns $2 or less a day, in the world of photovoltaic technology, that sum is low. SELCO is able to get the cost down by pruning the system so that it provides light but not much more. "We work with people to figure out what they need. Not what they *want*, but what they actually *need*," Hande explains. In other words, if they're willing to scale back, even the world's poorest can have renewable green power.

To see the offset-subsidized micro-solar systems in action, I go with my translator to the village of Nagarle, an hour's drive from SELCO's branch office in the city of Mysore. The company has assigned a young man named Sukumar K., the branch's executive of customer support, to act as my guide. He's a little shy, has a pockmarked face and bright eyes, and tells me that he does sales, installation, and maintenance across the region. The journey to Nagarle takes us along bony, rotten roads, dodging herds of sheep and perilously overstuffed buses whimsically decorated with tassels and flowers.

The large village of Nagarle is lively at midday. The sun is bright and high in the sky. Our first stop is a shop owned by a man named Maranayaka. The closet-size store is made of scraps of wood and bamboo with a roof of dried palm fronds. He sells eggs, rice, sweets, toothbrushes, cigarettes, alcohol, soap, SIM cards, and bright plastic, single-serving packets of cooking oil, pigment, and instant coffee. The stand is located on the main road, which is unpaved and shaded every so often by wide bodhi trees. Inside there's barely room for Maranayaka's aging body, let alone customers, so they must point to what they want from the other side of the narrow, well-worn wooden counter. He sees us coming—Sukumar brings visitors here with some regularity—and to demonstrate his sun-powered lights, he flicks on the two fluorescent bulbs that hang from the ceiling amid the shiny plastic packets.

Before getting his photovoltaic panel, the shopkeeper didn't have electricity, so after nightfall he was reliant on kerosene, which emits greenhouse gases when it's burned. The emissions that are saved when SELCO customers such as Maranayaka use solar instead of kerosene generate the credits that TCNC procures from SELCO. In turn, SELCO uses that offset revenue to subsidize 3 percent of the interest on loans people in non-electrified areas take out to buy its solar kits. For Maranayaka it's meant he didn't need a chunk of money to buy the system outright and could instead pay it off in installments over three years. Sukumar from SELCO says the shopkeeper's two-light, single-panel unit is cost competitive with kerosene when the payments are spread out over time. Once the solar setup is paid off, the energy will be virtually free for the remainder of the unit's life, which is about twenty years. Maranayaka brags to me that he's got only six months of payments left, then he'll have seventeen years of energy free and clear.

I walk around back to find the photovoltaic cell. The sleek rectangle sits incongruously atop Maranayaka's ramshackle hut; it is a collision of eras. (The previous day, my translator had said that India exists in many centuries at once.) Wires run from the twenty-watt photovoltaic panel down through one of the gaps in the back wall to what looks like a car battery sitting behind the counter at Maranayaka's feet. Each day the battery soaks up enough juice to brighten his lights for the three or so hours he's open after dark.

SELCO installs between ten and eleven thousand solar lighting units each year in remote villages as well as in more accessible spots, some of which are wired to central power lines. But the company sells CO_2 credits to TCNC only from systems bought by people who don't already have grid power. SELCO offers up credits generated by just two thousand of the sets it sells annually. TCNC tells me that SELCO reserves an additional thousand units on top of that to buffer against overcounting of carbon credits that might happen when systems fall out of use, say, if power lines are brought in. Compared to other CO_2 ventures, SELCO doesn't appear to be inflating its offset credits or leveraging them to pump up profits. As Harish Hande told me in our interview, "We use the CO_2 money to get projects off the ground, then we move on and put the money into a new project. We don't just keep collecting on the same project—I'm not using CO_2 offsets to boost my bottom line." He also voiced concern over offset money as a stable means of shifting to renewable energy. "I'm worried that once this [CO_2 offset] bubble bursts the money will dry up. . . . Then you'll have all these solar systems and wind farms that will be abandoned."

According to SELCO, half of its installations are in places hooked up to the grid; the other half are in places with no access. Nagarle is a mix of the two. Although SELCO and TCNC don't appear to be selling CO_2 credits from systems in homes already wired, the stories in Nagarle offer important insights into emerging clean-energy systems in one of the world's fastest-growing economies. The situation raises two crucial questions: What comes of photovoltaics when electricity generated at coal-fired plants shows up? Conversely, is people's use of grid power lessened when photovoltaics become available?

A group of men and children has gathered in front of the shop, but Maranayaka doesn't like people hanging around so he shoos them away. A man who is sitting in a lawn chair tilts back on its plastic legs and announces in English that he can stay because he's rich. The man is tossing peanuts carelessly into his mouth. He has silver hair and wears gold jewelry. When he speaks, bits of half-chewed peanuts fly from his lips and he doesn't care. He announces that he has a SELCO system at his house—

a more expensive two-panel, four-bulb unit—and blurts out that the lights aren't bright enough so he doesn't use them regularly, only when the electricity is out. It's then that I realize the village is wired; it's just the shacks like this shop that have squatted along the roadside and a smattering of houses that lack electricity. I find out that Maranayaka uses grid power at home, no solar. The shopkeeper next door also has a panel for his business but not for his house.

The rich man sends us to his house to see the SELCO system. Mahadevi, his wife, answers the front door in a flowing blue sari. She leads us through the cool, plaster, two-story dwelling to the garden and points to the two panels that adorn the roof. The photovoltaics are hooked up to four interior lights, each mounted in a different room: an office, a bedroom, the foyer, and the kitchen. Lightbulbs glow throughout the house, a ceiling fan whirs in the sitting room, and appliances, including a television and a refrigerator, hum in the kitchen. But none of it is powered by solar even though there's barely a cloud in the sky. On our way out, Mahadevi hits the switch in the foyer to show us that the solar light works, then she turns it off.

I ask Sukumar from SELCO if most people use their systems merely as a reserve for when the grid seizes up. He says people here do use solar over grid power and takes me to the house of another family to prove his point. We knock, and a quiet man in his early twenties named Suresh invites us in. In sharp contrast to Mahadevi's home, this dwelling has only one room and a nook for the kitchen. The cramped space is shared by four adults: Suresh, his older brother, and their parents. The brick-and-mud house is windowless but has two small rectangles cut into its roof that beam sunlight down onto where we sit.

As we settle in, Sukumar boasts that this is the first installation SELCO did in Nagarle and demonstrates the two-bulb, single-panel unit. The solar light flickers on, dim and metallic. To Sukumar's chagrin, Suresh echoes Mahadevi: his family only uses solar power when the grid falters. Because blackouts (or "load shedding" as it's often called) occur daily— typically during peak times, for a few hours in the morning and a few in the evening—the home solar systems in Nagarle are regularly used. But it seems that once the power comes back on, the sun-run lights are flipped off. The people I talk to in Nagarle say they don't rely more on emissions-free electricity because the voltage from the systems they can afford is too weak. At full capacity, the standard solar unit simply doesn't produce enough juice to power the basics such as a radio and hot plate while also keeping the lights on.

Nagarle presents a telling picture of what small-scale green energy systems are up against. When such projects are installed in villages with few prospects of connecting to the grid, they offer the biggest benefit. But when the units are installed in areas such as Nagarle where electricity is accessible, their efficacy drops precipitously. Maranayaka and his neighboring shopkeeper don't have solar at home because power from the grid is so cheap, domestic prices being heavily subsidized by the government. As a result, there's no economic reason for them to switch. The low-watt solar systems for their shops will pay off in savings on kerosene. But the cost difference between the outlay on the more extensive gear they'd need to generate equivalent solar power to what they get from the central lines just doesn't add up.

Another crucial issue these projects raise is who should pay for renewable energy hardware—rural people in developing countries, most of whom are impoverished, or governments that instead currently fund major expansions in coal-fired power plants? Suresh tells me that his family got the solar unit four years ago because his brother, Kumar, thought it was a good idea. Kumar convinced them to work with SELCO to secure a loan with a nearby bank so they could make the purchase. However, since then the family's finances have soured. After Kumar took a steady job— of all things—installing transmission lines that bring voltage from central power plants to the area's villages, the younger sibling followed him into the vocation. But a year and a half ago Suresh fell from a pole and sustained major injuries, including breaking most of the ribs on his left side. He spent three weeks in the hospital and another three months in bed and was on a steady diet of painkillers. His family is still struggling to pay down the resulting medical bills. Due to the effects of his injuries Suresh can't go back to his old job, so now he works with his parents at their restaurant in a shack a few doors down from Maranayaka's shop. The twelve to fourteen hours they put in shopping, cooking, and cleaning every day only reap a total of two hundred to three hundred rupees, or about US$2 each. Suresh tells me it's hard to get out from under all the debt. "We want to pay this [the medical bill] off before we pay for the solar system—I just told the bank we can't pay it now," he says with irritation. "The solar panel is my brother's problem."

The financial aspect of SELCO's project is complex. Sometimes the financing arrangement works, as with Maranayaka, but when it doesn't, this renewable green energy can become a burden. Suresh tells me that if they didn't have all the debt—another loan for his sister's wedding was only recently paid off—his family would have bought some land to build a house with more space. Not only does their current dwelling offer no privacy, but it also has no toilet or indoor running water.

Consumers in the West clicking onto TCNC's website might come across a description of SELCO's work and think that by chipping in they would be contributing to building a renewable energy infrastructure in India. And they can believe that carbon offset money plays a key role in getting these efforts off the ground, working around a stubborn lack of government support. But if green energy (CO_2 offset funded or not) is primarily tapped when more polluting systems go down, or is abandoned when conventional power plants go up, and if the financing of such systems is from unstable or inconsistent sources that aren't part of a long-term policy, then these endeavors won't be a bridge to cleaner energy. Many villages in India don't have access to electricity and won't for years to come; providing light to study and work by in such places is laudable and deeply humane. But we often assume the environmental benefits are just as abundant, which can be far from the truth because these clean-energy systems are designed to replace candles and kerosene lamps, not coal-fired power plants.

The reach of low-power energy such as SELCO's systems in Nagarle is inherently limited, V. Santhakumar, author of an analysis of electricity deregulation in India and an assistant professor at the Center for Development Studies, an economics graduate school in the southern state of Kerala, tells me. "It is not a very socially efficient solution because it doesn't meet their needs," he explains when we speak. The type of solar unit most rural dwellers can afford is one that, like SELCO's, produces a weak current compared to grid power. The professor says that's precisely why these micro off-the-grid options aren't remaking how energy is generated in India. Absent more comprehensive, integrated renewable energy infrastructure programs, when people such as those in Nagarle gain access to central lines, they'll most likely abandon their lower-quality, higher-cost micropower systems. "If I'm putting it bluntly, these types of projects lack the ability to shift people from fossil-fuel energy to renewable energy,"

Santhakumar tells me. Micro-solar and similar low-power systems can fill a need when no electricity is available. But as soon as Suresh's brother and his coworkers roll in with the power lines, the twenty-watt photovoltaics will most likely lose out to fossil fuels. As for people who already access the grid, installing solar photovoltaics to generate electricity is a discretionary cost many won't take on.

Building renewable energy systems needed to "leapfrog" dirty energy is a much larger and politically complex undertaking that requires community members, local leaders, and the Indian government getting on board and forging a far-reaching, well-funded program (subsidized by the world's most developed countries). A serious transformation would come from installing enough renewable energy capacity to eliminate the need to run grid power to these villages at all. Instead, bureaucrats, elected officials, and influential energy companies plow ahead with fossil fuels; India's Electricity Act of 2003 pledges to plug in the entire country by 2010. Although this goal won't be achieved on time, the tight schedule means the plan implicitly relies on fossil fuels, not renewables. A week after I go to Nagarle, the state of Karnataka announces the approval of two new six-hundred-megawatt power stations that will run on coal.

POLLUTER PAYS

So many endeavors coming up short begs the question, is it possible to do a carbon-offset project right? Perhaps, but some serious obstacles have to be overcome. The offset mechanism rests on two rather wobbly legs, "baseline" and "additionality." Without these it is impossible to quantify any benefits delivered by offsetting—necessary to sell the credits—however, it's impossible to firmly establish either.

Baseline is a predicted measurement of emissions that would be released if development continued under a "business as usual" scenario. Both voluntary and official Kyoto projects need to establish a baseline to measure how many credits will be generated by the project, and hence how many can be sold. Involving a huge amount of guesswork, baseline is supposed to pinpoint something quite convoluted: what would have happened if something else didn't happen, and what might that have led to?

It's murky business indeed, and a perfect breeding ground for venality. In Bangalore I hear stories of NGOs that offer generous baseline interpretations that serve to inflate the amount of CO_2 a project might realistically offset, therefore augmenting revenues. If an offset venture claims to be clearing more greenhouse gases than it can, it's obviously bilking consumers, but it's also failing to rein in carbon. (Similarly, and infamously, under the official Emissions Trading Scheme established by Kyoto, baselines were so grossly overestimated that within its first year of implementation, 2006, the bottom dropped out of the carbon market, while emissions continued to escalate.) On top of all this, it is impossible to track the accuracy of carbon credits assigned to the projects I saw because there are no requirements to keep such records.

As for additionality, it easily slips into equally confusing and counterproductive terrain. Additionality tries to establish whether a project would have happened without offset money. If, say, a biomass plant had already secured its funding through investors, then sought offset money, the project would be deemed illegitimate because its costs were already covered. It's only acceptable to ask for carbon funding before a venture is fully financed, the idea being to support endeavors that wouldn't otherwise have been realized. (This is why companies such as DESI get their offset funds *before* they build their projects.) But because additionality is so tricky to nail down, renewable energy companies and other projects that get voluntary, as well as official CDM, money are now factoring the pollution payment into the business plan from the start. In 2005, James Cameron, a London-based carbon trader with Climate Change Capital and a lawyer involved in Kyoto negotiations, said, "You are forcing investors in these projects to lie . . . they have to tell their financial backers that the projects are going to make lots of money, but you have to tell the [UN] that they wouldn't be financially viable" without the subsidies.

Another glitch is that an offset firm cannot know its efforts are truly additional. This is what happened in Guguletu, a decrepit apartheid-era township twenty kilometers outside Cape Town, South Africa. According to an article by Trusha Reddy in the *New Internationalist,* in 2005 the UK-based offset company Climate Care partnered with a local energy consultancy to hand out power-saving compact fluorescent lightbulbs to households in Guguletu. It seemed additional because most residents wouldn't have been able to afford a CFL bulb, which costs about five times more than a standard incandescent. Plus at the time no stores in the area sold them. However, not long after the CO_2 offset–funded bulbs were distributed, due to extensive blackouts the township's energy supplier,

Eskom, adopted an efficiency program that included distributing 5 million CFLs to low-income households. Eskom gave lightbulbs to eighty-six thousand homes in Guguletu, covering the same turf as Climate Care. The complexity and indirectness of the system hobbles its ability to effectively address global warming; since Eskom's initiative reduced the same CO_2 as Climate Care's, the emissions offsets that the company sold were not in fact offset.

Another aspect of additionality is that it can slow the growth of sensible options to fossil-fuel-generated electricity. In reading Malavalli's most recent verification form I come across a line confirming the project's additionality: "It can also be concluded that there are no new policies or regulations, which would mandate the implementation of the project activity." In other words, no laws have been enacted since the last verification that would require this type of renewable energy generation. If national or state laws establish such rules to help build an alternative low-carbon energy supply, then the CO_2 offset industry would suffer. The Indian government, through its Ministry of Environment and Forests, has set up a CDM Authority to streamline approval of projects and facilitate their implementation, with the aim of attracting foreign investors. The authority has already approved more than twelve hundred offset ventures, only four hundred of which have received full accreditation by the UN. India's CDM Authority states on its website that if the UN approves the remainder and the resulting credits are sold at the "conservative" price of $10 each, India will see "an overall inflow of approximately US$5.73 billion in the country by the year 2012." By keeping its energy system dirty, India promotes the value of its carbon market. If the government mandates green energy, on the other hand, fewer projects will be deemed additional, and the country will lose profitable offset projects to competing countries such as China.

According to the logic of the offset trade, both voluntary and mandated, the market creates incentives that will drive the discovery of the most cost-effective ways to cut greenhouse gas emissions. This is seen as more efficient than imposing regulations on sectors such as manufacturing and power generation, which many claim would cripple the economy. A look at official CDM offsets is revealing about what the emissions market can deliver.

Consider trifluoromethane, or HFC-23, which is a virulent greenhouse gas that also depletes ozone. It's related to the banned chemical chloro-fluorocarbon (CFC) and is similarly used to make refrigerants for appliances such as air conditioners. Eliminating the use of HFC-23s creates tradable emissions reductions under Kyoto's CDM. But rather than fix the problem, this seems to be helping support a dirty industry. According to Michael Wara, a carbon-trading lawyer interviewed in a 2006 *New York Times* article, the offset money chemical companies receive is helping finance the expansion of existing factories and build new ones that make HFC-23s. These factories aim to increase production of the chemical to lure even more offset money to boost the bottom line.

EcoSecurities, among the world's largest carbon-offset project implementation firms, which does most of its work in India, says that 80 percent of its endeavors are HFC-23 eradication projects. "There are imperfections" in the offset system, explains Bruce Usher, EcoSecurities CEO, when I hear him speak at a conference in the summer of 2008. He says that the CDM and offsets in general were promoted to help build a renewable energy network in developing countries, but that hasn't happened. Because the offset system encourages finding the cheapest solution, "everyone removed HFCs." As of 2006 two-thirds of all CDM projects were HFC-23 reduction ventures, which pulled in $3 billion in investments that year alone. There's no way to know how many current projects are treating HFC-23 from factories built with the very offset money meant to eradicate the chemical.

Even if carbon offsetting won't thrash the economy (which remains to be seen), it doesn't seem particularly helpful to the environment. The various projects I visited might contribute to the low-carbon energy infrastructure of tomorrow if they were being done well and as part of a larger, coordinated program. There are ecologically beneficial, or potentially beneficial, aspects to all of the projects I saw. Yet the drawbacks are many and don't seem to be flaws with just these few projects, but rather with the process itself.

The renewable energy venture in those one hundred villages in Bihar could hook people up to a truly green and reliable system. It could bring economic activity and from that better access to education, health care, and more comfortable living conditions. Regardless, what DESI is up to is obscure, whether by accident or design. The workings of the offset mechanism don't seem to facilitate transparency.

Micro-solar is useful for delivering voltage to remote villages with no access to the power grid, and for offsetting CO_2 emissions from items such as kerosene lamps. Small-scale solar also has the potential to cultivate a familiarity with and acceptance of renewable energy as part of daily life. Projects such as the one in Nagarle deliver electricity, but inadequate quantities of it even once people have reduced their consumption. The renewable energy hardware required to supplant fossil fuels is simply beyond the reach of the world's poorest who buy the products of a company like SELCO. And why should the rural poor—not the planet's wealthiest countries and companies—pay for the construction of a green energy network?

Burning plant matter to generate power is carbon neutral, so MPPL's Malavalli station could be ecologically sound. To do that it would need to incinerate only material that was truly waste. If this power station were part of a hybrid system that integrated other types of renewable energy such as solar, then there would likely be less pressure on the ecosystem. A biomass plant such as MPPL's also has the potential to provide quality jobs and real social engagement. But the game is such that doing those things costs more, impeding expansion to the next offset project and the next.

While I'm in Bangalore, I meet a man who owns a small solar-panel company. He tells me that Bangalore has the highest concentration of the devices in India. Amid its birth as a tech haven over the last decade and a half, Bangalore's population has mushroomed, stretching its power supply beyond the limit. In response, the city began encouraging residents to install solar water heaters. Almost everyone I meet in Bangalore now has one; washing with water warmed by the sun has become a mundane part of life. All of these people have shifted to solar but they didn't do so for carbon credits nor with an eye on potential offset money. They've embraced heating their water with solar rays instead of fossil fuels because it works, both at delivering heat to the faucet and reducing power consumption. This initiative doesn't require wading into the morass of calculating baseline or establishing additionality, no certification agent must be brought in, no abstract swapping of pollution for credits. The carbon credit system—a series of convoluted financial instruments that serve Wall Street and the City by allowing them to use the earth's atmosphere as a casino—is poised for mass adoption worldwide with the successor agreement to the Kyoto Protocol. But what if sunny towns in Western countries went ahead, as Bangalore did, with the truly voluntary installation of solar water heaters? Greenhouse gases would fall and jobs would be created for manufacturing, installing, and maintaining the equipment. Internationally, what if the West authentically supported developing countries in creating viable, sustainable, and integrated renewable energy networks today? This is the type of direct change that carbon offsetting can easily distract us from.

Assessment

When I set out on this journey, I'd never been to most of the places I visited. The rain forest was an abstraction, as was organic farming in the global south. Countless times I'd noticed various countries' names on the oval label stuck to the organic apples I would buy at the supermarket. Because of the dearth of reporting on how these growers operated, I could only wonder what such farms might be like. I'd seen dramatic pictures of clear-cut tropical rain forests in magazines such as *National Geographic,* but never thought I'd witness this firsthand. Carbon-offset projects were obscure as well. They seemed ethereal and convoluted, yet possibly leading to climate-protective progress on the ground. Eventually, I found that imagining these places and events wasn't enough. The blind spots in the stories we've been telling ourselves about how we're saving the planet were too big. I made this journey in an attempt to witness and better understand the concrete ways we're addressing today's grave ecological turmoil.

Everywhere I traveled I saw that the social and environmental are intimately linked. Talking about the damaging effects of monocropping in Paraguay is impossible without also discussing the economic prospects of the campesino farmers. On Borneo, ecological upheaval is inseparable from the division and betrayal within indigenous communities. Likewise, the decline of the island's rain forests and wetlands is intertwined with the opportunism and corruption of many government officials, plantation firms, and multinational corporations. From these remote locations all the way to the Hudson Valley of New York State, the interconnectedness of humans and the environment was inescapable. The way the New York small farmers tend their land and animals is about how humans connect to cultivation. And the eco-villages in Freiburg wouldn't successfully have been conceived, built, and maintained without social movements and community engagement.

When some people think about nature, they imagine a sandy beach with crystal clear water or perhaps a mountain peak surrounded by pristine forest. Typically these scenes include no humans. But people have always coexisted with nature, each influencing the other. Protecting the environment isn't about ending this connection, but instead apprehending it more fully as an interaction. The point is not to leave nature untouched; removing people from forests or any other ecosystem is not a real solution. A different approach could be to work with nature in an authentic way so that we can take what we need to live without trashing the place.

Keeping our attention trained on what we purchase can make a difference, to be sure. I shop my conscience when I can afford it, and I believe that doing so can have a positive impact. But these consumer-based actions lack the ability to reach the goals we're aiming for. Convincing ourselves that we're solving our environmental problems when we aren't is a catastrophic game of denial; the problems run deep and so must the solutions.

The new green economy operates on a lot of assumptions and misperceptions, often emanating from advertisements, corporate boardrooms, and politicians' offices. Consumers might trust that any food labeled organic is good for the earth, and that crop-based fuels are ecologically smart. People may believe they can erase their CO_2 emissions with the click of a mouse. Just as many might accept that green transport, eco-architecture, and renewable energy aren't available to the masses because the technology is flawed or still prohibitively expensive. The public is encouraged to believe that some solutions are successful when they can't possibly be, and that other clearly feasible options are unattainable. In researching this book I found solutions that work and saw that we know how to implement them—truly organic farming, green architecture, and energy-efficient transportation. But instead, political and corporate leaders, and some in the environmental establishment, are putting aside what works in exchange for what poses the least challenge to established power structures.

Large-scale organic exemplifies this dynamic. Although Azucarera Paraguaya's mammoth sugar plantation doesn't spray its organic acreage with chemicals, it does monocrop, uses chicken manure from factory poultry farms as fertilizer, and is benefiting from the felling of trees to expand its organic cropland. The small farmers who supply the company also seem to be cutting down diverse native forest and replacing it with fields of cane. Further, being registered Fair Trade offers no guarantee that the campesinos will earn more—or any—money from their crops. Even though its representative in Paraguay knows what's happening, Imperial Sugar's Wholesome Sweeteners continues buying AZPA's product. Yes, the events in Paraguay could be anomalous, but they're probably not. Because AZPA is one of the biggest suppliers of organic sugar globally and is certified by Quality Assurance International, among the largest validation firms in the world, what happens in the sugar maker's fields reflects at least some of what goes down in the organic trade more broadly. As organic goes mainstream, its methods increasingly resemble the environmentally disastrous commercial practices it was meant to challenge. This is the result of choices organic farmers and processors must take based on economic sense, which apparently limits how green they can be.

Among the most disastrous solutions out there, crop-based biofuels come at a dear ecological and social price. On Indonesian Borneo I met Dayak communities that were being driven from their ancestral lands by agribusiness firms growing oil palm used for making biodiesel. I witnessed a plantation company clear-cutting a community's forest. I met small farmers who were working under what amounts to a sharecropper system, obliged to sell their fruit strictly to a single processor—a major multinational corporation partly owned by Archer Daniels Midland. I talked to men and women being threatened and harassed by the police and military for opposing plantations in their forests. What I saw dispelled thoughts I had that maybe the deforestation was for crops not intended for biofuels, or maybe the forest destruction was an exaggeration. The ecological and social toll exacted by this "green" fuel is extreme. Precisely when we need forests to stay intact and perform the vital function of absorbing and storing CO_2, they're being ripped away in the name of stopping global warming.

With carbon offsetting I found blatant failures, and some projects that showed degrees of success. The biomass power station in Malavalli, MPPL, which bears the coveted Gold Standard assuring integrity and is supported with funds from the offset firm Myclimate, looks promising on paper. However, the energy plant doesn't live up to its online profile. Even though the company wasn't directly delivering electricity to the surrounding villages, it continued for years to say it did on its website. And although both MPPL and Myclimate dispute these claims, from what I saw and was told, the biomass plant has questionable working conditions and has created an incentive for people to cut healthy trees to sell either to the station as fuel or to villagers as firewood. The micro-solar project that receives funds from The CarbonNeutral Company brings much-needed light to villages with limited or no access to electricity. As such, the project is effective at replacing CO_2-generating kerosene lamps. But because this type of effort cannot compete in terms of price and performance with energy from coal-fired power plants, its reach is limited.

When considered in the larger context of national energy generation and concerted, committed global adoption of renewable power technologies, CO_2 offsets are troubling. Continuing to release carbon with the expectation that it will be balanced out, or even erased, at some other time in some other place is a dubious enterprise. Once carbon is emitted, it contributes to global warming today; projects that might compensate indirectly and decades from now are no substitute for a committed program to reduce greenhouse gases in the first place. Offset projects and CO_2 credit-generation ventures, meant to spur the shift to clean energy in developing countries, might just be inhibiting authentic long-term planning and construction of coordinated renewable energy systems. Relying on CO_2 credit trading and offsets to smooth a transition to a low-carbon future is unwise. Unfortunately, the successor agreement to the Kyoto Protocol and U.S. cap-and-trade legislation both lean heavily on these mechanisms.

What I learned is that the outcome of industrial organic, commodity biofuels, and CO_2 offsetting isn't authentic protection and stewardship of the environment. What's transpiring is a tailoring of environmental crises so they can be dealt with in ways today's economic and political structures deem least threatening to the status quo.

Fortunately, some solutions have real potential to work, provided they're given adequate backing. The small local farms I visited raise crops and animals without chemicals, cultivate nutritive soil, and foster biologically rich ecosystems. Against all odds they have forged a way of growing food to get what we need without stripping the biosphere of its life. Similar to how Dayaks on Borneo practice agroforestry, these beyond-organic farmers have tapped into a wealth of knowledge that stretches back well before factory farming. Dayaks as well as the New York growers base their methods neither on abstention from extracting resources, nor on a leveling and remaking of entire ecosystems to suit the mechanisms of mass production. They work based on formulating and maintaining farming methods and the social infrastructure needed to care for the environment, raise healthy food, and get it to people.

We tend to oversimplify the way deeper change is made, however. Since these farmers are the ones bucking the industrial food behemoth, the thinking goes, all we need to do is buy their produce. But even when we purchase their greens, eggs, and chops, I found, many of them are still struggling to get by. I didn't meet a single farmer who said, "Oh, yeah, business is booming, everything's great!" Business was booming, but no one was earning a living wage from farming alone. The obstacles and barriers were many, including the burdensome debt of mortgages, ever-increasing local taxes, lack of access to processing and distribution, and little to no cooperation from government agencies such as the USDA. Without a greater support structure, these producers will remain relegated to a high-end niche market, and many may go out of business. In the final stages of writing this book, I send Morse Pitts an e-mail with a few follow-up questions. He's already told me he hasn't found a new location for Windfall, two years after I first visited the place. In response to my questions he sends a text message explaining that he sees no other option than to sell his land and transition to something else. "Turns out my dream of leaving a farm for the next farmer was kind of silly." Just because their cultivation methods may be ecologically superior to industrial organic growers—who often abide by the lowest standards possible—doesn't mean beyond-organic farmers will prevail. The rules of the marketplace support the big guys; small farmers typically can't make a larger environmental impact because our political and economic system won't let them.

In London and Freiburg I saw that ecologically advantageous housing is up and running, and it works. By living in a super-low-energy apartment I experienced that this type of architecture isn't culturally exclusive or unfamiliar, nor is it awkward or uncomfortable. I went to places where thousands of regular people occupy these green homes, raising their families and leading utterly normal lives. Even amid this success, the impediment of cost persists. Primarily, not everyone can afford to build a new house, and because existing structures account for the great majority of all dwellings, new construction is only a small part of the picture, even in Freiburg. Retrofitting buildings to be more energy-sparing is often seen as an unnecessary expense, a cost beyond the reach of the homeowner, even if it will pay for itself over the long run. From these projects I also learned that a lack of technology or know-how isn't what's keeping energy-efficient architecture from widespread adoption in countries besides Germany. According to how value is allocated in the current economic framework, renewable energy and low-pollution buildings come with higher price tags, which keep them from being more widely accessible. That doesn't have to remain the case; as Freiburg demonstrates, political and economic obstructions to greener energy and homes can be challenged and overcome.

As for what we drive, the first eco-car to make it to the mainstream was Toyota's gas-electric hybrid Prius. But even as waiting lists for the Prius grew longer and demand for smaller, less polluting cars shot up, U.S. auto firms continued to lag. When I went to Detroit, I discovered that the world's top manufacturers haven't meaningfully produced green cars because these vehicles don't make them as much money as the gas hogs. As with superefficient architecture, the right equipment and engineering for fuel-sipping rides already exists. The holdup isn't for technology that produces fewer greenhouse gases, but for the auto firms to figure out how to squeeze higher margins from it. Even as the big automakers mass-produce eco-friendlier machines, this fundamental logic remains unchanged. That means technologies that are least profitable, whether they're environmentally sound or not, will have to wait.

Only when their economic and political options began to run out did the U.S. auto majors start dedicating serious resources to greener vehicles. But the efficacy of their domestic efforts remains to be seen. GM's much vaunted plug-in hybrid, the Chevy Volt, seems to be the most promising green tech on the road in the United States. Yet only a few hundred are slated to go on sale this year, and they come with a higher sticker price than nonhybrids. Left to the market, it will take decades for car owners to replace higher-emission vehicles with more efficient rides. Even when that happens, triple-digit mpg, as GM promises with the Volt, is not guaranteed. Additionally, with plug-in hybrids as well as full electrics, it is imprudent to place our transportation future on juice from coal-burning power plants since generating electricity is the most CO_2-intensive endeavor in the United States today.

One remedy is tighter rules on emissions and mpg, as in the form of a carbon tax, which could be levied on transportation fuels as well as power plants. The key with a carbon tax is that the revenue must be invested in developing renewable, clean energy. If the money is spent otherwise, say, as giveaways to industry to soften the blow, such a program will prove fruitless. In Europe, where taxes on gas and diesel are much higher than in the United States, companies including Ford and GM manufacture and profitably sell superefficient vehicles. To cut greenhouse gases Americans—the world's biggest polluters—must have affordable access to far less wasteful cars. We must also have fine-tuned mass transit and truly safe roadways for bicycles. The market's inability to deliver these choices is a strong signal that the system isn't working.

In researching this book I kept coming across third-party certification outfits, including Quality Assurance International for organic food, the Roundtable on Sustainable Palm Oil (RSPO) in Southeast Asia, and the Gold Standard for CO_2 offsets globally. These types of bodies are ostensibly formed to ensure consumers are getting what they pay for by keeping producers honest, and in response to outcry from environmental and social NGOs over destructive practices. But the role they play isn't so straightforward.

The RSPO was established by the World Wildlife Fund with Unilever (because palm oil is used in many processed foods), a handful of European food manufacturers, and Southeast Asian oil palm firms, in the midst of activist campaigns in the EU drawing attention to the crop's extravagant ecological and social costs. Today the RSPO counts the agribusiness giants Archer Daniels Midland and Cargill, the dominant palm oil producer Wilmar, and the World Bank's International Finance Corporation among its members. The RSPO presents itself as a legitimate overseer that encourages sustainable cultivation practices. However, on Borneo the RSPO seems either impotent or acquiescent in the face of its members' continuing to clear-cut and burn the rain forest while displacing indigenous and peasant communities.

This can happen because most of these oversight bodies are essentially accountable to no one. Even when they are, as with organic certification in the United States, a paucity of enforcement exists. Consequently, companies such as AZPA in Paraguay and Wilmar in Indonesia can carry on selling purportedly eco-friendly goods grown where diverse native ecosystems once stood, and carbon offsetters, including Myclimate, can continue selling credits for problematic projects. A third-party certifier's "trust mark" can soothe a nervous public by communicating that ecosystems are being taken care of even if they're not. Growers, food processors, builders, and carbon offsetters have access to a host of certifications, and we consumers can buy an increasing range of products bearing these logos, but none of it matters if real changes aren't being made on the ground.

Some certification programs, especially those that are community-based, may be more effective than what I found, but third-party certification often serves to patch the cracks in the dam rather than deal with the underlying forces that are driving ecological decline. Certification as practiced by most licensing bodies today can't truly deliver cleaner, greener goods because the system focuses on symptoms instead of causes of ecological harm. The only way to successfully take care of the environment is to remove the motivation to destroy it. This can't be achieved through current forms of monitoring because the incentives to exploit nature remain in place. If profits result most readily from pillaging ecosystems, then the destruction will continue. Therefore we must reconsider how we define profitability. By telling ourselves that certification bodies and their seals can and will defend the biosphere, we forfeit the chance to establish real solutions to environmental disaster.

All the billboards, T-shirts, logos, and ads that declare buying this brand at that store will help save the environment can persuade us that it's possible to shop our way out of global warming—and it brings a sense of relief because doable solutions exist! But many of us know, or at least suspect, that purchasing the "right" goods isn't enough, even if we're too freaked out to admit it. In reality much of what manufacturers tell us about the provenance of the items we buy is more akin to ad copy than honest information. We would be well served to consider that all those messages of doing right by the planet, and all those eco-products on sale that are supposed to get us to a bright green future, might just be a form of appeasement.

When I went to the places where green products are made, I encountered industries with an insatiable appetite for raw materials. I saw corporations collaborating with government officials who abused their power to facilitate unfettered resource extraction that also mauled indigenous and peasant communities. I witnessed the unremitting evisceration of native forestlands, and the broadsiding of successful solutions such as beyond-organic farming and low-emissions vehicles. While in developing countries, I glimpsed how plundering ecosystems continues to make perfect economic sense, even for businesses that are green. Environmental responsibility practiced this way looks more like camouflage to enable ongoing destructive practices rather than a break from the toxic past.

The dysfunctional medical apparatus in the United States offers an illuminating parallel to our system's inability to implement solutions that work. Quality health care exists, and tremendous breakthroughs happen all the time. But lifesaving treatments remain inaccessible to tens of millions in America, and hundreds of millions worldwide, because people can't afford them. As a result in the United States, families needlessly go bankrupt, the sick unnecessarily endure physical pain, and, in the worst cases, people die. Correspondingly, in developing countries, millions of pointless deaths from easily curable diseases such as malaria and diarrhea, as well as senseless suffering from incurable but treatable illnesses such as AIDS, persisted for years and in some places still does because pharmaceutical companies resist any lowering of profits. Confining treatment to those who can afford it makes economic sense, but it's brutally irrational based on measures that put human health before profits.

The 2008–9 economic meltdown provides another useful analogy, this time relating to the effectiveness of current solutions to ecological destruction. The seeds of the financial crisis were sown when banks began issuing what are called subprime home mortgages, loans given on onerous terms often to borrowers who could not possibly pay them back. The debts were then bundled and sold in financial markets, where respected rating agencies consistently gave them top scores, signaling nice returns with relatively low risk. This triggered a frenzy of investing that sent money gushing into Wall Street. When, after years of booming returns, investors started cashing in their bets, the most elite financial firms were so spectacularly overleveraged that the whole system came crashing down. Hundreds of billions of dollars that industry experts assured investors were stable simply didn't exist. Now the world is wracked with financial hardship and incomprehensible debt.

You could say we're similarly leveraged on greenhouse gases. Although catastrophic levels of toxic emissions have already been released, we're at the point where we can still get away with polluting and convincing ourselves that things will be fine. Depicting the economy as secure was politically and socially feasible right up until we were thrown into the full impact of the crash. The market and its regulatory lapdogs failed to contain predatory profit seeking in large part because the most powerful interests were making a killing. For similar reasons regulatory forces that lack real independence are incapable of quelling the ravaging of nature because it's so lucrative. As for the rest of us, with so many political, business, and industry leaders, and, of course, celebrities, claiming that we're saving the planet, we can more easily let ourselves believe. But if emissions reductions are fabricated, as was true of so much wealth in the precrash stock market, then as our global-warming debt comes due, we will suffer all the more cruelly. If we've made our environmental investments in false solutions, we will lose, big-time.

CAPITALISM'S NATURE

Much of the thinking behind current solutions to environmental crisis is the philosophy that's referred to as natural, or green, capitalism. Embraced—consciously or not—by many nonprofit groups, businesses, and some in government, natural capitalism says we can use the levers of the market to fix ecological breakdown. According to natural capitalism, going green by saving energy, cutting out waste, and using more sustainable materials and methods will give companies an edge on their rivals as natural resources inevitably dwindle. This approach likely informs Barack Obama's moves toward creating green jobs, encouraging energy conservation, and investing in renewable power. While visionaries have called for getting away from ecologically destructive practices for generations, over the past ten to fifteen years more people have embraced natural capitalism as the best, most realistic way to set things right.

Popularized by Amory Lovins and L. Hunter Lovins, founders of the resource policy center the Rocky Mountain Institute, and entrepreneur and writer Paul Hawken in their widely read 1999 book, *Natural Capitalism: Creating the Next Industrial Revolution*, the philosophy entreats business owners and CEOs to align their firms' goals with the well-being of the planet. Expanding the concept of socially responsible business, natural capitalism promotes what's called the "triple bottom line," a form of accounting that prioritizes not only profits, but also people and the planet. Other treatises have appeared in recent years including Thomas Friedman's *Hot, Flat, and Crowded*; *Cradle to Cradle* by Michael Braungart and William McDonough (who's responsible for the Ford Rouge renovation); and *Green to Gold* by business writers Daniel C. Esty and Andrew S. Winston. These books argue that, counter to common assumptions, profits won't suffer but will flourish by adopting greener practices. And, vitally, companies and countries that take an eco-friendly route will gain competitive advantage. Natural capitalism promises big wins to those who make the change because, according to its calculus, what's good for the environment is good for business.

Since the inception of industrial production, companies have regularly sought cost savings by streamlining manufacturing, but natural capitalism takes such improvements a step further. In addition to basic efficiency upgrades, natural capitalism advises redesigning products and processes to copy nature's ingeniously waste-free, energy-saving ways, a concept known as biomimicry. Consider the spiderweb. The silk of arachnids is tougher than Kevlar, a synthetic fiber used in military body armor. And, while spiders spin their webs from digested flies and other insects, making petroleum-based Kevlar requires high levels of energy and hazardous chemicals. Biomimicry is meant to push industrial production in a more biological direction.

Natural capitalism also promotes compelling ideas about the "flow" of goods. Centrally, instead of buying, we could lease products we need, such as refrigerators or cell phones, for the service they offer—in this case keeping our food cold and allowing us to stay in touch. When these devices break, the manufacturer repairs or replaces them, and when they die, the company takes them back to either reuse the parts in new machines or recycle the materials. Xerox does this type of "service leasing" with its Document Centre line of digital copiers. Such a program allows a company to scale back product obsolescence by expanding serviceability and remanufacturing using salvaged components. Consequently, profitability hinges less on getting consumers to keep buying ever-newer units and chucking the ones they have, and more on delivering the needed service.

Business as usual isn't working, Hawken and the Lovinses rightly observe. This is so because, as they state, "[industrial capitalism] neglects to assign any value to the largest stocks of capital it employs—the natural resources and living systems, as well as the social and cultural systems that are the basis of human capital." This allows for what economists refer to as the externalization of costs onto the environment and the future, whereby businesses cash in the store of nature's wealth for themselves today. Hawken and the Lovinses explain the result is a gravely malfunctioning market. Due to distortions from perverse government subsidies and trade policies skewed in favor of the biggest corporate polluters, the authors contend, it's impossible for consumers to have what economists beginning with Adam Smith call full information. We often don't realize the limits of nature because low prices and abundant supplies—our grocery stores are packed to the gills, clean water flows from our taps, and the lights come on when we flick the switch—mask this reality. Consequently, we lack full information when we choose what food to eat, what house to buy, and which mode of transportation we'll take.

In previous writings, Hawken has argued that "cost/price integration"—referred to by many in environmental circles as true cost pricing—can remedy this core problem. With such accounting, the price tag on consumer goods would reflect the full cost of the resources that went into their manufacture, distribution, and disposal. Natural capitalism contends that creating such integration, which will require government intervention and regulation, will at last let markets work properly. When external costs are added into the price of food, fuel, and fiber, people will have full information and so will buy ecologically responsible goods because those will be the least expensive. When consumers demand more eco-friendly goods, due to market competition companies will have no choice but to oblige.

While it may seem straightforward, cost/price integration is tricky. Consider, say, a bag of potato chips. Do we begin this accounting in the factory, or the potato field with the fertilizer and the pesticides, or perhaps the farmer's tractor? Or do we go back further, to the mining of the metals to make the tractor? How do we value the suffering of people whose drinking water is polluted by the mine, or the asthma cases in neighborhoods near the steel plant? And how do we integrate the environmental and social costs of extracting the coal and oil needed for producing a bag of potato chips? If we truly factored in these elements, the market as we know it would seize up; almost everything would become impossibly expensive. Also, cost/price integration would need to happen on a global scale for economic and geopolitical reasons. If, say, the United States required its companies to internalize costs but the EU or Russia didn't, American firms would be driven out of business because they couldn't compete. Cost/price integration is an important concept that is useful to highlight our current, criminally negligent accounting system. It can lead us into the crucial discussion of where goods come from and how we determine prices—and wages. But we need to push the discussion further to include a questioning of the limits of market mechanisms as tools for curing environmental ills.

Another key aspect of natural capitalism as laid out by Hawken and the Lovinses is the idea that we can flip the economic equation so that business growth can be achieved by using *less* from the biosphere. As an example of how natural capitalism can work, in their book Hawken and the Lovinses point to the chemical company DuPont. In line with the goals of the Kyoto Protocol, in the late 1990s DuPont pledged to cut its greenhouse gas emissions to less than half its 1991 levels. Doing so was a smart move since for each ton of CO_2 the company said it was saving $6 in net costs. The authors explain this is the two-for-one we should be seeking. However, when a firm such as DuPont saves billions by reducing its energy footprint, it will funnel much of that money right back into making more goods to sell to more clients. Staying competitive demands ongoing expansion, so even though the energy *intensity* of a company's production may go down, its *scale* of production will continue to escalate. As such, natural capitalism is misleading. Hawken and the Lovinses tell us, "America could shed $300 billion a year from its energy bills using existing technologies. . . . The earth's climate can thus be protected *not at a cost but at a profit*." When that profit gets channeled back into polluting processes and products to keep a company financially fit, the larger environmental upsides the authors predict fail to materialize and the situation gets worse. This backfiring is known as the Jevons Paradox—a concept forged in the mid-nineteenth century by the economist William Stanley Jevons—whereby greater efficiencies lead to greater resource use rather than less. In a recent interview, Wes Jackson, a plant geneticist and president of the Land Institute, said, "When the Wal-Marts of the world say they're going to put in different lightbulbs and get their trucks to get by on half the fuel, what are they going to do with that savings? They're going to open up another box store somewhere. It's just nuts."

We would be well served to ask after the deeper reasons why our system functions this way, especially if we do so without reciting the well-worn lines that we as individuals are greedy and can't control ourselves. To be sure, humans seek material pleasures that give us satisfaction, but the quantity and toxicity of waste Westerners produce today is in no way normal or natural. We've had to learn to be like this, and companies looking to expand their market share have delighted in schooling us. For over half a century industry and commerce have unleashed their PR and marketing machines on the public with the explicit intention of teaching and encouraging us to burn through consumer goods (i.e., natural resources) with abandon. This is true for the simple reason that the more we consume, the higher the profits.

Or, to get some relief from the guilt of personal responsibility, our society tells itself that we're here because we believed—through stubbornness, ignorance, or wishful thinking—that the world's systems would always provide. For so long, the narrative goes, we thought we could dump pollution into the water, pour emissions into the sky, and pull raw materials from forests, mountains, and beneath the earth's crust. And now we're experiencing the rudest of awakenings.

Far from being unaware, however, people, including highly influential leaders, have for a long time understood that the earth can't give indefinitely. Amid periodic famines, eighteenth-century classical economists, namely Thomas Malthus, concerned themselves with the question of resource scarcity. Theodore Roosevelt, when he was president in the opening decade of the twentieth century, institutionalized resource and land conservation to restrain the exploitation of natural systems. Less grandiose expressions of this awareness existed at the time as well. In 1913 the popular magazine *Scientific American* published an issue on energy problems that observed, "The question of the possible exhaustion of the world's oil supply deserves the gravest consideration. There is every indication that we are face to face with this possibility." Other articles in the issue delved into technologies to capture the power of the sun, the wind, the tide, and even the earth's rotation. What's more, eighty years ago the godfather of electricity-intensive living—of all people—Thomas Edison told his friends Henry Ford and Harvey Firestone, "I'd put my money on the sun and solar energy. What a source of power! I hope we don't have to wait until oil and coal run out before we tackle that."

The obstacles to applying effective solutions to ecological degradation can be overcome, but we will fall short if we get stuck focusing on human nature as a prime barrier. As the stories in this book reveal, we will make headway only in the symbolic realm if we seek what George Orwell has called "a change of spirit rather than a change in structure." Even with greater public awareness, some pro-environment legislation (mostly in European countries), and the involvement of third-party certifiers, we're still operating under free market capitalism. In this economic setup, it continues to be highly profitable to strip natural systems of their resources, kick people out of their forests, and sell the world's wealthiest consumers endless streams of goods that in short order end up in the landfill.

When companies achieve greater efficiencies, those savings aren't retired, leaving an equivalent portion of natural resources untouched. While efficiency is crucial to saving the planet, it isn't enough on its own. The only way we can have any semblance of cost/price integration, and any way of keeping money from seeking out carbon dioxide, which it almost inevitably does, is through more comprehensive regulation of industry and a major rethinking of our political and economic structures. Otherwise, while there may be gradual shifts, we'll continue getting outcomes such as those I found in my research.

As negotiations for a successor agreement to the Kyoto Protocol, the current phase of which ends in 2012, grind on, powerful interests are lobbying hard for provisions that leave much control over greenhouse gas emissions to market forces. Most of the projects I saw in researching this book were born out of letting the market take the lead in solving ecological crisis, and they aren't working. Waiting to implement solutions to global warming and other major environmental troubles until these technologies and systems are profitable enough is reckless and bizarre in the extreme. Seeing our options through the lens of consumption, even when it's well intentioned, is keeping us from using tools we already have to protect the ecosystems everyone needs. "We have to ask ourselves, who are we as a society and what are the limits of the free market?" economist Frank Ackerman tells me. "What do we owe to nature and human health? You can't deduce it from the market. You have to come to the table with moral statements. These are not economic truths, they're pre-economic assumptions." We need to do this because, he explains, despite what many believe today, the market isn't able to adequately value environmental health. "The fascination with the market—and it is a fascinating thing—has run wild in society," Ackerman observes. "People imagine it can do much more than it can."

Shopping green is alluring in part because it is simple (albeit often expensive), unlike the messy business of working toward systemic change. But consumption as politics bypasses pushing for action that might bring substantive shifts, such as meaningful controls on greenhouse gas emissions, comprehensive programs that sustain holistic farming and food, support for establishing and distributing solar, wind, geothermal, and tide-based energy to power buildings and vehicles, major investments in mass transit, and undoing the economic incentives that encourage native-ecosystem destruction. Even when back-end remedies work—say, reforesting a stretch of land in Costa Rica—they simply can't keep pace with the degradation the current growth-based economic system leaves in its wake.

If improvements to the biosphere are based on the needs and caprices of corporations, financial market bubbles, and wrongheaded government policies, then global warming, dying oceans, and biodiversity loss will continue. As the notion of cost/price integration indicates, the way we currently assign value sets us up for ecological failure. To change course, we must create a new notion of growth, where personal gratification in terms of achievement and desire can be met, and where the security that money offers can be attained in ways other than liquidating nature and exploiting people. Meaningful transformation requires not just unconventional products, but the creation of an alternative logic, where consuming less would *improve* the standard of living and where success was defined quite differently. We live in a time of curtailed democracy in which average citizens are implored to "Vote with your wallet" rather than truly participate in the process of being citizens. This will work, we're told by today's eco-friendly marketplace, because supply and demand and market incentives are the most effective means of saving the planet. In the United States the top 20 percent of Americans own 85 percent of the wealth, and globally the scales are tipped even further. So we can vote with our wallets all we want, but the people with the most money—precisely those who lavishly benefit from a system built on ransacking nature—will inevitably control the most votes. Only when we rethink how and what we value—so that we no longer base well-being and quality of life on excess production, consumption, and wasting—will we truly be able to address global warming and other forms of ecological ruin.

Notes on the Possible

The Dayak community I visited in Pareh, like many others on Borneo, practices agroforestry, a complex system of cultivating crops for food, fuel, construction, medicine, and income within the existing forest. The goal of this farming method is to raise what the people need while maintaining the diverse biological web that supports the rain forest's bounty into the future. When I was in Pareh, Margareta and Momonus fed us mostly food either gathered from within the trees or picked from their garden; we also ate eggs from their chickens, plus one can of sardines. This is how the others in the village eat as well, primarily relying on farming and hunting methods that coexist with the native ecosystem. My guide from Walhí explained to me that during the Asian economic crisis of the late 1990s, many of the poorest city dwellers returned to their families in the rain forests, such as those on Borneo. "This was an important reason Indonesia could survive the crisis," he told me. "Out here there was plenty to eat, the forest was a safety net." No doubt the same safety net is being utilized as the current global recession wears on.

Cultivating biodiversity is just as central to this agricultural practice as cultivating food. Integral to the holistic farming of the Dayaks of Pareh is land management in which the forest at once belongs to everyone and no one. No individuals "own" specific plots, but each family has discrete parcels. Sharing the land—while maintaining boundaries between each other's crops within that arrangement—facilitates getting everyone fed while keeping the forest fertile and strong. When the soil grows depleted, typically after about three years, the community relocates their plots to a more nutritive area, letting the vacated land sit fallow to regenerate. This can take as long as fifteen years, after which point it can again be used to grow on. The vast majority of the forest remains open for hunting and gathering. Agroforestry as practiced by Dayaks on Borneo is so effective that for centuries it provided for many of their needs without tipping the rain forest's fragile balance.

A major argument against integrated methods such as those of the Dayaks is that they don't use land efficiently enough. With an exploding global population, common sense says, we need to produce as much per acre as possible. Following this logic, it's a waste of resources to let only a few hundred people use a relatively large swath of forest to meet their needs when that land could be producing high-yield crops to feed thousands. According to the calculations of Thomas Malthus, the eighteenth-century economist, the earth has a limited carrying capacity while humans have a relatively unrestrained ability to procreate. As a result, he predicted, we were on a collision course with scarcity. The threat of overpopulation was amplified in the late 1960s by Paul Ehrlich's bestseller *The Population Bomb*, in which he foresaw widespread human die-off from starvation. At the time this sentiment gained credence among prominent environmentalists and thinkers. Ehrlich's Malthusian argument has made a comeback in recent years, holding sway in much of today's analysis of ecosystem breakdown.

The question of population control is complex and can quickly veer onto racist ground. (*They* need to stop having so many babies.) In thinking about the possibilities perhaps we could allow ourselves to see other perspectives on the problem of meeting human wants and needs using the biosphere that we have. The planet has a lot of people, but a lot in relation to what? According to overpopulation theories, the problem is *that* we consume; the more of us there are, the scarcer resources will become. However, this approach fails to consider the more central question of *how* we consume. According to the World Resources Institute, the average American "consumes around twenty times more meat and fish and sixty times more paper, gasoline and diesel than the average Indian." The difference between wealthy countries and the very poorest, such as those in Africa, is even more extreme. Shocking as these numbers are, the point isn't simply that Westerners consume in such higher quantities than people in less developed countries. The point is that our economic and political system blocks the resources that exist from getting to the people who need them.

According to the Food Ethics Council, the fruits, vegetables, grains, meat, and other edibles that Europeans and North Americans throw away is enough to feed the world's 1 billion hungry people. The United Nations

Food and Agriculture Organization has reported that the primary reasons for food scarcity are not supply, but rather economic and political. In other words, the problem isn't a shortage of food, it's a shortage of money to buy it. The global food crisis of 2007–8 was linked to the diversion of edible crops for biofuels, but, we now know, the real problem wasn't a lack of supply, it was ever-skyrocketing prices. When we limit our options to technological fixes, such as agrochemical factory farming, and steer clear of the structural dimension, we undercut our ability to truly solve ecological and social crises. To feed a growing population, we can continue expanding an agricultural system that we know adds to greenhouse gas emissions, depletes soil, spoils rivers and oceans, and devours huge quantities of water and fossil fuels. Or we can more fully engage with our political and economic structures to deliver the food we already produce to the people who need it. This engagement gives us the opportunity to reorganize the model so that we can grow food—and build houses and transportation systems—in ways that foster biodiverse ecosystems and are inherently socially just. Today's environmental revolution does depend on technology to be successful; sophisticated farming and manufacturing methods and tools—a mix of old and new—are crucial. But the changes we need to make are absolutely reliant on how we as neighbors, community members, citizens, and humans put those technologies to work.

The holistic land stewardship that's employed by countless indigenous groups in a range of ecosystems helps demonstrate an alternative range of possibilities. This chapter considers options to what was investigated in the previous pages, offering solutions that allow us to see ourselves as more than just right-minded consumers. Below are examples of sustainable cultivation practices that can produce bountiful harvests and a good standard of living while attending to the biodiversity necessary for robust ecosystems. In addition, and crucially, these answers acknowledge the economic and political underpinnings of environmental degradation. Such possibilities begin to point to a more substantive and appropriate way forward and might provide a framework that could be applied in various global regions as well as in the spheres of shelter and transportation.

A balanced ecosystem can be achieved by understanding farmland as a complex bionetwork in constant interaction with human activity. Referred to as agroecology, this approach values not only the crops produced, but also the silent workings of nutrient-building life within the soil, the role of bugs, weeds, and animals, and the contribution of humans. Miguel Altieri, a leading figure in the field of agroecology and a professor of entomology at the University of California at Berkeley, draws the connection between socially just practices and a thriving agriculture. This dynamic view of raising crops is not just about chemical-free or locally grown food. As Altieri has written, "Agroecosystems are communities of plants and animals interacting with their physical and chemical environments that have been modified by people to produce food, fibre, fuel and other products for human consumption and processing." Agroecology sees farmland not as a homogenized, sterilized site of production, but as a place where natural processes continue to occur and cultivation becomes part of larger biological cycles. By practicing farming as such, Altieri's research has shown, productivity is markedly increased and sustains itself over time with fewer and far less toxic external inputs than are required by conventional methods. Agroecology debunks the claim that industrial farming is the only way to meet the needs of the planet's 6 billion people. By practicing agroecological methods, Altieri says, productivity of organic crops can be doubled, making them competitive with those grown with conventional, chemical-reliant techniques.

If agroecological methods can protect the environment while putting out enough produce to meet global demand, the question then follows, can this be done on sustainable economic terms? As we saw in New York State, many holistic farmers are unable to earn an adequate wage, let alone sell their goods to consumers outside an upper-end niche market. Agroecological methods include addressing the need for functional, affordable processing and distribution networks. And, in some places, agroecology includes the participation of consumers, ensuring their input on farming practices and food prices. Owing to agroecology's efficiency gains, the method also has the potential to outperform spurious large-scale "organic" farming such as what I found in Paraguay. Some examples of programs conducted over recent decades in Central America, and a current project in Brazil, help flesh out what alternatives might look like.

In Peru beginning in the early 1980s a group of anthropologists collaborated with local communities of the Andean plains to revive a lost form of agriculture. The ancient farming system, called Waru-Warus, or Waru-Warns in the Quechua language, is believed to have evolved three thousand years ago, although its exact age is uncertain. When the project started, traces of old Waru-Warus fields could be seen scattered across the plains. The practice had long been abandoned, first because of a centuries-long drought, then, in the mid-to-late twentieth century, due to agrochemical farming. The researchers and some of the villagers wanted to learn more about how the pre-Columbian system worked, so, using traditional farming implements including Andean foot plows, they began rebuilding the ancient croplands. Once harvest season rolled around, the farmers discovered a dramatic jump in yields compared to their conventionally raised plots; in some cases productivity doubled, in others it shot up as much as fourteenfold.

Waru-Warus consist of platform fields that are typically one yard high and can stretch up to a hundred yards long and ten yards wide. These beds are surrounded by canals, which harvest rainwater and are used for "splash irrigation." Farmers can recharge their soil with nutrients in the form of algae, which is easily collected from that growing in the canals. The raised fields bounded by waterways protects against harsh weather, curbing the effects of floods and droughts while maintaining warmer soil temperatures during the nighttime cold snaps common in the 12,500-foot-high altiplano. With such impressive results, the Peruvian government and several NGOs joined the program. For the ensuing twenty years these efforts fostered the reestablishment of Waru-Warus across the plains, much of which continues today. In bringing nontoxic, regenerative farming to the region, this project also helped increase farmers' livelihoods through greater social engagement. Without the social infrastructure formed by the participation of residents, government, the anthropologists, and NGOs, such a project would be much harder to sustain. By contrast, just across the border in Bolivia, where farming conditions are identical, Waru-Warus test plots were initiated, but neither the government nor private groups took up the venture. Today the fields are derelict.

Another government-NGO collaboration with Peruvian farmers entailed a restoration of ancient terraced fields. Their efforts led to an increase in yields of potato and oca (a tuber) by more than 50 percent. Over ten years this higher productivity boosted annual incomes from about $100 to $500. Farmers in Honduras had similar outcomes from a program to control erosion and reinvigorate depleted soils by using organic fertilization and by intermingling various crops. Consequently yields tripled, and in some cases quadrupled. Families shifted from subsistence farming to selling produce at local markets. Landless fieldworkers' income also went up by 50 percent, and dozens of jobs were created as villagers became extension workers teaching agroecological methods. Consequently, outmigration to urban slums reversed as people repopulated the countryside, restoring abandoned farms to take advantage of the earning potential. The social benefits of these projects aren't possible without the ecological improvements. And those wouldn't happen without the larger support and involvement of state agencies, environmental and social justice NGOs, and, of course, the farmers themselves.

Currently a similar movement is happening in the farming regions of southern Brazil, spearheaded by the Rede Ecovida de Agroecologia (Ecovida Agroecology Network), or Ecovida for short. Ecovida is a partnership of farmers, government bodies, scientists, environmental organizations, and the public that is building a community-based agroecological system. In the 1980s, Brazil's southernmost states of Paraná, Rio Grande do Sul, and Santa Catarina began shifting to alternative cultivation methods in reaction to the country's increasingly industrial agricultural policies. Underpinning those commercially oriented policies was a set of technologies pioneered in the United States and exported to developing countries known as the green revolution. These new practices primarily entailed increased application of large-scale monoculture farming that regarded the earth as a medium through which crops could be grown using chemical inputs; the very idea was to make soil health irrelevant. Abandoning this form of agriculture was supported by strains in the Catholic and Lutheran churches, trade unions, rural workers, and environmental groups. Ecovida is a product of this movement and was established in 1998.

Ecovida's purpose is to continue steering farming away from the rainforest-leveling, monocropping, petrochemical-doused, export-driven ways of agribusiness, and toward an integrated social-ecological system that serves the people of the region. Today the organization is set up as a network connecting fifteen hundred family farms with their wider community. Taking the process one step further, the state apparatus in Rio Grande do Sul has adopted a number of supports to help this biodiverse, socially integrated method of cultivation flourish.

A key component of Ecovida's work is its Association of Participatory Certification, which grants the group's organic seal. To earn the label, Ecovida farmers must follow their country's official organic standards, as in the United States. But these growers must also adhere to a set of operational and production principles established and managed by representatives of Ecovida's members—peer farmers, NGOs doing agro-ecology-related work, professional agroecologists, unconventional food processors and marketers, and consumers. So instead of securing certi-fication through a U.S.-style system freighted with conflicts of interest, the Ecovida program convenes an association of the various participants to review farmers' practices. This process fosters an ongoing exchange of cultivation techniques and feedback on their efficacy among growers as well as with experts. After review of a farm, the Ecovida certification body grants its approval or offers recommendations on how to improve or, when a grower continually fails to comply, takes disciplinary action, which farmers can appeal. Another important aspect of the Ecovida proj-ect is local distribution of its members' produce at an affordable price.

Working in a smaller geographical area allows for the various parties to be involved, sealing the social component. Aligning with Altieri's explana-tion of agroecology, Ecovida's approach integrates the ecological with the social and technological. In doing so, the participating Brazilian farmers and processors are less likely to take up the unseemly and at times fraud-ulent maneuvers U.S. and EU certification programs lend themselves to. Unlike the Western focus on organic *products,* Ecovida's approach, and agroecology in general, treats farming as a dynamic, culturally and bio-logically diverse *process.*

In the United States, related movements are happening that include more accountable certification bodies that differ sharply from the pri-vate inspection and licensing methods under USDA standards. Likewise, business models that allow companies to operate with greater ecological integrity are also in use and reaping benefits.

Certified Naturally Grown, or CNG, is a peer-led program that, simi-lar to Ecovida, bases itself on a combination of environmental and social practices that foster deeper stewardship of natural resources. CNG was started by a group of farmers led by Ron Khosla in response to the insti-tution of the 2002 official USDA organic standards. These growers were distressed by what they saw as the inadequacy of the new rules. If farm-ers can't afford the inspection fees or the time to maintain the excessive documentation, and they decide not to risk ruining their soils by follow-ing the USDA's homogenized guidelines that aren't appropriate for every ecosystem, then they can't label their goods organic, whether they grow organically or not.

Tailored to unconventional farmers who don't fit the USDA's idea of organic, CNG requires its participants to follow a more holistic methodology in their fields. Earning the seal costs between $50 and $175, as opposed to official organic fees that can easily crest $1,000, and calls for documentation better suited to smaller operations. Working as volunteers under safeguards to maintain the system's integrity, groups of farmers—not lone outsiders—inspect the operations of other farmers. CNG isn't just about keeping growers honest; it also aims to nurture the culture and community of local farmers. According to Khosla, CNG outfits have sprung up in all fifty U.S. states, as well as overseas.

Organic Valley, the largest farmer-owned cooperative in the United States, provides another glimpse at our options. Established in 1988 with just seven farmers, the co-op has expanded to include thirteen hundred members that produce milk, cheese, eggs, and more. Organic Valley supplies its small farmers with a range of supports including training and help transitioning to organic methods. The co-op's network of farmers stretches across thirty-two U.S. states, and their products are offered countrywide; the company did over $500 million in sales in 2008. Calling itself the "uncorporation," Organic Valley has a structure whereby management and member farmers have equal say in much of the decision-making. This setup of accountability seems to be effective, as two recent episodes reveal.

In 2004 Organic Valley canceled shipments to Wal-Mart at the behest of its farmers. The powerful discount retailer was pressuring the co-op to bump up production and do so for less money. Organic Valley's members decided that would drive the co-op toward the very factory processes they opposed. So Organic Valley ditched the deal. A few years later, the cooperative structure allowed the farmer-owners to block another attempt to erode its ecologically sound practices. But this time the pressure to compromise was coming from Organic Valley's own management. In 2008 the Cornucopia Institute busted the company for "quietly" buying milk from a seven-thousand-head factory dairy that had earned the organic seal even though it was using some industrial-feedlot methods. When the story broke, Organic Valley management refused to stop buying milk from the Texas dairy, saying it needed to augment supplies. When the member farmers got word, they forced Organic Valley to pull out of its contract with the operation. This decision didn't serve the bottom line—any corporation would have balked at such a move. But the accountability inherent in the cooperative structure enabled the farmers to valorize other aims, such as ecological well-being. Kevin Engelbert, an Organic Valley member farmer, commented at the time, "The farmers who own the co-op are the ultimate watchdogs."

In buying milk from the industrial dairy, Organic Valley was caving in to the growth imperative intrinsic to capitalism; the company needed to get bigger or it would lose customers to rivals. This economic force inevitably pushes producers to tend the balance sheet more diligently than the natural systems we all need. If Organic Valley doesn't have enough farmers who want to do the right thing, the company could easily slide into barely organic practices because that pressure is always there. The cooperative dairy owners are willing to stay involved and forgo some portion of potential profits to maintain ecological and social standards. In other words, they are creating a different economic logic. Ultimately, as agroecology in Latin America, participatory certification efforts such as Ecovida and Certified Naturally Grown, and the cooperative structure of Organic Valley show, a healthy biosphere is achievable. But to get there we can't simply turn our agency over to the market. Nor can we assign responsibility for environmental disaster, or health, to the actions and choices of individual consumers. Flourishing ecosystems will be the result of social structures that address a pillaged and polluted environment through an economic and political set of solutions.

Systemic approaches such as those described above can seem unfamiliar, or too complicated and unrealistic, but they don't have to be. Delineating some shifts that could take place in the current U.S. food system might make these ideas more concrete. Continuing in the sphere of agriculture, we could have greater ecological and economic efficiency by applying readily available solutions. Building and streamlining distribution for unconventional and organic local produce would allow farmers to get their goods to consumers at a lower cost and with a smaller environmental footprint. Likewise, reinventing food-safety rules so they're appropriate for, indeed encourage, small farmers and processors would give eaters greater access to affordable, ecologically healthy food. On their own such changes cannot undo the large-scale environmental destruction caused by a system that needs unfettered access to natural resources, but these alternatives can begin to lead us in a more generative direction.

Distribution is a major struggle for countless unconventional and organic growers and animal farmers today. It's tough finding and keeping channels that run from field to fork. Processors such as General Mills and retailers ranging from Wal-Mart to Whole Foods and the British supermarket chain Tesco prefer to work with one supplier rather than many small farmers because it's more cost-effective. Also these stores need consistent quantity and quality and won't risk what might be less uniform produce from a collection of small growers. An appropriate distribution system would begin to pry open the current arrangement that excludes small producers, denying them meaningful access to consumers. Keeping local unconventional farmers out of larger markets confines them to servicing the affluent and facilitates growers with less stringent methods in flooding the mainstream organic supply chains. Creating and supporting a system that helps local unconventional producers become even more ecologically sound, through coordinating the transportation of their goods, while maintaining a fair price, is a crucial component of environmental stewardship.

Another important step forward is to renovate food-safety rules to accommodate small growers and processors, and not just the big guys. This would make services that are often inaccessible, such as slaughtering, available and affordable to local all-natural farmers. Ironically enough, increased safety standards to minimize contaminants such as *E. coli* have eased the massive consolidation in U.S. meat processing. Such lethal contaminants weren't a serious problem before food began rolling down factory-farm assembly lines. Regardless, small slaughterhouses are now bound to identical rules to those of the majors; they must file all the same costly and complicated paperwork and buy expensive equipment that's excessive for their needs. These locally owned processors often can't afford to meet such demands and are forced to close. According to a 2009 story in *Mother Jones,* it costs on average $2 million more for a locally owned abattoir to build to USDA standards. This is a drop in the bucket for a Tyson or a Perdue, but a killer for any mom-and-pop. Implementing and overseeing a different system for small operators will increase administrative costs for the USDA, which will have to budget for more inspectors. But this seems justifiable as a responsible investment in ecologically and socially valuable farming, not to mention food security.

Additionally, as many others have pointed out, the U.S. farm bill, which is updated every five years, could start kicking in real support for organic and beyond-organic cultivation. Serious subsidies for research and development could foster a dynamic agroecological movement in the United

States, with a force of extension workers well trained in unconventional methods and the latest breakthroughs. The bill could also contain aid for first-time farmers to buy land, and low-interest loans for existing alternative growers forced to relocate due to exurban sprawl. Also vital are ongoing assistance in education, creating networks to foster social and environmental responsibility, as well as tax breaks and other economic incentives for established unconventional farmers—and not just those certified as organic. These changes could also include enticements to build and maintain effective and efficient distribution networks for alternative growers.

All these efforts involve a cast of players including individuals, community organizations, NGOs, social and environmental activists, researchers, academics, scientists, politicians, businesses, and, yes, consumers. We must consume, and that inescapably requires resources. But we can meet our needs in ways that are far less damaging, and at times even advantageous, to ecosystems. And we can readjust our conception that a high standard of living necessarily produces high levels of waste and pollution. To do right by the planet we're obliged to reflect on the ecological impacts of our food, shelter, and transportation, but not just as the result of individual choices. The quality and quantity we consume is a cultural practice, the outcome of our specific historical conditions. It isn't inherently human; it is learned behavior that we can change by adopting new behaviors.

Taking a socioecological approach asks us to more fully participate in our societies, to experience ourselves as actors in political life. It would be a major relief if we could buy our way out of global warming. When we try to do that, however, we get clear-cut rain forests for biofuels, organic food grown on vast stretches of monoculture where native ecosystems once flourished, and machinations such as carbon offsetting that cannot wipe out CO_2. Greater engagement can seem daunting, to be sure. Getting involved isn't nearly as accessible as buying something at the store. With all those green products and the resulting notions about how we've become more responsible, it's easy to be lulled into thinking we don't really need to do more.

When I was on Borneo, I met an anthropology Ph.D. student who was doing her fieldwork. She was on her second long-term stay in a Dayak village and was in Pontianak, the main town in western Borneo, for a week-end break. She told me that in her village an oil palm plantation was trying to break the community to get their land. One by one the villagers began making deals. Those who didn't want the plantation were rapidly being outnumbered as deception ripped through the families. The anthropology student said one reason so many people were taking the plantation's money was because the Dayaks of that village couldn't imagine that the forest wouldn't be there in the future. They see it as a place they can always go back to, she said, even if for now it will be used for oil palm. The rain forest's history is ancient, and it has always served the Dayaks. So even though the community knows the oil palm estate will level the native ecosystem, many believe they'll be able to return to the forest, that its abundance will never actually run out.

I later realized (while watching a documentary featuring the philosopher Slavoj Zizek) that in many ways Westerners aren't so different in how we regard the natural systems we need. Imagining life carrying on as we know it comes easily. But visualizing our quotidian environments wiped out, or eroded by the effects of global warming, is almost impossible; that level of disaster is still too abstract. Based on an evacuation map that the city of New York sent out not long after Hurricane Katrina, my house in Brooklyn will be among the first to go underwater if a hurricane hits, or, presumably, as sea levels rise. Not long after the city mailed out the map, the owners of the butcher shop around the corner told me their insurance company revoked the building's policy because of the newly assessed flood potential. Neither of us is leaving, though, because somehow such a catastrophe continues to seem profoundly unreal. Even though we hear the steady stream of reports about the latest ecological disasters, my neighbors and I wake up every morning to find the birds chirping, trees swaying in the breeze, people rushing down the sidewalks. Perhaps we share with the Dayak villagers an inability to comprehend the loss of the environment we live with every day.

Governments and major corporations in the most developed economies are fully apprised of the findings of the world's top climate scientists. Regardless, the majority of leaders continue with policies and practices that so obviously exacerbate the situation, including promoting ecologically themed but ineffective products. By accepting green consumer goods as a way out, we consent. Compared to the scale of the disaster, such solutions are extraordinarily inadequate—akin to a cancer patient fussing over a hangnail. Perhaps we are like the Dayaks in this regard as well. The community I met in Pareh believes it can use the chain saws it confiscated from the clear-cutting crews as leverage against the oil palm plantation and its multinational corporate partners. The feebleness of this strategy, however earnest, is not so different from Westerners' embrace of green goods as a way out of ecological calamity. But we can do things differently. Viable solutions in all realms are out there. We suffer no shortage of knowledge or ideas, no dearth of entirely levelheaded and realistic possibilities that aren't just a new range of products to buy.

Part of what's holding us back is a lack of political will. When that expression is used, it often evokes leaders who don't have the guts to stand up to the moneyed interests they rely on to get elected. However true this may be, political will comes not just from leaders. It also originates with a public that has the determination to push for fundamental transformation that can lead to real solutions. A crucial step in getting there is informing ourselves about what options exist. Industries such as oil, coal, automotive, agribusiness, and manufacturing and their friends in government have a lot to lose if things change too much. So, directly and indirectly, these powerful interests marginalize and muffle genuinely greener efforts. Perhaps practicing environmental responsibility means granting ourselves the time to find out who's doing what to help the planet, and if we want to participate, or study up on it, or create something of our own. The following appendix lists organizations and projects that I came across in writing this book. In no way is it a complete survey of what's out there—consider it a small contribution to the growing list. The current moment of environmental awareness, and people's excitement about finding answers to global warming and ecological degradation, is unprecedented, and because of that it is precious and must not be squandered. The solutions we seek today will have profound and lasting consequences for generations; let's make them good ones.

Acknowledgments

To come to fruition, all books require a host of people. Even though we writers spend so much time by ourselves at our desks, we cannot do this job alone. The scope of travel for reporting *Green Gone Wrong* meant that I relied all the more on support—emotional, intellectual, and financial—from many.

At various, and key, stages along the way Dara Greenwald and Emily DeVoti gave terrific input and cheered me on. Brenda Coughlin, who offered whip-smart contributions throughout the process, has been a wonderful friend and ally. My cousin Charlie generously shared his astute observations of farming and the emergent green economy; our many conversations helped spark important ideas. For his fertile ideas and more general support as I toiled away, I warmly thank Josh MacPhee. I'm also grateful to Anthony Arnove for his incisive feedback on the manuscript and overall enthusiasm for the project and my work more broadly. Patrick Bond provided valuable input that aided me in better understanding the oftentimes convoluted world of carbon offsetting. As the fact checker on the book, Jesse Finfrock was thoughtful, nuanced, and top-notch. Thanks to Elizabeth Hopkins for her attentive research. Having added to this effort in a range of meaningful ways, Meghan McDermott, Maddalena Polletta, Williams Cole, Atticus Cole, Walter Ludwig, Pedro Diez, Kevin Kaplicki, Eric Triantafillou, Igor Vamos, Joachim Koester, Shane McKenna, and Erin Durant are deserving of my appreciation.

I'm grateful to the Investigative Fund of the Nation Institute. Without its generous support most of the foreign reporting for this book would not have been possible. Thanks to Esther Kaplan and Joe Conason at the Investigative Fund and Hamilton Fish at the Nation Institute for their ongoing and crucial backup. Additionally, the Wallace Global

Fund provided substantial support for this project. WGF's contribution was vital as it allowed me the time I needed to do the hard work this book required.

Beth Wareham, Whitney Frick, and the team at Scribner have been great to work with. I appreciate Beth's ability to take up the project midstream with such gusto and interest. Thanks to Colin Robinson, who brought *Green Gone Wrong* to Scribner and was my editor during much of the writing. I'm grateful for his efforts toward getting this book out into the world. I appreciate Amber Husbands's sharp, thoughtful legal review. Mark Ellingham and Duncan Clark gave indispensable feedback on the initial manuscript. The book benefited from their fluency with popular discussions of environmental issues and their international perspective. Thanks to my agent, Andrew Wylie, as well as Rebecca Nagel and James Pullen at the Wylie Agency. Their help in getting this project off the ground and shepherding it along has been key. I'm also grateful for the support of the progressive think tank Demos and the Center for Economic Research and Social Change.

Leo Panitch and Colin Leys at the *Socialist Register* gave me an initial platform for formulating the threads of what developed into *Green Gone Wrong*. In the earliest stages of this project, Jason Schwartz bent the rules at Marlow & Sons, which meant I had enough time to write. Toward the completion of the manuscript, Laura Haber brought me in for a residency at Allen Hall's Unit One program at the University of Illinois, Urbana-Champaign. The stay was productive, giving me the opportunity to present and discuss many of the ideas in this book with an engaged group of students including Sam Siner and Eric Green.

Some parts of this book previously appeared in articles. Much of what came to be chapter 4 was first published as "Slash and Burn: Why Biofuels Are the Rainforest's Worst Enemy" in the March/April 2009 issue of *Mother Jones*. My editors there, Monika Bauerlein and Rachel Morris, took the time to help me articulate the complexities of the situation on Borneo. I learned a lot from them. Fragments that appear in chapter 5 and the "Assessment" were initially published as "Current Thinking: Was Thomas Edison, the godfather of electricity-intensive living, green ahead of his time?" in the June 3, 2007, *New York Times Magazine*. Thanks to Alex Star for his editorial input on that story.

Many people helped me on the ground in the various places I visited. Above all, I'm indebted to the numerous people who told me their stories;

they offered their time, thoughts, opinions, and often their gracious hospitality.

In New York, my multiple conversations with Morse Pitts and Tim Wersan at Windfall Farms, as well as with Ron Khosla of Huguenot Farms and Certified Naturally Grown, were invaluable. I'm also grateful to Jennifer Small and Michael Yezzi of Flying Pigs Farm, and Joshua and Jessica Applestone of Fleischer's Grass-Fed and Organic Meats. I'm fortunate to have had the opportunity to work with Caroline Fidanza, Andrew Tarlow, Tom Mylan, Dave Gould, Sean Rembold, and Mark Firth at Marlow & Sons; their perspectives on and knowledge of food aided me in understanding and appreciating the politics of unconventional farming.

In South America, I'm grateful for the time and insights of Emiliano Ezcurra, who was at Greenpeace Argentina when I was there. Although the reporting I did in Argentina didn't make it into this book, the experience was key in understanding the environmental and social dynamics of native ecosystem destruction. Thanks also to Joseph Huff-Hannon in New York, John Palmer in Tartagal, Argentina, and in Brazil, Osmar Coelho Filho.

In Germany, Elsa Gheziel, Andreas Delleske, Marcus Neumann, Freiburg FuTour, Olaf and Genvieve Zubers, Dr. Clemens Back, Doris Müller, and Achem Hombach were all giving with their time and contacts.

In Indonesia, particularly in Pontianak, several people at community-based and environmental organizations aided me in navigating the complicated geography of deforestation. I'm appreciative of the help extended by Shaban Stiawan, Ari Munir, and Torry Koswardono of Walhí; Lely Khairnur of Lembaga Gemawan; and Julia Kam and John Bamba of Institut Dayakologi. Also deserving of my gratitude are Leila Salazar-Lopez and Brihannala Morgan of the Rainforest Action Network, Elizabeth Linda Yuliani and Budhy Kristanti of the Center for International Forestry Research, as well as Sumi Rae, Adriani Zakaria, Michele Tambunan, and Wira Dinata.

I appreciate the help Dianne Feeley and Bec Young extended while I was in Detroit. Also thanks to Dan Georgakas.

In India, Nirmala Karunan of Greenpeace India was generous with her logistical support. Thanks as well to Leo Saldanha and Bhargavi Rao of the Environmental Support Group in Bangalore. I'm also indebted to Rakesh Kumar, who was a perceptive and adept interpreter and a great partner in the field.

When I was on the road and at home, my family helped me complete this project in myriad ways. I'm grateful to my father, Charlie, my sister, Holli, and my mother, Reese Ludwig, who all made contributions to this book both directly and indirectly. I'm grateful for their abiding encouragement, for keeping in touch when I was in remote places on my own, and offering suggestions, some of which proved extremely useful. My cousin Kelly, ever curious, was a thoughtful and ready sounding board. Last, but not least, I'm indebted to my uncle Mike for coming up with such a great title.

Appendix: Resources

Local Organic

Agroecology and Sustainable Agriculture Program, University of Illinois at Urbana-Champaign, www.asap.sustainability.uiuc.edu

Certified Naturally Grown, Stone Ridge, New York, www.naturallygrown.org

Cornucopia Institute, Cornucopia, Wisconsin, www.cornucopia.org

Fleisher's Grass-Fed and Organic Meat, Kingston, New York, www.grassfedmeat.net

Flying Pigs Farm, Shushan, New York, www.flyingpigsfarm.com

Growing Power Community Food Center, Milwaukee, Wisconsin, www.growingpower.org

Just Food, New York City, www.justfood.org

The Land Institute, Salina, Kansas, www.landinstitute.org

The Leopold Center for Sustainable Agriculture, Ames, Iowa, www.leopold.iastate.edu

National Sustainable Agriculture Coalition, Washington, D.C., www.sustainableagriculture.net

New York City Greenmarket, www.cenyc.org/greenmarket

Rodale Institute, Kutztown, Pennsylvania, www.rodaleinstitute.org

Windfall Farms, Montgomery, New York, www.windfallfarm.blogspot.com

Global Organic

Agroecology in Action, Miguel A. Altieri's website, www.agroeco.org

Alter Vida Centro de Estudios y Formación para el Ecodesarrollo, Asunción, Paraguay, www.altervida.org.py

Chacolinks, Oxford, United Kingdom, www.chacolinks.org.uk

Rede Ecovida de Agroecologia, Brazil,
www.ifoam.org/about_ifoam/standards/pgs_projects/pgs_projects/15649.php

The Soil Association, London, United Kingdom, www.soilassociation.org

SHELTER

BioRegional, Surrey, United Kingdom, www.bioregional.com

Fraunhofer Institute, Freiburg, Germany, www.ise.fraunhofer.de

Freiburg FuTour, Freiburg, Germany, www.freiburg-futour.de

Passivhaus Institut, Dresden, Germany, www.passiv.de

Rieselfeld, Freiburg, Germany,
www.freiburg.de/servlet/PB/menu/1179601/index.html

Vauban District, Freiburg, Germany, www.vauban.de/info/abstract.html

Wohnen und Arbeiten (Living and Working *Passivhaus* building), Freiburg,
Germany, www.passivhaus-vauban.de

TRANSPORTATION

Biofuels

Biofuel Watch, United Kingdom, www.biofuelwatch.org.uk

Center for International Forestry Research, Bogor, Indonesia, www.cifor.cgiar.org

Forest Peoples Programme, United Kingdom, www.forestpeoples.org

Institut Dayakologi, Pontianak, Indonesia, www.dayakology.org

KONTAK Rakyat Borneo, Indonesia, www.kontakrakyatborneo.blogspot.com

Lembaga Gemawan, Pontianak, Indonesia, www.gemawan.org

Milieudefensie (Dutch branch of Friends of the Earth), Amsterdam, The
Netherlands, www.milieudefensie.nl

Sawit Watch (Oil Palm Watch), Bogor, Indonesia, www.sawitwatch.or.id

Walhi (The Indonesia Forum for Environment, a branch of Friends of the
Earth), Indonesia, www.walhi.or.id

Green Vehicles

Back Alley Bikes and The Hub of Detroit, Detroit, Michigan,
www.thehubofdetroit.org

Boggs Center, Detroit, Michigan, www.boggscenter.org

California Air Resources Board, Sacramento, California, www.arb.ca.gov

Oil Change International, Washington, D.C., www.priceofoil.org

Transportation Alternatives, New York, New York, www.transalt.org

Carbon Offsetting

Carbon Trade Watch, Amsterdam, The Netherlands, www.carbontradewatch
.org

The Corner House, United Kingdom, www.thecornerhouse.org.uk

Durban Group for Climate Justice,
www.carbontradewatch.org/durban/index.html

Forests and the European Union Research Network (FERN), Brussels, Belgium,
www.fern.org

SinksWatch, United Kingdom, www.sinkswatch.org

Transnational Institute, Amsterdam, The Netherlands, www.tni.org

University of Oxford Environmental Change Institute, United Kingdom,
www.eci.ox.ac.uk/research/climate/cop07/offsets.php

GENERAL

Environmental Support Group, Bangalore, India, www.esgindia.org

Food First—Institute for Food and Development Policy, Oakland, California,
www.foodfirst.org

Friends of the Earth International, www.foei.org

Greenpeace Argentina, Buenos Aires, www.greenpeace.org/argentina

Greenpeace India, Bangalore, www.greenpeace.org/india

Greenpeace Southeast Asia, Jakarta, Indonesia, www.greenpeace.org/seasia/id

Institute for Local Self-Reliance, Minneapolis, Minnesota, and Washington,
D.C., www.ilsr.org

International Forum on Globalization, San Francisco, California, www.ifg.org

International Rivers, Berkeley, California, www.internationalrivers.org

Mongabay, online environmental magazine, Mongabay.com

Oxfam International's Climate Change Campaign,
www.oxfam.org/en/climatechange

Rainforest Action Network, San Francisco, California, www.ran.org

REDD-Monitor, www.redd-monitor.org

Rising Tide North America, www.risingtidenorthamerica.org

Rising Tide United Kingdom, www.risingtide.org.uk

Via Campesina, Jakarta, Indonesia, www.viacampesina.org

Wetlands International, Ede, The Netherlands, www.wetlands.org

WiserEarth, www.wiserearth.org

Notes

INTRODUCTION:
GREEN DREAMS

1 price freeze on corn: Heather Stewart, "High costs of basics fuels global food fights," *Observer* (UK), February 18, 2007.

1 violent unrest in over thirty countries: Alex Morales, "Argentina, Venezuela, Cuba, criticize UN Food-Summit declaration," Bloomberg, June 6, 2008, http://www.bloomberg.com/apps/news?pid=20601086&sid=aoXaCUUCto yc&refer=latin_america.

1 food prices peaked further still: Food and Agriculture Organization, http://www.fao.org/fileadmin/templates/worldfood/Reports_and_docs/Food_price_indices_data.xls.

1 half or more of their income to keep their families fed: Paul Krugman, Robin Wells, and Martha Olney, *Essentials of Economics* (New York: Macmillan, 2007), 122.

1 people were killed in Cameroon: Jesse Finfrock and Nichole Wong, "Pouring biofuel on the fire," *Mother Jones,* March/April 2009, 42.

1 prime minister was ousted and at least four rioters were shot and killed: "Food riots turn deadly," BBC, April 5, 2008, http://news.bbc.co.uk/2/hi/americas/7331921.stm.

2 stampede at a supermarket: Keith Bradsher, "A new, global oil quandary: Costly fuel means costly calories," *New York Times,* January 19, 2008.

2 eliminated by adding household bleach: Interview with Elizabeth Linda Yuliani, ecologist at the Center for International Forestry Research, May 4, 2008.

2 corn ethanol was a net loser: Susan S. Lang, "Cornell ecologist's study finds that producing ethanol and biodiesel from corn and other crops is not worth the energy," Cornell University News Service, July 15, 2005, http://www.news.cornell.edu/stories/july05/ethanol.toocostly.ssl.html.

2 two reports published in early 2008: cited in Elisabeth Rosenthal, "Biofuels deemed a greenhouse threat," *New York Times,* February 8, 2008.

2 deforestation rates in Brazil shot up sharply: Rory Carroll, "Brazilian officials

face charges over Amazon destruction caused by logging," *Guardian* (UK), September 30, 2008.

2 world's third-largest carbon dioxide emitter: *How the Palm Oil Industry Is Cooking the Climate,* Greenpeace International, 2007, 1.

3 likely intensified by the effects of global warming: "Katrina and global warming," Pew Center of Global Climate Change, http://www.pewclimate.org/specialreports/katrina.cfm.

3 industrialized society plays a significant role: *Climate Change 2007: Synthesis report,* Contribution of Working Groups I, II, and III to the Fourth Assessment Report of the Intergovernmental Panel on Climate Change, Core Writing Team, R. K. Pachauri and A. Reisinger, eds. (Geneva, Switzerland: IPCC, 2008), 37.

3 2007 State of the Union address: American Rhetoric, http://www.americanrhetoric.com/speeches/stateoftheunion2007.htm.

4 Whole Foods . . . Wall Street darling: Tradingmarkets.com, http://www.tradingmarkets.com/.site/quotescharts/?qm_page=41537&qm_symbol=WFMI.

4 Wal-Mart . . . top vendor of organic groceries: MSNBC, http://www.msnbc.msn.com/id/11977666/.

4 organic-foods industry expanded: Organic Trade Association, http://www.ota.com/organic/mt/business.html.

4 outstripping conventional food: Elizabeth Brewster, "Tough Times: Stuck in neutral, supermarkets continue to battle other channels for market share," *Refrigerated and Frozen Foods,* June 1, 2004.

5 demand for ecologically astute architecture: Daily Green, http://www.thedailygreen.com/green-homes/latest/2987.

5 real estate market overall is still struggling: "New residential sales in July 2009," press release, U.S. Census Bureau News, August 26, 2009, http://www.census.gov/const/www/newressalesindex.html. Also see "Strong gain in existing-home sales maintains upward trend," press release, National Association of Realtors, August 21, 2009, http://www.realtor.org/press_room/news_releases/2009/08/strong_uptrend.

5 BP has committed over $1.5 billion: Clifford Krauss, "Big oil warms to ethanol and biofuel companies," *New York Times,* May 26, 2009.

5 Keeping drivers on a liquid diet: Clara Jeffery, "Michael Pollan fixes dinner," *Mother Jones,* March/April 2009, 33.

5 mandates and subsidies in the United Kingdom: Jim Lane, "UK government sets 3.25 percent biofuels mandate from 2009–10, up from expected 3.00 percent," *Biofuels Digest,* February 2, 2009, http://www.biofuelsdigest.com/blog2/2009/02/02/uk-government-sets-325-percent-biofuels-mandate-from-2009-10-up-from-expected-300-percent.

5 parts of China: "China needs new policies to kickstart biofuel sector," Thomson Financial News, http://www.forbes.com/feeds/afx/2008/06/03/afx5073275.html.

5 biofuels are clearly here to stay: *Biofuels for Transportation: Selected trends*

and facts, Worldwatch Institute, June 7, 2006, http://www.worldwatch.org/node/4081. Also see Sam Nelson, "EPA ruling allays concerns over biofuels mandates," Reuters, May 5, 2009.

6 a prominent eugenicist: Wikipedia, http://en.wikipedia.org/wiki/Svante_Arrhenius.

6 "We would then have some right": Ian Sample, "The father of climate change," *Guardian* (UK), June 30, 2005.

6 Hansen told lawmakers: Chris Mooney, "Some like it hot," *Mother Jones,* May/June 2005, http://www.motherjones.com/environment/2005/05/some-it-hot.

7 double what it normally is: My typical annual emissions equate to five thousand tons of CO_2.

7 average American spits out almost twice the CO_2: Anja Kollmuss, Helge Zink, and Clifford Polycarp, *Making Sense of the Voluntary Carbon Offset Market: A comparison of carbon offset standards,* WWF Germany, March 2008, 41.

7 the world's largest economy: Economy Watch, http://www.economywatch.com/economies-in-top/.

7 20 percent of the planet's energy: *International Energy Outlook 2009,* Energy Information Administration, Report # DOE/EIA-0484(2009), May 27, 2009, http://www.eia.doe.gov/oiaf/ieo/world.html.

7 top emitter of greenhouse gases: "China overtakes U.S. as top CO_2 emitter: Dutch agency," Reuters, June 20, 2007.

9 world's top organic sugar producers and exporters: Alejandro Sciscioli, "Sweet experiment with organic sugar," *Tierramérica,* June 13, 2005, http://www.tierramerica.info/nota.php?lang=eng&idnews=927&olt=137.

10 buildings account for almost 40 percent of CO_2 emissions: U.S. Green Building Council, http://www.usgbc.org/DisplayPage.aspx?CMSPageID=1718.

10 fossil fuels . . . are the top source of greenhouse gases: *Inventory of U.S. Greenhouse Gas Emissions and Sinks: 1990–2007,* Environmental Protection Agency, April 15, 2009, ES-8.

10 sole remaining viable habitat for the . . . orangutan: Greenpeace, http://www.greenpeace.org/usa/news/the-orangutan-s-rainforest-hom/the-orangutan-under-threat.

11 strengthening fuel economy standards: Saqib Rahim, "White House proposes new, stricter national fuel efficiency standards," *New York Times,* May 19, 2009.

11 perplexingly low 38.3 mpg: John O'Dell, "GM's 230 MPG estimate for Volt works, or not, depending on the drive," Edmunds.com, August 11, 2009, http://blogs.edmunds.com/greencaradvisor/2009/08/gms-230-mpg-estimate-for-volt-works-or-not-depending-on-the-drive.html.

11 electricity generation accounted for 42 percent: *Inventory of U.S. Greenhouse Gas Emissions,* EPA, ES-8.

11 India . . . hosts more than 25 percent: United Nations Framework Convention

on Climate Change, Clean Development Mechanism, http://cdm.unfccc.int/ Statistics/Registration/NumOfRegisteredProjByHostPartiesPieChart.html.

12 lifetime of the trees: "Lifespan of common urban trees," CBC News Online, August 11, 2005, http://www.cbc.ca/news/background/environment/trees_ lifespan.html.

CHAPTER ONE
CLOSE TO HOME: LOCAL ORGANIC

17 one of the biggest such networks: New York State Department of Agriculture and Markets, http://www.agmkt.state.ny.us/AP/CommunityFarmers Markets.asp.

18 up by more than 150 percent: USDA Agricultural Marketing Service, press release no. 0488.09, October 2, 2009.

18 topped $1 billion: *USDA National Farmers Market Manager Survey 2006*, United States Department of Agriculture, Agricultural Marketing Service, May 2009, 7.

18 exceeded $17 billion: *The Organic Industry,* Organic Trade Association, 2008, 1.

18 organic market was worth $48 billion: "Organic food not healthier, study finds," Reuters, July 30, 2009, http://www.reuters.com/article/scienceNews/ idUSTRE56S3ZJ 20090730.

18 "70% of human water consumption": "Running dry," *Economist,* September 18, 2008, http://www.economist.com/world/international/displayStory .cfm?story_id=12260907.

18 fuels rampant algae growth: "Farm runoff worse than thought, study says," AP, June 14, 2005, MSNBC, http://www.msnbc.msn.com/id/8214501/.

18 mass underwater "dead zones": Eric Chivian and Aaron Bernstein, "How is biodiversity threatened by human activity?" in *Sustaining Life: How human health depends on biodiversity,* ed. Eric Chivian and Aaron Bernstein (New York: Oxford University Press USA, 2008), 52–53.

18 pesticides also linger as residues on food: Consumers Union, http://www .consumersunion.org/food/organicsumm.htm.

19 did not factor fertilizer and pesticide residues: Karen McVeigh, "Organic food not healthier, says FSA," *Guardian* (UK), July 29, 2009.

19 pesticides wreak havoc on human health: U.S. Environmental Protection Agency, http://www.epa.gov/pesticides/.

19 "Conventional farming is cheaper": Interview with Richard Pirog, August 7, 2007.

20 at around thirty months: Interview with David Huse, July 9, 2007.

20 as young as twelve months: *Fiscal 2008 Fact Book,* Tyson Foods, 7.

21 two thousand and thirty-five hundred other organic farms: Allen Salkin, "Leaving behind the trucker hat," *New York Times,* March 16, 2008.

22   "I transplanted mint": Interview with Morse Pitts, July 5, 2007.

22   praised by the likes of Alice Waters: Lesley Procelli, "The producers," *Gourmet,* October 2007, 220.

23   No one ever gets more than a week: Interview with Pitts, July 5, 2007.

23   keeps weeds from sprouting: Jill MacKenzie, "Green manure cover crops for Minnesota," University of Minnesota Extension Service, http://www.extension.umn.edu/yardandgarden/ygbriefs/H234greenman.html.

24   known as broadcasting: The One-Straw Revolution, http://www.onestrawrevolution.net/MasanobuFukuoka.htm.

24   "We plant tons of stuff": Interview with Pitts, July 5, 2007.

24   Two years later he died: Interview with Pitts, July 6, 2007.

25   They must keep detailed records: "Certification preamble," *Regulatory Text,* National Organic Program, 1, http://www.ams.usda.gov/AMSv1.0/ams.fetchTemplateData.do?template=TemplateF&navID=RegulationsNOPNationalOrganicProgramHome&rightNav1=RegulationsNOPNationalOrganicProgramHome&topNav=&leftNav=&page=NOPRegulations&resultType=&acct=noprulemaking.

25   "then you're not growing the food": Interview with Pitts, July 5, 2007.

25   problems with USDA certification: Interview with Ron Khosla, July 17, 2007.

26   require no soil samples or chemical-residue tests: "Certification preamble," National Organic Program, 2.

26   he called Gonzalez to repaint the sign: Interview with Pitts, July 5, 2007.

27   Among the new neighbors: Cardinal Health, http://www.cardinal.com/us/en/aboutus/.

27   warehouse covering twenty-three acres: Google maps, http://maps.google.com/maps?oe=utf-8&rls=org.mozilla:en-US:official&client=firefox-a&um=1&ie=UTF-8&q=%22cardinal+health%22+Montgomery,+ny&fb=1&split=1&gl=us&ei=gcpcSoOuA4v8MM-dsa4C&sa=X&oi=local_group&ct=image&resnum=4.

27   "Farms are just gone from here": Interview with Pitts, July 6, 2007.

28   "If you're going to employ people here": Ibid.

28   "It's not a living, it's a life": Interview with Pitts, July 5, 2007.

29   "It's basically not": Interview with Pitts, July 6, 2007.

29   build a lasting market for humanely raised: http://grassfedmeat.net/about_fleishers.html.

29   trials of being butchers: Interview with Joshua Applestone and Aaron Lenz, September 6, 2007.

30   "If people are under forty": Interview with Eric Shelley, August 31, 2007.

30   top four companies slaughtered: Eric Schlosser, *Fast Food Nation: The dark side of the all-American meal* (New York: Perennial, 2001, 2002), 137–38.

32   fifty different types of grasses: Interview with David Huse, September 6, 2007.

32   Overgrazing has multiple ecological effects: Michael Pollan, *The Omnivore's Dilemma: A natural history of four meals* (New York: Penguin, 2006), 189–90.

32 "The coevolutionary relationship": Ibid., 70.

33 Methane is over twenty times: "Global warming culprits: Cars and cows," ABC News, December 13, 2006, http://abcnews.go.com/Technology/GlobalWarming/Story?id=2723201&page=1.

33 fifth-largest beef processor: Smithfield News, http://www.smithfieldfoodsnews.com/VolumeIV_NumberI/index.html.

33 bought out the regional slaughterhouse: Smithfield Foods Company, http://www.smithfieldfoods.com/our_company/Timeline_Print.aspx.

34 "I'm shipping to one little butcher shop": Interview with Huse.

34 A 2007 study: Ron Strochlic and Luis Sierra, *Conventional, Mixed and "Deregistered" Organic Farmers: Entry barriers and reasons for exiting organic production in California* (California Institute for Rural Studies, February 2007), 22–23.

35 over twenty thousand customers: Reference for Business, http://www.referenceforbusiness.com/history2/20/United-Natural-Foods-Inc.html.

35 "purchase of the last two natural-food-distribution cooperatives": Samuel Fromartz, *Organic, Inc.: Natural foods and how they grew* (New York: Harcourt, 2006), 189.

36 profile of a farmer named John Wing: Tracy Frisch, "The missing link for locally raised meats?" *Hill Country Observer,* August 2007, 16.

37 "USDA makes it so hard": Interview with Huse.

37 HACCP was adopted and refined: Schlosser, *Fast Food Nation,* 198–99.

37 "The earliest case [of *E. coli*]": Marion Nestle, *Safe Food: Bacteria, biotechnology, and bioterrorism* (Berkeley, Los Angeles, London: University of California Press, 2003), 42.

37 just fourteen meatpacking facilities: Bonnie Azab Powell, "This little piggy goes home," *Mother Jones,* March/April 2009, 39.

38 "because you should leave the earth": Interview with Frank Johnson, July 9, 2007.

38 According to the USDA Economic Research Service: Carol A. Jones, Hisham El-Osta, and Robert Green, *Economic Well-Being of Farm Households* (United States Department of Agriculture Economic Research Service, March 2006), 2.

39 "Nothing," he tells me: Phone call with USDA NOP receptionist, August 23, 2007.

40 key post of head of Compliance and Enforcement sat vacant: Richard H. Mathews, "National Organic Program: Structure, responsibilities, goals," National Organic Program, PowerPoint presentation, November 12, 2008, slide 16.

40 Compliance and Enforcement's stated goals: Ibid.

40 NOP budget: E-mail correspondence with Joan Shaffer, USDA Agriculture Marketing Service Public Affairs, July 20, 2009.

40 all-time high of fourteen: Ibid.

40 farm bill rings in at about $300 billion: Michael Doyle, "When Congress

had a chance, food safety wasn't its choice," *McClatchy,* June 10, 2008, http://www.mcclatchydc.com/227/story/40536.html.

40 fivefold increase: USDA Economic Research Service, http://www.ers.usda.gov/FarmBill/2008/Titles/TitleVIIResearch.htm#organic.

41 Some now criticize Cascadian Farm's: Pollan, *Omnivore's Dilemma,* 161–62.

41 "As the organic industry matures": Kimberly Kindy and Lindsey Layton, "Purity of federal 'organic' label is questioned," *Washington Post,* July 3, 2009.

41 working for the establishment compromises him: Interview with Peter LeCompte, October 16, 2007.

CHAPTER TWO
ALL THE WORLD'S A GARDEN: GLOBAL ORGANIC

43 Paraguay was among the first: Maps of the world, http://www.mapsofworld.com/paraguay/travel/transport.html.

43 among the most biodiverse: "Paraguay: Zero Deforestation Law contributes significantly to the conservation of the Upper Paraná Atlantic Forest," *Leaders for a Living Planet,* World Wildlife Fund, August 30, 2006, 2.

43 home to a wealth of plants: Ibid.

43 soy, wheat, and, increasingly, sugarcane: "Economic sectors: Agriculture country profile select," *Economist Intelligence Unit Ltd.,* April 23, 2008.

43 The native Atlantic Forest once carpeted: USAID, http://paraguay.usaid.gov/environment/forest.html.

43 one of the highest deforestation rates: Ibid.

43 just 8 percent of the primary . . . ecosystem remains: Ibid.

43 slowed the felling of trees: "Paraguay: Zero Deforestation Law," World Wildlife Fund, 1.

44 leading organic sugar producers and exporters: Farm online, http://fw.farmonline.com.au/news/nationalrural/sugar/general/paraguay-the-worlds-largest-organic-cane-sugar-producer/62572.aspx.

44 provides a third of all organic sugar: Interview with Dario Zaldivar, October 30, 2007.

44 subsidiary of Imperial Sugar: Imperial Sugar Annual Report 2007, 7.

44 used by top processors: Interview with Zaldivar, October 29, 2007.

45 consumption of all-natural goods has slowed: Nigel Hunt and Brad Dorfman, "How green is my wallet? Organic food growth slows," Reuters UK, January 28, 2009.

45 continues its ongoing expansion: Organic Trade Association, http://www.organicnewsroom.com/2009/05/us_organic_sales_grow_by_a_who.html.

45 supplies stretched thin: "UK organic food sales soar, supply fails to keep up," Reuters, March 9, 2007.

45 Organic Valley ended its lucrative deal: Kermit Pattison, "Wal-Mart loved

Organic Valley's milk, so why cut off the flow?" *Inc.*, July 1, 2007, http://www
.inc.com/magazine/20070701/casestudy.html.

45 Soil Association reasoned: Caroline Stacey, "Food Miles," BBC Home, http://
www.bbc.co.uk/food/food_matters/foodmiles.shtml#top.

45 divulges the total greenhouse gases: Carbon Label, http://www.carbon-label
.com/individuals/label.html.

45 Participants in the program: John Russell, "Greening the chain—we are all
farmers now," *Ethical Corporation*, May 15, 2009, http://www.wbcsd.org/
plugins/DocSearch/details.asp?type=DocDet&ObjectId=MzQ0NzQ.

46 Versions of the Carbon Reduction Label: CimateChangeCorp, http://www
.climatechangecorp.com/content.asp?ContentID=5828.

47 biggest Paraguayan customers: Interview with Raúl Hoeckle, December 5,
2007.

47 rapidly expanding its operations: Interview with Zaldivar, October 29, 2007.

47 is instead establishing new organic fields: Interview with Hoeckle.

47 his responsibilities are increasing: Interview with Rubén Darío Ayala,
November 3, 2007.

48 To qualify a farm must: Sections 205.205 and 205.206, Electronic Code of
Federal Regulations, http://ecfr.gpoaccess.gov/cgi/t/text/text-idx?type=sim
ple;c=ecfr;cc=ecfr;sid=4163ddc3518c1ffdc539675aed8efe33;region=DIV1
;q1=national%20organic%20program;rgn=div5;view=text;idno=7;node=7
%3A3.1.1.9.31#7:3.1.1.9.31.3.342.6.

48 established in 1989 and owned by: NSF International, http://www.nsf.org/busi
ness/quality_assurance_international/index.asp?program=QualityAsInt.

48 two-thirds of all certified organic food: Bill Alpert, "Ethical consumerism is
in," *Barron's*, November 12, 2007.

49 "Sustainability depends on": Richard P. Tucker, *Insatiable Appetite: The
United States and the ecological degradation of the tropical world* (Berkeley:
University of California Press, 2000), 62.

49 biggest underground stores of freshwater: *Guaraní Aquifer System: Environ-
mental protection and sustainable development of the Guaraní Aquifer System,*
Organization of American States Office for Sustainable Development and
Environment, Water Project Series no. 7, October 2005, 1.

49 legal text that delineates NOP standards: Electronic Code of Federal Regulations.

50 "If you have a requirement": Interview with Luis Brenes, December 17, 2007.

50 "That sounds like a bit of a cop-out": Interview with Jim Riddle, July 28, 2008.

50 NOP regs make no distinction: "Production and handling preamble," *Regulatory Text*, National Organic Program, 3. See USDA Agriculture Marketing Service National Organic Program, http://www.ams.usda.gov/AMSv1.0/
ams.fetchTemplateData.do?template=TemplateF&navID=RegulationsNOP
NationalOrganicProgramHome&rightNav1=RegulationsNOPNational
OrganicProgramHome&topNav=&leftNav=&page=NOPRegulations&result
Type=&acct=noprulemaking.

51 manure from animals fed such substances: E-mail correspondence with Miles McEvoy, deputy administrator, NOP, via Joan Shaffer, October 29, 2009.

51 "What kind of organic farm": Interview with Zaldivar, October 29, 2007.

51 "Organic is becoming exactly": Ibid., October 28, 2007.

51 "I don't do politics anymore": Ibid.

52 "mostly in the last five years": Ibid., October 30, 2007.

52 "Ten years ago": Interview with Avelino Vega, November 4, 2007.

53 "It's very difficult to fight": Interview with Flor Fretes, November 4, 2007.

53 AZPA cultivates twenty-seven thousand acres: "Paraguay introduces new varieties of sweet cane developed in Brazil," Rediex, http://www.rediex.gov .py/index.php?Itemid=190&id=327&option=com_content&task=view.

53 twenty-five thousand acres: Interview with Hoeckle, December 5, 2007.

53 serves at the Network on Investment and Export: "Paraguay introduces new varieties of sweet cane," Rediex.

54 "This is the problem of how farmers interpret": Interview with Salvador Garibay, October 27, 2009.

54 "What incentive do organic producers have to not clear land?": E-mail correspondence with Laura Raynolds, October 28, 2009.

54 QAI is also supposed to inspect: QAI, http://www.qai-inc.com/3_3_0_0.php.

54 "opportunistic ecosystem removal": *D2 Draft Biodiversity and Landscape Standards: Background of the development of draft biodiversity and landscape standards,* International Federation of Organic Agriculture Movements, 3, http://www.google.com/search?hl=en&client=firefox-a&rls=org .mozilla%3Aen-US%3Aofficial&hs=VIV&q=%22opportunistic+ecosystem +removal%22+ifoam&aq=f&oq=&aqi=.

54 "has been an advocate": E-mail correspondence with Jaclyn Bowen, September 22, 2009.

55 farmers pool their money to pay the certifier: *Certifying Operations with Multiple Production Units, Sites and Facilities Under the National Organic Program,* National Organic Standards Board Compliance, Accreditation and Certification Committee, November 19, 2008, 2.

55 their single largest fixed cost: Interview with Zaldivar and Ferriera, October 30, 2007.

56 license belongs to the trader: Interview with Zaldivar, October 30, 2007.

57 Ibarra grows five acres: Interview with Eber Ibarra, November 3, 2007.

57 about $265 per month: *2008 Human Rights Report: Paraguay,* U.S. Department of State, February 2009, http://www.state.gov/g/drl/rls/hrrpt/2008/ wha/119169.htm.

57 sometimes collected just two loads: Interview with Ibarra and Luis Gonzalez, November 3, 2007.

58 "I feel like I've been ripped off": Interview with Gonzalez, October 30, 2007.

58 about 70 percent of its members: Interview with Ferriera, October 30, 2007.

58 "AZPA would drop them": Interview with Zaldivar, October 30, 2007.

58 20 percent of their crops: *Shaping Global Partnerships,* FLO International Annual Report 2006/2007, 12.

59 AZPA performs the inspections: *Certifying Operations with Multiple Production Units,* 2.

59 the more money it costs the certifier: Ibid., 7.

60 "arguably the most devastated": Carlos Galindo-Leal and Ibsen de Gusmão Câmara, "Atlantic Forest hotspot status: An overview," in *The Atlantic Forest of South America: Biodiversity status, threats, and outlook,* ed. Galindo-Leal and Câmara (Washington, D.C.: Island Press, 2003), 3.

61 "This land is owned by": Interview with Mariano Martinez, November 4, 2007.

61 "When we started": Interview with Zaldivar, October 29, 2007.

62 an array of directives in a piecemeal system: Organic Trade Association, http://www.ota.com/pp/legislation/backgrounder.html.

62 it issues licenses to private certification companies: USDA Agriculture Marketing Service National Organics Program, http://www.ams.usda.gov/AMSv1.0/nop.

62 QAI is no longer AZPA's certifier: E-mail correspondence with Bowen.

62 AZPA spent about $25,000 annually: Interview with Zaldivar and Ferriera, October 30, 2007.

63 its milk is sold in cartons bearing: Liane Kufchock, "Aurora organic milk class-action suits to be heard in St. Louis," Bloomberg, February 26, 2008.

63 over a dozen "willful violations": USDA, http://www.usda.gov/wps/portal/!ut/p/_s.7_0_A/7_0_1OB?contentidonly=true&contentid=2007/08/0228.xml.

63 According to the investigation: Ibid.

63 it's implausible that QAI could have missed: "USDA finds largest organic dairy perpetrating fraud," press release, Cornucopia Institute, September 13, 2007.

63 QAI spoke in Aurora's defense: "USDA dismisses complaints against Aurora Organic Dairy," press release, Aurora Organic Dairy, August 29, 2007.

63 Aurora signed a consent agreement: USDA, http://www.usda.gov/wps/portal/!ut/p/_s.7_0_A/7_0_1OB?contentidonly=true&contentid=2007/08/0228.xml.

63 "People are really hung up on regulations": Quoted in Kimberly Kindy and Lyndsey Layton, "Purity of federal 'organic' label is questioned," *Washington Post,* July 3, 2009, http://www.washingtonpost.com/wp-dyn/content/article/2009/07/02/AR2009070203365.html?sid=ST2009070203371.

63 "If somebody wants to cheat": Interview with Peter LeCompte, June 19, 2008.

64 "Most consumers are simple minds": Bruno Fischer speaking at BioFach, São Paulo, Brazil, October 16, 2007.

64 "I can't think of the future": Interview with Zaldivar, October 29, 2007.

CHAPTER THREE
THE GREENHOUSE EFFECT: ECO-ARCHITECTURE

69 jobs such as manufacturing or behind clerk's desks: Interview with John Shakespeare, January 9, 2009.

69 BedZED is higher density: Bioregional, http://www.bioregional.com/pro gramme_projects/ecohous_prog/bedzed/bedzed_hpg.htm. Also see Green-roofs, http://www.greenroofs.com/projects/pview.php?id=547.

70 Highgrove sits amid thirty-seven acres: The Prince of Wales, http://www .princeofwales.gov.uk/personalprofiles/residences/highgrove/.

70 radically reconceptualizing home energy: Interview with Jennie Organ, January 9, 2009.

70 40 percent of all carbon dioxide emissions: U.S. Green Building Council, http://www.usgbc.org/DisplayPage.aspx?CMSPageID=1718.

70 36 percent in the European Union: European Commission, http://ec.europa .eu/research/industrial_technologies/lists/energy-efficient-buildings_ en.html#1.

70 half in the United Kingdom: Communities and Local Government, http:// www.communities.gov.uk/planningandbuilding/theenvironment/energy performance/.

71 "living machines," a technology pioneered in the United States: Nancy Jack Todd and John Todd, *From Eco-cities to Living Machines: Principles of ecological design* (Berkeley, CA: North Atlantic Books, 1993), xvii.

73 profiles Kathy Baur: Laura Nesbitt, "Earthships offer the ultimate in eco-living," *Mountain View Telegraph,* January 18, 2009.

73 "When we speak of a good value": LivingHomes, http://www.livinghomes .net/priceValue.html.

73 The company's smallest: Ibid. For lowest-cost home, see http://www.living-homes.net/homesCommunities.html. For highest-priced home, see http:// www.livinghomes.net/budget.html?model=rk1.

74 building systems' design has resulted in: Pelli Clarke Pelli Architects, http:// www.pcparch.com/#/projects/hotelresidential/the-solaire/description/.

74 Monthly rent at the Solaire: City Realty, http://www.cityrealty.com/new-york-city/apartment/rentals/for-rent/the-solaire-20-river-terrace/26573.

74 BedZED . . . demographic consists of: Interview with Shakespeare.

75 One in every hundred: Caroline Bayley, "Germany's sunny revolution," BBC Radio 4, January 10, 2008.

76 "Do you know what a heat-exchanger": Interview with Dr. Marcus A. Neumann, January 14, 2009.

76 retain 90 percent of its heat: Elisabeth Rosenthal, "No furnaces but heat aplenty in 'passive houses,' " *New York Times,* December 26, 2008.

76 in the United States 56 percent of all power: U.S. Department of Energy, http://www.energy.gov/heatingcooling.htm.

76 in the UK it's 58 percent: *Energy Consumption in the United Kingdom,* Department of Trade and Industry, 23, www.berr.gov.uk/files/file11250.pdf.

76 in Germany . . . closer to three-quarters: German Federal Ministry for the Environment, Nature Conservation and Nuclear Safety, http://www.bmu.de/english/energy_efficiency/household/doc/38272.php.

77 "I think when people are properly informed": Interview with Andreas Delleske, January 14, 2009.

77 Delleske recounts the early days: Interview with Delleske, January 19, 2009.

77 four barracks buildings to SUSI: Interview with Jörg Lange, January 20, 2009.

77 Forum Vauban won a sizable grant: Hannes Linck, *Quartier Freiburg Vauban: A guided tour of the district* trans. Moshe Haas and Ian Harrison (Freiburg: Stadtteilverein Vauban e.V., February 2008), 30–31.

78 the group set up an office: Interview with Lange.

78 up to between 60 and 80 percent: U.S. Environmental Protection Agency, http://www.epa.gov/CHP/basic/efficiency.html.

79 half the national average: Linck, *Quartier Freiburg Vauban,* 16–17.

79 who continue to insist more cars: Interview with Lange.

79 bureaucrats had unilaterally decided: Linck, *Quartier Freiburg Vauban,* 8–9.

80 "Minimizing the surface area": Interview with Michael Gies, January 16, 2009.

82 the most efficient buildings are made: Chris Goodall, *Ten Technologies to Save the Planet* (London: Profile, 2008), 122–33.

82 Feist's technology improved on efforts: Rosenthal, "No furnaces but heat aplenty."

82 Structures built to *Passivhaus* specifications: Goodall, *Ten Technologies,* 124.

82 energy consumption can't surpass six kilowatt-hours: Rieselfeld Projekt Group in Department 1, "The new district of Freiburg-Rieselfeld: A case study of successful, sustainable urban development," January 2009, 3, http://www.freiburg.de/servlet/PB/show/1180731/rieselfeld_en_2009.pdf.

83 it's being adopted as a standard: Walter Aussenhofer, "Carbon-neutral urban development: A German role model," PowerPoint presentation, City of Freiburg Environmental Protection Agency, 11–12.

83 the 1992 low-energy standard: Ibid., 8.

83 more than a quarter of all transport: Ibid., 30.

83 upped the low-energy rule: Ibid., 8.

84 thirty thousand people took part: Roger S. Powers, William B. Vogele, Christopher Kreugler, and Ronald M. McCarthy, *Protest, Power and Change: An encyclopedia of nonviolent action from Act-Up to women's suffrage* (New York: Garland, 1997), 104.

84 blocking the planned nuclear station: Judy Taylor, "Filming the anti-nuke movement," *Jump Cut* 24–25 (March 1981): 4–5, http://www.ejumpcut.org/archive/onlinessays/JC24-25folder/anti-nukeDocs.html.

84 similar demonstrations against nearby chemical plants: BUND (Friends of the Earth), http://vorort.bund.net/suedlicher-oberrhein/freiburg-environment-ecology.html.

84 six thousand youths lay down: Interview with Thomas Dresel, January 15, 2009.

85 more radioactive than Hiroshima: Richard Stone, "The long shadow of Chernobyl," *National Geographic,* April 2006, http://ngm.nationalgeographic.com/2006/04/inside-chernobyl/stone-text/2.

85 "really a triggering moment": Interview with Professor Eicke Weber, January 30, 2009.

85 Nuclear Exit Law: Michael Levitin, "Germany says auf Wiedersehen to nuclear power, guten Tag to renewables," *Grist,* August 12, 2005, http://www.grist.org/article/levitin-germany/.

86 14 percent of the country's electricity: Federal Ministry for the Environment, Nature Conservation and Nuclear Safety, http://www.bmu.de/english/climate/downloads/doc/40589.php.

86 on course to meet 25–30 percent: Groshschel_Geheeb_Responsible Branding GmbH, ed., *EEG—the Renewable Energy Sources Act: The success story of sustainable policies for Germany* (Federal Ministry for the Environment, Nature Conservation and Nuclear Safety, 2007), 4.

86 dearth of oil and natural gas: Frank Dohmen, Alexander Jung, Wolfgang Reuter, and Hans-Jürgen Schlamp, "Germany's energy 'wake-up call,'" *Spiegel Online,* January 10, 2006, http://www.spiegel.de/international/0,1518,394403,00.html.

86 "The real cost is": Interview with Elsa Gheziel, January 14, 2009.

88 utilities are obliged to purchase green power: Groshschel_Geheeb_Responsible Branding GmbH, ed., *EEG,* 7.

88 covers wind, solar, hydropower, biomass, geothermal: Ibid., 5.

89 renewable energy fed into Germany's grid: "Feed-in tariff for grid-connected solar systems," Energy Matters, http://www.energymatters.com.au/government-rebates/feedintariff.php.

89 "The oil companies are the most powerful": Interview with Rolf Disch, January 16, 2009.

89 In 2008 he launched a campaign: Dr. Tobias Bube, "The PlusEnergyHouse for every community," Büro Rolf Disch.

89 two hundred municipalities responded: E-mail correspondence with Dr. Tobias Bube, January 16, 2009.

90 Russia blocked gas exports to the EU: Luke Harding, "EU cautions after Putin and Ukraine PM outline gas agreement," *Guardian* (UK), January 19, 2009.

90 natural gas imported from Russia via Ukraine: Interview with Dresel. Also see Dohmen, Jung, Reuter, and Schlamp, "Germany's energy 'wake-up call.'"

90 Obama administration is showing interest: Mridul Chadha, "International renewable energy agency launched, U.S. and U.K. opt out," Red Green and

Blue, January 27, 2009, http://redgreenandblue.org/2009/01/27/interna tional-renewable-energy-agency-launched-us-and-uk-stay-out/.

90 The body is charged with spurring . . . renewable energy: Worldwatch Institute, "75 countries sign onto new clean energy agency," Environmental News Network, http://www.enn.com/climate/article/39242.

91 bombarded and leveled during World War II: Solar Region Freiburg, http://www.solarregion.freiburg.de/solarregion/freiburg_solar_city.php.

91 she . . . mentions Whyl: Interview with Hedda Jarvis, January 20, 2009.

92 73 percent of existing housing: German Federal Ministry of Transport, Building and Urban Affairs, http://www.bmvbs.de/en/artikel-,1872.983325/ The-programme-to-reduce-CO2-em.htm.

92 5 percent of all homes: *American Housing Survey for the United States: 2007* (U.S. Department of Housing and Urban Development and U.S. Department of Energy, September 2008), x, 1.

92 first multifamily *Passivhaus* structures: Wohnen und Arbeiten, http://www .passivhaus-vauban.de/passivhaus.en.html.

93 For Lange, an ecologically sane future: Interview with Lange.

93 the 2,000-Watt Society: K. John Morrow Jr. and Julie Ann Smith-Morrow, "Switzerland and the 2,000-watt society," *Sustainability* 1, no. 1 (February 2008): 32–33.

93 Current energy-consumption levels: "Earth Trends," World Resources Institute, http://earthtrends.wri.org.

93 70 percent of all economic activity: "Facts on policy: Consumer spending," Hoover Institute, http://www.hoover.org/research/factsonpolicy/ facts/4931661.html.

CHAPTER FOUR
THE FUEL OF FORESTS: BIODIESEL

97 Duta Palma Nusantara, was seizing their land: "Request for consideration of the situation of indigenous peoples in Kalimantan, Indonesia, under the United Nations Committee on the Elimination of Racial Discrimination's Urgent Action and Early Warning Procedures," Committee on the Elimination of Racial Discrimination Seventy-first Session, July 30–August 18, 2007, submitted July 6, 2007, 58–59.

97 PTLL's aim was to establish: Ibid., 58.

97 customers is Wilmar International Ltd.: Letter from Forest Peoples Programme to the Compliance Advisor/Ombudsman for the International Finance Corporation, August 12, 2008, http://www.forestpeoples.org/docu ments/ifi_igo/ifc_wilmar_fpp_cao_let_aug08_eng.pdf.

97 Archer Daniels Midland holds a 16 percent stake: Archer Daniels Midland 2007 Annual Report, 4.

97 certain rights under Indonesian law: "Customary right to land," Interna-

tional Development Law Organization, February 6, 2008, http://www.idlo
.int/docNews/Customary%20right%20to%20land.pdf.

98 Ethanol . . . emits 20 percent less carbon dioxide: U.S. Department of Energy,
http://www.afdc.energy.gov/afdc/ethanol/emissions.html.

98 Biodiesel . . . releases just a quarter the carbon: Ibid., http://www.afdc.energy
.gov/afdc/fuels/biodiesel_benefits.html.

98 half of all new automobiles and a third of the entire fleet: European Automobile Manufacturers' Association, http://www.acea.be/index.php/news/
news_detail/economic_report_passenger_car_production_stable_over_
first_quarter_2008.

98 consumption of biodiesel is set to triple: "Directive 2003/30/EC of the
European Parliament and of the Council of 8 May 2003 on the promo-
tion of the use of biofuels or other renewable fuels for transport," European
Parliament and the Council of the European Union, *Official Journal of the
European Union*, May 17, 2003, L 123/45.

99 $400 billion between 2006 and 2022: Doug Koplow, *A Boon to Bad Biofuels:
Federal tax credits and mandates underwrite environmental damage at tax-
payer expense* (Earth Track and Friends of the Earth, April 2009), 22.

99 Obama . . . aims to up the mix of biofuels: "Barack Obama and Joe Biden:
New energy for America," Obama-Biden campaign press release, August
2008, 5.

99 some biofuels may actually emit more carbon: Joseph Fargione, Jason Hill,
David Tilman, Stephen Polasky, and Peter Hawthorne, "Land Clearing and
the Biofuel Carbon Debt," *Science* 319, no. 5867 (February 29, 2008): 1235–
38.

99 Although peatlands cover just 3 percent: *Assessment on Peatlands, Biodiversity and Climate Change* (Global Environment Center, Wetlands International, 2007), v.

99 one ton of palm oil can generate thirty-three tons of carbon dioxide: Eric
Holt-Giménez and Isabella Kenfield, *When Renewable Isn't Sustainable*,
Food First Policy Brief No. 13, March 2008, 8.

100 Indonesia . . . the world's third-largest emitter of CO_2: *How the Palm Oil
Industry Is Cooking the Climate* (Greenpeace International, 2007), 1.

100 its current 16 million acres: Marcus Colchester et al., *Promised Land: Palm
oil and land acquisition in Indonesia: Implications for local communities and
indigenous peoples* (Forest Peoples Programme and Perkumpulan Sawit
Watch, November 2007), 25.

100 26 million by 2015: Evita H. Legowo, "Blueprint of biofuel development"
(PowerPoint presentation on behalf of Ministry of Energy and Mineral
Resources, Republic of Indonesia, May 15, 2007).

100 98 percent of Indonesia's forest . . . will be degraded or gone: Jack Santa Bar-
bara, *The False Promise of Biofuels* (International Forum on Globalization
and the Institute for Policy Studies, 2007), 12.

100 "For the permit certification": Interview with Ong Kee Chao, May 5, 2008.

100 "Oil palm is one of our areas": Interview with Dr. Herry Purnomo, May 6, 2008.

101 At that time a vicious conflict erupted: Nancy Lee Peluso and Emily Harwell, "Territory, custom, and the cultural politics of ethnic war in West Kalimantan, Indonesia," in *Violent Environments,* ed. Nancy Lee Peluso and Michael Watts (Ithaca, NY: Cornell University Press, 2001), 83–84.

101 Dayaks of today deploy their warrior reputation: Nancy Lee Peluso, "Weapons of the wild: Strategic uses of violence and wildness in the rain forests of Indonesian Borneo," in *In Search of the Rain Forest,* ed. Candace Slater (Durham and London: Duke University Press, 2003), 236.

104 agreement . . . known as a plasma scheme: *Ghosts on Our Own Land: Indonesian oil palm smallholders and the Roundtable on Sustainable Palm Oil* (Forest Peoples Programme and Sawit Watch, 2006), 18.

104 One of the leaders of Muara Ilai: Interview with Asmoro, April 28, 2008.

105 require palm oil companies . . . to secure a series of permits: Eric Wakker, *Greasy Palms: The social and ecological impacts of large-scale oil palm plantation development in Southeast Asia* (Friends of the Earth, January 2005), 27.

105 devolve power to the provincial and district levels: Colchester et al., *Promised Land,* 46.

106 "No one can force communities": Interview with Tri Budiarto, May 2, 2008.

106 conglomeration of trading firms used terror and brute force: Wikipedia, http://en.wikipedia.org/wiki/Dutch_East_India_Company.

106 Dutch colonial government declared all unclaimed land: Colchester et al., *Promised Land,* 52–53.

106 Dutch control continued through the 1940s: Wikipedia, http://en.wikipedia .org/wiki/Dutch_Empire#Decolonisation_.281942.E2.80.931975.29.

106 bloody communist purge: Richard Lloyd Parry, "Suharto fears the 'Pinochet effect,'" *Independent* (UK), August 17, 1999.

106 welcoming . . . the American mining giant Freeport-McMoRan: Lisa Pease, "JFK, Indonesia, CIA & Freeport Sulphur," http://www.realhistoryarchives .com/collections/hidden/freeport-indonesia.htm.

106 direct payments for protection of the mine: Jane Perlez and Raymond Bonner, "The cost of gold, the hidden payroll," *New York Times,* December 27, 2005.

106 planet's largest gold mine: "Two wounded in Papua near Freeport's big gold mine," *Wall Street Journal,* July 16, 2009.

107 the intimidation he's experiencing began: Interview with Norman Wicaksono, April 28, 2008.

107 "The companies are not allowed": Interview with Cion Aleksander, April 28, 2008.

108 4 percent of the world's total greenhouse gas emissions: *Cooking the Climate,* 13.

108 the country's decades-old transmigration program: Wikipedia, http:// en.wikipedia.org/wiki/Transmigration_program.

109 he supposes he's fifty-five: Interview with Nazit, April 29, 2008.

109 even though he's grateful to have work: Interview with Rahmat, April 29, 2008.

109 price of crude palm oil had almost doubled: Index Mundi, http://www .indexmundi.com/commodities/?commodity=palm-oil&months=300.

110 "I've been traumatized": Interview with Marnaki, April 29, 2008.

110 higher yields per acre than any other oilseed crop: RSPO, http://www.rspo .org/About_Sustainable_Palm_Oil.aspx.

110 what he earns from his harvests isn't enough: Interview with Jhari, April 29, 2008.

111 65 percent of maintenance costs on petrochemical fertilizers: Interview with Chau, May 5, 2008.

112 among its members Wilmar, Duta Palma, Archer Daniels Midland, and Cargill: *Cooking the Climate*, 3.

112 among the biggest consumers of palm oil: Ibid.

112 played key roles in establishing the RSPO: Ibid.

112 RSPO website states its aim: RSPO, http://www.rspo.org/Our_Aspirations .aspx.

112 "No new plantings are established": "RSPO Principles and Criteria for Sustainable Palm Oil Production," Roundtable on Sustainable Palm Oil, 2006, 42.

112 Other criteria pledge to: Ibid., 33, 40, 42–43.

113 "The RSPO is a voluntary": E-mail correspondence with Sarala Aikanathan, September 24, 2009.

113 The document details illegal acts: Lely Khairnur, Claudia Theile, and Adriani Zakaria, *Policy, Practice, Pride and Prejudice: Review of legal, environmental and social practices of oil palm plantation companies of the Wilmar Group in Sambas District, West Kalimantan (Indonesia)* (KONTAK Rakyat Borneo, Lembaga Gemawan, and Milieudefensie, 2007), 5–6.

113 Wilmar's own social-responsibility policies: Wilmar International Ltd., http://www.wilmar-international.com/about_socialresponsibility.htm.

113 provided Wilmar tens of millions of dollars: International Finance Corporation, http://www.ifc.org/ifcext/spiwebsite1.nsf/0/64d0058360ce6dbc85256d d6005e35e0?opendocument; http://www.ifc.org/ifcext/spiwebsite1.nsf/f451 ebbe34a9a8ca85256a550073ff10/68bdeb3d4fe3b5d38525738e0050bd85?op endocument.

113 IFC is also a member of the RSPO: *Audit Report: CAO audit of IFC*, Compliance Advisor/Ombudsman, C-I-R6-Y08-F096, June 19, 2009, 19.

113 a low-level manager who illuminated: Interview with Wilmar employee, April 28, 2008.

113 RSPO . . . gave Wilmar the all clear: E-mail correspondence with Sharon Chong, CSR Manager, Wilmar International Ltd., January 19, 2009.

113 "For more than twenty years": *Audit Report: CAO audit of IFC*, 2.

114 failed to ensure that Wilmar was in compliance: Ibid., 2–3.

114 "deal making prevailed": Ibid., 2.

114 "This is a long process": Interview with Lely Khairnur, May 2, 2008.

114 including the Sierra Club: Raya Widenoja, *Destination Iowa: Getting to a sustainable biofuels future* (Sierra Club and Worldwatch Institute, October 2007), 4.

114 Obama's own energy secretary, Steven Chu: Fiona Harvey, "Second generation biofuels—still five years away?" *Financial Times* blogs, May 29, 2009, http://blogs.ft.com/energy-source/2009/05/29/second-generation-biofuels-still-five-years-away/.

114 "a bridge to the next generation of biofuels": Timothy Gardner, "U.S. drafts rule to lower CO_2 output from biofuels," Reuters, May 5, 2009.

114 set to increase under current policy: Ibid.

114 U.S. government also committed support to automakers: Ibid.

115 over $126 billion on post-Katrina reconstruction: "Fact sheet: Rebuilding the Gulf Coast," White House, http://georgewbush-whitehouse.archives .gov/news/releases/2008/08/20080820-5.html.

115 "nowhere near what there needs to be": Interview with Purnomo.

115 displacement and clear-cutting . . . declared ecologically sustainable: REDD Monitor, http://www.redd-monitor.org/redd-an-introduction/.

CHAPTER FIVE
GREEN MACHINES: ECOLOGICAL AUTOMOBILES

117 had to join waiting lists . . . it cost about $3,000 more: Alex Taylor III, "Toyota: The birth of the Prius," *Fortune*, February 21, 2006, http://money .cnn.com/2006/02/17/news/companies/mostadmired_fortune_toyota/ index.htm. Also see "Worldwide Prius sales top 1 million mark," Toyota press release, May 15, 2008.

118 60 percent of the global Prius market: Taylor, "Toyota."

118 combined average fuel economy of 46 mpg: Environmental Protection Agency, http://www.fueleconomy.gov/feg/hybrid_sbs.shtml.

118 oil prices nearing $150 per barrel: "Oil prices fall below $65 despite OPEC's production cut; gas drops," *USA Today*, October 24, 2008.

118 nudge past General Motors: "Worldwide Prius sales top 1 million mark." Also see Chris Isidore, "GM loses sales title to Toyota," CNNmoney.com, January 21, 2009, http://money.cnn.com/2009/01/21/news/companies/gm_ toyota_sales/index.htm.

118 installing the technology in their ever-more-enormous . . . trucks and SUVs: General Motors, http://www.gm.com/vehicles/results.jsp?brand =gmc&evar10=hompage_vehicles_browsebybrand&fromHome=true.

118 "an interesting curiosity": Taylor, "Toyota."

119 Wagoner unveiled a concept car: Michelle Krebs, "General Motors' first

plug-in hybrid," Edmunds.com, January 7, 2007, http://www.edmunds.com/insideline/do/Features/articleId=119088.

119   200 mpg in the city and would sell for $40,000: Bill Vlasic and Nick Bunkley, "GM puts electric car's city mileage in triple digits," *New York Times,* August 12, 2009.

119   forty miles before any gas is needed: Scott Doggett, "Update: Range of Chevy Volt extended-range PHEV not shortened," Edmunds.com, July 9, 2008, http://blogs.edmunds.com/greencaradvisor/2008/07/update-range-of-chevy-volt-extended-range-phev-not-shortened.html.

119   eight hours for the Volt: Vlasic and Bunkley, "GM puts electric car's city mileage."

120   SUVs and light trucks accounted for half: "Americans might like these fuel-sipping cars," *BusinessWeek,* http://images.businessweek.com/ss/08/07/0731_europe_gas_sippers/index.htm?campaign_id=msn.

121   among the top advertising spenders in the United States: "TNS Media Intelligence reports U.S. advertising expenditures declined 14.2 percent first quarter 2009," TNS Media Intelligence press release, June 10, 2009, http://www.tns-mi.com/news/06102009.htm.

121   a few hundred dollars in profits: John Cloud et al., "Why the SUV is all the rage," *Time,* February 24, 2003, http://www.time.com/time/magazine/article/0,9171,1004283 -6,00.html.

121   over 80 mpg: Ford UK, http://www.ford.co.uk/Cars/NewFiesta/NewFiesta ECOnetic.

122   tax credits for plug-in hybrid purchasers: Scott Doggett, "Obama administration sparks battery gold rush as states, firms vie for $2.4 billion," Edmunds .com, May 26, 2009, http://blogs.edmunds.com/greencaradvisor/2009/05/obama-administration-sparks-battery-gold-rush-as-states-firms-vie-for-24-billion.html.

122   Obama raised fuel efficiency standards: Saqib Rahim, "White House proposes new, stricter national fuel efficiency standards," *New York Times,* May 19, 2009.

122   worldwide auto production: International Organization of Motor Vehicles, http://oica.net/category/production-statistics/.

122   more than 800 million cars and trucks . . . 1 billion by 2020: Plunkett Research Ltd., http://www.plunkettresearch.com/Industries/Automobiles Trucks/AutomobileTrends/tabid/89/Default.aspx.

123   brought in . . . William McDonough: "Ford's Rouge redesign," *Business-Week,* November 13, 2000, http://www.businessweek.com/archives/2000/b3707132.arc.htm.

123   Unveiled in 2004: "Ford overhauls historic factory to be green," MSNBC, April 27, 2004, http://www.msnbc.msn.com/id/4843708/.

123   a carpet of dense sedum: The Henry Ford, http://www.thehenryford.org/rouge/leedlivingroof.aspx.

124   "[The company] wants every owner of one of these cars": Quoted in Susan

Strasser, *Waste and Want: A social history of trash* (New York: Henry Holt, 1999), 194.

124 The average mpg for a 2008 Ford F-150 . . . is just under fifteen: *Model Year 2008 Fuel Economy Guide* (U.S. Department of Energy, Office of Energy Efficiency and Renewable Energy, U.S. Environmental Protection Agency, 2008), 15.

125 arguably worsened by the Explorer's top-heavy vehicle design: Keith Bradsher, *High and Mighty: The dangerous rise of the SUV* (New York: Public Affairs, 2002), 328.

125 $5,000 or more in pure profit: Cloud et al., "Why the SUV is all the rage."

125 American automakers had free rein: Bradsher, *High and Mighty*, 11–13.

125 SUVs qualify for a U.S. federal tax deduction: Jeff Plungis, "SUV, truck owners get a big tax break," *USA Today*, December 18, 2002.

125 Under the code the full price of an SUV: "Tax preferences for sport utility vehicles (SUVs): Current law and legislative initiatives in the 109th Congress," Congressional Research Service Report for Congress, March 21, 2005, 21.

126 the company's fantastic financial losses: Stockcharts.com, http://www.chartingstocks.net/wp-content/uploads/2009/03/ford_stock.png.

126 ecologically responsible innovations Ford is currently working on: Interview with John Viera, February 18, 2008.

126 EcoBoost technology in a few models so far: Ford website, http://media.ford.com/article_display.cfm?article_id=29681; http://media.ford.com/article_display.cfm?article_id=30663; and http://media.ford.com/article_display.cfm?article_id=29944.

126 In 2008 the company will sell almost 3 million: Ford Motor Company 2008 annual report, inside cover.

126 "Without the credits": Laura Meckler, "Fill up with ethanol? One obstacle is big oil," *Wall Street Journal*, April 2, 2007.

127 car companies receive CAFE credits regardless: Ibid.

127 1.3 gallons of corn-based ethanol be refined: National Geographic, http://ngm.nationalgeographic.com/2007/10/biofuels/biofuels-interactive.

127 would have 250,000 hybrids on the road: Ford, http://media.ford.com/article_display.cfm?article_id=21627.

127 The goal was quietly dropped: Bryce G. Hoffman and Deb Price, "Ford bails out on hybrid promise," *Detroit News*, June 29, 2006.

127 Escape, which gets about 33 mpg: EPA, http://www.epa.gov/fueleconomy/class-high.htm.

128 GM focuses mostly on the near term: Interview with Terry Cullum, February 19, 2008.

129 hydrogen fuel supply is derived . . . from natural gas: Jeremy Rifkin, *The Hydrogen Economy: The creation of the worldwide energy web and the redistribution of power on earth* (New York: Jeremy P. Tarcher/Penguin, 2002), 186–87.

129 "We are nowhere [near] where we need to be": Edward Taylor and Mike Spector, "GM, Toyota doubtful on fuel cells' mass use," *Wall Street Journal*, March 5, 2008.

129 the article is singularly focused on the Volt: Katie Merx, "In charge of Chevy Volt," *Detroit Free Press*, February 24, 2008.

130 a veteran worker at GM: Interview with Miguel Chavarria, February 20, 2008.

131 strictly the miles racked up commuting from home to work: Bureau of Transportation Statistics, http://www.bts.gov/publications/omnistats/vol ume_03_issue_04/html/figure_02.html.

131 fuel economy of the Volt plunges to 38.3 mpg: John O'Dell, "GM's 230 mpg estimate for Volt works, or not, depending on the drive," Edmunds.com, August 11, 2009, http://blogs.edmunds.com/greencaradvisor/2009/08/gms-230-mpg-estimate-for-volt-works-or-not-depending-on-the-drive.html.

131 she indulged in more trips: E-mail correspondence with Megan Prelinger, May 2007.

132 "total crock of shit": "GM exec stands by calling global warming a crock," Reuters, February 22, 2008, http://www.reuters.com/article/latestCrisis/idUSN22372976.

132 keeping the auto industry on its highly polluting course: Bradsher, *High and Mighty*, 46–47.

132 his private helicopter . . . his own fighter jet: Di Freeze, "Bob Lutz: Guts in the sky as well," *Airport Journals*, May 2005, http://www.airportjournals.com/Display.cfm?varID=0505007.

133 10 percent of Americans owned cars: Eric Schlosser, *Fast Food Nation: The dark side of the all-American meal* (New York: Houghton Mifflin, 2002), 26.

133 created a company called National City Lines: Edwin Black, *Internal Combustion: How corporations and governments addicted the world to oil and derailed the alternatives* (New York: St. Martin's Press, 2006), 244.

133 grew by acquiring local routes everywhere: Schlosser, *Fast Food Nation*, 16.

133 paving over trolley tracks and tearing down overhead electrical cables: Ibid.

133 "In the event we maintain a 5 cent fare": Black, *Internal Combustion*, 246.

133 the companies were found guilty of conspiring: Ibid., 245.

134 routes in more than eighty U.S. towns: Jim Motavalli, *Forward Drive: The race to build "clean" cars for the future* (San Francisco: Sierra Club Books, 2001), 26.

134 88 percent of those surveyed wanted more: Ibid.

134 the Porsche hybrid: Ibid., 11–12.

134 small companies . . . turned out EVs and hybrids: Ibid., 14–15.

134 both drove Detroit Electrics: Black, *Internal Combustion*, 143.

134 Americans were buying gas-saving compact: Motavalli, *Forward Drive*, 16.

134 GM made a hybrid prototype: Ibid., 66.

135 the EV1 and its successor, the EV2: Ibid., 128–29.

135 The public-private partnership . . . entailed $1.5 billion: Bradsher, *High and Mighty*, 406.

136 GM's top lobbyist in D.C.: Ibid., 390.

136 announced that the PNGV was over: Ibid., 406.

137 focused on improved gasoline engines: Interview with Reginald Modlin, February 26, 2008.

137 scrapping of its entire hybrid program: Mike Ramsey, "Chrysler to drop first hybrids, after October debut," Bloomberg, October 28, 2008, http://www .bloomberg.com/apps/news?pid=20601087&sid=aoEM.2RDUzU8&refer= home#.

137 comprised about three-quarters of its sales: Stephen Power, Gina Chon, and Neal E. Boudette, "Daimler opens doors to Chrysler," Wall Street Journal, February 15, 2007.

138 For every increase of five miles per gallon: Peter Miller, "Saving energy, it starts at home," National Geographic 215, no. 3 (March 2009): 71.

138 U.S. carbon dioxide releases have surged by 17 percent: Inventory of U.S. Greenhouse Gas Emissions and Sinks: 1990–2007, U.S. Environmental Protection Agency, April 15, 2009, ES-3.

138 consumers haven't been willing: Interview with John German, February 21, 2008.

139 shows me where the tests are conducted: Interview with Jeff Alson, February 21, 2008.

140 "broad consensus for . . . fuel efficiency increases": Pew Campaign for Fuel Efficiency, http://www.pewfuelefficiency.org/pr_2007-07-23.html.

141 Rivera ended up spending almost a year: Don Gonyea, "Detroit industry: The murals of Diego Rivera," NPR, April 22, 2009, http://www.npr.org/tem plates/story/story.php?storyId=103337403.

141 Economist magazine referred to Ovshinsky: "The Edison of our age?" Economist, November 30, 2006, 33–34.

141 His latest innovation: Interview with Stanford R. Ovshinsky, March 13, 2008.

142 the F3DM, as it's called: Michael Graham Richard, "F3DM: The second, smaller plug-in hybrid by China's BYD," Treehugger.com, March 18, 2008, http://www.treehugger.com/files/2008/03/byd-f3dm-plug-in-electric- hybrid-china.php.

142 three years' wages to buy one: Marc Gunther, "Warren Buffett takes charge," Fortune, April 13, 2009, http://money.cnn.com/2009/04/13/technology/ gunther_electric.fortune/index.htm.

142 Nissan with its Leaf: Green Car Congress, http://www.greencarcongress .com/2009/ 08/nissan-leaf-20090801.html.

143 The G-Wiz: Goingreen, http://www.goingreen.co.uk/store/pick_new.

143 Mitsubishi's i MiEV: Seth Fletcher, "Mitsubishi's i MiEV all-electric car goes on sale next month," Popsci.com, June 5, 2009, http://www.popsci.com/cars/ article/2009-06/mitsubishi%E2%80%99s-electric-car-goes-production.

143 The Th!nk City: Th!nk, http://www.think.no/think/TH!NK-city/Buy-a- TH!NK/Price-info.

143 cost around US$20,000: Sebastian Blanco, "Think City coming to the U.S.,"

Autobloggreen, March 12, 2009, http://green.autoblog.com/2009/03/12/think-city-coming-to-the-u-s-info-overload/.

143 monthly battery rental fee: Sebastian Blanco, "Think City might cost $49,500 (U.S.) in Holland without leasing battery," Autobloggreen, March 30, 2009, http://www.autobloggreen.com/2009/03/30/think-city-might-cost-49-500-u-s-in-holland-withouth-leasin/.

143 ringing in at $109,000: Tesla Motors, http://www.teslamotors.com/perfor mance/perf_specs.php.

143 planning a global rollout: Better Place, http://www.betterplace.com.

143 opened its first switching post: Ariel Schwartz, "Better Place unveils EV battery swap station in Japan," Fast Company, May 13, 2009, http://www .fastcompany.com/blog/ariel-schwartz/sustainability/better-place-takes-first-step-towards-electric-car-infrastructure.

143 Edison envisioned public charging points: Heather Rogers, "Current think-ing," New York Times Magazine, June 3, 2007, 18.

144 the world's most efficient cars: Roland Jones, "U.S. 'stuck in reverse' on fuel economy," MSNBC.com, February 28, 2007, http://www.msnbc.msn.com/id/17344368/.

144 petrol taxes are about 60 percent: "Carmakers lean toward higher gas tax to fuel small-car sales," USA Today, January 13, 2009.

144 13 percent in federal and state tariffs: Energy Information Administration, http://www.eia.doe.gov/bookshelf/brochures/gasolinepricesprimer/.

144 burns 30 percent cleaner: Michael Kanellos, "Diesel: The next big thing in America?" Greentech Media, September 23, 2009, http://www.greentech media.com/articles/read/diesel-the-next-big-thing-in-america.

144 50 percent of all new vehicles in Europe: European Automobile Manufactur-ers' Association, http://www.acea.be/index.php/news/news_detail/trends_in_new_car_characteristics.

144 88 mpg on the freeway and 61 in the city: Ford UK, http://www.ford.co.uk/Cars/NewFiesta/NewFiestaECOnetic.

144 car can seat five: Ibid.

144 starts at about $17,500: "Americans might like these fuel-sipping cars," Busi-nessWeek, http://images.businessweek.com/ss/08/07/0731_europe_gas_sip pers/11.htm.

144 fuel economy in the low 30s: Ben Mack, "Ford's ECOnetic Fiesta gets 65 mpg. You can't have one," Wired, February 10, 2009, http://www.wired.com/autopia/2009/02/ford-will-give/.

144 juicing up a plug-in electric with coal-fired energy: John Voelcker, "Con-sumer Reports questions plug-in practicality," Hybridcars.com, January 7, 2009, http://www.hybridcars.com/news/consumer-reports-questions-plug-practicality-25392.html.

144 three-quarters of its electricity from coal: Chi-Chu Tschang, "China looks to coal bed methane," BusinessWeek, January 3, 2008, http://www.business

week.com/globalbiz/content/jan2008/gb2008013_784582.htm?campaign_id=rss_as.

144 more than half its voltage from the black stuff: U.S. Department of Energy, http://www.energy.gov/energysources/coal.htm.

144 more than 40 percent of the world's electricity: World Coal Institute, http://www.worldcoal.org/coal/uses-of-coal/coal-electricity/.

145 a quarter of the energy used in industry: Energy Information Administration, http://www.eia.doe.gov/oiaf/ieo/coal.html.

145 poised for a steep rise: Ibid.

145 deserted en masse after World War II: Interview with John Mogk, February 20, 2008.

CHAPTER SIX
THE PRICE OF AIR: CARBON OFFSETS

149 to plant ten thousand mango trees: Amrit Dhillon and Toby Harnden, "How Coldplay's green hopes died in the arid soil of India," *Sunday Telegraph* (London), April 30, 2006. On exchange rate, see St. Louis Federal Reserve, http://research.stlouisfed.org/fred2/data/EXUSUK.txt.

149 "You can dedicate more saplings": Dhillon and Harnden, "How Coldplay's green hopes died." Also see The CarbonNeutral Company, http://www.carbonneutral.com/casestudies/client.asp?id=880.

151 promising the farmers a small sum: Dhillon and Harnden, "How Coldplay's green hopes died."

151 Only eight thousand trees were ever distributed: Ibid.

151 "I was promised two thousand rupees": Ibid. On exchange rate, see FX Street, http://www.fxstreet.com/fundamental/economic-time-series/data/fedstl/exinus.aspx.

151 the "Durban Declaration on Carbon Trading": "Climate Justice Now! The Durban Declaration on Carbon Trading," signed in Durban, South Africa, October 10, 2004.

152 made up for the loss elsewhere: TCNC, http://www.carbonneutral.com/pages/Whatweinvestin.asp.

152 "The first step you can take": TerraPass, http://www.terrapass.com/.

152 "Reduce what you can": Carbonfund.org, http://carbonfund.org/.

152 reassuringly tenders "climate protection": Myclimate, http://www.myclimate.org/en.html.

152 "because it should be easier": TCNC, http://www.carbonneutral.com/pages/whyweareinbusiness.asp.

153 worth $4 billion by 2010: Fiona Harvey and Stephen Fidler, "Industry caught in carbon smokescreen," *Financial Times,* April 25, 2007.

153 three options that range in price: TCNC, http://www.carbonneutral.com/cncalculators/flightcalculate.asp.

153 To do the same job, Myclimate charges: Myclimate, http://www.myclimate .org/nc/en/offsetting/co2-calculator/calculator.html?tx_myclimateiframe_ pi1[type]=flight.

154 could be one hundred years or more: "Life span of common urban trees," CBC News Online, August 11, 2005, http://www.cbc.ca/news/background/ environment/trees_lifespan.html.

154 CO_2 absorption is lower in saplings: Amelia Ravin and Teresa Raine, "Best practices for including carbon sinks in greenhouse gas inventories" (paper presented at 16th Annual International Emission Inventory Conference, May 14–17, 2007), 6, http://www.epa.gov/ttn/chief/conference/ei16/index.html.

154 TCNC uses both varieties: TCNC, http://www.carbonneutral.com/projects/ projects.asp?id=897.

154 "I can now say that producing this album": Natasha Courtenay-Smith, "Your Planet—Part 2," *Independent* (UK), September 20, 2005.

155 India is host to more than a quarter: United Nations Framework Convention on Climate Change, Clean Development Mechanism, http://cdm.unfccc.int/ Statistics/Registration/NumOfRegisteredProjByHostPartiesPieChart.html.

157 chaired by Anandi's father, Dr. K. S. Sharan: "Current Climate Issues," Anandi Sharan's blog, http://bloganandi.blogspot.com/2008/12/normal-0- false-false-false.html.

157 owned by Dr. Sharan's brother: Interview with Aklavya Sharan, November 13, 2008.

157 CER India Private Ltd.: Interview with Kaveri Uthaiah, November 13, 2008.

158 "Our grandfather was a lawyer": Interview with Sharan.

159 DESI gets 50 percent of its investments: "DESI to take EmPower project to 10 more locations," *Hindu*, March 18, 2008.

160 Karnataka Renewable Energy Development Ltd. liked the plan: Interview with V. P. Hiremath, KREDL Managing Director, November 10, 2008.

160 no such project had been developed: Interview with P. Sekhar, Director, MPPL, November 10, 2008.

161 "We are planning on building two more": Ibid.

161 MPPL has received money . . . from several other offset entities: Carbon Catalog, http://www.carboncatalog.org/projects/malavalli-biomass-power- plant/.

162 earn about US$1.50 per day: Interview with family in Chikke Gowda Halli, November 11, 2008.

162 When he started at MPPL: Interview with Sakash, November 11, 2008.

162 Neither did Amalendu: Interview with Amalendu, November 18, 2008.

162 the facility provides hard hats and goggles: E-mail correspondence with K. Krishan, September 19, 2009.

162 photos of the facility posted: Myclimate, http://www.myclimate.org/en/ carbon-offset-projects/international-projects/detail/mycproject/1/95.html.

163 a charge neither MPPL nor Myclimate disputes: E-mail correspondence with Dellantonio, September 15, 2009, and Krishan, September 19, 2009.

163 MPPL denied my request: Only after I asked for comment from MPPL on my findings, at which time I was no longer in India, did the company finally invite me to visit the factory.

163 "rural electricity distribution": Malavalli Power Plant Private Ltd., http://www.mpppl.com/.

163 "provides reliable energy": "A case study: Malavalli Power Plant, Mysore, India," brochure, Gold Standard, 3.

163 650 new jobs: Myclimate, http://www.myclimate.org/en/carbon-offset-projects/international-projects/detail/mycproject/1.html.

164 the firm has been "remiss": E-mail correspondence with K. Krishan, September 19, 2009.

164 Krishan says the company employs twenty workers: Ibid.

164 It's in the village of Heggur: E-mail correspondence with MPPL spokesperson, September 22, 2009.

164 slightly high but nevertheless realistic: Interview with Suresh and Puttaswamy, contractors who haul crop wastes, November 13, 2008.

165 people such as Manini: Interview with Manini in Heggur, November 11, 2008.

165 "not at all contribute to residents cutting": E-mail correspondence with Krishan, September 19, 2009. Myclimate also claims felling trees to sell as fuel isn't going on in Malavalli: e-mail correspondence with Dellantonio.

165 "ensure top quality projects": World Wildlife Fund, http://www.panda.org/what_we_do/how_we_work/businesses/business_industry/offsetting/gold_standard/.

165 GS has yet to issue its license to MPPL: E-mail correspondence with Jasmine Hyman, September 21, 2009.

166 "It's a load of rubbish": Interview with Harish Hande, November 10, 2008.

166 He's a little shy: Interview with Sukumar K., November 13, 2008.

167 only six months of payments left: Interview with Maranayaka, November 13, 2008.

168 According to SELCO: E-mail correspondence with Sarah Alexander, September 22, 2009.

169 Mahadevi, his wife, answers the front door: Interview with Mahadevi, November 13, 2008.

169 To Sukumar's chagrin: Interview with Suresh, November 13, 2008.

171 The reach of low-power energy: Interview with V. Santhakumar, December 23, 2008.

172 two new six-hundred-megawatt power stations: "Nod for 2 thermal power plants, 10 other projects," Deccan Herald, November 20, 2008.

172 NGOs that offer generous baseline interpretations: Interview with Hande.

173 "forcing investors in these projects to lie": Fiona Harvey, "Stumbling block that poses threat to Kyoto Protocol," Financial Times, February 15, 2005.

173 Climate Care partnered with a local energy consultancy: Trusha Reddy, "Blinded by the light," New Internationalist, July 2006, http://www.newint.org/features/2006/07/01/south-africa.

174 offsets that the company sold were not in fact offset: Graham Erion, Larry Lohmann, and Trusha Reddy, "The South African projects," in *Climate Change, Carbon Trading and Civil Society: Negative returns on South African investments*, ed. Patrick Bond, Rehana Dada, and Graham Erion (South Africa: University of KwaZulu-Natal Press, 2007), 76–78.

174 "It can also be concluded": *Validation Opinion for Crediting Period Renewal: 4.5 MW biomass (low density crop residues) based power generation unit of Malavalli Power Plant Pvt Ltd*, Det Norske Veritas, Report no. 2008-10565, January 26, 2009, 6.

174 "inflow of approximately US$5.73 billion": CDM India, http://cdmindia.nic .in/index.html.

175 increase production of the chemical to lure: Keith Bradsher, "Outsize profits, and questions, in effort to cut warming gases," *New York Times*, December 21, 2006.

175 "There are imperfections": Bruce Usher speaking at Columbia University Graduate School of Journalism International Journalism Seminar, June 9, 2008.

ASSESSMENT

183 "Turns out my dream": Text message from Morse Pitts, July 27, 2009.

184 generating electricity is the most CO_2-intensive: *Inventory of U.S. Greenhouse Gas Emissions and Sinks: 1990–2007*, Environmental Protection Agency, April 15, 2009, ES-8.

188 going green . . . will give companies an edge on their rivals: Paul Hawken, Amory Lovins, and L. Hunter Lovins, *Natural Capitalism: Creating the next industrial revolution* (New York: Little, Brown and Company, 1999), xiii.

188 "triple bottom line": "Q&A: John Elkington," *Fast Company*, February 11, 2008, http://www.fastcompany.com/social/2008/articles/john-elkington.html.

189 concept known as biomimicry: Hawken et al., *Natural Capitalism*, 10.

189 high levels of energy and hazardous chemicals: Ibid., 15.

189 When these devices break: Ibid., 134.

189 Consequently, profitability hinges . . . on delivering the needed service: Ibid., 78, 138.

189 "[industrial capitalism] neglects to assign any value": Ibid., 5.

189 the result is a gravely malfunctioning market: Ibid., 265.

189 Due to distortions: Ibid., 160, 262–66.

190 "cost/price integration": Paul Hawken, *Ecology of Commerce: A declaration of sustainability* (New York: HarperBusiness, 1993), 81–82.

190 When external costs are added into: Ibid., 81.

191 saving $6 in net costs: Hawken et al., *Natural Capitalism*, 258.

191 "America could shed $300 billion": Ibid., 243, emphasis in original.

191 the Jevons Paradox: Wikipedia, http://en.wikipedia.org/wiki/jevons_paradox.

191 "When the Wal-Marts of the world": Jesse Finfrock, "Q&A: Wes Jackson," *Mother Jones,* October 29, 2008, http://www.motherjones.com/environment/2008/10/qa-wes-jackson.

192 the question of resource scarcity: Wikipedia, http://en.wikipedia.org/wiki/Malthusian_catastrophe.

192 Roosevelt . . . institutionalized resource and land conservation: Wikipedia, http://en.wikipedia.org/wiki/Theodore_Roosevelt.

192 "The question of the possible exhaustion": Cited in Heather Rogers, "Current Thinking," *New York Times Magazine,* June 3, 2007, 18.

192 "I'd put my money on the sun": Ibid.

192 "a change of spirit rather than": Quoted in Malcolm Gladwell, "The courthouse ring," *New Yorker,* August 10 and 17, 2009, 32.

193 keeping money from seeking out carbon dioxide: Finfrock, "Q&A: Wes Jackson."

193 "We have to ask ourselves": Interview with Frank Ackerman, February 24, 2009.

194 top 20 percent of Americans: Who Rules America?, http://sociology.ucsc.edu/whorulesamerica/power/wealth.html.

NOTES ON THE POSSIBLE

195 "This was an important reason": Interview with Ari Munir, April 28, 2008.

195 This can take as long as fifteen years: JoAnn Kawell, "For an agriculture that doesn't get rid of farmers: An interview with Miguel Altieri," http://www.agroeco.org/doc/crp.html.

196 widespread human die-off from starvation: Paul R. Ehrlich, *The Population Bomb: Population control or race to oblivion?* (New York: Ballantine, 1968), 17.

196 "consumes around twenty times more": World Resources Institute, http://earthtrends.wri.org/updates/node/236.

196 According to the Food Ethics Council: Adam Vaughan, "Elimination of food waste could lift 1bn out of hunger, say campaigners," *Guardian* (UK), September 8, 2009.

197 the primary reasons for food scarcity: "Reducing food insecurity via distributive access: Land, gender rights and food," *State of Food and Agriculture 2000,* Food and Agriculture Organization of the United Nations, 2000, http://www.fao.org/docrep/x4400e/x4400e00.HTM.

197 the problem isn't a shortage of food: Frederick Kaufman, "Let them eat cash," *Harper's,* June 2009, 51.

198 the connection between socially just practices: Miguel A. Altieri, "Agroecology: Principles and strategies for designing sustainable farming systems," electronic version, not dated, 2, http://www.agroeco.org/doc/new_docs/Agroeco_principles.pdf.

198 "Agroecosystems are communities": Ibid.

198 productivity is markedly increased and sustains itself: Ibid.

198 productivity of organic crops can be doubled: Kawell, "For an agriculture that doesn't get rid of farmers."

198 ancient farming system, called Waru-Warus: Miguel A. Altieri and Clara I. Nicholls, *Agroecology and the Search for a Truly Sustainable Agriculture* (Mexico City: United Nations Environment Programme, 2005), 160. Also see Organization of American States, http://www.oas.org/dsd/publications/Unit/oea59e/ch27.htm.

199 they began rebuilding the ancient croplands: Drew Benson, "Peru resurrects ancient ways of farming," *Los Angeles Times,* August 10, 2003.

199 a dramatic jump in yields: Miguel A. Altieri, "Applying agroecology to enhance the productivity of peasant farming systems in Latin America," *Environment, Development and Sustainability* 1 (1999): 206, http://www.agroeco.org/doc/LApeasantdev.pdf.

199 Waru-Warus consist of: Benson, "Peru resurrects ancient ways."

199 the reestablishment of Waru-Warus: Ibid.

199 increase farmers' livelihoods through greater social engagement: Altieri, "Applying agroecology to enhance productivity," 206–7.

199 Today the fields are derelict: Benson, "Peru resurrects ancient ways."

199 from about $100 to $500: Altieri, "Applying agroecology to enhance productivity," 207.

200 outmigration to urban slums reversed: Ibid., 204.

200 Brazil's southernmost states . . . began shifting: Ari Henrique Uriartt, Sonia Regina de Mello Pereira, and Xavier Simón, *Building participative processes: The case of the "Rede Ecovida de Acroecologia" in the Southern region of Brazil,* not dated, 15.

200 churches, trade unions, rural workers, and environmental groups: Ibid., 3.

200 Ecovida is a product of this movement: Ibid., 11.

200 network connecting fifteen hundred family farms: Ibid., 14.

200 Rio Grande do Sul has adopted: Ibid., 9–11.

200 But these growers must also adhere to a set of . . . principles: Ibid., 12.

201 Ecovida certification body grants its approval: Ibid., 17–18.

201 CNG was started by a group of farmers: Interview with Ron Khosla, June 26, 2009.

202 Tailored to unconventional farmers: Certified Naturally Grown, http://www.naturallygrown.org/requirements.html.

202 The co-op's network of farmers: Organic Valley, http://www.organicvalley.coop/newsroom/press-releases/details/article/california-hens-welcomed-to-organic-valley-brood.

202 management and member farmers have equal say: Organic Valley website, http://www.organicvalley.coop/our-story/our-cooperative/.

202 Organic Valley canceled shipments to Wal-Mart: Kermit Pattison, "Wal-Mart loved Organic Valley's milk, so why cut off the flow?" *Inc.,* July 1, 2007, http://www.inc.com/magazine/20070701/casestudy.html.

202 Organic Valley ditched the deal: Jim Hightower and Susan Demarco, "How to swim against the current," *Nation*, March 6, 2008, http://www.thenation.com/doc/20080324/hightower_demarco.

202 the Cornucopia Institute busted the company: "Organic Valley halts milk purchases with Texas dairy," press release, July 17, 2008, http://www.commondreams.org/news2008/0717-02.htm.

203 "The farmers who own the co-op": "Farmers at Organic Valley assert control to maintain high ethics standards at co-op," press release, June 19, 2008, http://www.commondreams.org/news2008/0619-17.htm.

204 $2 million more for a locally owned abattoir: Bonnie Azab Powell, "This little piggy goes home," *Mother Jones,* March/April 2009, 39.

206 a documentary featuring the philosopher Slavoj Zizek: *Examined Life: Philosophy is in the street,* Astra Taylor, director, 2009.

Index